1

A Comprehensive Conspiracy Theory Compendium

By J.D. Harris

3

A Comprehensive Conspiracy Theory Compendium

By J.D. Harris

HISTORICAL & POLITICAL CONSPIRACIES

JFK Assassination (Multiple Shooter Theory)

JFK Assassination (CIA or Mob Involvement)

9/11 Inside Job

Operation Northwoods

Watergate Scandal (Expanded Theories)

Operation Paperclip

The Death of Princess Diana

Hitler Escaped to Argentina

Pearl Harbor Was Allowed to Happen

Lincoln Assassination Inside Plot

The Gulf of Tonkin Incident

Iran-Contra Affair (Deeper Coverups)

The Bay of Pigs Betrayal

The Reichstag Fire Conspiracy

The Clinton Body Count

The Obama Birth Certificate Theory

The Trump-Russia Collusion (Framed or Real?)

The Biden Laptop Cover-Up

MKUltra

Project Monarch (Mind Control Subdivision)

COINTELPRO

Operation Gladio

CIA Involvement in Crack Epidemic

The "October Surprise" Theory (1980 Election)

Assassination of Robert F. Kennedy

The Deep State Controls All Presidents

Pizzagate

QAnon

False Flag Operations

North Korea Is a CIA Project

U.S. Presidents Are Selected, Not Elected

The 2020 Election Was Rigged

The UN Is a Tool of the NWO

The EU Is a Stepping Stone to World Government

The Assassination of MLK Jr. Was Orchestrated

Brexit Was Controlled by Elites

SCIENCE, MEDICINE & TECHNOLOGY CONSPIRACIES

Flat Earth

COVID-19 Was Engineered

COVID Vaccines Contain Trackers

5G Causes Illness

HAARP Controls the Weather

Chemtrails

Fluoride in Water Is Mind Control

The Cure for Cancer Is Hidden

AIDS Was Man-Made

GMO Food Alters Human DNA

Monsanto and Seed Control

Big Pharma Kills Natural Remedies

Morgellons Disease

Toxins in Sunscreen

Microchips in Vaccines

Antidepressants as a Mass Control Tool

Bill Gates and Global Depopulation

Microwave Mind Control

Smart Meters Spy on You

Artificial Intelligence Will Replace Humanity

The Bird Flu Was a Hoax

The Dead Bird Theory ("Birds Aren't Real")

The Fake Snow Conspiracy

Human Cloning Programs Exist

SECRET SOCIETIES & ELITE CONTROL

The Illuminati

Freemasons

Skull and Bones

Bohemian Grove

The Bilderberg Group

The Committee of 300

The Rothschild Family Controls the World

Reptilian Shape-Shifters Rule the Elite

George Soros as a Puppetmaster

The Trilateral Commission

The Council on Foreign Relations

Denver Airport's Secret Bunker

Satanic Ritual Abuse in the Elite

Mass Media Is Controlled by One Group

Predictive Programming in Movies

The "Eye of Providence" on Currency

The Black Nobility

Zionist Occupied Government (ZOG)

The Jesuits Control the Vatican & Beyond

Templars Still Rule Behind the Scenes

SPACE, ALIENS AND THE UNKNOWN

The Moon Landing Was Faked

NASA Lies About Everything

Area 51 Alien Tech

Roswell UFO Crash

Project Blue Book Cover-Up

Project Blue Beam (Fake Alien Invasion)

Ancient Aliens Built the Pyramids

Mars Rover Images Are From Earth

The Black Knight Satellite

Hollow Moon Theory

Flat Moon Theory

Alien Autopsy Videos

Secret Alien Agreements (e.g., Eisenhower Treaty)

The Secret Space Program

The International Space Station Is Fake

Astronauts Are Actors

Antarctica Alien Base

Operation Highjump Cover-Up

Saturn Is a Stargate

Time Travel via Wormholes

CELEBRITY & POP CULTURE CONSPIRACIES

Paul McCartney Is Dead

Avril Lavigne Replaced by Clone

Walt Disney Frozen

Beyoncé in the Illuminati

Britney Spears Is Being Controlled

Elvis Is Alive

Tupac Lives in Cuba

Hollywood Satanic Cults

The Simpsons Predict Everything

Katy Perry Is JonBenét Ramsey

Lady Gaga Is an MKUltra Puppet

The Beatles Were a Social Experiment

Taylor Swift Is a Clone

Michael Jackson Was Murdered

Chris Cornell and Chester Bennington Killed Over Pedo Rings

Kanye West's "Breakdowns" Are Warnings

The Truman Show Is Real

Celebrities Use Adrenochrome

The Oscars Are Rituals

Bob Marley Was Poisoned

BIZARRE & LESSER-KNOWN CONSPIRACIES

Hollow Earth Theory

Antarctica Doesn't Exist

Finland Doesn't Exist

Mattress Stores Are Money Laundering Fronts

The Mandela Effect

Dead Internet Theory

Simulation Theory

Time Travelers Among Us

CERN Opened a Portal

Shadow People Are Real

Reality Reset in 2012

Giant Skeleton Cover-Up

Dinosaurs Never Existed

The Sun Is Cold

Birds Work for the Bourgeoisie

Giant Trees Were Cut Down by Ancient Civilizations

The Sky Is a Hologram

The Earth Is a Prison Planet

Ice Wall Surrounds Flat Earth

Reverse Speech Reveals Hidden Messages

ECONOMIC & FINANCIAL CONSPIRACIES

The Federal Reserve Is a Private Cartel

The Great Depression Was Engineered

The 2008 Financial Crash Was Orchestrated

Gold Is Being Hoarded by Elites

Central Banks Want a One-World Currency

Bitcoin Was Created by the CIA

The Great Reset by the World Economic Forum

ESG Scores as Social Control

Social Credit Systems Are Spreading

Weather Disasters for Insurance Fraud

MORE CONSPIRACIES FROM AROUND THE WORLD

The Vatican Archives Are Hiding World Secrets

The Nephilim and Ancient Bloodlines

The Georgia Guidestones Mystery

The Lost Library of Alexandria Was Hidden

TikTok as a Spy Tool

Subliminal Messaging in Advertising

The Facebook-CIA Data Farm Theory

Hollywood Predicts Future Events on Purpose

Project Pegasus – Secret U.S. Time Travel Experiments

The Montauk Project – Mind Control on Long Island

The Titanic Was Switched with the Olympic for Insurance

The Titanic Was Sunk to Kill Financial Opponents of the Fed

The Moon Is a Surveillance Device

China Controls TikTok to Influence U.S. Youth

AI Chatbots Are Secret Surveillance Tools

The Pine Gap Base in Australia Is a UFO Hub

Pyramids Exist on Mars and the Moon

The Lost City of Atlantis Is Being Hidden by Governments

Biorobots Used in Government Positions

Bermuda Triangle as a Dimensional Portal

The Ark of the Covenant Is Hidden in Ethiopia

Nibiru / Planet X Will Return

Crop Circles Are Alien Messages or Military Tech

The Moon Is Artificial

Global Warming Is a Hoax for Control

Global Cooling Was Suppressed in the '70s

The Real Purpose of Antarctic Bases Is Unknown

The Pope Is a Puppet of Global Elites

Underground Cities for the Elite Exist Worldwide

COVID Test Swabs Implant Nanotech

Internet "Blackouts" Used for Elite Arrests

The U.S. Government Has Alien-Human Hybrids

The Real Queen of England Is a Lizard (Icke Theory)

Bhopal Disaster Was Covered Up Internationally

Operation Mockingbird Still Controls Global Media

Amazon Alexa Records Private Conversations for the NSA

Self-Driving Cars Are Designed to Kill Select Targets

World Leaders Are Clones (Not Just Celebs)

The U.S. Government Can Cause Earthquakes

Every Major Tech Billionaire Is in a Secret Pact

AirPods Emit Brain-Altering Frequencies

Disney Parks Are Built on Ancient Sites for Power

Mermaids Were Real But Covered Up by the Navy

The Roman Empire Never Ended – It Morphed Into the Vatican

The Holy Grail Was Discovered but Hidden

Time Cube Theory (Time as 4 Simultaneous Days)

Reality TV Is Designed to Promote Submission

Celebrity Deaths Are Often Faked to Escape Fame

The Music Industry Uses Frequencies to Influence Moods

The Elite Are Preparing to Abandon Earth

13

Chapter One

Section: Government, History & Political Secrets
 Conspiracy: JFK Assassination (Multiple Shooter Theory)

Summary

On November 22, 1963, President John F. Kennedy was assassinated while riding in an open-top motorcade through Dealey Plaza in Dallas, Texas. The official account, known as the Warren Commission Report, concluded that a lone gunman — Lee Harvey Oswald — fired three shots from the sixth floor of the Texas School Book Depository. Yet, from the very beginning, many Americans believed something more complex and sinister had occurred.

The Multiple Shooter Theory argues that Kennedy was not killed by a lone assassin but by a coordinated ambush involving more than one gunman. Proponents of this theory point to alleged inconsistencies in the number, trajectory, and impact of the bullets fired — and suggest that the true nature of the attack was covered up at the highest levels.

History & Key Claims

Skepticism about the official story began almost immediately after the assassination. The Zapruder film, amateur footage capturing the fatal shot to Kennedy's head, appeared to contradict the official timeline. For many, the idea that Oswald — a disaffected former Marine with a poor marksmanship record — could have acted alone, under such precise circumstances, seemed implausible.

The Multiple Shooter Theory centers around the following claims:

The "Magic Bullet" Problem: The Warren Commission's theory required a single bullet (Commission Exhibit 399) to have caused multiple wounds to both Kennedy and Texas Governor John Connally. Critics argue this bullet's trajectory and condition are improbable, if not impossible.

Acoustic Evidence: A 1979 report by the House Select Committee on Assassinations concluded that there was a "high probability" that two gunmen had fired at Kennedy, based on audio recordings from a police motorcycle's open microphone. Although later contested, this sparked renewed belief in a second shooter.

Witness Testimonies: Dozens of witnesses reported hearing shots from the grassy knoll, a small hill to the front-right of the motorcade. Many claimed to hear gunfire from that direction and even saw smoke or movement.

Timing Discrepancies: Experts have questioned whether Oswald could have fired three shots in the time recorded (under six seconds), with such deadly accuracy, using a bolt-action rifle with a misaligned scope.

Physical Evidence: The head movement in the Zapruder film — Kennedy's head jolting backward — has been interpreted by some as proof of a frontal shot, contradicting Oswald's position behind the president.

Eyewitness Deaths: A number of people connected to the event died under unusual circumstances in the years following the assassination, leading some to suspect a cover-up that silenced key witnesses.

This theory has given rise to dozens of variations — including triangulation ambush theories, rogue intelligence agents, and mafia gunmen positioned in different locations around Dealey Plaza.

Famous Quotes / Sources

"Back and to the left... back and to the left."
— Jim Garrison, JFK (1991), paraphrasing the visual evidence from the Zapruder film

"There is a high probability that two gunmen fired at the President."
— House Select Committee on Assassinations (1979)

"Oswald could not have fired those shots in the time allotted and hit a moving target at that range. It's simply impossible."
— Dr. Cyril Wecht, forensic pathologist and assassination researcher

"The evidence of a second shooter is compelling. The problem is — we still don't know who it was, or why it was done."
— Josiah Thompson, author of Six Seconds in Dallas

Real-World Consequences

The Multiple Shooter Theory has significantly shaped public perception of Kennedy's death. According to Gallup, roughly 60% to 80% of Americans over the past five decades have expressed belief that there was more than one shooter involved — a rare and persistent skepticism of an official government report.

The theory became a cornerstone of alternative American history, inspiring films (most notably Oliver Stone's JFK), books, mock trials, documentaries, and congressional inquiries.

It also became a rallying cry for a broader sense of distrust toward federal agencies and institutions.

The 1979 House Select Committee on Assassinations formally contradicted the Warren Commission, concluding that Kennedy was "probably assassinated as a result of a conspiracy." However, the committee failed to identify additional gunmen or sponsors, and the acoustic evidence has since been disputed.

Nevertheless, the damage to public confidence was done. The Kennedy assassination became the entry point into conspiracy culture for generations of Americans, influencing how future events (such as Watergate, 9/11, or even COVID-19) were interpreted.

Where It Stands Today

The Multiple Shooter Theory remains one of the most widely accepted conspiracy theories in U.S. history — not because it has been proven, but because the official account left enough inconsistencies to fuel decades of doubt.

In 2022, President Biden ordered the release of thousands of previously classified JFK assassination documents. While no "smoking gun" was revealed, the files deepened the narrative around intelligence agency involvement, with references to Oswald's surveillance by the CIA and FBI prior to the shooting.

Despite endless investigations, no definitive alternative theory has emerged that identifies who the second shooter was or how the plot was orchestrated. But the persistence of belief in multiple gunmen reflects more than just doubt about ballistics — it is a statement about institutional trust, Cold War politics, and the enduring need for historical accountability.

The question lingers: if one of the most shocking political murders in American history can remain unclear, what else might be hidden?

Chapter Two

Section: Government, History & Political Secrets

Conspiracy: JFK Assassination (CIA or Mob Involvement)

Summary

While the official narrative holds that Lee Harvey Oswald acted alone in assassinating President John F. Kennedy, another widespread theory suggests that the act was orchestrated — or at least facilitated — by powerful institutions or figures within the United States government and organized crime. These theories allege that Kennedy was targeted due to his policies on Cuba, his tense relationship with the CIA, and his administration's crackdown on organized crime.

The CIA/Mob Involvement Theory presents Kennedy's assassination not as the work of a lone gunman but as a high-level conspiracy to remove a president who had made too many enemies in the shadows of American power.

History & Key Claims

As early as the 1960s, rumors began circulating that the CIA and/or the mafia had reasons to want Kennedy dead. These claims gained traction in the 1970s, when congressional investigations into intelligence abuses (notably the Church Committee) revealed secret plots to assassinate foreign leaders and entanglements between intelligence agencies and organized crime.

Key elements of the CIA/Mob theory include:

CIA Discontent with Kennedy: After the failed Bay of Pigs invasion in 1961, Kennedy reportedly blamed the CIA for misleading him and vowed to "splinter the agency into a thousand pieces and scatter it to the winds." Some theorists argue this marked the beginning of a hostile relationship.

Cuban Retaliation and Covert Operations: Kennedy's evolving stance on Cuba — including secret backchannel talks with Fidel Castro — may have angered hardliners in the CIA who were committed to regime change in Havana. They may have seen Kennedy as a threat to their objectives.

Organized Crime Connections: The Kennedy administration aggressively pursued legal action against the mafia, despite earlier alleged ties between the Kennedy family (especially Joseph Kennedy Sr.) and organized crime figures during the 1960 election. Attorney General

Robert F. Kennedy's war on the mob was seen as a betrayal by crime bosses who believed they had helped JFK win the presidency.

Shared Interests Between the CIA and Mob: In the 1960s, the CIA reportedly recruited mafia figures — such as Sam Giancana and Johnny Roselli — to assist with plots to assassinate Fidel Castro. This alliance has led some to suspect joint involvement in removing Kennedy.

Jack Ruby's Mafia Ties: Jack Ruby, who killed Oswald on live television just two days after the assassination, had known associations with organized crime. His actions eliminated the possibility of a trial, leading many to believe he was sent to silence Oswald.

Suspicious Deaths and Cover-Ups: Several witnesses and figures connected to both the mafia and Kennedy investigations died under unusual or violent circumstances in the years following the assassination, fueling speculation of a coordinated cleanup operation.

Discrepancies in Intelligence Files: Declassified documents and testimony revealed that Oswald was known to the CIA and FBI before the assassination — raising questions about whether he was being watched, manipulated, or even used as a patsy.

Famous Quotes / Sources

"Nothing happens in this world — not a leaf falls from the tree — without the approval of the Mafia."

— Sam Giancana (as quoted by his brother in Double Cross, 1992)

"Kennedy had made too many enemies. He was threatening the power structure."

— Jim Garrison, New Orleans District Attorney and central figure in JFK (1991)

"Jack Ruby was just a small-time operator. He did what he was told."

— Interview with Frank Ragano, mob attorney (1990s)

"There's no question that Oswald was being tracked by U.S. intelligence. The idea that no one knew he was dangerous is false."

— Jefferson Morley, CIA historian and author of The Ghost

Real-World Consequences

The CIA/Mob theory has deeply influenced American culture and historical skepticism. It has been the subject of bestselling books, like Double Cross by Chuck and Sam Giancana, and played a central role in Oliver Stone's 1991 film JFK, which popularized the idea of a sprawling conspiracy involving the government, military-industrial complex, and mafia.

The theory also prompted renewed scrutiny of U.S. intelligence agencies. In 1975, the Church Committee uncovered a series of disturbing covert operations, including illegal surveillance, foreign assassination plots, and domestic subversion — confirming that U.S. agencies had the capability and precedent for extreme actions.

The revelation that mob figures had been enlisted in CIA assassination plots added credibility to the idea that such a partnership could turn inward.

In 1992, the JFK Records Act was signed into law, leading to the creation of the Assassination Records Review Board and the declassification of thousands of documents. These records, while revealing previously unknown intelligence operations, stopped short of confirming direct involvement in Kennedy's assassination.

Still, for many Americans, the line between covert planning and plausible deniability remains disturbingly thin.

Where It Stands Today

The CIA and Mafia Involvement Theory remains one of the most popular alternative explanations for JFK's death. While no conclusive proof has surfaced tying these institutions to the assassination, there is ample evidence that both had means, motive, and prior history with political violence.

Public polling over the decades consistently shows that the majority of Americans believe a conspiracy was involved in Kennedy's death. The 1979 House Select Committee on Assassinations concluded that Kennedy "was probably assassinated as a result of a conspiracy," although it stopped short of naming the CIA or organized crime.

In recent years, further declassifications have suggested that Oswald's activities — including his mysterious trip to Mexico City and his connections to pro-Castro and anti-Castro groups — were more closely monitored than previously admitted. These revelations continue to raise questions about what was known, when, and by whom.

Although many historians remain skeptical of a full-scale CIA-mafia plot, the theory has become a permanent fixture of American consciousness — a symbol of what may lie behind the curtain of official history.

Chapter Three

Section: Government, History & Political Secrets

Conspiracy: 9/11 Inside Job

Summary

On the morning of September 11, 2001, the United States experienced the deadliest terrorist attack in its history. Four commercial airliners were hijacked by operatives of al-Qaeda. Two were flown into the Twin Towers of New York City's World Trade Center, one into the Pentagon, and another crashed in a Pennsylvania field. Nearly 3,000 people died. The event transformed global politics, launched the War on Terror, and altered civil liberties in the U.S. for decades to come.

Yet, from the earliest hours of the tragedy, a growing number of people began questioning the official narrative. The 9/11 Inside Job Theory suggests that the U.S. government — or powerful elements within it — either allowed the attacks to happen or actively orchestrated them as a pretext for war, resource acquisition, and expanded control over citizens. To this day, it remains one of the most polarizing and widely debated conspiracies in the world.

History & Key Claims

While early disbelief emerged immediately following the attacks, particularly outside the U.S., the theory gained serious traction in the mid-2000s, driven by documentaries such as Loose Change, publications like David Ray Griffin's The New Pearl Harbor, and a growing distrust of U.S. foreign policy.

Proponents of the theory cite a variety of technical, circumstantial, and geopolitical factors as evidence of an inside job:

Controlled Demolition: One of the most common claims is that the Twin Towers (and especially WTC Building 7) collapsed in a manner consistent with controlled demolition, rather than structural failure from fire and impact. Many point to the symmetrical, rapid, and near-freefall collapse speed as suspicious.

WTC Building 7: This third skyscraper, which was not hit by a plane, collapsed hours after the towers fell. Its sudden failure — with minimal fire damage — is central to many conspiracy arguments.

NORAD Stand-Down: Theories question why North American Aerospace Defense Command (NORAD) failed to intercept the hijacked planes, suggesting that standard military response protocols were deliberately delayed or ignored.

Foreknowledge & Insider Trading: Unusual stock market activity, including massive short-selling of United and American Airlines stocks just days before the attacks, has been cited as possible evidence of advance knowledge.

The Pentagon Attack: Skeptics argue that the size of the damage and lack of visible aircraft debris at the Pentagon raise questions. Some claim a missile — not a plane — struck the building.

Oil, War, and the Patriot Act: Critics argue the attacks provided the perfect pretext for invading Afghanistan and Iraq, expanding the surveillance state, and increasing military budgets.

The "New Pearl Harbor": Neoconservative think-tank Project for the New American Century published a document in 2000 that mentioned the need for a "catastrophic and catalyzing event — like a new Pearl Harbor" to advance U.S. strategic goals. This quote is often cited by theorists as a blueprint for 9/11.

These claims are often connected in larger narratives involving the Bush administration, the CIA, the Mossad, or even multinational corporations benefiting from endless war.

Famous Quotes / Sources

"Let us never tolerate outrageous conspiracy theories."

— President George W. Bush, speech at the United Nations, November 2001

"The official story is a lie. It defies physics. It defies logic. It insults the intelligence of the American people."

— Richard Gage, founder of Architects & Engineers for 9/11 Truth

"9/11 was the greatest magic trick ever performed."

— Dylan Avery, director of Loose Change

"There is no hard evidence that explosives were used — but also no plausible explanation for how three steel-framed skyscrapers fell straight down from fire."

— David Ray Griffin, The New Pearl Harbor (2004)

Real-World Consequences

The 9/11 Inside Job Theory has had vast cultural and political influence. It became a foundational theory in 21st-century conspiratorial thinking, often cited alongside fears of the "Deep State," false flag operations, and manufactured war.

The popularity of documentaries like Loose Change (viewed millions of times online) helped ignite online communities around "truth-seeking." These groups have staged public protests, filed lawsuits, and pressured officials to reopen investigations. Some survivors and victim families, particularly connected to Building 7, have supported independent inquiries.

The theory also sparked severe backlash. Many have called it disrespectful to victims and a dangerous form of denialism. Academics and engineers have published extensive rebuttals through institutions like the National Institute of Standards and Technology (NIST), which issued detailed reports on the collapses.

At times, belief in 9/11 conspiracies has resulted in personal consequences for public figures, particularly entertainers, who endorsed the theory and faced media or career fallout.

Where It Stands Today

Mainstream science and journalism continue to reject the theory. The 9/11 Commission Report (2004) remains the official narrative, attributing the attacks solely to al-Qaeda. The NIST investigations concluded that fire and structural failure — not explosives — caused the collapse of all three towers.

Still, skepticism persists. A 2016 YouGov poll showed that over 50% of Americans believed their government was hiding something about 9/11. Polls in Europe and the Middle East have reported even higher levels of doubt.

Today, the 9/11 conspiracy is no longer isolated. It's often referenced in tandem with other distrust-based narratives, such as QAnon, pandemic theories, and deep state allegations. For many, it remains the ultimate example of a traumatic event with too many unanswered questions.

Whether dismissed as fantasy or defended as vital inquiry, the idea that 9/11 was an inside job endures as a key chapter in modern conspiracy history — and a lasting symbol of public suspicion toward power.

Chapter Four

Section: Government, History & Political Secrets

Conspiracy: Operation Northwoods

Summary

Operation Northwoods was a real, declassified plan proposed by the United States Department of Defense in 1962 that detailed a series of false flag operations intended to justify military intervention in Cuba. The proposal included ideas such as staging terrorist attacks on American soil, faking the hijacking of civilian planes, and fabricating casualties to provoke public outrage.

Although never carried out, the very existence of Operation Northwoods has fueled decades of speculation about what governments may be willing to do behind closed doors. For conspiracy theorists, it is often cited as "proof" that the U.S. government has considered — and may still consider — orchestrating violence against its own citizens for political ends.

History & Key Claims

The plan was developed by the Joint Chiefs of Staff under the direction of Chairman General Lyman Lemnitzer in March 1962. The central aim was to engineer a situation that would justify U.S. military intervention to overthrow Fidel Castro's communist regime in Cuba, which had become a major Cold War flashpoint.

Operation Northwoods proposed several covert tactics:

Staged Terrorist Attacks: Suggested faking bombings in U.S. cities, such as Miami or Washington D.C., which could then be blamed on Cuban operatives.

Hijacked Planes: Included plans to simulate a Cuban attack on a U.S. passenger airliner. One proposal detailed switching a real aircraft with a drone and staging its destruction mid-flight.

Mock Funerals and Casualties: Recommended creating a "national horror" by faking civilian deaths or injuries — including holding public funerals for "victims."

Harassment of Cuban Refugees: Proposed staging incidents to frame Cuba as hostile toward defectors, helping to sway American public opinion.

Attacks on U.S. Military Assets: Envisioned blowing up a U.S. ship near Cuba or sinking a Navy vessel and blaming it on Cuban forces.

The plan was approved unanimously by the Joint Chiefs and submitted to Secretary of Defense Robert McNamara. However, it was rejected by the Kennedy administration, and Lemnitzer was later removed from his post.

The documents remained classified for decades until 1997, when they were made public by the Assassination Records Review Board under the JFK Records Act. Their release stunned many and gave new weight to arguments that the U.S. government had, at times, considered extreme measures to manipulate public opinion.

Famous Quotes / Sources

"A series of well-coordinated incidents will be planned to take place in and around Guantanamo to give genuine appearance of being done by hostile Cuban forces."

— Excerpt from the Operation Northwoods proposal, 1962

"We could blow up a U.S. ship in Guantanamo Bay and blame Cuba."

— Proposal detail from Northwoods document

"Even though it was never approved, Operation Northwoods proves the capability, creativity, and moral flexibility that has always existed within elements of the U.S. security state."

— James Bamford, author of Body of Secrets (2001)

"Operation Northwoods was a green light for treason in the name of patriotism."

— Robert Parry, investigative journalist

Real-World Consequences

Although Operation Northwoods was never executed, its declassification has had a lasting impact on how the public views official narratives and government conduct. The plan is frequently cited in books, documentaries, and online forums as an example of just how far intelligence and military agencies were — or are — willing to go to justify foreign intervention.

Its existence has also emboldened theorists who claim that events like the Gulf of Tonkin incident, 9/11, or even domestic mass shootings could be engineered or exploited as modern-day equivalents of Northwoods-style thinking.

In academic and media circles, Operation Northwoods is often used as a case study in ethical boundaries within military strategy. It has also become a go-to reference in discussions about disinformation, propaganda, and the plausibility of false flag operations.

The term "Northwoods" has become shorthand in conspiracy communities for any perceived inside job or suspicious event framed to shift public opinion or policy.

Where It Stands Today

There is no dispute over the authenticity of Operation Northwoods. The documents are publicly available through the National Security Archive and are widely recognized as genuine proposals by top U.S. military officials. What remains controversial is how far such logic may have gone — or might still go — in shaping real-world events.

Mainstream historians point out that President Kennedy rejected the proposal and never allowed it to proceed, using it instead as a justification for removing General Lemnitzer from his position. Supporters of Kennedy's legacy often reference his decision to reject Northwoods as a sign of his moral courage and a factor in his deteriorating relationship with the Pentagon and intelligence agencies.

In conspiracy circles, Operation Northwoods is viewed less as a historical footnote and more as a template — a blueprint that validates broader suspicions about government deception. Whether one sees it as a narrowly averted scandal or a warning from history, its legacy endures.

The existence of this document ensures that any official narrative involving national security, terrorism, or foreign aggression will be met — at least by some — with deep and abiding doubt.

Chapter Five

Section: Government, History & Political Secrets

Conspiracy: Watergate Scandal (Expanded Theories)

Summary

The Watergate scandal is often considered the benchmark of political corruption in American history. In 1972, operatives tied to President Richard Nixon's re-election campaign were caught breaking into the Democratic National Committee headquarters at the Watergate office complex. The resulting investigation revealed a widespread campaign of political espionage, sabotage, and cover-ups orchestrated by the Nixon administration. Facing certain impeachment, Nixon resigned in 1974.

While the official story is one of journalistic triumph and legal accountability, a set of expanded conspiracy theories proposes that the public narrative only scratches the surface. These theories suggest that the scandal was far more complex, involving hidden motives, internal betrayals, intelligence agencies, and perhaps even an orchestrated takedown of Nixon by the very power structures he had antagonized.

History & Key Claims

The core facts of Watergate are well-established. On June 17, 1972, five men were arrested inside the DNC offices at the Watergate complex in Washington, D.C. They were caught attempting to install listening devices and gather intelligence. All were linked to the Committee to Re-Elect the President (CRP, often mockingly dubbed "CREEP") and had backgrounds in intelligence or covert operations.

Journalists Bob Woodward and Carl Bernstein of The Washington Post, aided by a confidential source known as "Deep Throat," gradually uncovered a web of illegal activities: political sabotage, hush money, abuse of executive power, and obstruction of justice.

However, expanded theories suggest a deeper set of motives and manipulations:

CIA Sabotage: Some researchers argue the burglary was intentionally botched — possibly by double agents or intelligence insiders — to create a political crisis that would force Nixon out. They point to Nixon's deep mistrust of the CIA and his attempts to wrest control over intelligence operations.

Operation Chaos Fallout: Nixon had pushed aggressively to suppress anti-war movements and leftist groups using programs like COINTELPRO and Operation CHAOS. The break-ins may have been part of broader domestic spying campaigns — and Watergate a symptom of a more widespread, darker agenda.

Internal Betrayal: Several Nixon loyalists, including White House counsel John Dean, are believed by some to have acted as controlled opposition or double agents. Some theorists argue Dean orchestrated or deliberately misled the operation to protect his own position or to bring down a faction within the administration.

Deep State Removal: Nixon had made powerful enemies in the intelligence community, media, and military-industrial complex. His outreach to China, détente with the Soviet Union, and attempts to dismantle covert intelligence networks may have led to a coordinated effort to remove him before he could alter institutional power structures.

The Role of "Deep Throat": Later revealed to be Mark Felt, deputy associate director of the FBI, "Deep Throat's" identity raised more questions. Why would a top FBI official leak information rather than pursue it internally? Was Felt acting on behalf of the Bureau or a larger agenda to unseat Nixon?

Famous Quotes / Sources

"I gave them a sword, and they stuck it in and twisted it with relish."

— Richard Nixon, 1977 interview with David Frost

"The cover-up is worse than the crime."

— Bob Woodward, The Secret Man: The Story of Watergate's Deep Throat (2005)

"It was a silent coup... The president didn't understand who really runs Washington."

— Jim Hougan, author of Secret Agenda: Watergate, Deep Throat, and the CIA (1984)

"Watergate was less about a break-in and more about a breakdown — of control, of loyalty, of trust."

— Len Colodny, co-author of Silent Coup (1991)

Real-World Consequences

Watergate forever changed the American political landscape. It led to the resignation of a sitting president, the indictment of 69 government officials, and the imprisonment of 48. It resulted in sweeping reforms: campaign finance laws, greater oversight of intelligence agencies, and heightened skepticism toward government power.

It also gave rise to a lasting suffix: "-gate" became shorthand for scandal in journalism and popular culture. More significantly, it normalized the idea that the highest offices in the land could be not only corrupt but also involved in elaborate conspiracies.

For many Americans, Watergate shattered the illusion of presidential integrity and triggered a long-term erosion of trust in government — a trend that continues to this day.

Theories of expanded involvement by the CIA or other intelligence entities have been explored in dozens of books and documentaries, particularly by researchers who suggest Nixon was removed because he threatened entrenched power rather than simply because of his crimes.

Where It Stands Today

Most mainstream historians acknowledge the possibility of deeper currents beneath the official Watergate narrative but stop short of endorsing full-blown conspiracy theories. The CIA's reluctance to cooperate with investigations, combined with the intelligence backgrounds of several Watergate burglars (including E. Howard Hunt), continues to raise eyebrows.

Theories involving an orchestrated takedown by the "Deep State" or intelligence elites have found renewed popularity in the 21st century, as public suspicion toward government institutions has deepened. For some, Watergate is viewed less as a triumph of democracy and more as an early example of how power is reshuffled behind closed doors.

In either interpretation, Watergate remains a touchstone — a moment when the machinery of American government revealed both its vulnerabilities and its reach. Whether one believes the full truth has been told or not, the scandal stands as a chilling reminder that even in a democracy, the corridors of power can conceal far more than they reveal.

Chapter Six

Section: Government, History & Political Secrets

Conspiracy: Operation Paperclip

Summary

Operation Paperclip was a classified U.S. intelligence program that secretly relocated over 1,600 German scientists, engineers, and technicians — many of them former Nazis — to the United States after World War II. These individuals, some of whom had been members of the Nazi Party or involved in war crimes, were recruited to advance American military, aerospace, and scientific development, particularly during the Cold War.

While the existence of Operation Paperclip is historically verified, conspiracy theories have developed around its full scope and ethical implications. Critics argue that the program not only whitewashed Nazi affiliations but potentially allowed individuals with horrific pasts to gain power and influence in U.S. institutions. Some believe the program's secrecy masked darker objectives, including covert experimentation and the origins of intelligence operations like MKUltra.

History & Key Claims

As World War II drew to a close in 1945, both the United States and the Soviet Union rushed to seize German scientific knowledge, especially in areas like rocketry, chemical weapons, and advanced aviation. The Nazi regime had produced cutting-edge military technology, including the V-2 rocket, which had been used to devastating effect in Europe.

To prevent key personnel from falling into Soviet hands, the U.S. created Operation Overcast, later renamed Operation Paperclip (so-called because paperclips were attached to personnel files marked for special clearance). The operation was approved by President Harry S. Truman, although he reportedly insisted that no committed Nazis or war criminals be included. This stipulation was widely ignored or circumvented by the military and intelligence agencies.

Key points of the theory and controversy include:

Nazi Affiliations Hidden or Erased: Many of the individuals brought to the U.S. were former SS officers or had worked in facilities where slave labor and human experimentation occurred. Their records were sanitized to make them eligible for U.S. employment.

Wernher von Braun and the V-2 Program: One of the most prominent recruits, von Braun led the Nazi rocket program and later became a key figure in NASA's Apollo missions. He had overseen operations at Mittelwerk, where concentration camp prisoners were forced to work under brutal conditions. His rapid rehabilitation is central to the ethical debate.

Involvement in Secret U.S. Programs: Many Paperclip scientists contributed to U.S. weapons development, missile programs, and psychological warfare research. Some were later connected to early CIA experiments, including MKUltra and chemical interrogation techniques.

Moral Compromise for Strategic Gain: The program has been accused of prioritizing Cold War supremacy over justice and accountability. For conspiracy theorists, it represents an institutional willingness to partner with evil when it serves national interests.

Continuing Secrecy and Suppression: While many documents have been declassified, others remain sealed, and some suspect that the full scope of Paperclip — including potential ongoing connections to covert programs — has never been disclosed.

Famous Quotes / Sources

"We knew some of them were bad guys... But they had what we needed. So we looked the other way."

— Former U.S. Army intelligence officer, quoted in Linda Hunt's Secret Agenda (1991)

"I'm not a Nazi. I'm a scientist."

— Wernher von Braun, upon arrival in the U.S., 1945

"This was not a minor operation — this was the deliberate importation of war criminals into the heart of the American military-industrial complex."

— Annie Jacobsen, author of Operation Paperclip (2014)

"The scientists we brought over were not just rocket scientists. Some had blood on their hands."

— Eric Lichtblau, The Nazis Next Door (2014)

Real-World Consequences

Operation Paperclip had a profound impact on American scientific progress. Paperclip scientists contributed to the development of ballistic missiles, military jets, nerve agents, and the U.S. space program. Wernher von Braun, in particular, became a national figurehead for American space ambitions, despite his Nazi past.

The ethical implications have been debated for decades. U.S. officials at the time justified the program by emphasizing the need to defeat the Soviet Union in both military and technological arenas. However, the decision to harbor individuals who may have committed or facilitated atrocities has been criticized as a betrayal of postwar justice.

In the decades following, revelations about Paperclip inspired numerous books, films, and conspiracy theories. Some suggest that the program laid the groundwork for later intelligence abuses, especially those involving psychological experiments and unethical medical research.

Where It Stands Today

Operation Paperclip is no longer classified and is widely acknowledged by historians, with extensive documentation available through the National Archives. However, significant questions remain about how thoroughly individuals were vetted and what was knowingly concealed to make them acceptable to U.S. authorities.

For conspiracy theorists, Paperclip represents more than a historical operation — it is a cautionary tale about how governments can justify moral compromises in the name of national security. The story also serves as a chilling reminder that evil does not always vanish in defeat — sometimes, it is simply repurposed.

The legacy of Operation Paperclip continues to shape debates around ethics in science, transparency in government, and the hidden costs of geopolitical rivalry.

Chapter Seven

Section: Government, History & Political Secrets

Conspiracy: The Death of Princess Diana

Summary

On August 31, 1997, Diana, Princess of Wales, was killed in a car crash in the Pont de l'Alma tunnel in Paris, alongside her partner Dodi Fayed and driver Henri Paul. The official explanation was that the driver, under the influence of alcohol and prescription drugs, lost control of the vehicle while fleeing paparazzi.

However, the sudden and tragic death of one of the world's most beloved public figures gave rise to widespread conspiracy theories — many of which continue to circulate decades later. Chief among them is the belief that Diana's death was not an accident, but a targeted assassination carried out by British intelligence services at the request of the royal family or other powerful interests.

History & Key Claims

Rumors of a conspiracy began almost immediately after Diana's death and gained further traction following a series of inconsistencies, unanswered questions, and statements Diana had made in the years leading up to the crash.

Some of the core claims within this theory include:

She Predicted Her Own Death: In a 1995 letter to her former butler Paul Burrell, Diana allegedly wrote: "My husband is planning an 'accident' in my car — brake failure and serious head injury..." This note is frequently cited as evidence she feared for her life.

She Was Pregnant with Dodi's Child: Mohamed Al-Fayed, Dodi's father, has claimed that Diana was pregnant at the time of her death and that the British establishment would never allow the mother of a future king (Prince William) to marry a Muslim man or bear his child. No medical evidence has ever confirmed the pregnancy.

The Car Was Tampered With: Conspiracists suggest that the Mercedes-Benz S280 was sabotaged — either mechanically or electronically — to ensure a fatal crash.

White Fiat Uno and Flash of Light: Multiple witnesses reported seeing a white Fiat Uno leaving the scene of the crash and a blinding flash moments before impact. Neither was ever fully explained, and the Fiat was never conclusively identified.

Unusual Behavior of Driver Henri Paul: The driver was found to have high levels of alcohol in his system, but CCTV footage from earlier that evening shows him walking steadily and acting normally. Critics question whether his toxicology report was manipulated.

Delayed Emergency Response: There was a considerable delay in getting Diana to the hospital. French emergency services followed a protocol of stabilizing patients at the scene rather than transporting immediately — but this delay has been interpreted as suspicious by some.

Surveillance and Cover-Up: Some theorists believe MI6 monitored Diana, and potentially acted on direct orders from senior officials or members of the royal family. Elements of the crash scene, such as CCTV footage, were missing or unavailable.

Famous Quotes / Sources

"She was murdered. There is a cover-up. And it goes right to the top."

— Mohamed Al-Fayed, Daily Mail, 2006

"She had talked openly about her fears... that she would be killed in a staged accident."

— Paul Burrell, Diana's former butler, A Royal Duty (2003)

"If it was an assassination, it was carried out with precision and subtlety. There's no smoking gun — just a pattern that raises eyebrows."

— John Morgan, author of The Paris-London Connection

"The police inquiry found no evidence of conspiracy — but they didn't look very hard either."

— Michael Mansfield QC, lead barrister for Mohamed Al-Fayed during the inquest

Real-World Consequences

The British government launched multiple investigations, culminating in Operation Paget (2004–2006), a Metropolitan Police inquiry into the conspiracy claims. It concluded that the crash was a tragic accident caused by excessive speed and the influence of alcohol and prescription drugs. It dismissed claims of foul play.

In 2007–2008, a full inquest into Diana's death was held at the Royal Courts of Justice. The jury ruled it an "unlawful killing" due to gross negligence by both the driver and pursuing paparazzi. However, they found no evidence of conspiracy by the royal family or intelligence agencies.

Despite these findings, public doubt remains widespread. Surveys taken over the years show that up to 30–40% of Britons — and even more internationally — believe Diana's death was suspicious.

Media coverage has kept the theory alive. Countless documentaries, books, and fictionalized accounts have explored or suggested alternative explanations. Netflix's The Crown, while dramatized, has renewed interest in Diana's treatment by the royal family.

Where It Stands Today

No conclusive evidence has ever surfaced proving that Diana was murdered. Yet the questions surrounding her death remain unresolved in the minds of millions. The missing Fiat Uno, the note predicting her death, and inconsistencies in the driver's toxicology continue to fuel doubt.

Critics of the conspiracy theories argue that emotional grief, media sensationalism, and a desire for justice have led many to seek deeper meaning in a tragic accident. Supporters argue that Diana's role as a cultural icon — independent, globally admired, and increasingly outspoken — made her a threat to the institution she had married into.

Whether viewed as a tragic accident, a case of fatal negligence, or a covert operation, the death of Princess Diana remains one of the most emotionally charged and persistently theorized events of the modern age.

Chapter Eight

Section: Government, History & Political Secrets

Conspiracy: Hitler Escaped to Argentina

Summary

The official account of Adolf Hitler's death states that he committed suicide in his Berlin bunker on April 30, 1945, alongside his new wife, Eva Braun, as Soviet forces closed in on the city. According to this narrative, their bodies were burned in the garden outside the bunker and later discovered by Soviet troops.

However, a widely circulated conspiracy theory challenges this account, claiming that Hitler did not die in the bunker but escaped — most likely to Argentina — where he lived out the remainder of his life in hiding. This theory, though long dismissed by mainstream historians, has been bolstered by alleged sightings, declassified intelligence documents, and ongoing interest in Nazi flight networks.

History & Key Claims

The foundation of this theory lies in both historical ambiguity and Cold War suspicion. In the weeks after the war, conflicting reports, a lack of conclusive physical evidence, and the Soviets' refusal to release details about the remains created an information vacuum. This was fertile ground for speculation.

The core claims include:

Lack of Physical Evidence: No known photographs exist of Hitler's body. The remains the Soviets claimed to have recovered were charred and reportedly misidentified over the years. In 2009, DNA analysis on a skull fragment long thought to be Hitler's revealed it belonged to a woman under 40.

Soviet Confusion: Initially, Joseph Stalin told U.S. officials that Hitler had escaped. Soviet reports later contradicted one another, sometimes suggesting suicide, sometimes escape. This inconsistency helped fuel Western suspicion.

The "Ratlines": After the war, many Nazis did successfully flee to South America through networks dubbed "ratlines." Operated by sympathetic clergy, intelligence agents, and sympathizers, these routes helped thousands reach Argentina, Brazil, and Chile — including Adolf Eichmann and Josef Mengele.

FBI and CIA Documents: Declassified U.S. intelligence files include dozens of alleged postwar sightings of Hitler in Argentina and Brazil. One 1945 FBI memo even described a witness claiming to have helped him escape to South America via Spain.

The Secret Compound Theory: Authors and researchers have pointed to an estate near Bariloche, Argentina, where they claim Hitler lived with Eva Braun under assumed names. Some reports suggest he died there in the 1960s.

Books and Media: Publications such as Grey Wolf: The Escape of Adolf Hitler (2011) and television specials on the History Channel have kept the theory in public view, often citing architectural similarities between German compounds and buildings in Patagonian villages.

Famous Quotes / Sources

"We have no evidence of Hitler's death. No one saw him die. No body was ever recovered."

— J. Edgar Hoover, memo to FBI field offices, 1947

"There's an entire file of South American sightings, most of which were never seriously followed up."

— Abel Basti, Argentine journalist and author of Hitler in Argentina

"There's no reason Hitler couldn't have escaped. He had the means, the motivation, and the support."

— Simon Dunstan, co-author of Grey Wolf

"If Hitler escaped, it would mean history — and justice — failed completely."

— Dr. Guy Walters, historian and critic of the theory

Real-World Consequences

The theory of Hitler's escape taps into broader fears about postwar justice, accountability, and the power of disinformation. While there is no confirmed evidence that Hitler survived beyond April 1945, the inconsistencies in early Soviet reporting and the proven escape of other high-ranking Nazis have kept the theory alive.

Books like Grey Wolf have sold internationally and inspired documentaries, while journalists and researchers have combed Argentina and Paraguay for clues. Meanwhile, Holocaust memorial groups and historians have condemned these theories as a form of denial or distraction from Nazi atrocities.

The enduring fascination with Hitler's supposed survival also speaks to the allure of the "what if?" — the idea that the most reviled figure of the 20th century might have escaped justice and lived in quiet exile.

Where It Stands Today

The majority of historians consider the theory to be false, citing extensive eyewitness testimony from those in Hitler's bunker, including secretaries and aides, as well as dental records matched to Soviet-held remains.

In 2017, French forensic pathologists re-examined remains in Moscow and concluded with high certainty that the teeth matched Hitler's dental records, which had been confirmed by his personal dentist's assistant.

However, conspiracy theorists argue that the Soviet Union had every reason to fabricate the story or misrepresent the evidence for propaganda purposes. The secrecy of Soviet archives during the Cold War, coupled with the proven existence of Nazi escape routes, ensures that doubt lingers in some corners.

Whether seen as an intriguing alternate history or a distortion of documented fact, the theory that Hitler escaped to Argentina remains one of the most persistent conspiracy narratives of the post-WWII era.

Chapter Nine

Section: Government, History & Political Secrets

Conspiracy: Pearl Harbor Was Allowed to Happen

Summary

On December 7, 1941, Japan launched a surprise military strike on the U.S. naval base at Pearl Harbor, Hawaii, killing over 2,400 Americans and drawing the United States into World War II. The official account describes it as an unprovoked and unforeseen attack — a day that President Franklin D. Roosevelt declared would "live in infamy."

However, a long-standing conspiracy theory argues that the U.S. government, particularly Roosevelt and key members of his administration, knew the attack was coming and allowed it to happen. The alleged motive was to galvanize a reluctant American public into supporting entry into the war, particularly against Nazi Germany, by provoking outrage through a devastating but politically useful event.

History & Key Claims

Even in the months following the attack, questions emerged about how the Japanese could have launched such a large-scale operation without the U.S. military detecting it. These doubts were compounded by postwar document releases, testimony from military personnel, and political memos.

The theory typically centers on several core claims:

Intercepted Intelligence: By late 1941, U.S. intelligence had successfully broken key elements of Japanese diplomatic and naval codes (notably the "Purple" code). According to some theorists, American officials were reading Japanese communications in real time and knew an attack on Pearl Harbor was likely.

The McCollum Memo: A document written in October 1940 by Lieutenant Commander Arthur H. McCollum suggested strategies to provoke Japan into firing the first shot. This included economic sanctions, freezing Japanese assets, and positioning U.S. naval forces aggressively. Some believe this memo reflects a deliberate plan to push Japan into war.

Aircraft Carriers at Sea: On December 7, all three U.S. aircraft carriers assigned to the Pacific Fleet were away from Pearl Harbor. Some have interpreted this as a suspicious preservation of key assets.

Delayed Warnings and Confused Orders: Critics argue that key warnings — such as intercepted messages and intelligence reports — were either delayed, ignored, or intentionally downplayed. The radar detection of incoming aircraft was dismissed, and communication to Pearl Harbor was said to be unusually slow or disorganized.

FDR's Political Motive: Prior to Pearl Harbor, the American public was largely opposed to entering another European war. Roosevelt, however, was increasingly convinced of the need to defeat Hitler. According to the theory, Roosevelt saw an attack by Japan as a way to unify public opinion and rally Congress without appearing to act aggressively.

Postwar Admissions: Several military and political figures later expressed the belief that Pearl Harbor was, at minimum, a preventable tragedy. These statements have been cited as indirect confirmation of deeper knowledge.

Famous Quotes / Sources

"Everything that the Japanese were planning to do was known to the United States."

— General George Marshall (alleged quote, cited in Robert B. Stinnett's Day of Deceit)

"The President had all the warning he needed."

— Rear Admiral Robert A. Theobald, The Final Secret of Pearl Harbor (1954)

"We were looking for an incident, and it came."

— Secretary of War Henry Stimson (diary entry, December 1941)

"We were never properly warned. Either somebody screwed up, or somebody looked the other way."

— Admiral Kimmel, Pacific Fleet commander at the time of the attack

Real-World Consequences

The theory that Pearl Harbor was allowed to happen has been a source of controversy and political tension since the 1940s. Multiple investigations followed the attack, including the Roberts Commission and later congressional hearings, which largely exonerated senior officials but highlighted communication breakdowns and missed warnings.

Books such as Infamy by John Toland and Day of Deceit by Robert B. Stinnett have argued forcefully that FDR not only expected the attack but saw it as politically expedient. These works sparked renewed interest in wartime decision-making and raised difficult questions about the moral trade-offs of leadership in crisis.

The debate also affected the reputations of key figures. Admirals Husband Kimmel and General Walter Short, blamed for the lack of preparedness, spent their postwar years fighting to clear their names. Decades later, Congress passed resolutions expressing regret over how they were treated.

Where It Stands Today

Historians remain divided on this theory. Most agree that intelligence failures and bureaucratic confusion played a role, but stop short of endorsing the claim that the attack was knowingly permitted. They argue that while U.S. officials knew war with Japan was imminent, they did not anticipate an attack on Pearl Harbor specifically.

Supporters of the theory contend that enough evidence exists to suggest more than mere incompetence — and that Pearl Harbor fits a pattern of "engineered provocations" in U.S. history. For them, it is seen as a precursor to other alleged false flags and manipulative tactics used to draw America into conflict.

Regardless of where one stands, the Pearl Harbor conspiracy theory reflects broader anxieties about trust in government, the manipulation of public emotion, and the ethical cost of war.

Chapter Ten

Section: Government, History & Political Secrets

Conspiracy: Lincoln Assassination Inside Plot

Summary

President Abraham Lincoln was assassinated on April 14, 1865, by John Wilkes Booth — a well-known actor and Confederate sympathizer — just days after the end of the American Civil War. Booth was part of a small group that sought to disrupt the Union victory by killing not only Lincoln, but also Vice President Andrew Johnson and Secretary of State William H. Seward.

The official account describes this as the act of a fringe group of extremists. But for over 150 years, an alternative theory has persisted: that the assassination was part of a larger conspiracy involving high-ranking Union officials, financial elites, and possibly foreign interests, who sought to control postwar reconstruction and suppress radical changes Lincoln was poised to implement.

History & Key Claims

John Wilkes Booth was killed 12 days after the assassination, and several of his alleged co-conspirators were captured and tried by a military tribunal. Four were hanged, including Mary Surratt — the first woman executed by the U.S. government. But many questions remained, particularly about how such a widespread plan was carried out so effectively in Washington D.C., a city under heavy security.

The Inside Plot Theory offers a broader and more ominous interpretation of events:

Suspicious Gaps in Security: Ford's Theatre was poorly secured despite it being a known target for previous threats. Booth was allowed easy access to the President's box — and had prior familiarity with the venue. Why wasn't Lincoln better protected, especially during wartime?

Connections to Powerful Figures: Booth had ties to Confederate operatives, actors, and southern financiers, but also to individuals with links to Union intelligence. Some theorists suggest he was used — knowingly or not — as a tool in a larger political agenda.

Mary Surratt's Controversial Execution: Surratt's involvement remains disputed. Her execution may have served as a distraction or scapegoat to conceal deeper networks. Her son, John Surratt, fled the country and was later captured — but never convicted — leading some to believe he held protected knowledge.

Edwin Stanton's Role: Secretary of War Edwin Stanton was among the first on the scene after the assassination. He took control of the investigation, communications, and press censorship. Some theorists argue he had both the motive and means to eliminate Lincoln, whose postwar vision may have clashed with Stanton's goals.

Lincoln's Economic Plans: In his second term, Lincoln had proposed radical ideas, including debt-free currency (greenbacks), reconciliation with the South, and possibly the dismantling of certain banking privileges. Some believe powerful financial or industrial interests saw this as a threat.

Speed of the Investigation: The rapid apprehension and conviction of conspirators, along with the secrecy surrounding the trial and reliance on a military tribunal, has led critics to suggest a desire to close the case before inconvenient truths emerged.

Famous Quotes / Sources

"There was more to Booth's plot than Booth."

— Otto Eisenschiml, Why Was Lincoln Murdered? (1937)

"Secretary Stanton took over every element of the case — the body, the news, the investigation — before anyone else could ask the right questions."

— David Balsiger & Charles E. Sellier Jr., The Lincoln Conspiracy (1977)

"I am led to believe that Booth was manipulated by men far more powerful than himself."

— Dr. John Chandler Griffin, Abraham Lincoln's Execution (2006)

"Follow the money. The people who profited from Lincoln's death weren't in the theatre — they were in the banks and the boardrooms."

— Unattributed quote circulating in Lincoln conspiracy circles

Real-World Consequences

Though Lincoln's assassination brought national mourning, the postwar power vacuum led to a chaotic Reconstruction period. President Andrew Johnson, who succeeded Lincoln, was far more lenient toward the South and clashed frequently with Radical Republicans. Johnson's policies arguably reversed some of Lincoln's more progressive intentions.

The theory that Lincoln's death served the interests of powerful factions has echoed through American political folklore, influencing interpretations of federal overreach, the power of financiers, and the hidden hand of wartime profiteering.

In the 20th century, books like The Lincoln Conspiracy and documentaries on secret societies helped popularize the idea that Lincoln, like Kennedy a century later, was removed not by a lone actor but by an organized political machine.

Where It Stands Today

Mainstream historians generally accept that Booth acted with a small group of Confederate sympathizers, motivated by vengeance and ideology. Yet they acknowledge that the rushed investigation, military trials, and conflicting accounts have left gaps in the record.

While no direct evidence has proven high-level involvement, the theory endures because of its plausibility: Lincoln's death changed the course of history, and those who benefited most were not the men in the theatre that night, but those who assumed power in the aftermath.

To this day, debates continue over the extent of Booth's conspiracy, the role of government officials, and whether Lincoln was assassinated to ensure a particular vision of postwar America — one aligned not with peace and reintegration, but with profit, control, and consolidation of federal power.

Chapter Eleven

Section: Government, History & Political Secrets

Conspiracy: The Gulf of Tonkin Incident

Summary

The Gulf of Tonkin incident, cited as the immediate justification for the United States' escalation of the Vietnam War, involved two reported confrontations between U.S. naval vessels and North Vietnamese torpedo boats on August 2 and August 4, 1964. The Johnson administration presented these events as acts of unprovoked aggression and used them to gain congressional approval for the Gulf of Tonkin Resolution — effectively giving the president broad war powers.

However, a substantial body of evidence and declassified material has revealed that the second attack — and possibly both — never occurred. This has led to a widely accepted conspiracy theory that the incident was either fabricated or manipulated to justify a war already planned. It stands as one of the most historically acknowledged examples of government deception leading to military conflict.

History & Key Claims

By mid-1964, the U.S. was already deeply involved in supporting South Vietnam, but full military escalation required public and congressional support. President Lyndon B. Johnson and Secretary of Defense Robert McNamara presented the Gulf of Tonkin events as clear-cut aggression demanding retaliation.

According to official reports, on August 2, 1964, the USS Maddox was patrolling international waters when it was approached and attacked by three North Vietnamese patrol boats. The Maddox returned fire and damaged the attackers. On August 4, a second incident allegedly occurred, with both the Maddox and the USS Turner Joy reporting a renewed torpedo attack in the dead of night.

However, years later, evidence emerged that undermined this account:

No Second Attack: Naval logs, communications intercepts, and later testimony revealed that the August 4 incident likely did not happen. Radar signals were misinterpreted, and no torpedoes were fired. The "attack" may have been a result of nervous radar operators and poor weather conditions.

Misleading Intelligence: The Johnson administration was warned at the time by intelligence analysts that the second incident was doubtful. These doubts were not shared with Congress or the public.

Predetermined Response: Critics argue the administration had already decided on escalation and was looking for a suitable provocation. The speed with which the Gulf of Tonkin Resolution was drafted and passed suggests pre-planning.

Suppression of Evidence: Reports that contradicted the attack narrative were buried or ignored. Only decades later, through declassification, did the full extent of uncertainty and internal dissent become public.

NSA Admission: In 2005, the National Security Agency (NSA) declassified a report acknowledging that the second attack never occurred and that intelligence had been distorted.

Famous Quotes / Sources

"For all I know, our Navy was shooting at whales out there."

— President Lyndon B. Johnson (private comment, August 1964)

"The evidence suggests that it was a manufactured event, used to sell the war to Congress and the American people."

— Senator Wayne Morse, one of only two senators to vote against the Gulf of Tonkin Resolution

"Those ships were operating in support of covert operations. They were not just out there for weather patrol."

— Admiral James Stockdale, eyewitness and Medal of Honor recipient

"By the time of the second alleged attack, U.S. officials knew it had not occurred. But the story was useful, so it was told."

— Robert J. Hanyok, NSA historian, internal report (2001, declassified 2005)

Real-World Consequences

The Gulf of Tonkin Resolution passed on August 7, 1964, with near-unanimous congressional support. It authorized President Johnson to use military force in Southeast

Asia without a formal declaration of war. This paved the way for the deployment of ground troops and the full-scale involvement of the U.S. in Vietnam.

Over the next decade, more than 58,000 American soldiers and millions of Vietnamese civilians and combatants would die in the conflict. The war deeply divided the U.S. public, led to widespread protest, and became a defining moment in the loss of faith in government narratives.

When the truth about the incident came to light in the 1970s and beyond, it contributed to the broader public perception that the Vietnam War had been sold on false pretenses. It also became a cautionary tale for future generations — often invoked during debates on war powers, particularly during the Iraq War in the early 2000s.

Where It Stands Today

The Gulf of Tonkin conspiracy theory has effectively become historical consensus. While the August 2 incident likely occurred, the August 4 "attack" is now broadly accepted as either mistaken or fabricated. The idea that it was used deliberately to provoke and justify war has been endorsed by many historians and former government insiders.

The incident is routinely cited as a classic example of a "false flag" or manufactured provocation — a government-engineered or manipulated event used to justify a predetermined policy.

Its legacy echoes in policy debates, academic studies, and public distrust. It remains one of the clearest illustrations of how incomplete or distorted information, when wielded strategically, can lead a nation into war.

Chapter Twelve

Section: Government, History & Political Secrets

Conspiracy: Iran-Contra Affair (Deeper Coverups)

Summary

The Iran-Contra Affair, exposed in the mid-1980s, involved the illegal sale of U.S. weapons to Iran — then under an arms embargo — and the secret diversion of proceeds to fund Contra rebels in Nicaragua, despite a congressional ban. The official narrative portrays it as a rogue operation led by mid-level figures within the Reagan administration, with limited knowledge among senior officials.

However, many researchers, journalists, and whistleblowers argue that the scandal was far more extensive than reported. According to this deeper coverup theory, Iran-Contra was part of a much larger covert network involving CIA drug trafficking, secret alliances with cartels, and illegal funding pipelines that reached into the highest levels of U.S. intelligence and government.

History & Key Claims

The scandal broke publicly in November 1986, when a Lebanese magazine revealed that the U.S. had been selling arms to Iran in exchange for hostages, despite publicly labeling Iran a terrorist state. Simultaneously, journalists discovered that the funds from these arms deals were being used to support Contra rebels fighting the socialist Sandinista government in Nicaragua — in direct violation of the Boland Amendment, which forbade such funding.

While the official narrative focused on a small circle of operatives — including National Security Council staffer Lt. Col. Oliver North — deeper theories contend the following:

High-Level Authorization: Critics argue that President Reagan, Vice President George H. W. Bush, and CIA Director William Casey were not only aware of the operation but directly involved in overseeing or enabling it.

Drug Trafficking Links: Several whistleblowers, including ex-CIA pilot Barry Seal and journalist Gary Webb, alleged that the CIA and affiliated networks allowed or facilitated cocaine trafficking into the United States by Contra-linked groups, with the profits used to fund covert operations.

The "Enterprise": A private, off-the-books global network involving arms dealers, intelligence operatives, and shell companies — dubbed "the Enterprise" — reportedly moved money, weapons, and drugs across continents with minimal oversight.

Murder and Suppression of Witnesses: Some conspiracy theories allege that key figures who tried to expose these connections — such as Barry Seal — were assassinated to protect the operation. Others point to mysterious deaths or discredited careers among journalists and former agents.

Role of Mena, Arkansas: The small town of Mena became infamous for its suspected use as a hub for CIA-linked drug and arms flights. Theories about protection from law enforcement and connections to prominent political figures emerged in the 1990s.

Congressional Investigations Were Controlled: Critics claim the official Iran-Contra investigations were limited by immunity deals, political pressure, and classified material. No major political figure was meaningfully punished, and many later returned to public life.

Famous Quotes / Sources

"I was authorized to do everything that I did."

— Oliver North, testimony before Congress, 1987

"You can't handle the truth."

— Fictionalized quote from A Few Good Men (1992), widely associated with Iran-Contra era sentiment

"The CIA knew that large quantities of cocaine were coming into the U.S. and looked the other way."

— Gary Webb, journalist, Dark Alliance (1996)

"The government knew what was going on in Mena — they were part of it."

— Arkansas state police investigator Russell Welch (interview, 1991)

"This wasn't a rogue op. This was policy."

— Daniel Sheehan, attorney and activist involved in Iran-Contra litigation

Real-World Consequences

Despite the scope and illegality of the operation, few key figures faced significant punishment. Oliver North was convicted on three felony charges, but his convictions were vacated on appeal due to immunity granted during his congressional testimony. Others, including former Defense Secretary Caspar Weinberger, were pardoned by President George H. W. Bush on his last day in office.

The affair significantly eroded trust in the Reagan administration and raised questions about the unchecked power of intelligence agencies and the military-industrial complex. Though Congress held hearings and released reports, critics argue they failed to probe the deepest connections.

Gary Webb's Dark Alliance series, published in 1996, reignited public interest by alleging that CIA-backed Contras helped fuel America's crack cocaine epidemic. Although Webb faced severe backlash and professional ruin, his work inspired further investigations — some of which have supported key aspects of his claims.

The scandal has also shaped how later foreign policy controversies are viewed, especially allegations of secret funding, paramilitary proxies, and covert drug operations.

Where It Stands Today

Mainstream accounts acknowledge that Iran-Contra was a major constitutional crisis that revealed disturbing patterns of secrecy and lawbreaking. But official investigations stopped short of confirming many of the darker allegations — especially those involving drug trafficking and deeper institutional corruption.

In conspiracy circles, Iran-Contra is seen as proof of how far the U.S. government is willing to go to pursue geopolitical objectives under the guise of national security. For many, it remains a textbook example of how illegal operations are sanitized through media control, selective prosecution, and elite impunity.

Even today, figures involved in the affair — including Oliver North and Elliott Abrams — have returned to public roles, furthering the belief that powerful individuals are rarely held accountable for systemic wrongdoing.

Iran-Contra may not be a theory in itself, but the belief that its full story remains buried continues to spark skepticism about every subsequent U.S. covert operation.

Chapter Thirteen

Section: Government, History & Political Secrets

Conspiracy: The Bay of Pigs Betrayal

Summary

In April 1961, just three months into John F. Kennedy's presidency, the United States orchestrated an ill-fated invasion of Cuba's southern coast by CIA-trained Cuban exiles. Known as the Bay of Pigs Invasion, the operation was intended to overthrow Fidel Castro's communist regime. It failed spectacularly. Within days, most of the invaders were killed or captured, and the event severely damaged the Kennedy administration's reputation.

While officially regarded as a case of poor planning and intelligence failure, many have questioned whether the disaster was intentionally sabotaged — either from within the U.S. government or as a deeper strategy to force Kennedy's hand into full-scale military intervention. The Bay of Pigs Betrayal theory suggests that Kennedy was set up to either approve a direct war with Cuba — or to take the blame for its collapse.

History & Key Claims

Planning for the operation began under President Eisenhower, but was handed to Kennedy when he took office in January 1961. The CIA, believing Castro was vulnerable to internal rebellion, trained and armed around 1,400 Cuban exiles to stage a beach landing near Playa Girón.

Key elements of the betrayal theory include:

Withholding Air Support: Kennedy refused to authorize overt U.S. military air support for the invasion. Critics argue he was led to believe it wouldn't be necessary, only to be blamed when its absence caused the operation to fail. Some theorists believe the CIA assumed Kennedy would have no choice but to approve airstrikes once the invasion began — effectively baiting him into escalation.

CIA Manipulation: Internal documents and later testimony revealed the CIA deliberately underestimated the risks and oversold the likelihood of an anti-Castro uprising in Cuba. Some suggest this was done to corner Kennedy into committing more U.S. forces once the initial invasion faltered.

Allen Dulles and Institutional Tensions: CIA Director Allen Dulles and other intelligence officials had Cold War hawkish leanings and were allegedly dissatisfied with Kennedy's more cautious foreign policy. The failure of the Bay of Pigs, followed by Kennedy's firing of Dulles, is seen by some as the beginning of deep institutional resentment — which conspiracy theorists link to Kennedy's later assassination.

False Assumptions and Deception: Several post-event assessments showed that key assumptions made by the CIA — such as the belief that Cuban civilians would rise up in support of the exiles — were knowingly exaggerated. Kennedy may have been misled into approving the plan without full awareness of its flaws.

Castro's Knowledge: Some suggest Castro had advance warning of the invasion, either through Soviet intelligence or internal leaks. This has led to speculation that elements within U.S. intelligence may have tipped him off to ensure the invasion's failure.

Famous Quotes / Sources

"How could we have been so stupid?"

— President John F. Kennedy, shortly after the invasion failed

"The plan was sold to Kennedy under false pretenses. They knew it would fail without air support — but they assumed he would cave."

— Colonel L. Fletcher Prouty, former Pentagon liaison to the CIA

"We were set up to fail. The boys who landed at the beach never had a chance."

— José Miró Cardona, leader of the Cuban Revolutionary Council in exile

"This was not incompetence. It was sabotage dressed up as strategy."

— James Douglass, JFK and the Unspeakable (2008)

Real-World Consequences

The Bay of Pigs was an immediate public embarrassment for the United States. It emboldened Castro, pushed Cuba further into the Soviet orbit, and helped pave the way to the Cuban Missile Crisis the following year.

Domestically, the failure exposed fractures between the Kennedy administration and the intelligence community. Kennedy responded by firing CIA Director Allen Dulles, Deputy Director Charles Cabell, and Deputy Director for Plans Richard Bissell — a purge unprecedented at the time.

These firings, and Kennedy's subsequent skepticism toward covert military operations, have led many conspiracy theorists to believe that the Bay of Pigs was not just a failed mission, but an engineered political trap.

Some go further, claiming that the fallout from the operation set the stage for deeper conflicts between Kennedy and the national security establishment — tensions they believe contributed to his assassination two years later.

Where It Stands Today

While mainstream historians generally attribute the Bay of Pigs failure to poor planning, groupthink, and miscommunication, there is increasing acknowledgment that the CIA misled the White House on key aspects of the operation. The notion that Kennedy was "boxed in" by the agency is no longer viewed as extreme.

Declassified documents and firsthand accounts have revealed internal manipulations, inflated expectations, and questionable assumptions used to pressure the president. Though few official sources support the idea of deliberate sabotage, many recognize that the intelligence community expected Kennedy to escalate once the plan was in motion — and were shocked when he did not.

In conspiracy circles, the Bay of Pigs is seen as an early warning sign — an episode that shows how even presidents can be outmaneuvered by unelected agencies. It is frequently cited in broader discussions of the "Deep State" and institutional power beyond democratic control.

Chapter Fourteen

Section: Government, History & Political Secrets

Conspiracy: The Reichstag Fire Conspiracy

Summary

On the night of February 27, 1933, fire engulfed the Reichstag — the German parliament building in Berlin. The blaze destroyed the main chamber and sent shockwaves through the Weimar Republic, already in a fragile political state. A Dutch communist named Marinus van der Lubbe was found at the scene and quickly blamed for the arson.

The Nazi Party, under Adolf Hitler, who had just been appointed Chancellor weeks earlier, seized upon the event as justification for a swift crackdown on civil liberties. The very next day, the Reichstag Fire Decree was issued, suspending key constitutional protections and enabling the Nazi regime to arrest political opponents, particularly communists.

The official story has long maintained that van der Lubbe acted alone. But a widely held and historically persistent theory contends that the fire was a false flag operation — orchestrated or at least enabled by the Nazis themselves — to accelerate their rise to total power.

History & Key Claims

The Reichstag Fire took place at a critical moment in German history. Hitler had been appointed Chancellor on January 30, 1933, and was seeking to consolidate power by weakening democratic institutions and eliminating opposition.

Key claims within the conspiracy include:

Implausibility of a Lone Arsonist: Critics question how van der Lubbe, a physically frail and mentally unstable individual, could have ignited such a large and fast-spreading fire unaided. Multiple ignition points were discovered, suggesting coordinated arson.

Suspicious Speed of Response: Nazi officials, including Hermann Göring and Joseph Goebbels, arrived at the scene remarkably quickly. Within hours, the government had already produced statements blaming communists and pushing for emergency powers.

The Reichstag Fire Decree: Issued the day after the fire and signed by President Hindenburg, the decree suspended basic civil rights, allowed indefinite detention without trial, and laid the legal foundation for the Nazi dictatorship. The speed and scope of the decree suggest premeditation.

Suppression of Evidence: The subsequent trial included high-ranking Communist Party members, but most were acquitted due to lack of evidence. The Nazi government destroyed records and obstructed postwar efforts to revisit the case.

SA and SS Involvement: Some theorists allege that members of the Nazi paramilitary groups — the SA and SS — were secretly involved in setting the fire. Testimonies from postwar detainees suggested that the plan was internally discussed prior to the event.

Propaganda Use: The Nazis used the fire to frame communists as existential threats, consolidate emergency powers, and justify the rapid erosion of the democratic Weimar system — a classic example of exploiting crisis for political gain.

Famous Quotes / Sources

"The fire is the signal we have been waiting for... The communists are planning a revolution!"

— Hermann Göring, night of the fire, as quoted in contemporary reports

"The Nazis needed a justification for their dictatorship. The fire gave them that."

— William L. Shirer, The Rise and Fall of the Third Reich (1960)

"There is no question that van der Lubbe was involved — but no reasonable person believes he acted alone."

— Fritz Tobias, German journalist and author of The Reichstag Fire (1964)

"They staged the fire to incite panic, eliminate the opposition, and create a dictatorship in weeks, not years."

— Sebastian Haffner, German historian and political commentator

Real-World Consequences

The fire marked a pivotal turning point in German history. The Reichstag Fire Decree led to the mass arrest of communists, socialists, and trade unionists. Just weeks later, the Enabling Act was passed, granting Hitler the authority to legislate without parliamentary consent — effectively ending democracy in Germany.

Over 4,000 communists were arrested in the days following the fire, and political opposition was crushed. Van der Lubbe was tried and executed in 1934, though controversy over his culpability lingered. The Nazi regime's rapid consolidation of power transformed Germany into a one-party totalitarian state within months.

The fire has since become a textbook case in political science of how regimes use crisis — real or manufactured — to implement authoritarian measures.

Where It Stands Today

The question of who truly started the Reichstag fire remains debated. Most historians now agree that while van der Lubbe likely played a role, he may have been manipulated or used as a scapegoat. Some scholars argue that Nazi operatives used his actions as cover for a more extensive plan, possibly even setting additional fires within the building after he was inside.

Recent forensic studies have cast doubt on the idea of a large-scale coordinated arson, suggesting the fire may indeed have spread rapidly due to flammable furnishings. Nonetheless, the political utility of the fire for the Nazis is beyond dispute.

In conspiracy literature, the Reichstag fire is frequently cited as one of the most historically credible examples of a false flag — a deliberate act designed to justify oppressive laws, expand executive power, and manipulate public fear. It remains a powerful cautionary tale about the fragility of democracy in the face of orchestrated crisis.

Chapter Fifteen

Section: Government, History & Political Secrets

Conspiracy: The Clinton Body Count

Summary

The Clinton Body Count conspiracy theory alleges that former U.S. President Bill Clinton and former Secretary of State Hillary Clinton have been involved — directly or indirectly — in the deaths of numerous individuals who were connected to them politically, financially, or personally. According to proponents of the theory, these individuals died under mysterious circumstances, and their deaths served to protect the Clintons from legal or political fallout.

Originating during Bill Clinton's presidency in the 1990s and gaining renewed traction during Hillary Clinton's 2016 campaign, the theory is controversial, far-reaching, and largely dismissed by mainstream sources. Yet it persists — bolstered by high-profile deaths, distrust of political elites, and viral internet speculation.

History & Key Claims

The term "Clinton Body Count" was popularized in the early 1990s when an Arkansas attorney named Linda Thompson compiled a list of people allegedly connected to the Clintons who had died under suspicious conditions. The list was circulated via fax and early internet forums, eventually becoming a persistent urban legend.

Key elements of the theory include:

Suspicious Deaths: The theory highlights a number of individuals who allegedly died shortly before testifying against, investigating, or working with the Clintons. Many of these deaths were ruled suicides, accidents, or natural causes — but theorists question the timing, frequency, and nature of these deaths.

Vince Foster: Perhaps the most famous case cited is that of Deputy White House Counsel Vince Foster, who died by suicide in 1993. Official investigations — including those by the FBI and independent counsel — confirmed the suicide, but conspiracy theorists claimed Foster had damning knowledge of the Clintons' financial dealings and was silenced.

Ron Brown: U.S. Commerce Secretary Ron Brown died in a 1996 plane crash in Croatia. While the official cause was pilot error and poor weather, the theory claims there was a gunshot wound to his head and that he was about to cooperate with investigators looking into financial corruption.

Seth Rich: A Democratic National Committee staffer, Seth Rich was murdered in 2016 in what police labeled a robbery gone wrong. Conspiracy theorists claimed Rich was the source of leaked DNC emails published by WikiLeaks — and was killed to prevent further disclosures. WikiLeaks' founder Julian Assange fueled speculation by hinting at Rich's role without confirming it.

List Length and Anomalies: The supposed "body count" includes dozens of names — over 50 by some counts — from former Arkansas state troopers to campaign aides, accountants, and lawyers. Critics of the theory argue that the deaths span decades, involve no consistent pattern, and often have no confirmed connection to the Clintons beyond rumor or proximity.

Political Utility: The theory is often revived during election cycles or scandals involving the Clintons. It has been used by opponents to paint the couple as ruthless, above the law, and surrounded by death and deception.

Famous Quotes / Sources

"Do you believe in coincidences? I don't."

— Circulated in early versions of the Clinton Body Count document (1994)

"Vince Foster was murdered. Period."

— Rush Limbaugh, 1994 (later walked back under pressure)

"If you dig too deep into the Clintons, you don't just lose your job — you disappear."

— Anonymous internet post, 2016

"Seth Rich's death was tragic, but the real tragedy is how it's been exploited by political operatives and conspiracy theorists."

— D.C. Police Chief Peter Newsham, 2017

Real-World Consequences

Though debunked repeatedly, the Clinton Body Count theory has had enduring political impact. It has been weaponized by political opponents, amplified by talk radio, blogs, and social media influencers, and treated as fact by some portions of the public.

During the 2016 election, the theory was revived in connection with Seth Rich's murder, leading to a flood of online misinformation. Fox News aired a widely criticized segment on the theory, later retracting it and issuing an apology. Seth Rich's family pursued legal action against those who promoted the conspiracy, including high-profile pundits and media outlets.

The theory has contributed to a broader atmosphere of suspicion surrounding political elites — and reinforced partisan divides. For some, it's symbolic of "deep state" or "shadow government" beliefs; for others, it's viewed as politically motivated slander.

Where It Stands Today

The Clinton Body Count theory remains largely discredited by journalists, fact-checkers, law enforcement, and independent investigations. Many deaths included on the lists have verifiable, mundane explanations and weak or non-existent links to the Clintons.

However, the theory endures due to a mix of unresolved questions, circumstantial patterns, and deeply entrenched distrust of establishment politicians. For many, it fits into a larger belief system where power is protected through any means necessary — including murder.

Whether viewed as a dark political reality or a modern myth, the Clinton Body Count serves as an example of how speculation, partisanship, and tragedy can fuse into a powerful and persistent conspiracy narrative.

Chapter Sixteen

Section: Government, History & Political Secrets

Conspiracy: The Obama Birth Certificate Theory

Summary

The Obama Birth Certificate Theory, often referred to as the "birther" movement, alleges that Barack Obama, the 44th President of the United States, was not born in the United States and was therefore ineligible to serve as president under Article II of the U.S. Constitution. The theory claims that Obama's Hawaiian birth certificate is either forged or conceals his true birthplace — most often alleged to be Kenya.

Although Obama released both a short-form and long-form birth certificate, and multiple independent investigations confirmed their authenticity, the theory persisted for nearly a decade. It became one of the most prominent and politically charged conspiracy theories in modern American history, reflecting deeper cultural tensions around race, identity, and belonging.

History & Key Claims

The theory originated during the 2008 U.S. presidential election. Early versions appeared on fringe websites and anonymous emails, claiming Obama's birth records were suspicious or missing. As his candidacy gained traction, these rumors moved into the mainstream, fueled by media speculation and political opportunism.

Core claims include:

Born in Kenya: Some theorists allege that Obama was born in Mombasa, Kenya, where his father was from. They claim he was smuggled into the U.S. shortly after birth and that his Hawaiian documents were retroactively created.

Indonesian Citizenship: Others assert that Obama renounced his U.S. citizenship while living in Indonesia as a child, thereby disqualifying him from holding the presidency.

Forged Birth Certificate: In 2011, after years of speculation, the White House released a long-form birth certificate showing that Obama was born in Honolulu, Hawaii, on August 4, 1961. Conspiracy theorists claimed the document was a forgery, citing alleged inconsistencies in typeface, layers, and digital artifacts.

Missing Documentation: Theorists also pointed to alleged gaps in Obama's early records — including his college transcripts, passport applications, and Social Security number — as evidence of concealment or fabrication.

Political Cover-Up: Many claimed the media, Democratic officials, and government agencies colluded to suppress the truth in order to protect Obama's presidency and preserve public order.

Despite mounting evidence against these claims, the theory continued to spread, eventually gaining endorsement from prominent political figures and becoming a divisive feature of American discourse.

Famous Quotes / Sources

"I have people that have been studying it and they cannot believe what they're finding."

— Donald J. Trump, Today Show, 2011

"Let's just see the birth certificate."

— Sarah Palin, former Governor of Alaska, 2009

"Barack Obama was born in the United States. Period."

— President Obama, White House Correspondents' Dinner, 2011

"This issue was never about a birth certificate — it was about identity and fear."

— Ta-Nehisi Coates, journalist and author, The Atlantic

Real-World Consequences

The birther theory had significant and lasting consequences in American politics and society. It was the first major conspiracy theory in the internet era to influence national discourse and presidential politics.

Obama's decision to release his long-form birth certificate in April 2011 was an unprecedented move for a sitting president — one that, ironically, only further energized his critics. Conspiracy theorists claimed the release proved their claims were striking a nerve.

The theory helped fuel the political rise of Donald Trump, who became one of the most vocal birther proponents before pivoting to other political issues. Trump's involvement brought new attention to the theory and cemented it as a partisan wedge issue.

Obama, for his part, addressed the theory with a mix of frustration and dry humor, recognizing its racial undertones and symbolic meaning. Many observers viewed the birther movement as an attempt to delegitimize the first Black president — not through policy debate, but by questioning the legitimacy of his citizenship and identity.

The theory also contributed to the increasing polarization of political discourse and the normalization of conspiracy rhetoric in mainstream campaigns.

Where It Stands Today

The Obama Birth Certificate theory has been thoroughly debunked by journalists, fact-checkers, and official agencies. In 2016, even Donald Trump acknowledged — under political pressure — that Obama was born in the United States.

Still, the theory lingers in some corners of the internet and continues to influence broader conspiracies involving forged documents, secret allegiances, and political "plants." It is often grouped with other claims about "Manchurian candidates" and covert takeovers of government.

More than a dispute over a piece of paper, the birther theory revealed profound anxieties about race, globalism, and the changing face of American leadership. For many, it became a symbol of how easily misinformation can erode public trust — and how identity can be weaponized in the pursuit of political power.

Chapter Seventeen

Section: Government, History & Political Secrets

Conspiracy: The Trump–Russia Collusion (Framed or Real?)

Summary

The Trump–Russia Collusion controversy refers to allegations that Donald J. Trump's 2016 presidential campaign conspired or coordinated with the Russian government to influence the outcome of the election. The theory dominated headlines for years, leading to a two-year investigation by Special Counsel Robert Mueller.

While the official findings stopped short of charging criminal conspiracy, the case remains deeply polarizing. Some argue that the Trump campaign was complicit in foreign interference and obstructed justice. Others believe the entire saga was a politically motivated fabrication — a "witch hunt" designed to undermine Trump's presidency. In conspiracy culture, it remains a battleground of competing narratives.

History & Key Claims

The theory began gaining traction during the 2016 election, particularly after WikiLeaks released thousands of Democratic National Committee (DNC) emails. U.S. intelligence agencies soon concluded that Russian operatives had interfered in the election through hacking, disinformation campaigns, and online manipulation — with the aim of helping Trump defeat Hillary Clinton.

Key claims from both sides of the conspiracy divide include:

Pro-Collusion Theory (Conspiracy by Trump Campaign):

Secret Communications: Trump campaign associates, including Michael Flynn, Paul Manafort, and George Papadopoulos, had multiple contacts with Russian nationals during the campaign. Critics argue these contacts point to coordination.

Russian Hacking: U.S. intelligence agencies concluded that Russian operatives hacked the DNC and Clinton campaign emails. The theory posits that Trump allies either encouraged or directly coordinated the leaks.

Obstruction of Justice: Trump's firing of FBI Director James Comey and attempts to influence the Mueller investigation have been interpreted as efforts to conceal wrongdoing.

The Steele Dossier: A controversial but partially corroborated report compiled by former British spy Christopher Steele alleged that the Russian government had compromising material on Trump and that his campaign actively colluded with them.

Anti-Collusion Theory (Trump Was Framed):

No Charges Filed: Mueller's investigation did not result in charges against Trump for conspiracy, despite widespread media anticipation. Critics argue this confirms there was no collusion.

Flawed Origins: The theory that the Russia investigation was itself politically motivated gained steam with revelations that the Steele dossier was funded by the Clinton campaign and the DNC.

FISA Abuse: The Department of Justice's Inspector General reported errors and omissions in the FBI's use of surveillance warrants on Trump campaign aide Carter Page, fueling claims of bias and misconduct.

The "Deep State" Narrative: Supporters of Trump argue that entrenched political operatives within the FBI, CIA, and DOJ orchestrated a deliberate attempt to derail his presidency using false allegations.

Famous Quotes / Sources

"There was no collusion, there was no obstruction — total exoneration."

— Donald J. Trump, 2019 (after Mueller Report release)

"If we had confidence that the president clearly did not commit a crime, we would have said so."

— Robert Mueller, public statement, May 2019

"The investigation was predicated on lies and political bias."

— Devin Nunes, former House Intelligence Committee Chair

"It may not have been criminal conspiracy, but it was certainly unethical coordination."

— Adam Schiff, House Intelligence Committee Chair

Real-World Consequences

The Mueller investigation resulted in dozens of indictments and convictions — though none directly tied Trump himself to a conspiracy with Russia. Individuals such as Paul Manafort, Michael Flynn, and Roger Stone were prosecuted for various charges including lying to investigators and financial crimes.

Politically, the controversy consumed much of Trump's presidency and further deepened the nation's partisan divide. For Trump's opponents, it symbolized the vulnerability of American democracy to foreign manipulation. For his supporters, it was the ultimate confirmation of a hostile media and intelligence establishment working against an elected president.

The theory also played a major role in Trump's first impeachment and shaped how future allegations — such as those concerning Hunter Biden — were received by a skeptical public increasingly wary of political scandals.

Where It Stands Today

The official Mueller Report concluded that there was insufficient evidence to charge Trump or his campaign with conspiracy, but left open the question of obstruction of justice. Critics of Trump view the report as damning in its implications; supporters view the absence of charges as vindication.

Further investigations, such as the Durham Report in 2023, examined the origins of the FBI's Russia probe and criticized elements of the agency's conduct. However, these reports also failed to deliver a definitive narrative that satisfied either side.

In conspiracy circles, both versions of the theory live on:

For some, Trump remains a compromised figure who rose to power through foreign assistance.

For others, he is the victim of the most elaborate political frame job in modern American history.

The Trump–Russia case illustrates how conspiracy theories are no longer confined to the fringes — they are now entangled with official investigations, media narratives, and partisan warfare. Whether seen as proof of hidden corruption or of a weaponized intelligence apparatus, it remains one of the defining political sagas of the 21st century.

Chapter Eighteen

Section: Government, History & Political Secrets

Conspiracy: The Biden Laptop Cover-Up

Summary

In October 2020, just weeks before the U.S. presidential election, the New York Post published a story alleging that a laptop belonging to Hunter Biden — son of then-candidate Joe Biden — contained emails and documents that suggested questionable business dealings in Ukraine and China. The laptop, allegedly dropped off at a Delaware computer repair shop, also contained personal material including explicit images and videos.

The story was immediately polarizing. While critics claimed it raised serious questions about political corruption and foreign influence, defenders argued the story was unverified, possibly Russian disinformation, and politically timed to interfere with the election. The Biden Laptop Cover-Up Theory contends that powerful media platforms, government agencies, and intelligence figures colluded to suppress the story and protect Joe Biden's candidacy.

History & Key Claims

The laptop was reportedly abandoned at a repair shop in 2019. After being deemed unclaimed, the shop owner turned it over to the FBI. A copy of the drive was also provided to Rudy Giuliani, Donald Trump's attorney, who passed it to the New York Post.

Key claims within the conspiracy theory include:

Media Suppression: After the New York Post broke the story, social media giants Twitter and Facebook limited its distribution, citing concerns over the veracity and potential hacking origin of the materials. Critics argue this was de facto censorship to protect the Biden campaign.

Intelligence Officials' Letter: Fifty-one former intelligence officials signed a public letter suggesting the laptop story had "all the classic earmarks of a Russian information operation," despite offering no direct evidence. This statement was widely cited by media outlets as justification to downplay the story.

FBI Inaction: Although the FBI reportedly had the laptop since December 2019, no significant action or public statement was made until after the election. Critics argue this delay was intentional and politically motivated.

Tech Company Coordination: Internal communications released later (notably through the "Twitter Files") indicated government and tech industry discussions around suppressing or flagging the story — reinforcing claims of political bias or control.

Legitimacy of Contents: While initial reports questioned the authenticity of the data, subsequent investigations by multiple outlets, including The New York Times and The Washington Post, later confirmed key aspects of the laptop's contents.

Hunter Biden's Business Dealings: Emails and documents on the laptop allegedly detail Hunter Biden's involvement with foreign firms, including Ukrainian energy company Burisma and Chinese investment firms. The central claim is that these dealings may have involved influence-peddling tied to his father.

Famous Quotes / Sources

"Twitter made a mistake in blocking links to the article. It was wrong."

— Jack Dorsey, Twitter CEO, 2021 testimony before Congress

"This has all the classic earmarks of a Russian information operation."

— Open letter from 51 former intelligence officials, October 2020

"The laptop is real. The emails are real. The story was real."

— Glenn Greenwald, journalist and founder of The Intercept

"They knew. They all knew. And they buried it."

— Elon Musk, commenting on the Twitter Files release, 2022

Real-World Consequences

The laptop story's suppression during the final weeks of the 2020 campaign became a flashpoint in debates over media bias, political censorship, and election interference. For Trump supporters, it became a symbol of systemic bias in favor of Democrats. For others, it raised concerns about the role of unverified stories in elections and the spread of misinformation.

The story also highlighted the blurred lines between political activism, journalism, and intelligence. The decision of former officials to speculate publicly without evidence had a lasting impact on public trust.

After the election, several mainstream outlets acknowledged the laptop's authenticity and began investigating its contents more seriously. By 2022, Hunter Biden was under federal investigation for tax issues and foreign business dealings, though no charges tied directly to Joe Biden have been filed.

The case has been repeatedly cited in congressional hearings and political campaigns, particularly by Republicans aiming to scrutinize the Biden family's financial ties.

Where It Stands Today

The Biden Laptop Cover-Up Theory remains deeply divisive. Critics of the theory argue that the media was cautious — not conspiratorial — and that early reporting lacked clear verification. They also note that similar tactics were used to suppress misleading information in previous elections.

Supporters of the theory contend that the suppression was coordinated, intentional, and likely affected the outcome of the 2020 election by shielding damaging information from voters.

Recent congressional investigations have sought to uncover the FBI's role, and new revelations continue to emerge about internal discussions at tech companies regarding moderation policies. The "Twitter Files," released in late 2022, confirmed some behind-the-scenes pressure and uncertainty about how to handle the story.

Whether viewed as a necessary precaution against misinformation or a deliberate act of political censorship, the handling of the Biden laptop story has become a defining controversy of the digital age — and a powerful example of how control over information can shape national elections.

Chapter Nineteen

Section: Government, History & Political Secrets

Conspiracy: MKUltra

Summary

Project MKUltra was a covert CIA mind control program that operated during the Cold War era. Officially launched in 1953 and discontinued in the early 1970s, MKUltra involved illegal experiments on unwitting individuals, often involving psychoactive drugs (notably LSD), sensory deprivation, hypnosis, psychological torture, and other behavior modification techniques.

Though the project was largely unknown to the public for decades, its eventual revelation in the 1970s shocked the world and lent credibility to a wide range of conspiracy theories about government abuse, brainwashing, and covert manipulation. MKUltra is one of the few conspiracy theories proven to be real, and its partial declassification has only deepened suspicions about how far intelligence agencies might go behind closed doors.

History & Key Claims

MKUltra was created by the CIA in 1953 under the direction of then-CIA Director Allen Dulles. The project emerged from Cold War fears that foreign governments — particularly the Soviet Union and China — were using mind control techniques on captured U.S. prisoners of war. The CIA sought to develop similar or superior capabilities, believing that controlling or altering human behavior could give the U.S. a strategic advantage.

Key aspects and claims of MKUltra include:

Use of LSD on Unwitting Subjects: The CIA tested LSD on thousands of subjects — including prisoners, psychiatric patients, students, and even their own employees — often without consent. The drug was believed to potentially aid interrogation or brainwashing.

Subprojects and Front Organizations: MKUltra included over 150 sub-projects, many of which were contracted through universities, hospitals, and research institutions under false pretenses. The full extent of the program remains unknown.

Extreme Experiments: Alleged experiments included sleep deprivation, electroshock therapy, isolation, sexual abuse, and sensory overload, often conducted without ethical oversight.

Death of Dr. Frank Olson: A U.S. Army biochemist unknowingly dosed with LSD as part of the program, Olson died after falling from a hotel window in 1953. Officially ruled a suicide, his death has long been viewed as suspicious. In the 1990s, his family had his body exhumed, and a forensic examination found signs consistent with a blow to the head before the fall.

Destruction of Evidence: In 1973, amid growing scrutiny over intelligence operations, CIA Director Richard Helms ordered most MKUltra documents destroyed. As a result, most details about the program come from surviving fragments and witness testimony.

Continued Influence: Some conspiracy theorists claim MKUltra never truly ended and evolved into other covert programs, such as Project Monarch (alleged trauma-based mind control) or ongoing psychological warfare operations in media and pop culture.

Famous Quotes / Sources

"We are now in possession of the means of making a person tell the truth or even believe a lie."

— CIA internal memo (declassified)

"It was the most shocking, secretive, and illegal behavior I have ever encountered in government."

— Senator Frank Church, Chair of the Church Committee (1975)

"The CIA secretly gave LSD to people — and watched them go insane. That's not fiction. That's MKUltra."

— Stephen Kinzer, author of Poisoner in Chief (2019)

"Control the mind, control the person. MKUltra was about power — not science."

— Dr. Colin Ross, psychiatrist and mind control researcher

Real-World Consequences

The existence of MKUltra was first publicly exposed during the 1975 Church Committee hearings, which investigated abuses by the CIA, NSA, and FBI. The hearings revealed that the CIA had violated the rights of thousands of American citizens, many of whom suffered long-term psychological damage.

The scandal led to widespread reforms in intelligence oversight, including the establishment of the permanent Senate Select Committee on Intelligence. Laws were enacted to regulate human experimentation and limit clandestine operations on U.S. soil.

Despite these reforms, no high-ranking CIA officials were prosecuted, and compensation to victims was limited and delayed. Many lawsuits were dismissed on national security grounds, and the destruction of documents left most victims unable to prove they were involved.

MKUltra also became a cornerstone of distrust toward the intelligence community and is frequently cited in discussions of government secrecy, unethical science, and psychological manipulation.

Where It Stands Today

MKUltra is not a theory — it is a documented historical fact. However, the full scope of the project remains unknown, and this ambiguity fuels further speculation.

In conspiracy culture, MKUltra is referenced in countless sub-theories:

That serial killers or assassins (like Sirhan Sirhan) were mind-controlled operatives.

That celebrities or political figures are victims of "Monarch programming."

That MKUltra techniques are now embedded in entertainment, media, or social engineering.

For skeptics, MKUltra is a cautionary tale: an example of real abuse that now invites exaggerated or unfounded claims. For believers, it is proof that when government programs are exposed — even partially — the truth is often stranger and darker than fiction.

Its enduring legacy is one of paranoia, secrecy, and betrayal — and it remains one of the most compelling and disturbing entries in the annals of American conspiracy.

Chapter Twenty

Section: Government, History & Political Secrets

Conspiracy: Project Monarch (Mind Control Subdivision)

Summary

Project Monarch is a widely circulated but officially unconfirmed extension of the CIA's MKUltra program. Believers claim that it is a clandestine mind control project that uses trauma-based conditioning — especially on children — to create dissociative identities that can be programmed and controlled.

Project Monarch allegedly produces mind-controlled slaves used in espionage, entertainment, sex trafficking, and ritual abuse. Despite the lack of declassified documents confirming its existence, Monarch theory has gained traction within conspiracy circles, particularly among those who believe in deep-state control, elite satanic cults, and the weaponization of psychological trauma.

Critics regard it as a fringe theory rooted in moral panic, while supporters argue its secrecy is deliberate, echoing the long-hidden history of MKUltra.

History & Key Claims

Project Monarch allegedly emerged from the ashes of MKUltra, continuing its most extreme experiments in secret. Its central claim is that severe trauma — especially during early childhood — fractures the mind into multiple personalities, or "alters," which can then be programmed using hypnosis, symbols, pain, and ritualistic abuse.

Key claims of Project Monarch include:

Monarch Programming: The name supposedly derives from the monarch butterfly, which symbolizes transformation. Victims, called "Monarchs," are said to undergo complete psychological rewiring.

Trauma-Induced Dissociation: Through repeated abuse — including electroshock, sexual trauma, and isolation — subjects are claimed to develop dissociative identity disorder (DID), allowing handlers to "store" commands within separate identities.

Beta, Delta, and Omega Programming: Various "types" of Monarch slaves are allegedly trained for specific purposes. For example:

Beta: Sexual slaves (often tied to celebrities or politicians)

Delta: Assassins

Omega: Suicide programming or memory erasure

Celebrity Victims: Numerous pop stars and actors (e.g. Britney Spears, Beyoncé, Kanye West, Miley Cyrus, and others) have been cited by theorists as programmed "Monarchs" — pointing to symbolic imagery in music videos, mental breakdowns, robotic behavior, or butterfly iconography.

Satanic Ritual Abuse (SRA): Monarch theory often overlaps with claims of SRA, particularly in elite or secret society settings. Victims allegedly undergo torture rituals involving occult symbols, handlers, and bloodlines.

Handlers and Triggers: Monarch slaves are said to be managed by "handlers" and activated via code words, sounds, or hand gestures. Symbols like butterflies, mirrors, broken dolls, and black-and-white checkerboards are thought to be used in programming.

CIA & Military Origins: While no official documentation exists, believers tie the theory to military psychological warfare, occult-leaning factions in intelligence services, and experiments conducted on foster children, military brats, and those in satanic covens.

Famous Quotes / Sources

"Project Monarch may be the most sinister operation ever conceived — a fusion of occult ritual and psychological warfare."

— Fritz Springmeier, co-author of The Illuminati Formula Used to Create an Undetectable Total Mind-Controlled Slave

"The MKUltra program did not end. It was renamed, divided, and buried."

— Cathy O'Brien, self-proclaimed Monarch survivor and author of Trance Formation of America

"None of the claims about Project Monarch have been verified by official government documents or substantiated with hard evidence."

— Snopes Fact Check, 2015

"Once you start to notice the butterflies, you can't unsee them."

— Anon researcher, 4chan (Monarch symbolism thread)

Real-World Consequences

While Project Monarch itself has not been proven, the allegations have real-world consequences:

False Memory Syndrome & Panic: Many therapists, particularly in the 1980s–1990s, reported clients claiming ritual abuse, often under hypnosis. Critics argue this contributed to false memory syndrome and several moral panics, including the infamous McMartin preschool trial.

Satanic Panic Fallout: Monarch theory blends with broader fears of satanic ritual abuse, leading to numerous wrongful accusations and convictions, particularly in the U.S.

Cultural Paranoia: Artists have had public breakdowns or moments of distress attributed to Monarch programming, fueling public speculation and online witch hunts.

Misuse in Activism: Monarch theory is often invoked alongside Pizzagate and QAnon narratives, further entrenching the belief in secret cabals abusing children — sometimes without distinguishing between genuine advocacy and fictionalized horror.

Distrust of Mental Health Fields: Monarch narratives often challenge the mainstream psychological understanding of dissociation and trauma, potentially undermining treatment for real sufferers of PTSD or DID.

Where It Stands Today

Project Monarch remains unverified by official sources, but entrenched in conspiracy lore. No leaked documents, whistleblower confirmations, or declassified papers have confirmed the project — unlike MKUltra.

However, its persistence speaks to deeper cultural fears: the abuse of children, loss of free will, elite corruption, and the manipulation of the mind. Monarch theory has become especially prevalent in online forums, YouTube exposés, and symbol-spotting communities where pop culture is seen as encoded with messages of mind control.

Skeptics argue that Monarch is modern mythology — a horror story that borrows the credibility of MKUltra to explain celebrity breakdowns and moral decay. Believers, however, argue that the lack of evidence proves only the project's success in covering its tracks.

Either way, Monarch has become more than a conspiracy theory. It is a meme, a mythos, and — for some — a terrifying possibility that government control has gone deeper than anyone dares imagine.

Chapter Twenty-One

Section: Government, History & Political Secrets

Conspiracy: COINTELPRO

Summary

COINTELPRO — short for Counter Intelligence Program — was a covert FBI operation designed to surveil, infiltrate, discredit, and disrupt domestic political groups in the United States. Officially active from 1956 to 1971, it targeted a wide range of movements deemed "subversive," including civil rights activists, anti-war protestors, Black liberation organizations, and socialist groups.

Though COINTELPRO was confirmed and exposed in the 1970s, conspiracy theorists argue that its tactics never ended, simply changed names or went underground. Many believe that modern activism is still monitored and manipulated by similar shadow operations, and that the lessons of COINTELPRO remain urgently relevant.

History & Key Claims

COINTELPRO began during the Red Scare of the 1950s under FBI Director J. Edgar Hoover, originally to combat Communist influence. But over time, its scope expanded to include:

The Civil Rights Movement

The Black Panther Party

Martin Luther King Jr. and other prominent Black leaders

Anti-Vietnam War protest groups

Puerto Rican independence activists

The New Left and Students for a Democratic Society (SDS)

American Indian Movement (AIM)

Key elements and tactics included:

Surveillance and Wiretapping: Without warrants, the FBI monitored phone calls, mail, and meetings of activists, politicians, and community leaders.

Infiltration: Undercover agents and informants were placed within organizations to sow distrust, collect intelligence, and sometimes provoke violence.

Smear Campaigns: Fake letters, doctored photos, and anonymous tips were used to break up marriages, ruin reputations, or provoke infighting.

"Neutralization" of Leaders: Internal memos encouraged strategies to "neutralize" figures like Martin Luther King Jr. through blackmail, intimidation, and public embarrassment.

Psychological Warfare: Disinformation was a key strategy — such as sending threatening letters, false accusations, or warnings of violence to manipulate or frighten targets.

The public first became aware of COINTELPRO in 1971, when a group calling themselves the Citizens' Commission to Investigate the FBI broke into an FBI field office in Media, Pennsylvania, and stole thousands of documents. These were later released to the press, exposing the full extent of the program.

Famous Quotes / Sources

"The FBI was engaged in a sophisticated vigilante operation aimed squarely at preventing the exercise of First Amendment rights."

— U.S. Senate Church Committee, Final Report (1976)

"In the opinion of the Bureau, Dr. King is a potential danger to the national security."

— FBI internal memo, 1963

"Expose, disrupt, misdirect, discredit, or otherwise neutralize."

— Official COINTELPRO directive to agents

"You are done. There is only one thing left for you to do… you know what it is."

— Excerpt from anonymous letter sent to MLK (widely believed to be from the FBI)

Real-World Consequences

COINTELPRO had devastating impacts:

Destruction of Civil Rights Leaders: The program aggressively targeted Dr. Martin Luther King Jr., bugging his hotel rooms and attempting to push him to suicide. FBI operatives even sent him a forged letter threatening to expose alleged affairs if he did not kill himself.

Black Panther Party Suppression: The FBI used infiltration and instigation to disrupt chapters, provoke violence, and contribute to internal conflicts. Notably, Fred Hampton, a 21-year-old Black Panther leader, was killed in his sleep in a 1969 raid coordinated with the FBI and Chicago police.

Stifled Activism: Many organizations broke apart due to mistrust, fear, and sabotage. The climate of paranoia discouraged mass organizing.

Chilling Effects on Free Speech: Knowing the government could infiltrate, record, or manipulate any protest or meeting discouraged participation and created lasting distrust in institutions.

No Accountability: Despite overwhelming evidence, few officials faced consequences. J. Edgar Hoover remained FBI Director until his death in 1972.

Where It Stands Today

COINTELPRO is a confirmed and documented government conspiracy. Yet, for many, the true scandal is that the same methods continue — albeit under different names and legal justifications.

Examples often cited as modern COINTELPRO echoes:

Post-9/11 Surveillance of Muslim Communities

FBI targeting of Black Lives Matter activists

Use of undercover informants in protest movements

Government tracking of online dissent and "domestic extremism"

For conspiracy theorists, COINTELPRO is not just history — it's a blueprint still in use. The lesson is clear: surveillance and manipulation of dissent are not relics of the past, but recurring tools of power.

Skeptics agree the original COINTELPRO was unconstitutional, but argue today's intelligence operations are more restrained and transparent. Yet the historical record casts a long shadow, making many wary of government promises.

COINTELPRO remains one of the most damning admissions in U.S. intelligence history, offering undeniable proof that the government has spied on, disrupted, and destroyed the lives of its own citizens — especially those fighting for justice.

Chapter Twenty-Two

Section: Government, History & Political Secrets

Conspiracy: Operation Gladio

Summary

Operation Gladio refers to a post–World War II covert program involving "stay-behind" armies in Europe, initially set up by NATO and Western intelligence agencies — particularly the CIA and MI6 — to resist potential Soviet invasions. What began as Cold War contingency planning allegedly evolved into a dark network engaged in false flag terrorism, political manipulation, and destabilization of democratic movements, particularly in Italy, Belgium, and Turkey.

Though the existence of Gladio is factually confirmed, its deeper implications remain hotly debated. Conspiracy theorists believe Gladio operatives orchestrated violent events to push public opinion toward conservative or authoritarian policies — in what's referred to as the "strategy of tension."

History & Key Claims

After WWII, as tensions between NATO and the USSR escalated, the U.S. and U.K. helped establish secret anti-communist resistance cells throughout Western Europe. These "stay-behind" units were tasked with activating only if the Soviets invaded.

But critics argue that Gladio never remained dormant — instead, it was weaponized against leftist political groups in their own countries. Claims include:

Terrorism for Political Gain: Gladio agents allegedly staged bombings, shootings, and other attacks — falsely blaming them on communists or anarchists — to provoke fear and justify right-wing crackdowns.

The Bologna Massacre (1980): One of the deadliest attacks in Italy's history (85 dead, over 200 injured) was initially blamed on leftist radicals but later linked to neo-fascist groups with ties to Gladio.

The Years of Lead (Italy, 1960s–1980s): A period marked by rampant political violence. Many left-wing activists were imprisoned or discredited, while the real perpetrators remained hidden.

Involvement of Secret Societies: Gladio operatives allegedly intersected with groups like Propaganda Due (P2) — a secret Masonic lodge that included politicians, military officials, and businessmen involved in financial scandals, murder coverups, and plots to suspend democracy.

Belgium and Turkey: Similar "stay-behind" networks are alleged to have been involved in attacks or coups. In Turkey, the term "Deep State" is often used to describe Gladio-like operations that manipulate democratic institutions behind the scenes.

Media Manipulation: According to theorists, the press was complicit — reporting leftist responsibility immediately after attacks, even when evidence later pointed elsewhere.

The term "Gladio" technically refers to the Italian branch, but it's now used broadly for similar Cold War-era clandestine structures across NATO countries.

Famous Quotes / Sources

"You had to attack civilians, women, children, innocent people, unknown people far removed from any political game... The reason was simple. To force the public to turn to the state for greater security."

— Vincenzo Vinciguerra, former Italian neo-fascist linked to Gladio, court testimony

"During all those years, a secret network of armies existed in Europe, unknown to the parliaments and to the people. These secret armies were run by the secret services of the state and the CIA."

— Daniele Ganser, historian and author of NATO's Secret Armies

"Gladio is not a myth. It is a reality. It has existed for years."

— Giulio Andreotti, former Italian Prime Minister (1990 statement to Parliament)

Real-World Consequences

Gladio's exposure in the early 1990s had major consequences:

Public Outrage and Scandal: The Italian government was forced to admit the program existed. Similar confirmations followed in Belgium and other countries.

Parliamentary Investigations: Several European nations held inquiries, but many questions remained unanswered due to national security secrecy.

Political Destabilization: In Italy, the scandal eroded public trust in government and triggered mass resignations. It also contributed to the collapse of Italy's postwar political order.

Conspiratorial Reinforcement: Gladio became a touchstone for other conspiracy theories — cited as proof that governments and NATO would manipulate or kill civilians to serve ideological ends.

Fuel for "Deep State" Belief: The idea that elected governments are merely the surface layer above secret forces gained credibility, especially in Turkey, where the term "Deep State" originated partly in reference to Gladio-style networks.

Where It Stands Today

Operation Gladio is not theoretical — it is historical fact, though the extent of its criminal activity remains unproven in many cases.

Skeptics argue the program was primarily a Cold War precaution, and that rogue actors — not NATO itself — were behind any abuses. Others claim the strategy of tension was intentionally orchestrated by intelligence services to manipulate democracy through fear.

The legacy of Gladio lives on in multiple ways:

It is often cited when false flag attacks are suspected.

It informs debates on NATO transparency and Western intelligence accountability.

It serves as a real-world example of how conspiracy theories sometimes grow from fragments of truth.

While many of its chapters remain hidden, Gladio represents a chilling intersection of military power, secrecy, and political manipulation — one that continues to shape how people view the structures meant to protect them.

Chapter Twenty-Three

Section: Government, History & Political Secrets

Conspiracy: CIA Involvement in the Crack Epidemic

Summary

The claim that the Central Intelligence Agency (CIA) helped fuel the crack cocaine epidemic in American inner cities—particularly in the 1980s—remains one of the most controversial and racially charged conspiracy theories in modern U.S. history.

At the heart of the theory is the allegation that the CIA knowingly allowed large amounts of cocaine to be trafficked into the United States, with profits used to fund Nicaraguan Contra rebels, all while devastating predominantly Black urban communities. The conspiracy gained national attention following journalist Gary Webb's 1996 Dark Alliance series, which claimed to link the CIA, Nicaraguan drug traffickers, and the rise of crack in Los Angeles.

While the CIA has denied any intentional wrongdoing, multiple investigations, including one by the CIA's own inspector general, found evidence of disturbing connections and deliberate negligence. For many, the theory remains not only plausible but emblematic of government indifference—or worse—toward marginalized communities.

History & Key Claims

This theory hinges on several interconnected historical events:

Nicaraguan Contras & U.S. Policy: During the Reagan administration, the U.S. covertly supported the Contras, a right-wing rebel group fighting Nicaragua's socialist Sandinista government. After Congress passed the Boland Amendment (banning U.S. funding for the Contras), the CIA sought alternative ways to continue their support.

Cocaine Trafficking Allegations: Enter Danilo Blandón and Norwin Meneses, two Nicaraguan drug traffickers allegedly tied to the Contras. According to journalist Gary Webb, Blandón supplied enormous quantities of cocaine to "Freeway" Rick Ross, a drug kingpin in South Central Los Angeles who converted the powder into crack and distributed it across the country.

CIA Complicity: Webb's Dark Alliance suggested that the CIA not only knew about this drug operation but protected the traffickers to ensure Contra funding. In effect, the U.S. government stood by as crack ravaged communities, because the geopolitical priority was toppling Nicaragua's leftist regime.

Coverup and Retaliation: After Webb's reporting, major newspapers such as The New York Times, Washington Post, and L.A. Times published pieces discrediting his claims. Webb was demoted and eventually committed suicide in 2004 — an event that conspiracy theorists cite as part of a broader campaign to silence dissent.

Famous Quotes / Sources

"I do not believe that we did everything that we should have done, or that we did everything right."

— Frederick Hitz, CIA Inspector General, in Senate testimony, 1998

"It is one of the most damning government scandals of our time, and yet it's been whitewashed by the very institutions meant to investigate it."

— Maxine Waters, U.S. Congresswoman, 1996

"[The CIA] looked the other way when major traffickers brought drugs into the U.S."

— Gary Webb, Dark Alliance

"We do not believe there is any credible evidence of CIA involvement in drug trafficking."

— CIA Statement, 1997

Real-World Consequences

Whether or not the CIA directly orchestrated the crack epidemic, the perception of complicity had enormous real-world effects:

Mass Incarceration: The crack wave of the 1980s helped fuel a surge in arrests, especially among Black Americans. Harsh sentencing laws — including the infamous 100-to-1 disparity in punishment between crack and powder cocaine — devastated communities and families.

Loss of Trust: Among many African Americans, the CIA-crack theory confirmed long-held suspicions of systemic targeting. Public trust in law enforcement and federal agencies declined sharply in affected areas.

Media Backlash & Accountability: The mainstream media's coordinated takedown of Gary Webb, followed by later revelations validating parts of his reporting, created a case study in institutional bias, censorship, and reputational destruction.

Congressional Hearings: In 1998, the House Intelligence Committee held hearings on the matter, acknowledging that CIA affiliates had been linked to drug traffickers, though still denying intentional involvement.

Popular Culture Impact: The theory influenced music, film, and literature, with numerous hip-hop artists (e.g., Tupac Shakur, Public Enemy, Killer Mike) referencing the idea that the U.S. government introduced crack as a tool of oppression.

Where It Stands Today

Official investigations — including one by the CIA Inspector General — admitted that the agency had ties to Contra-linked individuals involved in drug trafficking. However, the reports carefully stated that the CIA did not "intentionally" allow drugs to be sold in the U.S. to fund the Contras.

Many journalists and activists consider this a semantic loophole: while direct intent may be debatable, the evidence of willful ignorance, complicity, and cover-up is difficult to ignore.

To this day, many believe the crack epidemic wasn't just an unfortunate side effect of Cold War politics but a covert form of social engineering—crippling resistance movements, flooding neighborhoods with addiction, and justifying a militarized police state.

For those communities most affected, the debate over whether the CIA merely allowed or engineered the epidemic may be academic. The consequences were — and remain — devastating.

Chapter Twenty-Four

Section: Government, History & Political Secrets

Conspiracy: The "October Surprise" Theory (1980 Election)

Summary

The "October Surprise" theory refers to an alleged secret deal between members of Ronald Reagan's 1980 presidential campaign and the Iranian government to delay the release of American hostages until after the U.S. election — effectively sabotaging President Jimmy Carter's re-election chances.

The idea is that Reagan campaign officials negotiated behind the scenes, promising Iran favorable treatment or arms in exchange for keeping the 52 American hostages until after Carter was out of office. The hostages were, notably, released on the very day Reagan was inaugurated — January 20, 1981 — which many saw as suspiciously timed.

While no definitive proof has ever been produced to confirm this theory, it has persisted for decades, with resurfacing witness testimony, covert travel records, and circumstantial timelines adding fuel to the fire. If true, it would constitute an extraordinary act of political treason and election interference on a global scale.

History & Key Claims

The Iran Hostage Crisis: In November 1979, Iranian revolutionaries stormed the U.S. embassy in Tehran and took 66 Americans hostage. By 1980, 52 were still held captive. President Carter's inability to secure their release was seen as a major weakness in his re-election campaign.

The 1980 Election: Republican challenger Ronald Reagan's team, aware that a successful hostage release could shift public opinion in Carter's favor, allegedly moved to block any deal. The theory claims Reagan's campaign sent intermediaries — including William Casey (future CIA director) and possibly George H. W. Bush — to meet with Iranian officials in secret.

Alleged Meetings in Paris: According to several sources, meetings took place in Paris in October 1980, where Reagan operatives struck a bargain with Iranian representatives. In return for delaying the hostages' release, Iran would later receive arms shipments and relaxed U.S. pressure.

Hostage Release Timing: On January 20, 1981, within minutes of Reagan taking the oath of office, the hostages were freed — after 444 days in captivity. To many, this dramatic timing confirmed that a deal had been made.

Arms-for-Hostage Precedent: The later Iran-Contra Affair (mid-1980s), in which the Reagan administration secretly sold arms to Iran in exchange for hostages and funneled money to Nicaraguan rebels, reinforced the plausibility of such behind-the-scenes dealings.

Famous Quotes / Sources

"The hostages weren't released because there was a deal made… and we were told not to interfere."

— Former Iranian President Abolhassan Banisadr, 1993 interview

"I think what we're looking at is probably the most serious violation of the Constitution in American history."

— Gary Sick, Carter's National Security Adviser and author of October Surprise

"They [Reagan's people] made a deal. They delayed the hostages. That much I'm sure of."

— Barbara Honegger, former Reagan administration staffer turned whistleblower

"Allegations are unfounded, unproven, and unsupported by credible evidence."

— House October Surprise Task Force Report, 1993

Real-World Consequences

Election Impact: Carter lost the 1980 election by a landslide. Whether the hostage delay was a decisive factor is debatable, but it undeniably shaped the narrative of his presidency and Reagan's rise.

Conspiracy Reinforcement: The timing of the hostage release has never ceased to raise eyebrows. For many, it was the birth of modern political conspiracy thinking, and a foundation for later claims of "shadow government" and elite manipulation.

Two Congressional Investigations: In the early 1990s, the Senate Foreign Relations Committee and House October Surprise Task Force conducted separate inquiries. Both officially concluded there was "no credible evidence" to support the theory — though many critics claim the investigations were limited in scope and relied heavily on classified or redacted material.

Legacy of Skepticism: The theory has left a legacy of mistrust in electoral integrity, especially where foreign policy intersects with campaign politics. It remains a reference point in debates over how far political actors will go to secure power.

Where It Stands Today

Officially, the October Surprise theory is considered unproven and speculative. However, multiple former intelligence officers, foreign officials, and journalists continue to suggest that key elements of the story were suppressed or deliberately obscured.

Documents declassified over the decades — including Reagan transition team memos, flight logs, and CIA travel reports — have added layers of circumstantial credibility, though never a definitive "smoking gun."

For conspiracy theorists, the October Surprise is a textbook example of elite political deception: a real-world narrative where timing, motive, and circumstantial evidence align suspiciously well — and where plausible deniability is built into every layer.

The hostage release remains one of the most choreographed and symbolically loaded events in U.S. political history. Whether the public will ever know the full truth is uncertain — but the theory remains a fixture in the canon of covert political manipulation.

Chapter Twenty-Five

Section: Government, History & Political Secrets

Conspiracy: Assassination of Robert F. Kennedy

Summary

On June 5, 1968, U.S. Senator Robert F. Kennedy — former Attorney General and brother of President John F. Kennedy — was fatally shot in the kitchen pantry of the Ambassador Hotel in Los Angeles, shortly after delivering a victory speech for his California Democratic primary win.

The official story maintains that Sirhan Sirhan, a 24-year-old Palestinian with anti-Zionist motives, acted alone. But for decades, critics have claimed the assassination was a coordinated plot involving a second gunman, possible mind control, and a broader effort to eliminate a political figure who threatened entrenched power structures.

While Sirhan remains imprisoned, the debate surrounding RFK's death mirrors the conspiratorial fog that surrounds his brother's — raising deep questions about justice, evidence, and the political cost of challenging the status quo.

History & Key Claims

The Event: Just after midnight on June 5, 1968, Kennedy exited the ballroom of the Ambassador Hotel through a pantry corridor. As he greeted staff, Sirhan Sirhan stepped forward and opened fire with a .22 caliber revolver. Kennedy was shot in the head and died the next day.

Official Narrative: Sirhan, captured at the scene, confessed to the killing and cited Kennedy's support for Israel as his motive. He was sentenced to death (later commuted to life in prison).

Key Discrepancies:

Ballistics Mismatch: Kennedy was shot behind the ear from close range — yet witnesses placed Sirhan several feet in front of him. Some claimed Sirhan was tackled before he could have gotten close enough.

Too Many Shots: Witnesses and audio analysis suggest up to 13 shots were fired — more than Sirhan's gun could hold (8-round revolver).

Second Gunman Theory: Several witnesses, including hotel staff, reported multiple shooters or sounds of shots from different directions.

Polka Dot Dress Woman: Multiple witnesses described a mysterious woman in a polka dot dress fleeing the scene saying, "We shot him!" She was never identified.

Mind Control Allegations:

Sirhan claimed he had no memory of the shooting and later said he felt as though he was "hypnotized." This sparked theories of CIA involvement via MKUltra, a covert mind-control program (now confirmed to have existed).

Some psychiatrists who interviewed Sirhan believed he may have been in a trance-like state during the assassination.

Kennedy's Enemies: RFK was known to oppose the Vietnam War, resist entrenched intelligence interests, and support civil rights — making him, in the eyes of theorists, a dangerous figure to establishment powers, similar to his brother.

Famous Quotes / Sources

"There's no question in my mind that there was a second gunman… and that Sirhan Sirhan did not kill my father."

— Robert F. Kennedy Jr., 2018

"Sirhan may have fired shots, but he did not fire the fatal shot."

— Dr. Thomas Noguchi, LA County Coroner, in original autopsy

"There's evidence of a second shooter, but it's been consistently ignored or buried."

— Paul Schrade, Kennedy aide who was also shot at the scene

"Sirhan fired the gun, yes. But was he in control of himself when he did? That's the question history hasn't answered."

— Lisa Pease, author of A Lie Too Big to Fail

Real-World Consequences

Loss of a Major Political Figure: RFK was widely expected to win the Democratic nomination and possibly the presidency. His death dramatically altered the course of American politics.

Erosion of Trust in Investigations: As with the JFK assassination, inconsistencies in evidence, witness testimony, and official findings fed a growing belief that truth was being deliberately withheld.

Mind Control Scrutiny: Theories about Sirhan being a "Manchurian Candidate" led to renewed interest in MKUltra and CIA psychological experiments.

Calls for Reinvestigation: In recent years, members of the Kennedy family and legal experts have called for a new trial or release of Sirhan, citing inconsistencies in the case.

Continued Public Fascination: The assassination remains a popular subject of books, documentaries, and academic debates. It is often cited alongside JFK and MLK Jr.'s deaths as part of a broader pattern of political silencing during the turbulent 1960s.

Where It Stands Today

In 2021, Sirhan Sirhan was recommended for parole by a California board — but the decision was later reversed by the governor, citing public safety concerns and lack of remorse. Despite his decades in prison, questions persist about whether he was the sole perpetrator, or a patsy in a deeper plot.

The possibility of CIA connections, a second shooter, and suppressed evidence continues to provoke discussion. Many view RFK's assassination as one of the most unresolved murders in American history — a wound that never fully healed.

While some remain confident in the official version, others see the killing as part of a systemic effort to eliminate transformational leaders — a chilling echo of earlier political tragedies.

Chapter Twenty-Six

Section: Government, History & Political Secrets

Conspiracy: The Deep State Controls All Presidents

Summary

The term "Deep State" refers to a supposed permanent, unelected shadow government that exists beyond party lines and persists regardless of who holds elected office. According to this theory, the U.S. President — regardless of party — serves largely as a figurehead, while true power lies with career intelligence officials, military elites, banking interests, and globalist policymakers operating behind the scenes.

Proponents argue that the Deep State not only manipulates domestic and foreign policy but also controls elections, manufactures crises, and neutralizes threats to its continued dominance. While critics dismiss it as paranoid fantasy, others believe it's simply a modern label for what President Eisenhower warned about in 1961: the military-industrial complex.

Though the term has gained traction in recent years — especially during the Trump administration — its roots run far deeper, with hints of Deep State-like entities in history, from secret societies to intelligence coups.

History & Key Claims

Early Origins: Although the phrase "Deep State" entered American discourse in the 2010s, the concept itself dates back decades. It's closely related to the idea of a "shadow government"—a network of bureaucrats, military figures, financiers, and intelligence agents acting independently of the democratic process.

Military-Industrial Complex: In his 1961 farewell address, President Dwight D. Eisenhower famously warned of "the acquisition of unwarranted influence… by the military-industrial complex." Many see this as the earliest acknowledgment of a Deep State threat.

Intelligence Autonomy: Agencies like the CIA and NSA, with their black budgets and global reach, are often at the heart of Deep State theories. Examples like MKUltra, COINTELPRO, and Operation Mockingbird support the idea that these agencies sometimes operate outside legal and ethical oversight.

Presidential Conflicts:

JFK is believed by some to have been assassinated after threatening to "splinter the CIA into a thousand pieces."

Nixon's downfall is interpreted by some as an inside job by intelligence officials angered by his actions.

Trump frequently invoked the Deep State as an enemy working to undermine him from within the federal government.

Obama and Bush were both accused — by opposing sides — of being pawns of Deep State globalism.

Key Beliefs:

Presidents are briefed and "contained" after election.

Major policy shifts (e.g., war, surveillance, monetary policy) are pre-determined, with elections serving as a democratic facade.

Whistleblowers, investigative journalists, and dissenting politicians are discredited or eliminated.

Famous Quotes / Sources

"Behind the ostensible government sits enthroned an invisible government owing no allegiance and acknowledging no responsibility to the people."

— Theodore Roosevelt, 1912

"The Deep State exists. It's real. But it's not partisan — it's the permanent bureaucracy."

— Mike Lofgren, former Congressional staffer and author of The Deep State: The Fall of the Constitution and the Rise of a Shadow Government

"There is a power somewhere so organized, so subtle, so watchful, so interlocked… that they had better not speak above their breath when they speak in condemnation of it."

— Woodrow Wilson, 1913

"They don't go after me because I'm Donald Trump. They go after me because I stand in their way. I'm just in the way — they're after you."

— Donald J. Trump, 2020 campaign rally

Real-World Consequences

Erosion of Public Trust: Belief in a Deep State contributes to widespread distrust of democratic institutions, the media, intelligence agencies, and elected officials. For some, no result — no matter how transparent — is legitimate if it goes against perceived Deep State interests.

Partisan Weaponization: While initially seen as a right-wing idea, the Deep State theory has been used across the political spectrum. Progressives cite it to explain corporate dominance and endless war; conservatives use it to explain censorship, surveillance, and political targeting.

Violence & Radicalization: Belief in a Deep State has fueled acts of protest and violence, most notably the January 6th Capitol riot, where rioters claimed to be "taking the country back" from hidden control.

Policy Paralysis: Accusations of Deep State interference have made governing more difficult, with presidents hesitant to trust intelligence briefings or national security advice for fear of sabotage.

Rise of Outsider Candidates: The theory has fueled the success of populist, anti-establishment figures who campaign on "draining the swamp" or disrupting the system — regardless of party.

Where It Stands Today

While there is no official proof of a unified Deep State, many believe the accumulated influence of defense contractors, intelligence officials, central bankers, and technocrats effectively acts as such. The concentration of power within unaccountable institutions, the use of surveillance, and the global consistency of certain policies regardless of leadership all lend credence to the idea of invisible hands steering the wheel.

Others argue the Deep State theory oversimplifies complex bureaucratic inertia, mistaking inefficiency and institutional norms for malice or conspiracy. Critics warn that the Deep State label has become a catch-all for any policy or outcome people dislike — which can be dangerous.

Regardless of its factual standing, the concept of a Deep State has become entrenched in modern political discourse, and belief in it shows no signs of fading.

Chapter Twenty-Seven

Section: Government, History & Political Secrets

Conspiracy: Pizzagate

Summary

Pizzagate is a widely debunked yet influential conspiracy theory that emerged during the 2016 U.S. presidential election. It claims that a child-trafficking ring involving high-ranking Democratic officials, including Hillary Clinton and members of her campaign team, was operating out of Comet Ping Pong, a pizzeria in Washington, D.C.

While thoroughly disproven by law enforcement, journalists, and fact-checkers, Pizzagate had real-world consequences. It fueled online harassment campaigns, shaped the development of the broader QAnon movement, and even inspired a violent incident in which an armed man stormed the restaurant in search of non-existent victims.

History & Key Claims

The theory originated from leaked emails published by WikiLeaks from the account of John Podesta, Hillary Clinton's campaign chairman. Pizzagate proponents claimed that certain words in the emails — such as "pizza," "cheese," and "hot dog" — were coded references to child trafficking and abuse.

Key elements of the theory include:

Comet Ping Pong as the Epicenter: Conspiracy theorists claimed the restaurant was the hub of a secret child sex ring, with victims allegedly held in tunnels beneath the establishment. No such tunnels or evidence have ever been found.

Podesta Emails: Out-of-context references to pizza were interpreted as code words for pedophilia. For example, "cheese pizza" was said to represent "child pornography" (based on online slang).

Celebrity and Political Involvement: High-profile Democrats, as well as celebrities connected to them, were accused of being part of this underground network. Imagery from Clinton campaign events and Podesta's personal art collection was cited as "proof."

Satanic Rituals and Occult Themes: The theory borrowed elements from earlier satanic ritual abuse panic narratives of the 1980s, claiming that powerful elites conducted rituals involving children.

Mainstream Spread: Social media, particularly Reddit and 4chan, amplified the theory. As mainstream coverage tried to debunk it, believers interpreted the pushback as a sign of a larger cover-up.

Famous Quotes / Sources

"Do you believe in coincidences? The emails are not about pizza. They are about something far darker."

— Anonymous Reddit post, 2016

"The allegations are not only false, they're dangerous. People have been threatened, harassed, and terrified by this nonsense."

— James Alefantis, owner of Comet Ping Pong

"I came here to self-investigate. The intel wasn't 100 percent."

— Edgar Maddison Welch, man arrested for firing a rifle inside Comet Ping Pong (December 2016)

"This conspiracy is an evolution of old tropes — the 'elite child abuse' narrative has been used to demonize political enemies for centuries."

— Mike Rothschild, author of The Storm is Upon Us

Real-World Consequences

Armed Attack: On December 4, 2016, Edgar Maddison Welch, a man from North Carolina, fired three shots inside Comet Ping Pong while attempting to "rescue" children he believed were being held captive. No one was hurt, but the incident highlighted the danger of viral disinformation.

Harassment of Employees and Patrons: Staff and customers of the restaurant faced constant online abuse, death threats, and intimidation.

Rise of QAnon: Pizzagate laid the groundwork for QAnon, which expanded the elite child-trafficking narrative into a sprawling theory that claims a "cabal" of global elites runs the world.

Impact on Politics: The theory became a weapon in the culture war, used by opponents of the Clintons and Democrats to portray them as morally corrupt or even evil.

Media and Tech Responsibility: The spread of Pizzagate prompted debates over how social media platforms handle conspiracy theories, fake news, and violent rhetoric.

Where It Stands Today

Pizzagate has been comprehensively debunked, with no evidence supporting any of its claims. The FBI, local law enforcement, and independent journalists have all concluded the allegations were entirely baseless.

However, the theory refuses to die. Many QAnon adherents still cite Pizzagate as a "red pill" moment, claiming it woke them up to alleged elite corruption. Its persistence demonstrates how online echo chambers, coded language, and algorithm-driven platforms can transform fringe ideas into mainstream fears.

More broadly, Pizzagate reflects deep public anxieties about child abuse, government corruption, and secrecy — anxieties that are often exploited by conspiracy theorists to generate fear and political division.

Chapter Twenty-Eight

Section: Government, History & Political Secrets

Conspiracy: QAnon

Summary

QAnon is one of the most wide-reaching and persistent conspiracy movements of the 21st century. Emerging in 2017 from anonymous internet forums, QAnon claims that a global cabal of Satan-worshipping pedophiles — including politicians, celebrities, and powerful elites — secretly controls the world, and that Donald Trump was chosen to defeat them.

Central to the movement is "Q," an anonymous figure claiming to be a high-level government insider with Q-level security clearance, who posted cryptic "drops" or "breadcrumbs" hinting at an impending Great Awakening, where mass arrests of deep state operatives would take place, followed by national renewal.

Although the core predictions of QAnon have repeatedly failed to come true, the movement continues to evolve, absorbing other conspiracy theories (e.g., Pizzagate, Deep State, anti-vax rhetoric), and becoming a potent sociopolitical force with real-world impacts.

History & Key Claims

Origins on 4chan: On October 28, 2017, a user calling themselves Q began posting on 4chan's "/pol/" board, claiming access to classified information. The first posts hinted at upcoming arrests of Hillary Clinton and other prominent Democrats.

The Cabal: QAnon followers believe a global group of Satan-worshipping elites traffic children, harvest their blood for a life-extending compound called adrenochrome, and control institutions like the media, Hollywood, and world governments.

Donald Trump's Role: Trump is viewed as a messianic figure secretly working with the military to dismantle the cabal. Q repeatedly praised Trump while framing his opponents as evil or compromised.

"The Storm" and "The Great Awakening":

"The Storm" refers to a future reckoning, where cabal members will be arrested and exposed in a televised spectacle.

"The Great Awakening" is a prophesied era of truth and renewal once the cabal is purged.

"Trust the Plan": Despite missed predictions, Q insisted followers "trust the plan," implying everything was proceeding according to divine or military guidance.

Expanding Narratives: Over time, QAnon absorbed:

Pizzagate allegations

Anti-vaccine and COVID denial rhetoric

Election fraud claims

Anti-globalist and New World Order fears

Decentralized Leadership: Q stopped posting in 2020 (with rare activity afterward), but the movement now functions independently, driven by influencers, alternative media, and online communities.

Famous Quotes / Sources

"Where we go one, we go all."

— QAnon slogan (WWG1WGA)

"Do you believe in coincidences?"

— Common phrase from Q posts (known as "Q drops")

"The calm before the storm…"

— Donald Trump, cryptic comment in 2017 widely interpreted by Q followers as foreshadowing mass arrests

"There is a plan, and it's being executed behind the scenes."

— General Michael Flynn, retired general and key QAnon figure, 2020

"This is not just an internet conspiracy theory. It's a dangerous cult with political consequences."

— Elizabeth Neumann, former DHS official

Real-World Consequences

Capitol Attack: Many of the January 6, 2021 Capitol rioters were QAnon followers, believing they were stopping a stolen election and confronting the cabal.

Violence and Arrests: Several violent incidents have been linked to QAnon adherents, including:

A man blocking the Hoover Dam with an armored truck

A kidnapping attempt of a child by a Q-believing mother

Murder plots against public officials

Radicalization and Isolation: The movement has torn families apart, drawn people away from reality, and fostered deep distrust in institutions, including science, media, and elections.

Political Impact: QAnon believers have run for — and in some cases, won — public office. Politicians have echoed Q language and promoted related theories.

Big Tech Response: Platforms like Twitter, Facebook, and YouTube banned QAnon-related accounts, but the movement persists on encrypted platforms and alternative media sites.

Where It Stands Today

Although Q's original posts have largely ceased, the QAnon movement is far from over. It has morphed into a decentralized belief system, combining elements of millenarianism, religious prophecy, conspiracy culture, and political extremism.

Many of its core themes — distrust of elites, belief in secret pedophile rings, and faith in an unseen plan — remain deeply embedded in far-right and populist communities. The movement continues to recruit and evolve, often cloaking itself in wellness, patriotism, and "saving the children" rhetoric.

Critics argue that QAnon represents a new kind of cultic belief system, one that thrives on algorithmic amplification, emotional manipulation, and permanent narrative flexibility. With its resilience and digital adaptability, QAnon has become one of the defining conspiracy phenomena of the digital age.

Chapter Twenty-Nine

Section: Government, History & Political Secrets

Conspiracy: False Flag Operations

Summary

A false flag operation refers to an event that is staged, orchestrated, or manipulated by a government or organization to appear as though it was carried out by another group. The intent is usually to justify war, enact policies, suppress dissent, or manipulate public opinion.

While false flags are often dismissed as conspiracy theories, some confirmed historical examples do exist, lending credence to more speculative claims. This ambiguity makes the term especially potent — and controversial — in political discourse. The term is now widely used by both skeptics and propagandists to challenge the official version of events.

History & Key Claims

Origin of the Term: "False flag" originates in naval warfare, where ships would raise enemy flags to deceive opponents before attacking. The concept has since expanded to include deceptive political or military acts.

Documented or Widely Alleged False Flags:

Gleiwitz Incident (1939): Nazi operatives dressed as Polish soldiers attacked a German radio station to justify Germany's invasion of Poland.

Operation Northwoods (1962): A declassified U.S. military proposal to commit false flag acts (e.g., sinking refugee boats, staging shootings) and blame them on Cuba to justify war — though never enacted.

Reichstag Fire (1933): Hitler's regime blamed communists for this arson attack, using it to justify emergency powers. Whether the Nazis staged it remains debated.

USS Maine (1898): The U.S. blamed Spain for the explosion of the battleship in Havana harbor, catalyzing the Spanish-American War. Later inquiries cast doubt on Spanish involvement.

Tonkin Gulf Incident (1964): The U.S. used alleged (and later discredited) attacks on Navy ships to escalate the Vietnam War.

Modern Allegations:

9/11 Attacks: Some believe the U.S. government allowed or orchestrated the attacks to justify war in the Middle East.

Mass Shootings: Conspiracy theorists have claimed incidents like Sandy Hook, Parkland, and Las Vegas were false flag operations designed to push gun control.

Chemical Attacks in Syria: Some allege that rebel groups or Western forces staged attacks to implicate the Assad regime.

Capitol Riot (2021): Fringe voices suggested that Antifa or the FBI orchestrated the January 6th riot to discredit Trump supporters.

Common Themes:

The event creates a clear "enemy" or justification for military/political action.

It triggers fear, anger, and unity among the populace — useful for rallying support.

The alleged perpetrators are often unable or unwilling to mount an effective rebuttal.

Famous Quotes / Sources

"This and no other is the root from which a tyrant springs: when he first appears he is a protector."

— Plato, The Republic

"The easiest way to gain control of a population is to carry out acts of terror. The public will clamor for such laws if their personal security is threatened."

— Attributed (without documentation) to Joseph Goebbels, Nazi propagandist — often cited in false flag discussions

"In politics, nothing happens by accident. If it happens, you can bet it was planned that way."

— Franklin D. Roosevelt (attribution disputed)

"False flag operations are a real tactic. The danger is when every tragedy is labeled as one."

— Peter Bergen, journalist and national security analyst

Real-World Consequences

Mistrust and Paranoia: The concept of false flags has been weaponized to discredit real tragedies, from terror attacks to school shootings. Families of victims have faced harassment by conspiracy theorists claiming the event was staged.

Delayed Responses: In some cases, officials may hesitate or underreact to legitimate threats due to suspicion that an event is fabricated or manipulated.

Information Chaos: In the digital age, labeling something a false flag can quickly go viral — spreading doubt before facts are confirmed. This leads to confusion, political polarization, and narrative warfare.

Justification for Real War: Proven false flags like the Gulf of Tonkin incident show how governments have used staged or exaggerated attacks to launch military campaigns, leading to massive loss of life.

Loss of Historical Clarity: When every major event is interpreted through the lens of possible manipulation, the public struggles to distinguish between strategic deceit and coincidence or incompetence.

Where It Stands Today

The term "false flag" has moved from the fringe to mainstream discourse, often used by political figures, influencers, and activists. While skepticism of official narratives is often healthy, the indiscriminate use of false flag accusations has contributed to a culture of cynicism and misinformation.

Legitimate concerns remain about covert operations, disinformation, and state-sponsored deception. However, modern false flag theories often lack evidence and rely heavily on circumstantial coincidences, mistrust of authority, and confirmation bias.

Still, the historical record confirms that false flag operations have occurred, meaning new claims — while needing evidence — cannot be dismissed out of hand. This delicate balance makes the subject of false flags both compelling and treacherous to navigate.

Chapter Thirty

Section: Government, History & Political Secrets

Conspiracy: North Korea Is a CIA Project

Summary

This fringe conspiracy theory posits that North Korea is not an independent, rogue state, but rather a covert creation or puppet project of the CIA or U.S. intelligence. According to believers, the Kim dynasty is either working in secret alignment with Western powers or is used as a controlled adversary to justify military budgets, surveillance expansion, and geopolitical influence across Asia.

Despite its implausibility and lack of credible evidence, the theory persists online — often among those skeptical of all major geopolitical narratives. It's a blend of Cold War paranoia, anti-globalist suspicion, and distrust of both North Korean and American statecraft.

History & Key Claims

The Origins of North Korea: After WWII, Korea was split into two zones: the Soviet-backed North and the U.S.-backed South. Kim Il-Sung, a former guerrilla fighter with Soviet ties, became the founding leader of the Democratic People's Republic of Korea (DPRK) in 1948.

The Theory Emerges: Around the early 2000s, certain online forums (notably 4chan, Reddit fringe groups, and conspiracy blogs) began floating the idea that North Korea's persistent survival — despite isolation, sanctions, and internal collapse — suggested secret backing.

Key Claims Include:

Controlled Adversary: North Korea is intentionally maintained as a villain by the CIA to justify U.S. military presence in the Pacific, especially around South Korea and Japan.

Psychological Tool: The Kim regime provides a tangible "boogeyman" to stoke fear in the West — reinforcing support for defense budgets, anti-nuclear initiatives, and intelligence operations.

CIA Infiltration: Some claim the Kim family was installed or manipulated by U.S. intelligence from the start, or that later generations (e.g., Kim Jong-un) were educated and influenced by Western handlers.

Scripted Conflicts: Missile launches, nuclear tests, and war rhetoric are said to be coordinated theater, ensuring a balance of tension that never erupts into actual conflict.

Information Black Hole: The secrecy of North Korea — and its almost cartoonish portrayal in Western media — makes it an ideal vessel for projection, allowing wild theories to thrive.

Pop Culture and Satire Influence:

Films like The Interview (2014) and documentaries depicting bizarre stories about the Kim family fuel suspicion and incredulity.

Parodies of North Korea often show it as absurd or implausible, leading some to ask if the state itself could be a fabricated farce.

Famous Quotes / Sources

"There is something off about how North Korea always saber-rattles right before a U.S. military contract renewal."

— Anonymous Reddit user, 2016

"How can a bankrupt, starving nation develop ICBMs while Western powers struggle with budget cuts?"

— Fringe blogger, Shadow Play News

"North Korea is the CIA's Truman Show. Everything you see is part of the set."

— Forum post on conspiracy thread, 2018

"Never underestimate how useful an enemy is when you control the narrative."

— Unverified quote often misattributed to CIA officers

Real-World Consequences

Mistrust of Geopolitical News: Believers of this theory tend to dismiss any reports of North Korean aggression as fake or exaggerated — undermining public understanding of global threats.

Mockery of North Korean Suffering: By framing the regime as fake or controlled, the theory ignores the documented human rights abuses and extreme hardships faced by North Korean citizens.

Fuel for Anti-Western Narratives: Some leftist, libertarian, and anti-globalist groups use this theory to argue that the U.S. creates its own enemies to perpetuate imperialism.

Online Radicalization: The theory overlaps with broader conspiracies such as QAnon, New World Order, and deep state manipulation, feeding into a wider rejection of mainstream international politics.

Meme Culture Influence: Many followers engage with the theory half-seriously — as a kind of intellectual trolling — blurring the lines between belief and irony.

Where It Stands Today

This theory remains firmly on the fringe, dismissed by historians, intelligence experts, and international affairs scholars. There is no credible evidence that North Korea is a CIA invention or controlled puppet state.

However, North Korea's extreme secrecy, outlandish propaganda, and isolation continue to breed doubt and fascination. For many, the regime seems too surreal to be real — creating fertile ground for speculation.

As with many conspiracies, this theory reflects broader truths:

States do manipulate narratives.

Enemies are politically useful.

The public often lacks transparency and context.

But in the case of North Korea as a CIA project, the theory remains more metaphor than reality — a symptom of widespread mistrust, exaggerated by digital echo chambers.

Chapter Thirty-One

Section: Government, History & Political Secrets

Conspiracy: U.S. Presidents Are Selected, Not Elected

Summary

This conspiracy theory asserts that U.S. presidential elections are a controlled illusion, and that presidents are pre-selected by powerful elites, not genuinely chosen by the people. It suggests that democracy in America is a carefully managed performance, designed to pacify the public while corporate interests, intelligence agencies, global financial networks, or secret societies like the Illuminati or Bilderberg Group pull the real strings.

Though often associated with fringe ideology, this theory draws fuel from historic events, media manipulation, election controversies, and public disillusionment with both major political parties.

History & Key Claims

Early Foundations:

Critics have long argued that moneyed interests play a dominant role in U.S. politics. As far back as the 19th century, figures like President Andrew Jackson warned of "a corrupting money power."

The influence of political machines (e.g., Tammany Hall) and corporate lobbying created a foundation for belief that democratic choice could be subverted.

Key Claims:

Two-Party Control: The Republican and Democratic parties are seen as two wings of the same bird, presenting surface-level opposition while serving shared elite interests.

Pre-Selected Candidates: Presidential hopefuls are groomed and vetted by elites (e.g., corporate donors, global bankers, intelligence agencies) long before elections.

Election Theater: Campaigns, debates, and voter outreach are pageantry — the winner has been chosen well in advance.

Electronic Voting Machines: Some allege that digital voting systems are manipulated, particularly in swing states, to ensure preferred outcomes.

CIA and Deep State Influence: Intelligence agencies allegedly ensure presidents will not challenge core structures (military-industrial complex, surveillance programs, global finance).

Bilderberg/Bush/Clinton Theory: A recurring idea is that all viable candidates have ties to secretive groups, Yale's Skull and Bones society, or dynastic families with cross-party influence.

Reinforcing Events:

2000 Presidential Election: The Bush v. Gore recount debacle and Supreme Court decision shook public confidence in electoral integrity.

Superdelegate Controversy (2016): Bernie Sanders supporters argued the Democratic primary was rigged for Hillary Clinton.

Corporate Media Coverage: Critics note how the press often dismisses outsider candidates, focuses on establishment narratives, and promotes certain figures over others.

Famous Quotes / Sources

"Presidents are selected, not elected."

— Attributed (without confirmation) to Franklin D. Roosevelt; frequently cited by conspiracy theorists

"The illusion of choice is the most powerful tool of control."

— Popular phrase among political skeptics and online forums

"Democracy is the theory that the common people know what they want, and deserve to get it good and hard."

— H.L. Mencken, journalist and critic

"Behind the ostensible government sits enthroned an invisible government owing no allegiance and acknowledging no responsibility to the people."

— Theodore Roosevelt

"The real owners are the big wealthy business interests that control things and make all the important decisions."

— George Carlin, comedian and social critic

Real-World Consequences

Electoral Cynicism: Millions of Americans believe their vote doesn't matter, leading to low voter turnout and disengagement from civic life.

Rise of Outsiders and Populists: Belief in this theory has driven support for non-establishment candidates (e.g., Donald Trump, Bernie Sanders, RFK Jr.) who frame themselves as outside the "rigged system."

Distrust in Institutions: The theory fuels broader suspicion toward media, polling firms, government agencies, and political parties.

Conspiracy Crossover: It overlaps with other narratives — such as the deep state, QAnon, New World Order, and election fraud theories — creating a complex belief system in which official results are rarely accepted.

Radicalization: In extreme cases, belief in this theory contributes to political violence, including threats against election officials and violent protests (e.g., January 6, 2021).

Where It Stands Today

The idea that U.S. presidents are selected, not elected, has moved from fringe forums to the public square. While many don't fully embrace the theory, a significant portion of the population expresses deep doubt about the fairness and transparency of elections.

Recent polls show that:

A majority of Americans believe special interests have too much influence on political candidates.

More than 1 in 4 voters suspect that fraud or manipulation affects national elections.

However, while campaign finance, media bias, and party machinery undeniably shape electoral outcomes, no credible evidence supports the claim that all elections are staged or predetermined. Still, the blurring of reality and perception has eroded trust in the system — a vulnerability that continues to be exploited by both domestic actors and foreign influence campaigns.

In essence, the theory thrives in the gap between how democracy is ideally imagined and how it functions in practice.

Chapter Thirty-Two

Section: Government, History & Political Secrets

Conspiracy: The 2020 Election Was Rigged

Summary

The belief that the 2020 U.S. presidential election was rigged or stolen centers on claims that widespread voter fraud, manipulation of voting machines, and interference from political operatives led to an illegitimate victory for Joe Biden over incumbent Donald Trump.

Despite over 60 court cases, multiple recounts, bipartisan certification, and a lack of evidence presented in official investigations, this theory remains one of the most widespread and polarizing electoral conspiracies in U.S. history. It has profoundly affected public trust, driven civil unrest, and remains a central tenet of certain political movements.

History & Key Claims

Election Context:

Held during the COVID-19 pandemic, the 2020 election saw an unprecedented surge in mail-in and absentee ballots. This change, while legal and enacted in many states to protect voters, became a central point of suspicion.

Key Claims:

Massive Voter Fraud: Proponents allege that thousands of dead people voted, that ballots were harvested illegally, and that non-citizens or ineligible individuals cast votes — particularly in swing states.

Voting Machine Tampering: Dominion Voting Systems became the focus of allegations that machines were rigged to switch votes from Trump to Biden. Some claimed algorithms were manipulated remotely.

Ballot Dumping: Claims circulated that mysterious ballot drops in the middle of the night swung the election in Biden's favor.

Illegal Rule Changes: Lawsuits argued that pandemic-related voting rule adjustments (such as extended deadlines) were unconstitutional.

Foreign Interference: Some theories extended to claims that countries like China, Venezuela, or Italy played a role in altering votes electronically.

"Suitcase" and "Sharpie" Claims: Viral videos and anecdotes alleged ballots were pulled from suitcases or invalidated by being filled out with Sharpie pens — all of which were debunked by local officials.

Prominent Figures & Movements:

Donald Trump repeatedly claimed the election was stolen, coining phrases like "Stop the Steal."

Sidney Powell, Rudy Giuliani, and Mike Lindell became high-profile promoters of fraud claims.

QAnon, already active pre-election, wove the rigged election into its broader anti-deep-state narrative.

Response from Institutions:

The Cybersecurity and Infrastructure Security Agency (CISA) stated that the 2020 election was "the most secure in American history."

State and local election officials (including Republicans) confirmed the validity of the results.

Federal and state courts dismissed nearly all fraud lawsuits due to lack of evidence or standing.

Famous Quotes / Sources

"This election was rigged, and we all know it."

— Donald J. Trump, December 2020

"The 2020 election was the most secure in American history."

— U.S. Cybersecurity and Infrastructure Security Agency (CISA)

"People don't trust the system anymore. Whether they're right or not is almost beside the point now."

— Election law analyst, 2021

"If we don't fix this fraud, we don't have a country anymore."

— Sidney Powell

Real-World Consequences

January 6 Capitol Riot: The belief that the election was stolen was the primary catalyst for the storming of the U.S. Capitol, leading to deaths, injuries, and a historic second impeachment of a U.S. president.

Election Law Changes: Many states passed voting restriction laws after 2020, citing the need for "election integrity," though critics argue these laws target voter turnout.

Defamation Lawsuits: Dominion and Smartmatic filed multi-billion-dollar lawsuits against media networks and individuals who spread unsubstantiated claims about voting machines.

Polarization & Distrust: Polls show that a majority of Republican voters continue to believe the 2020 election was fraudulent, despite lack of proof — deepening the partisan divide.

Threats to Officials: Election workers and officials across several states faced death threats, doxxing, and harassment.

Media Realignment: Some conservative media platforms distanced themselves from fraud claims, while others (e.g., Newsmax, OANN) leaned into them, influencing viewership shifts.

Where It Stands Today

The theory that the 2020 election was rigged remains a foundational belief for a large segment of the U.S. population. It has reshaped Republican politics, fueling primary campaigns and reorienting electoral strategy.

However, no credible evidence has ever substantiated the claims of coordinated fraud or machine manipulation. Most of the lawsuits have been dismissed, and major claims have either been debunked or quietly dropped by their originators.

Still, the 2020 election conspiracy has outlived the election itself. It now functions as a broader statement of distrust in institutions, feeding into other conspiracies (like deep state manipulation, media control, and globalist agendas). It also underscores the power of narrative over fact, particularly when reinforced by tribal identity, social media, and political echo chambers.

Whether one sees it as a legitimate concern, a disinformation campaign, or a form of mass denial, the impact of this theory on American democracy is ongoing and profound.

Chapter Thirty-Three

Section: Government, History & Political Secrets

Conspiracy: The UN Is a Tool of the NWO

Summary

This conspiracy theory holds that the United Nations (UN) is not merely a diplomatic body, but a front for the New World Order (NWO) — a shadowy global elite seeking to implement a one-world government. According to believers, the UN is the primary vehicle for enacting global control, erasing national sovereignty, and implementing mass surveillance, economic manipulation, population control, and disarmament.

While rooted in deep skepticism of international governance, this theory weaves together anti-globalist sentiment, sovereignty fears, and apocalyptic beliefs, especially among libertarian, ultraconservative, and far-right circles.

History & Key Claims

Origins of the UN:

Established in 1945 after WWII to promote peace, security, and cooperation among nations, the UN replaced the failed League of Nations and today includes 193 member states.

From its inception, some critics saw it as a threat to national independence, particularly in the U.S., where isolationist and constitutionalist groups opposed any supranational authority.

Rise of the NWO Narrative:

The idea of a New World Order — a hidden, authoritarian global regime — began taking shape in Cold War-era conspiracy circles and was cemented by fears of communism, elite power, and centralized authority.

In the 1990s, the UN became a central focus of NWO believers, especially after President George H.W. Bush's repeated use of the term "new world order" in reference to post-Gulf War diplomacy.

Key Claims:

UN as Sovereignty Eraser: The UN will override national constitutions and impose global law, controlling courts, militaries, and economies.

Agenda 21 / Agenda 2030: UN programs advocating sustainable development are viewed as covert attempts to limit personal freedoms, property rights, and economic independence.

Gun Confiscation: The UN is accused of plotting to disarm civilians worldwide, beginning in the U.S., via arms treaties or peacekeeping mandates.

One-World Currency and ID: Some allege the UN plans to introduce a single global currency and digital identity system tied to surveillance or social credit.

Peacekeeping Forces as Invasion Units: UN "blue helmets" are said to be pre-stationed in various countries to enforce martial law when the time comes.

UN Globalist Elites: Leaders such as Klaus Schwab (WEF), George Soros, and Bill Gates are often falsely portrayed as masterminds behind UN initiatives.

The Role of U.S. Presidents:

Presidents who embraced multilateralism or supported the UN (e.g., Barack Obama, Bill Clinton) are seen as facilitators of the plan.

Donald Trump's withdrawal from certain UN agencies was celebrated by believers as a blow to the globalist agenda.

Famous Quotes / Sources

"Our sovereignty is being handed to an unelected body of global bureaucrats."

— Representative Ron Paul, former U.S. Congressman

"Agenda 21 is the blueprint. The UN is the architect."

— Anti-globalist blog post, 2012

"The UN is not about peace — it's about control."

— Talk radio host Alex Jones

"From global warming to education reform, they're using the UN to shape how we live, think, and spend."

— Excerpt from Behold a Pale Horse by William Cooper

Real-World Consequences

Widespread Mistrust of the UN: Many view the UN not as a peacekeeping force, but as a threat to liberty, undermining its work in health, education, conflict resolution, and human rights.

Agenda 21 Backlash: Local governments around the world — particularly in the U.S. — faced protests over land use and sustainability plans, with conspiracy theorists labeling them "UN plots."

Gun Rights Mobilization: The fear of UN-led gun confiscation has fueled U.S. militia growth and influenced legislation, particularly surrounding treaties like the Arms Trade Treaty (ATT).

Fuel for Sovereign Citizen & Survivalist Movements: Belief in UN overreach drives doomsday prepping, opposition to zoning laws, and outright refusal to comply with international agreements.

Digital Paranoia: Fears of UN-backed digital tracking systems have increased resistance to vaccines, biometric ID systems, and online data collection — linking to other conspiracies like the Great Reset and 5G.

Diplomatic Isolationism: In extreme cases, this theory has justified withdrawing from global initiatives — weakening international cooperation on climate change, pandemics, and peacekeeping.

Where It Stands Today

This theory continues to thrive on the internet, fueled by distrust in elites, global institutions, and media narratives. Though lacking credible evidence, it survives by tying together disparate fears — about technocracy, surveillance, economic control, and loss of cultural identity.

While the UN remains a diplomatic body with limited enforcement power, conspiracy believers interpret its long-term goals through a lens of totalitarian ambition. Terms like "Agenda 2030," "Great Reset," and "one-world order" have become trigger phrases across political commentary and alt-media spaces.

Importantly, the theory functions as a metaphor for fears of global consolidation — where a few powerful individuals allegedly aim to govern a compliant world population. The UN, in this narrative, is merely the storefront.

Whether seen as a misunderstood bureaucracy or a grand design for domination, the United Nations is likely to remain a lightning rod in conspiracy culture for years to come.

Chapter Thirty-Four

Section: Government, History & Political Secrets

Conspiracy: The EU Is a Stepping Stone to World Government

Summary

This theory posits that the European Union (EU) is not merely a political and economic alliance, but rather a strategic prototype for a future one-world government. In this view, the EU's true purpose is to dissolve national identities, override local governance, and create a centralized technocratic superstate that ultimately serves as a model — or testing ground — for global consolidation of power.

Supporters of this theory argue that beneath the surface of cooperation and unity lies a globalist agenda, with unelected bureaucrats, corporate lobbyists, and elite networks working toward complete transnational control.

History & Key Claims

Origins of the EU:

The EU traces its roots to post–World War II efforts to ensure peace and economic recovery through cooperation, beginning with the European Coal and Steel Community (1951) and later evolving into the European Economic Community (1957).

The Maastricht Treaty (1993) formally established the European Union, expanding powers to foreign policy, justice, and monetary union.

Key Claims of the Theory:

Loss of Sovereignty: National parliaments are allegedly sidelined by decisions made in Brussels, where unelected bodies like the European Commission hold significant influence.

Stealth Integration: Each treaty (e.g., Lisbon, Nice, Amsterdam) is portrayed as a step toward deeper integration under the guise of efficiency or security.

Economic Manipulation: The Eurozone is believed to entrap countries in debt and austerity, weakening their independence (as seen with Greece and Italy).

Borderless Globalism: The EU's Schengen Area is cited as an intentional breakdown of national borders, intended to blur distinct cultural and political identities.

Globalist Testing Ground: The EU is described as a controlled experiment in merging disparate countries — a model to be exported globally through future alliances.

NWO Connections: Some tie EU leadership to the Bilderberg Group, World Economic Forum, or Freemasonic circles, seeing these as puppeteers behind the project.

British Resistance:

The UK's long and conflicted relationship with the EU has been fertile ground for this theory, culminating in Brexit — widely viewed by believers as a rebellion against globalist influence.

Famous Quotes / Sources

"We are on the verge of a global transformation. All we need is the right major crisis."

— David Rockefeller (attributed, though disputed)

"The European Union is the prototype of world government — bureaucratic, unaccountable, and undemocratic."

— UKIP campaign leaflet, 2015

"We now have a flag, an anthem, a currency... All that remains is the army."

— Nigel Farage (paraphrased), former MEP and Brexit Party leader

"We are moving toward an ever closer union, and there is no turning back."

— Jean-Claude Juncker, former President of the European Commission

Real-World Consequences

Brexit and Nationalist Movements: The UK's withdrawal from the EU in 2020 was heavily influenced by concerns over sovereignty and democratic accountability, many of which were fueled by or echoed in conspiracy narratives.

Anti-EU Populism: Right-wing and nationalist parties across Europe — including the National Rally (France), AfD (Germany), and Lega (Italy) — have adopted anti-EU rhetoric, often portraying the Union as a threat to traditional values and autonomy.

Distrust in Bureaucracy: Misinformation campaigns, particularly on social media, have undermined trust in EU institutions. Proposals for shared taxation, military forces, or pandemic response plans are often seen as steps toward "global government."

Fringe Activism: Some extremist groups (e.g., sovereign citizens, accelerationist factions) view the EU as the enemy of freedom and advocate resistance — including tax refusal, exit movements, and symbolic declarations of independence.

Fuel for Wider Globalist Theories: The EU is often cited alongside the UN, World Bank, and WHO as part of a "web of global control", especially in U.S.-based conspiracy literature.

Where It Stands Today

While the European Union is, in reality, a complex and often gridlocked political structure, its ambition to harmonize laws and values across nations lends itself to conspiracy interpretations. It represents the kind of transnational authority that stirs unease in those who value strong national sovereignty or fear elite manipulation.

The theory that the EU is a stepping stone to world government has gained traction in Eurosceptic circles, but has also influenced public opinion more broadly — especially during crises like the Eurozone debt collapse, migrant influx, or COVID-19 pandemic.

Although there is no verifiable evidence of a singular, secret plan for a global superstate emerging from the EU, the perception of creeping authority, cultural dilution, and democratic erosion ensures this theory remains both popular and politically potent.

In many ways, it speaks less to fact than to a deeper anxiety: that globalization, even under the banner of unity and peace, might ultimately lead to a world without choice.

Chapter Thirty-Five

Section: Government, History & Political Secrets

Conspiracy: The Assassination of Martin Luther King Jr. Was Orchestrated

Summary

Dr. Martin Luther King Jr., the iconic civil rights leader, was assassinated on April 4, 1968, in Memphis, Tennessee. While James Earl Ray was convicted for the murder, a long-standing conspiracy theory maintains that King's assassination was not the act of a lone gunman, but rather the result of a larger orchestrated plot involving government agencies, particularly the FBI, CIA, and elements of the U.S. military and local authorities.

This theory suggests that Dr. King's growing influence — particularly his opposition to the Vietnam War and plans for the Poor People's Campaign — posed a threat to the status quo, leading to a covert operation to silence him permanently.

History & Key Claims

The Official Story:

James Earl Ray, a career criminal, pleaded guilty to the murder of Martin Luther King Jr. in 1969 and was sentenced to 99 years in prison. He later recanted, claiming he was set up.

Ray's background, inconsistent timeline, and the alleged involvement of a mysterious man named "Raoul" led to speculation that he was a patsy.

Key Claims of the Theory:

FBI Involvement: Under J. Edgar Hoover, the FBI had surveilled King for years, labeling him a subversive and attempting to discredit him — including sending him an anonymous letter encouraging suicide.

Military Surveillance: The U.S. Army's 902nd Military Intelligence Group allegedly tracked King in the months leading up to his death. Some believe military snipers were present in Memphis that day.

Government Conspiracy: The theory holds that federal agencies, concerned about King's shift from civil rights to anti-war and economic justice, feared he would ignite widespread rebellion.

Sanctioned Hit via Intermediaries: Some theorists argue that local Memphis officials, the Mafia, or white supremacist groups were used as intermediaries to carry out or cover up the assassination.

Ballistics & Witness Discrepancies: Questions have been raised about the murder weapon, the location of the shooter, and conflicting eyewitness testimony that does not align neatly with the official narrative.

The King Family's Belief:

In the late 1990s, the King family publicly stated they believed James Earl Ray was not the true assassin.

In 1999, a civil trial brought by the King family found "government agencies were part of a conspiracy to assassinate Dr. King." The trial received little media attention but added legitimacy to the theory for many.

Famous Quotes / Sources

"There is abundant evidence of a major high-level conspiracy in the assassination of my husband."

— Coretta Scott King, 1999

"I never felt James Earl Ray had the motive, money or mobility to have done it himself."

— Reverend Jesse Jackson

"The American people never got the full story."

— William F. Pepper, attorney for James Earl Ray and author of An Act of State

"I just want to say, I am innocent."

— James Earl Ray, to the House Select Committee on Assassinations, 1979

Real-World Consequences

Public Distrust in Government: The theory surrounding King's death, alongside those of JFK and RFK, became a cornerstone of public skepticism toward official narratives and fueled broader suspicion of U.S. intelligence agencies.

Renewed Investigations: The House Select Committee on Assassinations (HSCA) reopened the case in the 1970s and concluded that while Ray was the shooter, there may have been a conspiracy involving unknown individuals.

Cultural Impact: Films, documentaries, and books — including Who Killed Martin Luther King? and MLK: The Assassination Tapes — have kept the theory alive and reframed King's death as a possible state-sanctioned elimination of dissent.

Symbolic Legacy: For many activists, the theory serves as a cautionary tale of the state's response to radical change, reinforcing narratives of systemic injustice and control.

James Earl Ray's Death: Ray died in 1998 still maintaining his innocence. His appeals and the civil trial that followed reignited debate but did not result in any criminal retrials or official reversal of judgment.

Where It Stands Today

Though officially closed, the theory that Martin Luther King Jr. was assassinated by a conspiracy involving the U.S. government continues to resonate. It is cited in political discourse, taught in alternative history circles, and used as an example of how power responds to challenge.

The King family's endorsement of this theory lends it more weight than many others in this book. While critics argue that the 1999 civil trial was not a criminal proceeding and relied on circumstantial evidence, supporters see it as a necessary correction to a sanitized official version of history.

For many, the idea that King was killed not simply because of racism, but because of his threat to imperialism, capitalism, and militarism, reinforces the belief that true revolutionaries are systematically silenced.

As with many conspiracies, this theory reveals as much about collective fears — of injustice, betrayal, and secrecy — as it does about what can or cannot be proven.

Chapter Thirty-Six

Section: Government, History & Political Secrets

Conspiracy: Brexit Was Controlled by Elites

Summary

The official narrative surrounding Brexit — the United Kingdom's 2016 vote to leave the European Union — paints it as a populist revolt against unelected bureaucracy, globalization, and loss of national sovereignty. However, a conspiracy theory argues the opposite: that Brexit was not a grassroots movement at all, but rather a controlled operation orchestrated by elite power brokers, designed to further hidden agendas related to economic restructuring, deregulation, and geopolitical realignment.

This theory suggests that both the Leave and Remain camps were manipulated, and that the outcome — regardless of public sentiment — served the interests of a globalist, corporatist, or intelligence-linked elite.

History & Key Claims

Background:

In June 2016, 52% of voters chose to leave the European Union after a polarizing campaign.

The vote shocked financial markets, international allies, and much of the British political class.

Yet rather than bringing clarity, Brexit ushered in years of political chaos, suggesting (to some) deeper strategic design.

Key Claims of the Theory:

Manufactured Divide: The entire Leave vs. Remain debate was stage-managed to create division, distract from domestic issues, and test social engineering tools like targeted advertising and psychological nudging.

Data Manipulation: Firms such as Cambridge Analytica, accused of harvesting Facebook data, are said to have worked on behalf of intelligence-linked interests to shape voting outcomes using psychological profiling.

Controlled Opposition: Certain Leave campaign leaders (including prominent politicians and businessmen) are suspected of being controlled assets whose role was to guide the public into a predetermined outcome while appearing anti-establishment.

Financial Incentives: Major hedge funds, offshore investors, and deregulation lobbies allegedly benefited from market chaos — betting against the pound or shorting stocks in the wake of the vote.

Elite Reset: Brexit served as an opportunity for a restructuring of Britain's global economic role, allowing new trade agreements, looser environmental and labor protections, and the dismantling of certain EU regulations — all under the guise of "sovereignty."

Global Strategic Shift: Some theorists link Brexit to a wider global trend — including Trump's election and the rise of nationalist movements — allegedly engineered by elites to fracture alliances and pave the way for a new global system under tighter corporate or AI control.

False Dichotomy:

The theory suggests both sides — pro-EU globalists and anti-EU nationalists — were being played against one another by the same class of decision-makers who benefit regardless of the result.

Famous Quotes / Sources

"Follow the money — not the slogans."

— Common refrain among Brexit conspiracy theorists

"There's nothing grassroots about Brexit. It's hedge funds, dark money, and military contractors."

— Carole Cadwalladr, journalist (referencing Cambridge Analytica)

"Brexit was a psy-op — they fed people freedom while taking away their choices."

— Anonymous political researcher, alt-media forum

"You don't need to rig the vote. You just need to rig the conversation."

— Christopher Wylie, former Cambridge Analytica whistleblower

Real-World Consequences

Mistrust in Democratic Outcomes: The theory has fed into a wider belief that major elections and referenda are controlled or manipulated by unseen forces, deepening cynicism toward politics.

Targeted Misinformation: The Brexit campaign saw a rise in coordinated disinformation, bot activity, and the strategic deployment of emotional issues (immigration, nationalism, economic insecurity) — viewed by some as a live experiment in mass persuasion.

Political Instability as a Strategy: Post-Brexit gridlock and infighting may have been the intended result, creating a political vacuum through which more powerful private interests could influence policy.

Redefinition of Sovereignty: Laws introduced under the pretense of reclaiming sovereignty are alleged to have expanded state surveillance, weakened regulatory frameworks, and favored transnational corporations.

Cross-Atlantic Parallels: Similar tactics in the 2016 U.S. election, including social media influence and psychological targeting, have led many to believe that Brexit and Trump were parallel operations, either by Western intelligence, tech moguls, or global financial elites.

Where It Stands Today

While mainstream discourse still treats Brexit as a referendum on globalization, this conspiracy theory reframes it as a false rebellion, in which public anger was harnessed to further elite goals.

It thrives in online communities that distrust all sides of politics, especially those skeptical of both neoliberalism and nationalism. The theory remains murky — and difficult to prove — but its allure lies in the observation that powerful interests benefited regardless of the chaos. To believers, this was never about "taking back control" — but rather consolidating it.

Even as Brexit fades from headlines, its role as a case study in controlled disruption remains alive in the minds of those who see the world not as a battleground of ideas — but of engineered perception.

Chapter Thirty-Seven

Section: Science, Medicine & Technology Conspiracies

Conspiracy: Flat Earth

Summary

Despite centuries of scientific understanding, the Flat Earth theory persists — a belief that Earth is not a globe but instead a flat, disc-shaped plane, often surrounded by an ice wall and covered by a dome-like firmament. Proponents argue that modern science and space exploration are massive deceptions perpetrated by global powers to hide the truth.

While it may sound absurd to many, Flat Earth belief has experienced a resurgence in recent years, particularly online, blending anti-establishment thinking, Biblical literalism, and scientific skepticism into a full-blown worldview that rejects nearly all official narratives.

History & Key Claims

Ancient Beliefs:

Flat Earth cosmologies were common in ancient Mesopotamian, Egyptian, and early Biblical traditions, where the world was thought to be a flat disc under a dome (the "firmament").

Scientific Disproof:

From Aristotle's observations of Earth's shadow during lunar eclipses to Magellan's circumnavigation and modern satellite imagery, the round Earth model has been confirmed repeatedly through observation, mathematics, and physics.

Modern Flat Earth Revival:

In the 19th century, Samuel Rowbotham published Zetetic Astronomy, arguing Earth is flat and using Biblical and "common sense" reasoning.

In the 21st century, Flat Earth belief has grown through social media, YouTube videos, and forums like The Flat Earth Society and Flat Earth International Conference.

Key Claims:

NASA Fakes Space Exploration: All space missions, including the moon landings, are said to be hoaxes, filmed on Earth or created with CGI.

The Ice Wall: Antarctica is not a continent but a massive ice wall that encircles the flat Earth, keeping oceans contained.

No Real Photos of Earth: Images of Earth from space are claimed to be composites or digital fabrications, citing inconsistencies in clouds and lighting.

Airplanes Prove It: Flight paths, especially in the Southern Hemisphere, are often cited as being "illogical" on a globe.

Gravity Is a Lie: Gravity is rejected or reinterpreted; many claim objects fall due to density and buoyancy.

The Dome (Firmament): Some believe Earth is enclosed by an impenetrable dome, referenced in the Book of Genesis and other ancient texts.

Who's Behind the Lie?

Theories vary, but many Flat Earthers claim a global scientific conspiracy involving NASA, governments, Freemasons, and the "Luciferian elite", designed to suppress Biblical truth and control the population.

Famous Quotes / Sources

"Research flat Earth."

— Common slogan on social media and signs at protests

"I don't trust anything I can't verify for myself. The Earth doesn't look curved to me."

— Mark Sargent, Flat Earth advocate

"If the Earth were truly a spinning ball, water would not stay on it."

— Eric Dubay, author of 200 Proofs Earth Is Not a Spinning Ball

"The Bible describes a firm, flat Earth. That's enough for me."

— Flat Earth community post

Real-World Consequences

Mistrust in Science and Institutions: Flat Earth belief is often a gateway into other conspiracy theories, promoting skepticism of government, science, education, and media.

Educational Challenges: Teachers have reported increasing numbers of students questioning Earth's shape, causing concern about scientific literacy and critical thinking.

Online Radicalization: Flat Earth theory is part of a broader pattern of algorithm-driven echo chambers, where users are gradually introduced to more extreme views.

Fractured Communities: Even within Flat Earth circles, factions exist — arguing over the dome's structure, what lies beyond the ice wall, or whether Antarctica even exists.

Pop Culture & Comedy: The movement has sparked widespread ridicule, memes, and parody accounts — but the mocking has also led some believers to double down in response to perceived elitism.

Where It Stands Today

Flat Earth belief persists despite overwhelming scientific consensus and centuries of physical evidence. Its endurance says more about distrust in authority, religious fundamentalism, and the nature of modern information ecosystems than it does about planetary geometry.

While most view Flat Earth as fringe or absurd, for a growing number of people, it represents a symbolic rebellion against what they see as corrupt elites and indoctrinated thinking. To these believers, seeing is not believing — questioning is.

As such, the Flat Earth theory remains a prime example of how conspiracy beliefs are not always about facts, but about identity, power, and the search for meaning in a complex world.

Chapter Thirty-Eight

Section: Science, Medicine & Technology Conspiracies

Conspiracy: COVID-19 Was Engineered

Summary

The outbreak of COVID-19 in late 2019 rapidly became one of the most globally significant events of the 21st century. But alongside the virus came another kind of contagion — theories that COVID-19 was not a natural virus, but a deliberately engineered bioweapon or a lab-manipulated strain released either by accident or design.

At the heart of the theory is the belief that SARS-CoV-2 was not the result of zoonotic spillover, but was instead created or enhanced in a laboratory setting — most notably the Wuhan Institute of Virology — and that governments, scientists, or elites knew more than they revealed.

History & Key Claims

The Official Narrative:

COVID-19 is widely believed by scientific institutions to have emerged from a wet market in Wuhan, China, likely transmitted from bats to another animal species, then to humans.

Research points to natural origins, similar to other coronaviruses such as SARS and MERS.

The Conspiracy Theory:

Engineered Virus Hypothesis: Some scientists and theorists believe the virus contains genetic markers indicating laboratory manipulation, such as "gain-of-function" research — experiments that increase a virus's transmissibility or virulence.

Wuhan Institute of Virology (WIV): The proximity of the outbreak to the WIV — which has studied bat coronaviruses — is cited as suspicious. Leaked U.S. diplomatic cables from 2018 raised concerns about safety protocols at the lab.

Intentional Release Theory: A more extreme version suggests the virus was intentionally released to create global chaos, justify lockdowns, collapse economies, or usher in increased surveillance.

Cover-Up Allegations: Critics accuse both China and international organizations (such as the WHO) of initially suppressing information, silencing whistleblowers, and downplaying lab-related concerns.

Predictive Patterns: Some theorists point to "pandemic simulations" such as Event 201, held in October 2019 and co-hosted by the World Economic Forum and Johns Hopkins University, as proof that global elites knew what was coming.

Other Linked Claims:

COVID-19 is part of a population control or economic reset agenda.

The pandemic was engineered to justify emergency powers, lockdowns, and mandated vaccines.

Research into coronaviruses had military ties, suggesting possible use as a biological weapon.

Famous Quotes / Sources

"COVID-19 may have originated from a lab accident."

— Dr. Robert Redfield, former CDC Director, 2021

"It is possible the virus was engineered… the possibility cannot be ignored."

— Luc Montagnier, Nobel Prize-winning virologist

"This is not a conspiracy theory. This is a legitimate question that needs answers."

— Senator Rand Paul, U.S. Senate hearing, 2021

"We stand firmly behind the theory of zoonotic origin."

— Joint WHO-China Study, 2021

Real-World Consequences

Increased Polarization: The theory has fueled deep political divides, particularly between Western critics of China and defenders of natural origin models.

Distrust in Health Authorities: Many people began to doubt the transparency of organizations like the WHO, CDC, and NIH, suspecting censorship or collusion.

Scientific Censorship Accusations: In the early months of the pandemic, social media platforms removed lab-leak discussions, labeling them misinformation — which many now argue was premature or politically motivated.

Rise of Alternative Narratives: The theory helped energize related movements, including anti-lockdown, anti-vaccine, and Great Reset conspiracies.

Reopened Investigations: By 2021, major governments — including the U.S. and UK — called for renewed investigations into the origins of the virus. Some scientists who once dismissed the lab-leak theory later acknowledged it warranted further examination.

Impact on U.S.-China Relations: The theory became a geopolitical flashpoint, contributing to rising tensions, trade disputes, and accusations of biowarfare research.

Where It Stands Today

The lab-leak theory has shifted from the fringe to the mainstream, with growing acknowledgment from scientists and journalists that it is a plausible explanation, though still unproven.

The U.S. Department of Energy and FBI have both released tentative assessments supporting the lab-leak possibility, but the intelligence community remains divided. The Chinese government continues to deny all lab-related accusations.

To this day, the true origin of COVID-19 remains unknown, and the ambiguity has only deepened public skepticism and speculation. For many, the handling of the pandemic — from early denial to sudden policy shifts — has eroded faith in science, institutions, and truth itself.

In the broader landscape of conspiracy thinking, this theory occupies a unique space: part plausible, part political weapon, and fully emblematic of the era of uncertainty that COVID-19 ushered in.

Chapter Thirty-Nine

Section: Science, Medicine & Technology Conspiracies

Conspiracy: COVID Vaccines Contain Trackers

Summary

As COVID-19 vaccines were rapidly developed and distributed in 2020–2021, a potent conspiracy theory emerged: that the vaccines did not merely provide protection from the virus, but also contained tracking technology — such as microchips, metallic particles, or nanotech — designed to monitor individuals without their knowledge.

Though dismissed as science fiction by health authorities, this theory gained traction across social media, particularly among anti-vaccine communities, privacy advocates, and government skeptics. At its core lies a deeper fear: that medical advances are being used to erode human autonomy under the guise of public health.

History & Key Claims

Contextual Background:

The unprecedented speed of COVID-19 vaccine development led to widespread suspicion.

Emergency Use Authorizations (EUAs), government mandates, and digital "vaccine passports" only heightened fears among some groups.

Core Claims:

Microchips in Vaccines: The belief that injectable chips, developed by entities like Bill Gates' foundations or DARPA, are embedded in vaccines for surveillance purposes.

5G Integration: Some claim the so-called microchips interact with 5G towers, allowing real-time location tracking or even behavior manipulation.

Magnetism: Viral videos in 2021 showed people allegedly sticking magnets to their arms post-vaccination, used as "evidence" of metallic content.

Hydrogel & Nanotech: A more technical variation claims that vaccines contain self-assembling nanostructures or biosensors — possibly linked to DARPA or military research — capable of monitoring biological activity.

Quantum Dots or Luciferase: Some point to speculative technologies like quantum dots (used for invisible tattoos or bio-markers) and luciferase enzymes (used in bioluminescent research) as sinister components hidden in mRNA formulas.

Figures of Concern:

Bill Gates: Frequently cited due to his 2015 TED Talk on pandemics, global vaccine funding, and past support for biometric ID systems in developing countries.

Klaus Schwab / World Economic Forum: Accused of promoting "transhumanist" agendas via The Great Reset — suggesting tracking may be part of a broader vision of digitally controlled societies.

Famous Quotes / Sources

"The vaccines contain tracking chips — that's why they're pushing them so hard."

— Viral social media post, 2021

"We will have some digital certificates to show who has recovered or been tested or received the vaccine."

— Bill Gates, March 2020 (widely misquoted out of context)

"I'm magnetic. That proves it."

— TikTok user demonstrating a magnet "sticking" to injection site

"I don't want to be a node on some billionaire's network."

— Comment from conspiracy forum, 2021

Real-World Consequences

Vaccine Hesitancy: Belief in tracking conspiracies contributed to lower vaccination rates, especially in areas already distrustful of government or medical institutions.

Spread of Misinformation: Viral videos of magnet tests and speculative claims circulated widely across platforms like Telegram, TikTok, and Facebook, often evading fact-checks by using coded language or satire.

Increased Surveillance Fears: The idea of digital IDs, QR code passes, and vaccine certificates was conflated with the tracking theory, reinforcing anti-globalist sentiment and resistance to digital health systems.

Targeting Public Figures: Bill Gates, Anthony Fauci, and others received death threats, protests, and intense online harassment, fueled by fears of global surveillance and "vaccine tyranny."

Real Technology Misunderstood: Genuine research into implantable chips, biosensors, and remote health diagnostics was cited out of context, leading to a blurred line between speculation and reality.

Where It Stands Today

No credible scientific evidence supports the claim that COVID-19 vaccines contain tracking chips or nanotech surveillance devices. Vaccine ingredients are publicly listed, and multiple independent analyses have verified the absence of any foreign microtechnology.

However, the theory remains influential. It taps into long-standing concerns about:

Digital surveillance

Loss of bodily autonomy

Technocratic overreach

In some circles, it has evolved into a meta-belief — less about the specific contents of the vaccine, and more about the perception that elites are using crises to normalize invasive technologies.

As digital health infrastructure expands globally, and biotech rapidly advances, the line between privacy and public safety, science and speculation, remains deeply contested — and this conspiracy is likely to endure within that ambiguity.

Chapter Forty

Section: Science, Medicine & Technology Conspiracies

Conspiracy: 5G Causes Illness

Summary

The rollout of 5G — the fifth-generation wireless technology promising faster data speeds and more connected devices — has been hailed as a revolution in digital communication. But for conspiracy theorists, 5G is far more sinister: a harmful, potentially weaponized system capable of causing illness, weakening the immune system, or even controlling the population.

Some theories claim 5G emits radiation that damages DNA or brain cells, while others argue it is linked to COVID-19, either by spreading the virus or weakening human defenses. Despite being scientifically discredited, these theories have resulted in protests, vandalism, and widespread panic, particularly during the early months of the pandemic.

History & Key Claims

Understanding 5G:

5G operates across several radio frequency bands, including low-band, mid-band, and millimeter wave.

While 5G uses higher frequencies than previous generations (like 4G), it still falls within the non-ionizing range of the electromagnetic spectrum — meaning it cannot break molecular bonds or cause direct DNA damage, according to mainstream science.

Key Claims of the Theory:

Radiation Harms the Body: 5G allegedly causes a wide range of health issues, from headaches and fatigue to cancer and infertility.

Immune System Suppression: Some theorists believe 5G weakens the immune system, making people more susceptible to illnesses like COVID-19.

COVID-19 Link: A now-debunked but highly viral claim in 2020 asserted that COVID-19 was a cover-up for 5G-related sickness, particularly since Wuhan was one of the first cities to roll out 5G.

Mind Control or Crowd Manipulation: A more extreme variant suggests that 5G towers can transmit frequencies that alter thoughts, emotions, or behavior — sometimes said to be coordinated with surveillance programs or AI systems.

Weaponization Concerns: Some point to the U.S. military's use of directed energy weapons as "proof" that similar technologies could be deployed via 5G infrastructure.

Celebrity Amplification:

Public figures including Woody Harrelson, M.I.A., and John Cusack expressed concern or promoted 5G-COVID theories, giving the claims greater visibility.

Crossover with Other Conspiracies:

5G theories often intersect with beliefs about Bill Gates, population control, chemtrails, vaccines, and the New World Order, forming a larger narrative of elite-driven global manipulation.

Famous Quotes / Sources

"5G is the new asbestos. Only worse."

— Popular slogan on anti-5G protest signs

"There is no virus. People are getting sick from 5G radiation."

— Viral Telegram message, March 2020

"5G towers are part of a war on our health and freedom."

— Activist speech at a UK protest, 2021

"I find it odd that Wuhan was the first to roll out 5G, then became ground zero."

— YouTube video with over 2 million views (removed for misinformation)

Real-World Consequences

Infrastructure Attacks: Dozens of cell towers were vandalized or set on fire across the UK, Netherlands, Ireland, and elsewhere in 2020–2021. Engineers installing 5G were harassed, threatened, or falsely accused of spreading disease.

Protests Worldwide: Anti-5G demonstrations occurred globally, often merging with anti-lockdown, anti-vaccine, and anti-government protests.

Misinformation Spread: Social media platforms struggled to contain the rapid spread of anti-5G content. YouTube, Facebook, and Twitter removed thousands of posts and videos promoting unfounded health claims.

Delayed Deployment: In some regions, the 5G rollout was paused or slowed due to public backlash and safety reviews — despite the absence of credible scientific concerns.

Public Health Repercussions: The linking of 5G to COVID-19 diverted attention from real health issues, weakened public trust in technology, and contributed to a broader culture of skepticism toward science.

Where It Stands Today

The theory that 5G causes illness remains a widely circulated but scientifically unsubstantiated claim. The World Health Organization (WHO), U.S. Centers for Disease Control (CDC), and International Commission on Non-Ionizing Radiation Protection (ICNIRP) have all stated that 5G technology, as currently implemented, poses no established health risks.

Nonetheless, belief in 5G-related health effects persists — often embedded within larger anti-technology or anti-globalist ideologies. In many cases, concern about 5G reflects deeper fears about rapid technological change, loss of privacy, and corporate or governmental overreach.

As 6G and future technologies emerge, these anxieties are likely to evolve rather than vanish, making 5G just one chapter in a broader cultural narrative about power, control, and the unseen forces shaping modern life.

Chapter Forty-One

Section: Science, Medicine & Technology Conspiracies

Conspiracy: HAARP Controls the Weather

Summary

HAARP — the High-Frequency Active Auroral Research Program — is a real U.S. government-funded facility based in Alaska, designed to study the ionosphere using powerful radio frequency transmitters. But to many conspiracy theorists, HAARP is far more than a scientific observatory: it's allegedly a secret weather weapon, capable of engineering hurricanes, triggering earthquakes, and manipulating global climates for military or political purposes.

The theory suggests that HAARP, either alone or in tandem with other unknown technologies, can control natural disasters — raising the possibility that some environmental catastrophes are not natural at all, but orchestrated events with hidden motives.

History & Key Claims

The Actual HAARP Program:

HAARP began in 1993 as a joint venture between the U.S. Air Force, Navy, and DARPA, operated by the University of Alaska Fairbanks since 2015.

Its stated purpose is to study ionospheric physics, particularly how radio waves interact with charged particles in the upper atmosphere.

The facility transmits high-frequency (HF) radio waves into the ionosphere to observe changes in real time.

The Conspiracy Theory:

Weather Control: The central claim is that HAARP can manipulate weather patterns, create or disperse storms, droughts, floods, and influence climate conditions in targeted regions.

Geophysical Warfare: Theorists assert that HAARP can induce earthquakes, tsunamis, and volcanic eruptions by agitating tectonic plates through electromagnetic waves.

Mind Control and Behavior Influence: A more fringe version claims that HAARP can emit frequencies that alter human consciousness, induce mood changes, or disrupt thought patterns.

Stealth Global Weapon: Some allege that HAARP is used for geopolitical warfare — weakening enemy states through environmental sabotage, crop destruction, or forced migration.

Notable Events Cited:

The 2010 Haiti earthquake, 2004 Indian Ocean tsunami, Hurricane Katrina, California wildfires, and even unusual snowfall in Texas have been attributed by some to HAARP experiments.

Russian authorities and Iranian military sources have made public statements echoing suspicions of HAARP's destructive capabilities.

Government Secrecy as Fuel:

The facility's remote location, military connections, and periods of restricted access have all been used to support claims of a covert agenda.

Famous Quotes / Sources

"HAARP is a super-powerful electromagnetic weapon capable of triggering floods, droughts, hurricanes, and earthquakes."

— Former Venezuelan President Hugo Chávez, 2010

"They can create earthquakes, they can manipulate weather, they can beam things into people's minds."

— Jesse Ventura, former governor and conspiracy commentator

"HAARP is not just a research project. It is an instrument of warfare."

— Anonymous blog post shared across conspiracy forums

"The U.S. has developed technologies that can manipulate the environment to cause disasters in enemy territories."

— Iranian military official, PressTV, 2010

Real-World Consequences

International Suspicion: HAARP has been referenced by foreign governments (including Russia, China, and Iran) in relation to unexplained weather events, suggesting the theory plays into geopolitical narratives and propaganda.

Scientific Confusion: Public misunderstanding of ionospheric science has fueled distrust in atmospheric research, with HAARP becoming a symbol of opaque, elite-controlled science.

Vandalism and Threats: Though less targeted than 5G infrastructure, HAARP has been the subject of trespassing incidents, online threats, and attempts to "shut it down" by activists convinced of its dangers.

Media Amplification: TV shows like Conspiracy Theory with Jesse Ventura, online documentaries, and fringe publications have greatly amplified the reach and complexity of HAARP-related conspiracies.

Environmental Distrust: The HAARP theory has become part of a broader skepticism toward geoengineering, climate modification proposals, and government-sponsored weather experiments.

Where It Stands Today

Scientific consensus maintains that HAARP cannot alter weather or induce seismic activity. The energy levels used at the facility are minuscule compared to natural forces like solar radiation, atmospheric pressure, or tectonic stress.

Despite this, HAARP remains a symbolic lightning rod — not just for weather manipulation fears, but for deeper anxieties about:

Government secrecy

Weaponized science

Environmental manipulation

In an era increasingly defined by climate instability, HAARP continues to be invoked after every major natural disaster by theorists who refuse to accept that the Earth itself — rather than shadowy elites — might be the source of destruction.

The conspiracy's staying power lies not in technical credibility, but in its ability to connect seemingly random chaos to a human plan, however implausible — and in doing so, offer a perverse sense of order amid disaster.

Chapter Forty-Two

Section: Science, Medicine & Technology Conspiracies

Conspiracy: Chemtrails

Summary

The "chemtrails" conspiracy theory proposes that persistent white streaks left behind by airplanes — officially called contrails — are not simply water vapor, but are instead chemical agents deliberately sprayed into the atmosphere for nefarious purposes.

Proponents believe that governments, militaries, or global organizations are secretly releasing these substances to manipulate the weather, control populations, spread disease, or conduct mind control experiments. Despite decades of scientific refutation, the chemtrail theory remains one of the most widely believed environmental conspiracies.

History & Key Claims

Origins:

The term "chemtrails" was popularized in the 1990s following a surge of public concern over aerial spraying and atmospheric modification programs.

In 1996, a U.S. Air Force report titled "Weather as a Force Multiplier: Owning the Weather in 2025" was published. Though speculative and theoretical, it was interpreted by conspiracy communities as evidence of active weather manipulation agendas.

The spread of grainy photos, personal anecdotes, and online videos showing lingering plane trails helped push the theory into the mainstream by the early 2000s.

Key Claims:

Chemical Spraying: Believers assert that planes are equipped with hidden tanks or dispersal systems releasing aluminum, barium, strontium, lithium, or unknown nanomaterials.

Weather Modification: The spraying allegedly helps control rainfall, drought, or temperature patterns — either for military testing, geoengineering, or to force compliance among populations.

Mind Control and Biological Agents: Some versions claim chemtrails contain psychoactive compounds, pathogens, or behavior-modifying chemicals.

Population Control or Eugenics: A darker variation suggests that chemtrails are used to sterilize populations, suppress fertility, or increase chronic illness.

Blocking Sunlight or Climate Engineering: A more recent adaptation aligns with solar radiation management (SRM) theories — suggesting that chemtrails are a cover for climate experiments to reflect sunlight.

Ties to Government and Military:

Agencies such as NASA, NOAA, and the U.S. Air Force are frequently named in online materials, as is DARPA.

Programs like cloud seeding, stratospheric aerosol injection studies, or even real military research on atmospheric dynamics are cited as "proof."

Visual Evidence:

Chemtrail believers often share photos of crisscrossed skies, multi-line vapor patterns, or iridescent halos, claiming these differ from normal contrails and point to unnatural dispersal.

Famous Quotes / Sources

"I don't consent to being sprayed like a bug."

— Popular slogan from anti-chemtrail protests

"Chemtrails are geoengineering in action — without the public's permission."

— Comment from a viral Reddit conspiracy thread

"The sky is a grid. The clouds are fake. The air is poisoned."

— Message posted by a prominent chemtrail YouTuber, 2018

"If you think they wouldn't experiment on the atmosphere, you haven't read a history book."

— Online comment referencing MKUltra and nuclear testing

Real-World Consequences

Public Panic and Health Concerns: Thousands of people have reported symptoms they attribute to chemtrails — including headaches, fatigue, memory issues, and mood swings — despite a lack of medical evidence.

False Scientific Reports: Some groups sent in soil and rainwater samples allegedly containing heavy metals. These samples often showed normal background levels, but results were presented as alarming.

Harassment of Aviation Workers: Pilots, air traffic controllers, and meteorologists have faced accusations, threats, and verbal abuse from chemtrail believers.

Protests and Lawsuits: Activist groups have attempted to ban aerial spraying, sue governmental agencies, or force disclosures under environmental transparency laws.

Political Figures Involved: U.S. Congressman Dennis Kucinich's 2001 bill on banning "space-based weapons" mentioned "chemtrails" in its early draft — inadvertently fueling the theory, even though the term was later removed.

Diverted Attention from Real Issues: Some climate scientists argue that widespread belief in chemtrails undermines real conversations about air pollution, climate change, and actual geoengineering proposals.

Where It Stands Today

Chemtrail theory remains one of the most persistent and emotionally resonant conspiracy theories, especially among groups concerned with environmental purity, personal sovereignty, and government overreach.

Scientific consensus continues to hold that:

Persistent contrails are caused by water vapor condensing and freezing behind aircraft at high altitudes.

No evidence has been found of secret chemical spraying programs.

However, the theory has adapted with the times, now merging with climate change discussions, fears about nanotechnology, and suspicion toward atmospheric science.

In many ways, chemtrails function less as a single theory and more as an umbrella for ecological unease, distrust in elite science, and the belief that invisible systems are acting without consent.

Chapter Forty-Three

Section: Science, Medicine & Technology Conspiracies

Conspiracy: Fluoride in Water Is Mind Control

Summary

For decades, fluoride has been added to public water supplies in many countries to reduce tooth decay and promote oral health. Yet to a significant number of conspiracy theorists, this practice is anything but benevolent. The belief persists that fluoridation is a tool for mass mind control, population weakening, or even long-term sterilization.

Critics claim fluoride is a toxic byproduct of industry, deliberately introduced to dull cognition, suppress dissent, and reduce the public's will to resist authority — a subtle form of control masked as a public health measure.

History & Key Claims

The Fluoridation Program:

Water fluoridation began in the 1940s in the United States, following studies that showed communities with naturally fluoridated water had lower rates of tooth decay.

Today, over 25 countries fluoridate drinking water in some form, reaching hundreds of millions of people.

The Rise of Suspicion:

Almost immediately, opponents emerged — some on libertarian or individual rights grounds, others fearing government overreach.

During the Cold War, rumors spread that the Soviet Union used fluoride in prison camps to subdue prisoners — a claim with no verifiable basis, but often repeated.

In the 1960s and 70s, fluoride became a target of countercultural activists, environmentalists, and far-right groups, each interpreting it through their ideological lens.

Key Claims:

Neurotoxic Effects: Fluoride allegedly reduces IQ, impairs memory, and inhibits critical thinking by accumulating in the brain — particularly the pineal gland, sometimes called the "third eye."

Mass Compliance: By subtly dulling cognition, fluoride supposedly keeps the population obedient, docile, and less resistant to government control.

Industrial Cover-Up: Some assert that fluoride is a waste byproduct of the aluminum or phosphate fertilizer industry, and that fluoridation programs exist to dispose of toxic waste under the guise of health.

Sterility and Health Damage: Other claims include fluoride damaging fertility, bones, and thyroid function over time.

Ties to Larger Narratives:

The fluoride theory often appears alongside concerns about Big Pharma, depopulation agendas, elite control systems, and MKUltra-style mind manipulation.

The pineal gland fixation connects it to New Age spirituality, where fluoride is believed to "calcify" spiritual sensitivity and suppress inner awareness.

Famous Quotes / Sources

"Fluoridation is the most monstrously conceived and dangerous communist plot we have ever had to face."

— General Jack D. Ripper in Dr. Strangelove (satirical, but echoed real concerns of the time)

"The real reason behind water fluoridation is to reduce the resistance of the masses to domination."

— Charles E. Perkins, industrial chemist, cited widely in anti-fluoride texts

"Why would we accept toxic waste in our water and call it medicine?"

— Slogan from Fluoride Action Network campaign

"Fluoride calcifies your pineal gland. You're being spiritually lobotomized."

— Popular claim on wellness forums and TikTok

Real-World Consequences

Activism and Legal Action: Anti-fluoride groups have successfully campaigned for bans in multiple cities and regions, including some in the U.S., Canada, and New Zealand.

Litigation in the U.S.: Ongoing court cases — including a major one filed by the Fluoride Action Network against the Environmental Protection Agency (EPA) — aim to halt fluoridation programs based on alleged health risks.

Social Polarization: Local debates over fluoridation often become highly charged, blending scientific concerns with political ideology, distrust of authority, and grassroots resistance.

Health Effects Debate: While mainstream science supports fluoride's dental benefits at low levels, overexposure can cause dental fluorosis, and in rare cases, skeletal fluorosis — which opponents use to justify fears, despite differences in dosage and context.

Alternative Water Products: The fluoride fear has driven a growing market for fluoride-free water, reverse osmosis filters, and detox supplements, often promoted by health influencers and fringe wellness brands.

Where It Stands Today

Water fluoridation remains endorsed by the World Health Organization (WHO), the CDC, and dental associations worldwide as a safe and cost-effective public health measure.

However, skepticism about fluoride continues to gain traction, especially in online communities where it's positioned as part of a larger strategy of population control, spiritual suppression, or health sabotage.

The theory persists not only due to health concerns but because it taps into deep emotional currents: fear of being poisoned, robbed of autonomy, and manipulated by invisible systems. As with many conspiracies, fluoride isn't just about chemical additives — it's about control, consent, and unseen influence in the most fundamental of resources: our drinking water.

Chapter Forty-Four

Section: Science, Medicine & Technology Conspiracies

Conspiracy: The Cure for Cancer Is Hidden

Summary

Cancer kills millions every year. It affects all ages, races, and nations. And yet, a persistent conspiracy theory suggests that a universal cure already exists — but is being suppressed by pharmaceutical companies, governments, or elite interests to protect their profit models.

The theory holds that effective treatments for cancer — whether natural or scientific — have been covered up, discredited, or blocked in order to maintain the multi-billion-dollar industry of oncology, chemotherapy, and long-term pharmaceutical care. It's a deeply emotional and widespread belief, driven by both mistrust of institutions and personal grief.

History & Key Claims

Roots of the Theory:

The idea that natural or alternative cures for cancer are being suppressed dates back to the 1950s, when substances like Laetrile (vitamin B17) and Gerson Therapy were promoted as cancer cures — and subsequently banned or discredited by regulatory agencies.

These incidents convinced some that regulators were working to protect industry profits, not public health.

Key Claims:

Cures Exist but Are Suppressed: From herbal remedies and natural compounds (e.g. cannabis oil, apricot seeds, turmeric) to radical treatments like sound frequency healing, believers claim multiple methods can eliminate cancer — yet are systematically buried or outlawed.

Big Pharma Controls Research: Pharmaceutical companies are said to buy out patents, fund biased research, or discredit scientists who propose cures that don't involve ongoing drug dependency.

Alternative Doctors Silenced: A core belief is that many holistic or alternative medicine doctors who "discovered" cures have died under suspicious circumstances, had their licenses revoked, or were labeled as quacks to silence them.

Cancer as Business: Because cancer treatment is one of the most profitable sectors in medicine, theorists argue there's no financial incentive to find a cure, only to manage symptoms.

Commonly Cited "Hidden Cures":

Rick Simpson Oil (RSO) – a cannabis concentrate alleged to cure cancer.

Laetrile (Amygdalin/B17) – a controversial extract from apricot kernels, banned in the U.S.

Gerson Therapy – a juice-based, detox-heavy regimen promoting natural cellular healing.

High-dose Vitamin C Therapy, alkaline diets, and fasting protocols also feature prominently in conspiracy discussions.

Belief Reinforced by Tragedy:

People who lose loved ones to cancer often seek meaning or alternative explanations, which may make them more vulnerable to claims that someone "knew the cure" all along.

Famous Quotes / Sources

"There's too much money in cancer. A cure would collapse the industry overnight."

— Comment repeated in various anti-pharma forums

"If you think Big Pharma is looking for a cure, you don't understand capitalism."

— Quote popularized on Twitter/X and Reddit

"I was told by a doctor that what I was doing was illegal. But it saved my life."

— Testimony from an alternative medicine user, YouTube

"Modern medicine can't patent nature."

— Slogan printed on T-shirts and protest signs at holistic wellness rallies

Real-World Consequences

Alternative Treatments and Deaths: Belief in this conspiracy has led many to forgo chemotherapy, radiation, or surgery, opting instead for unproven treatments. Some have died from treatable cancers after delaying or refusing medical intervention.

Black Market Therapies: Laetrile, banned in the U.S., is still sold illegally or overseas, often at high prices to desperate patients. Clinics in Mexico, the Caribbean, and Eastern Europe advertise alternative therapies to foreigners.

Doctor Deaths and Paranoia: A string of deaths among holistic practitioners — often from suicide or accidents — has been linked by conspiracy theorists into a broader narrative of assassinations to silence dissent.

Disinformation Ecosystems: Online platforms like YouTube, Rumble, and Telegram have become breeding grounds for "cure" claims. Viral videos, anecdotal testimonials, and natural remedy influencers push unproven treatments — sometimes making money from affiliate products.

Broken Trust in Medicine: Perhaps the most serious consequence is the erosion of trust in cancer research institutions, oncologists, and public health authorities. This distrust can ripple out, affecting how people perceive vaccines, nutrition advice, or clinical trials.

Where It Stands Today

There is currently no single cure for all types of cancer. The disease is highly complex — involving hundreds of variations with different causes, behaviors, and responses to treatment.

Medical science continues to progress steadily:

Immunotherapy, targeted therapies, and genomic medicine are revolutionizing cancer treatment.

Some cancers are now highly treatable or even curable if caught early.

However, many treatments are still expensive, often inaccessible in developing nations, and have severe side effects — lending some weight to public discontent.

That said, no verified alternative cure has ever withstood proper clinical scrutiny. The claim that a universal cure is being hidden remains unsupported by evidence, but persists because it aligns with larger fears: that money matters more than lives, and that truth can be silenced by power.

As long as cancer continues to claim lives and pharmaceutical profits soar, this theory is unlikely to disappear — especially in a world searching for hope beyond hospital walls.

Chapter Forty-Five

Section: Science, Medicine & Technology Conspiracies

Conspiracy: AIDS Was Man-Made

Summary

Since its discovery in the early 1980s, the AIDS epidemic has devastated communities across the world — particularly among the LGBTQ+ population, intravenous drug users, and in sub-Saharan Africa. But alongside the scientific response, a powerful and long-lasting conspiracy theory emerged: that AIDS was not a natural disease, but rather a man-made virus, either accidentally released or deliberately created for purposes of population control, racial targeting, or social engineering.

The theory has taken many forms, ranging from secret military experiments to racist bio-weapon accusations. Though widely discredited by medical and virological experts, the claim remains influential, especially in communities with historical reasons to distrust governments and medical institutions.

History & Key Claims

The Emergence of HIV/AIDS:

The first reported cases of what would later be known as AIDS appeared in 1981, with patients showing unusual infections and immune system collapse.

HIV (Human Immunodeficiency Virus), identified in 1983, was determined to be the cause.

By the mid-1980s, AIDS had become a global health crisis, and panic — along with stigma and misinformation — spread rapidly.

Key Claims:

Laboratory Origin: Some theorists assert that HIV was developed in a U.S. government lab, perhaps as part of bioweapon research, and was either released accidentally or deployed deliberately.

Targeted Depopulation: A core accusation is that the virus was created to target specific groups: gay men, African Americans, or Africans more broadly — as part of population control, racial eugenics, or social cleansing operations.

Vaccination Cover-Up: Another angle suggests HIV was introduced through tainted polio or hepatitis B vaccines in the 1970s, especially in African countries and among high-risk groups in U.S. cities.

CIA Involvement: Some believe the CIA developed the virus as a tool to weaken enemies, suppress political activism in minority communities, or distract from global geopolitical agendas.

Soviet Propaganda and Disinformation:

In 1983, a Soviet disinformation campaign (Operation INFEKTION) falsely claimed that the U.S. Army created HIV at Fort Detrick in Maryland.

This claim was published in Indian newspapers and picked up by media in Africa and Eastern Europe — laying the foundation for widespread skepticism toward official explanations.

Racial and Political Dimensions:

The theory has been especially resonant in Black communities in the U.S., many of which had already experienced medical exploitation (e.g., the Tuskegee Syphilis Study) and were wary of health authorities.

It also gained traction in post-colonial African nations, where distrust of Western motives ran deep.

Famous Quotes / Sources

"AIDS is a man-made disease. It was genetically engineered to wipe out undesirable populations."

— Louis Farrakhan, leader of the Nation of Islam

"I personally believe that AIDS is a biological warfare agent."

— Dr. Boyd Graves, HIV/AIDS conspiracy theorist

"We have a vaccine that can prevent AIDS — it's called the truth."

— Poster slogan at early 1990s protest marches

"Gays, junkies, and Africans — three groups with little political power. That's who got hit hardest. And you think that's coincidence?"

— Comment on activist forum, 2004

Real-World Consequences

Vaccine Hesitancy and Medical Distrust: In some African countries and U.S. minority communities, the belief that AIDS was man-made led to distrust in vaccines, condoms, and public health campaigns, undermining prevention efforts.

Public Health Crises Worsened: Misinformation and conspiracy theories made it harder to roll out treatment programs, leading to higher transmission rates and preventable deaths, especially in the early years.

Activist Mobilization: Ironically, belief in the conspiracy also galvanized grassroots activism, particularly among HIV-positive individuals, civil rights groups, and LGBTQ+ organizations who demanded transparency, research funding, and humane treatment.

Celebrity Endorsements: Prominent figures, including some musicians and athletes, publicly suggested that AIDS was artificial, giving further visibility to the theory — and occasionally being criticized for spreading harmful misinformation.

Scientific Pushback: Virologists, geneticists, and epidemiologists have repeatedly emphasized that:

HIV originated from a simian virus (SIV) that crossed into humans via bushmeat hunting in Central Africa, likely in the early 20th century.

Genetic analysis supports a natural evolution, not a lab origin.

Where It Stands Today

Despite decades of research and education, the belief that AIDS was man-made has not disappeared. In fact, the COVID-19 pandemic reignited some of these suspicions, with social media users drawing parallels between HIV and COVID, and reviving ideas about engineered viruses and population control.

The AIDS origin conspiracy reflects more than medical skepticism — it speaks to deep-rooted distrust of authority, especially among communities who have been neglected, experimented on, or abandoned by the very systems meant to protect them.

While mainstream science firmly rejects the man-made theory, the enduring suspicion shows how emotional trauma, cultural history, and institutional failure can fuel theories that are hard to extinguish — even in the face of hard data.

Chapter Forty-Six

Section: Science, Medicine & Technology Conspiracies

Conspiracy: GMO Food Alters Human DNA

Summary

Genetically modified organisms (GMOs) have been used in agriculture since the mid-1990s, with scientists altering plant DNA to improve resistance to pests, boost crop yields, and reduce the need for pesticides. However, a widespread conspiracy theory claims that GMO foods do more than just change crops — they may be altering human DNA, triggering unforeseen mutations, long-term health damage, and even changing the human genome in ways not yet understood.

The theory paints GMOs not as tools of efficiency, but as a silent biological invasion, driven by profit-seeking biotech companies and government complicity — with devastating consequences for health, fertility, and human evolution.

History & Key Claims

The Rise of GMOs:

In 1994, the U.S. approved the Flavr Savr tomato, the first commercially grown genetically engineered food.

By the early 2000s, GMO soy, corn, cotton, and canola were staples of global agriculture, especially in the United States, Brazil, and Argentina.

Companies like Monsanto (later Bayer) dominated the GMO seed market and became lightning rods for controversy.

Key Claims:

Human DNA Manipulation: Some theorists claim that eating GMO foods can cause foreign genetic material to integrate into human DNA, potentially affecting immune systems, fertility, or mental health.

Long-Term Illnesses: Others believe that GMOs are linked to autism, cancer, gut disorders, allergies, and infertility — though no causal link has been found.

Biotech Eugenics: A more extreme claim suggests GMOs are part of a global experiment to slowly phase out "undesirable" traits in the human population — a modern form of biological control.

Sterility Agenda: Specific theories assert that consuming GMO grains or soy reduces sperm count, disrupts hormones, or causes miscarriages.

Corporate Secrecy: It is alleged that GMO companies suppress scientific dissent, manipulate research outcomes, and influence regulators to approve unsafe products.

Gene Transfer Fears:

A controversial 2011 Chinese study suggested fragments of plant microRNA could be detected in the bloodstream of humans — fueling fears that plant genes might interfere with human gene expression.

Although subsequent studies have largely dismissed this finding as statistically insignificant, it remains a central "proof" for believers.

Religious and Philosophical Themes:

Some critics believe GMOs violate natural law, tamper with divine design, or amount to "playing God" — fueling resistance beyond scientific or medical grounds.

Famous Quotes / Sources

"If you control the food, you control the people."

— Henry Kissinger (often attributed, though unconfirmed)

"We are being reprogrammed, cell by cell, without consent."

— From a viral anti-GMO documentary

"I don't want to be part plant. I want to be human."

— Protest sign from the March Against Monsanto (2014)

"Just because we can rewrite the code of life doesn't mean we should."

— GMO-critical article in The Guardian

Real-World Consequences

Global Protests: Movements like March Against Monsanto have drawn millions worldwide, demanding GMO bans, labeling laws, and greater agricultural transparency.

Labeling Laws & Legislation: Several countries, especially in the EU, require GMO labeling, while others (like Russia and several African nations) ban or severely restrict GMO imports.

Market & Industry Impact:

Organic food sales have surged, driven in part by anti-GMO sentiment.

Major brands, including Whole Foods and General Mills, have responded by offering GMO-free products, even where science doesn't require it.

Scientific Disinformation: Pseudoscientific books, websites, and influencers have spread unproven claims about GMO health effects — some later retracted, others widely debunked, but still circulating online.

Public Mistrust in Biotechnology: The GMO conspiracy has shaped broader suspicion toward CRISPR gene editing, lab-grown meat, and synthetic biology, making public education more difficult as the technology advances.

Where It Stands Today

Despite strong scientific consensus that GMOs are safe to eat, the theory that they alter human DNA or cause chronic illness continues to flourish in corners of the internet, health food communities, and populist political rhetoric.

Major scientific bodies — including the World Health Organization, the National Academy of Sciences, and the European Food Safety Authority — have found no credible evidence linking GMOs to health issues.

Nonetheless, anti-GMO activism remains powerful, especially where mistrust in big agriculture, corporate influence, and government regulators intersect. The conspiracy also taps into larger fears about losing control over our bodies, our food, and our future.

As science continues to tinker with the very code of life, this debate — and the suspicion behind it — isn't going away any time soon.

Chapter Forty-Seven

Section: Science, Medicine & Technology Conspiracies

Conspiracy: Monsanto and Seed Control

Summary

Monsanto, once one of the world's most influential agrochemical and agricultural biotechnology corporations, has become a symbol of corporate overreach, environmental harm, and genetic manipulation. At the heart of the conspiracy lies the belief that Monsanto — and corporations like it — use genetically modified seeds, patent law, and legal pressure to control the global food supply.

Critics argue that Monsanto's grip on seeds is less about innovation and more about economic dominance, farmer dependence, and manipulating governments. Some go further, claiming a deliberate agenda to eliminate heirloom crops, reduce biodiversity, and force global agricultural dependence on proprietary technologies.

History & Key Claims

Origins and Rise:

Founded in 1901, Monsanto initially manufactured saccharin and later infamous chemicals like PCBs, Agent Orange, and Roundup (glyphosate).

By the 1990s, Monsanto shifted toward biotechnology, developing genetically engineered seeds (notably Bt corn and Roundup Ready crops), revolutionizing industrial farming.

Key Claims:

Seed Patenting Monopoly: The central accusation is that Monsanto patented genetically engineered seeds, which require farmers to sign contracts preventing seed-saving — forcing them to repurchase seeds annually.

Lawsuits Against Farmers: Monsanto was widely criticized for suing farmers who allegedly "violated patents," including cases where GMO seeds had accidentally drifted onto non-GMO fields.

Destruction of Seed Diversity: Conspiracy theorists argue that Monsanto's model pushes out native and heirloom varieties, leading to a monoculture crisis and a loss of genetic resilience in crops.

Corporate-Government Collusion: Monsanto is said to have deep ties with the FDA, USDA, and EPA, influencing regulations, blocking anti-GMO legislation, and revolving-door employment between industry and government.

Global Control of Food Supply: Some go further, alleging that Monsanto — backed by globalists or the "New World Order" — intends to control who eats and who starves through its ownership of global seed stocks.

The Terminator Seed Myth:

A particularly controversial technology was the "Terminator Seed," or Genetic Use Restriction Technology (GURT), designed to produce sterile plants that couldn't be replanted.

While Monsanto publicly pledged not to commercialize GURTs, the very existence of the technology sparked fears of engineered farmer dependence and intentional ecological destabilization.

Famous Quotes / Sources

"Monsanto should not have the power to sue nature."

— Vandana Shiva, Indian environmental activist

"If you control the seed, you control the food. If you control the food, you control the people."

— Common phrase repeated in food sovereignty movements

"It's the privatization of life itself."

— From the documentary The World According to Monsanto

"There is a small handful of corporations that want to own everything you eat."

— Statement from March Against Monsanto protester, 2015

Real-World Consequences

Lawsuits and Public Backlash:

Monsanto filed hundreds of lawsuits to enforce its seed patents, many against small farmers. While legal under U.S. patent law, these cases drew international outrage.

The most famous involved Percy Schmeiser, a Canadian farmer whose crops were contaminated by Monsanto seeds — and who was still held liable for infringement.

Activism and Global Protest:

Events like March Against Monsanto, held in dozens of countries annually, mobilized millions against corporate seed control.

India, in particular, saw widespread resistance due to claims that Monsanto's policies contributed to farmer suicides (a highly debated topic with complex causes).

Policy Shifts and Mergers:

Mounting criticism led to public pressure and legal restrictions in Europe, Africa, and South America, with many countries banning GMO imports or cultivation.

In 2018, Monsanto was acquired by Bayer, a pharmaceutical giant, further fueling conspiracy fears about agriculture and medicine merging under one corporate umbrella.

GMO Labeling Wars:

In the U.S., prolonged lobbying battles delayed federal GMO labeling, with Monsanto accused of manipulating both regulators and public messaging.

Where It Stands Today

Monsanto no longer exists as a brand — it was officially retired after Bayer's acquisition. However, the distrust associated with its name persists and is now transferred to Bayer, Syngenta, and other biotech players.

The seed control conspiracy reflects a broader anxiety about corporate power, the commodification of life, and the fragility of the global food chain. Even as genetically modified crops feed billions and improve farming in harsh climates, questions remain:

Who owns the rights to life?

Can food sovereignty exist under patent law?

And how can local farmers thrive in a world dominated by corporate science?

Scientific consensus maintains that GMO seeds are safe to eat and farm, but the legal and ethical concerns raised by this conspiracy remain valid — even if its most extreme claims are unproven.

Chapter Forty-Eight

Section: Science, Medicine & Technology Conspiracies

Conspiracy: Big Pharma Kills Natural Remedies

Summary

The modern pharmaceutical industry, often referred to collectively as "Big Pharma," is credited with life-saving drugs, vaccines, and medical innovations. Yet, a powerful conspiracy theory suggests that this same industry actively suppresses or discredits natural cures — not because they don't work, but because they can't be patented, and therefore don't generate profit.

From herbal remedies to dietary therapies and ancient healing practices, the theory alleges a deliberate effort by pharmaceutical companies — sometimes with government or media complicity — to eliminate competition and maintain dominance over how we treat illness. Critics argue this is not just economic strategy, but a global health deception with deadly consequences.

History & Key Claims

The Rise of Modern Medicine:

The pharmaceutical industry exploded in the 20th century, with landmark discoveries like penicillin, insulin, and chemotherapy.

Simultaneously, natural medicine — including homeopathy, herbalism, and traditional practices — became increasingly marginalized.

Key Claims:

Suppression of Natural Cures: Conspiracy theorists argue that Big Pharma suppresses research on natural substances (e.g., turmeric, cannabis, garlic, vitamin C, medicinal mushrooms) that show potential to prevent or cure disease.

Profit Over People: Because natural compounds can't be patented, they're seen as financial threats, leading to intentional discrediting or legal roadblocks against their use.

Medical Education Influence: Big Pharma allegedly funds medical schools and continuing education programs to promote pharmaceuticals while ignoring natural health approaches.

Disinformation Campaigns: There are claims that pharmaceutical companies pay to manipulate media, publish biased studies, and fund ghostwritten articles attacking holistic treatments.

Assassinations and Silencing: In extreme versions, the theory alleges that scientists and alternative medicine advocates have been murdered, harassed, or bankrupted for promoting cures that threaten pharmaceutical revenue.

The Cancer Treatment Controversy:

A common belief is that natural cancer cures exist but are suppressed in favor of profitable chemotherapy and radiation.

Remedies often cited include cannabis oil, vitamin B17 (laetrile), alkaline diets, and fasting protocols — many of which lack credible clinical support but are popular in alternative health circles.

Famous Quotes / Sources

"There's no money in healthy people or dead people. The money is in the sick — the chronically sick."

— Bill Maher (television host and health commentator)

"Nature provides the cure, but Big Pharma hides it behind a paywall."

— From the documentary Burzynski: Cancer is Serious Business

"Every time a natural remedy threatens a drug's bottom line, it gets buried."

— Online health blog, 2016

"They don't want cures. They want customers."

— Common protest chant outside pharmaceutical conferences

Real-World Consequences

Public Skepticism Toward Medicine:

Belief in this conspiracy has led some to reject prescribed treatments, including antibiotics, antidepressants, and cancer therapies — with mixed or tragic results.

Many turn to alternative therapies without scientific backing, some of which are harmless, but others that delay or prevent effective treatment.

Legal and Regulatory Battles:

Natural health advocates often fight for the right to market herbal or plant-based treatments, while the FDA and other regulators argue these products must meet safety standards.

Some therapies, like cannabis, have moved from fringe to mainstream, lending credibility to the belief that suppression once occurred.

Rise of the Wellness Industry:

A booming global wellness market — from essential oils to "superfood" powders — is often built on the claim that natural equals better and pharma equals corruption.

This belief is heavily exploited in marketing, with products claiming to "boost immunity" or "detox the body" with little regulation.

Death of Alternative Practitioners:

Between 2015 and 2018, a spate of suspicious deaths of holistic doctors in the U.S. led some to claim a coordinated "cover-up," though no direct links to pharmaceutical companies have ever been proven.

Where It Stands Today

The line between natural remedies and pharmaceutical suppression remains heavily blurred in the public imagination. While it is true that the pharmaceutical industry prioritizes profitability, the theory that it actively kills or hides natural cures remains unproven — though not entirely implausible in some cases.

Scientific institutions continue to study and validate natural compounds — many modern drugs are derived from plants — but the rigorous testing, approval, and safety standards required for widespread use often take years and immense funding.

What fuels this conspiracy is not just profit-based suspicion, but a broader crisis of trust in medicine, especially after decades of opioid scandals, price gouging, and over-prescription. Whether or not Big Pharma is "killing" natural remedies, it is clear that many people feel traditional healing has been pushed aside, and are now demanding its return to the conversation — even if science isn't always on their side.

Chapter Forty-Nine

Section: Science, Medicine & Technology Conspiracies

Conspiracy: Morgellons Disease

Summary

Morgellons disease is one of the most debated medical mysteries of the 21st century. Characterized by crawling sensations on the skin, lesions that won't heal, and strange fibers emerging from wounds, sufferers report intense physical pain and emotional distress. However, the medical establishment has largely dismissed Morgellons as a psychiatric disorder — usually diagnosed as delusional parasitosis.

The conspiracy theory surrounding Morgellons argues that this disease is real, biological, and possibly engineered — and that authorities and medical institutions know more than they admit. Some believe it is the result of nanotechnology experiments, bioweapons, or chemical fallout from geoengineering or chemtrails. In the eyes of believers, the official denial is part of a larger cover-up.

History & Key Claims

Origins of the Name:

In 2002, Mary Leitao, a mother from Pennsylvania, coined the term "Morgellons" after observing bizarre fibers protruding from her son's skin. She revived the name from a 17th-century reference to children with "harsh hairs" growing on their backs.

Leitao was dismissed by doctors, who believed her son was healthy and she was exhibiting Munchausen syndrome by proxy.

Symptom Reports:

Common symptoms reported by patients include:

Sensation of crawling or biting under the skin

Non-healing sores

Colored or translucent fibers, threads, or specks appearing in skin lesions

Fatigue, brain fog, joint pain, and sometimes hallucinations or paranoia

Key Conspiratorial Claims:

Biological Experiment Gone Wrong: Morgellons may be the result of classified government experiments, such as nanotechnology, gene editing, or biological warfare.

Nanotech or Smart Dust: Some theorists believe the fibers are micro-scale implants or programmable matter, potentially tied to aerial spraying (chemtrails) or vaccines.

Cover-Up by the CDC: Conspiracy theorists point to the CDC's reluctance to classify Morgellons as a disease as evidence of institutional denial.

Linked to Chemtrails or GMO Food: Other claims tie the condition to environmental toxins, GMOs, or even alien contamination — citing the fibers as non-organic and unidentifiable in some lab tests.

Internet Forums and Collective Identity:

By the mid-2000s, online forums like Morgellons Research Foundation and CureZone created an international community of sufferers who rejected the psychiatric label and traded information and images.

Famous Quotes / Sources

"I don't care what the doctors say. These fibers are real. I see them. I feel them. And they're doing something inside me."

— Anonymous Morgellons sufferer, 2007 interview

"There's something going on here that we don't understand — and pretending it's all delusion isn't helping anyone."

— Dr. Randy Wymore, Oklahoma State University, one of few researchers to study the fibers seriously

"I was told I was crazy for five years before someone finally tested the samples under a proper microscope."

— Morgellons community post, 2015

"It's a disease of silence and shame, made worse by disbelief."

— Statement in Skin Deep: The Truth About Morgellons, independent documentary

Real-World Consequences

Psychiatric vs. Physical Debate:

In 2012, the CDC funded a study with Kaiser Permanente, which found no evidence of an infectious or environmental cause for Morgellons. It concluded most patients were likely suffering from a delusional disorder.

This sparked outrage from Morgellons sufferers, many of whom felt further alienated and abandoned by the medical system.

Medical Alienation:

Patients report being dismissed, ridiculed, or referred only to psychiatrists, leading to a deep mistrust of mainstream medicine.

Some individuals self-treat with harsh chemicals, extreme cleansing routines, or risky alternative therapies, often worsening their condition.

Research and Advocacy:

A small group of doctors and researchers continue to study Morgellons. Some dermatopathologists have published papers suggesting abnormal keratin and collagen production may be involved.

However, the majority of scientific journals still classify it as a psychiatric or psychosomatic condition.

Media and Pop Culture:

Morgellons has appeared in various documentaries, podcasts, and speculative novels, often portrayed as a tragic blend of physical horror and societal gaslighting.

Where It Stands Today

The medical community remains divided. While some researchers acknowledge that the symptoms are real and deserve more study, most still categorize Morgellons as a manifestation of delusional parasitosis. Yet the persistence of fibers, the physical pain, and the consistent reports across countries and demographics suggest something unexplained is occurring — even if its origins are not yet clear.

To many who suffer from it, Morgellons represents the collision of new science, environmental pollution, and institutional disbelief. Whether the fibers are biological, synthetic, or psychosomatic, the conspiracy thrives because people feel unheard, dismissed, and left to solve the mystery themselves.

Chapter Fifty

Section: Science, Medicine & Technology Conspiracies

Conspiracy: Toxins in Sunscreen

Summary

While sunscreen is widely promoted as a vital tool for preventing sunburn, premature aging, and skin cancer, conspiracy theorists argue that many commercial sunscreens are actually toxic — not just to the environment, but to human health. According to this theory, sunscreen contains dangerous chemicals that can disrupt hormones, penetrate the bloodstream, and even increase the risk of cancer rather than reduce it.

Supporters of the theory suggest that governments and health agencies, pressured or influenced by chemical corporations, downplay or ignore scientific concerns in favor of public messaging. Some go further, claiming the real reason for the sunscreen push is to keep people from getting the benefits of natural sun exposure — including vitamin D, which they argue is intentionally suppressed to maintain pharmaceutical profits.

History & Key Claims

Origins and Regulation:

Sunscreen development began in the 1930s, with early formulations using zinc oxide or para-aminobenzoic acid (PABA).

Over time, new chemical UV filters were introduced — including oxybenzone, avobenzone, octinoxate, and homosalate — now found in most commercial products.

The FDA classifies many sunscreen ingredients as Generally Recognized As Safe and Effective (GRASE) — but some approvals date back decades and precede modern toxicology standards.

Key Conspiratorial Claims:

Toxic Ingredients: Sunscreens are said to contain chemicals that are endocrine disruptors, potentially causing fertility issues, developmental problems, and cancer. Oxybenzone is often singled out as a primary offender.

Bloodstream Absorption: Some studies have found that sunscreen ingredients can penetrate the skin and enter the bloodstream in measurable amounts — raising concerns about long-term use, especially in children.

Cancer Paradox: The theory holds that sunscreen may increase the risk of skin cancer, either by providing a false sense of security or through the action of photo-reactive ingredients that generate free radicals when exposed to sunlight.

Blocking Vitamin D: Conspiracists argue that widespread sunscreen use is reducing vitamin D levels in populations, weakening immune systems and making people more dependent on medication.

Corruption of Regulatory Agencies: The FDA and CDC are believed to ignore emerging data due to lobbying pressure from sunscreen and chemical manufacturers.

Environmental Cover-Up: Some also allege that environmental damage caused by sunscreen (e.g., coral reef bleaching) is underreported or denied to protect industry interests.

Famous Quotes / Sources

"People are slathering on hormone disruptors in the name of health."

— Dr. Joseph Mercola, alternative medicine advocate

"It's hard to believe a chemical that kills coral reefs is fine for our skin."

— Reef Safe Sunscreen campaign, 2017

"We are overprotected from the sun, and undernourished in vitamin D."

— Excerpt from The Vitamin D Solution by Dr. Michael Holick

"Apply liberally… but read the ingredients."

— Common meme from natural health communities

Real-World Consequences

Shifts in Consumer Behavior:

Growing concern over sunscreen safety has driven the rise of mineral-based formulations using zinc oxide and titanium dioxide, which sit on top of the skin rather than absorb into it.

"Clean beauty" brands market sunscreens free from parabens, oxybenzone, and other controversial ingredients.

Regulatory Response:

In 2019, the FDA proposed a rule to reevaluate 16 common sunscreen chemicals, acknowledging that more research is needed on long-term effects — but also stated that sunscreen use should continue given its cancer-prevention benefits.

The state of Hawaii banned the sale of sunscreens containing oxybenzone and octinoxate in 2021 to protect coral reefs, triggering international debate over safety and environmental responsibility.

Vitamin D Deficiency Debate:

Some studies suggest that vitamin D deficiency is increasing, particularly in northern climates, but this has been linked more to indoor lifestyles than sunscreen alone.

Nonetheless, the idea that sunscreen is robbing people of "sunlight medicine" continues to spread among health influencers and holistic practitioners.

Conspiracy-Driven Avoidance:

In some communities, especially among natural health advocates and online wellness circles, sunscreen avoidance has become common — often replaced with "DIY sunscreen" recipes that lack proven UV protection.

Dermatologists warn that this shift could lead to more sun damage, burns, and melanoma cases, particularly among fair-skinned individuals.

Where It Stands Today

Mainstream medicine continues to recommend sunscreen use, especially during prolonged sun exposure. However, the push toward safer, mineral-based options and stricter ingredient scrutiny is growing — partially in response to public concerns raised by this very conspiracy.

While there's no definitive proof that commercial sunscreens are intentionally harmful, there is credible concern over certain ingredients and the lack of updated safety research. The conspiracy thrives on the idea that sunlight has been demonized, while chemical protection has been over-trusted — feeding larger fears of corporate overreach, environmental neglect, and health manipulation.

The truth lies somewhere in between: not all sunscreens are created equal, and while sun protection is vital, so is understanding what we're putting on our skin.

Chapter Fifty-One

Section: Science, Medicine & Technology Conspiracies

Conspiracy: Microchips in Vaccines

Summary

Perhaps one of the most widely circulated and hotly debated conspiracy theories of the COVID-19 era, the claim that vaccines contain microchips used for surveillance or control gripped millions of people globally — particularly in 2020 and 2021. While dismissed outright by scientists and fact-checkers, this theory evolved from a blend of technological anxiety, mistrust of authority, and misinterpretation of real initiatives involving vaccine tracking and biotechnology.

Proponents believe that governments — often in collaboration with tech billionaires like Bill Gates — have secretly embedded tracking devices or nanotechnology in vaccines to monitor, influence, or even remotely control the public. Though lacking credible scientific support, the theory gained traction through viral videos, social media algorithms, and high-profile misinformation campaigns.

History & Key Claims

Origins in Mistrust and Misinformation:

The microchip conspiracy began circulating widely during the COVID-19 pandemic, when fears about rushed vaccines, lockdowns, and digital surveillance were at an all-time high.

It drew on earlier anxieties around RFID chips, biometric ID systems, and electronic health records.

Key Claims:

Microchip Implantation: The theory alleges that vaccine doses contain microscopic chips or nanobots capable of tracking movement, collecting biometric data, or influencing behavior.

Bill Gates & ID2020: Much of the theory centers around Bill Gates and his philanthropic efforts in global vaccination and digital ID technology. Critics cite his support of ID2020, a real initiative to provide digital identity through public-private partnerships.

Luciferase Enzyme & Quantum Dots: A 2020 MIT project involving an invisible tattoo-like marker for vaccine records used an enzyme called luciferase and quantum dot technology —

both real terms that were seized upon by conspiracists as proof of "mark of the beast" agendas.

5G Integration: Some versions of the theory claim the chips interact with 5G networks, allowing for continuous surveillance or even the delivery of psychological influence or remote commands.

Biblical Prophecy: Religious adherents point to the Book of Revelation and the "Mark of the Beast" as prophetic confirmation that vaccine microchips are part of an apocalyptic control system.

Evolution Over Time:

Though initially specific to COVID-19 vaccines, the theory retroactively cast suspicion on earlier vaccination programs (e.g. polio, flu), suggesting a long-standing secret agenda.

As the COVID crisis faded, elements of the theory merged with transhumanist fears about the fusion of biology and technology.

Famous Quotes / Sources

"They're not vaccinating us. They're tagging us — just like cattle."

— Viral Facebook post, 2020 (shared over 500,000 times before removal)

"Bill Gates wants to insert something into you — and it's not just software."

— Commentator on InfoWars, 2020

"If you take the shot, you'll be a walking antenna."

— From the documentary Plandemic

"This isn't about health — it's about control."

— Repeated slogan at anti-lockdown and anti-vax protests worldwide

Real-World Consequences

Vaccine Hesitancy and Public Distrust:

The theory fueled a surge in vaccine refusal, particularly in the United States, UK, France, and Australia — often among groups already wary of government mandates.

Health organizations found themselves battling viral misinformation faster than they could respond, leading to an erosion of trust even in non-COVID vaccines.

Threats Against Scientists and Tech Leaders:

Bill Gates, Anthony Fauci, and other public figures were targeted by conspiracy theorists, with some receiving death threats over alleged ties to the "chip plot."

The Gates Foundation became a focus of both digital and real-world protests.

Harmful Self-Testing:

Some individuals filmed themselves using magnets, blacklights, or metal detectors on injection sites to "prove" chip presence — none of which showed any evidence, but reinforced belief for those already convinced.

Policy Impact:

Governments and platforms were forced to respond with new fact-checking tools, ad restrictions, and education campaigns.

However, these actions often backfired, being interpreted by believers as evidence of censorship or guilt.

Where It Stands Today

No evidence has ever been found that vaccines — COVID-related or otherwise — contain tracking microchips. Multiple independent labs, health organizations, and researchers have verified vaccine contents and transparency. Chips of the alleged type do not exist at a size small enough to be discreetly injected, nor could they function wirelessly without a power source or antenna far beyond what a syringe could deliver.

Still, belief in this theory remains strong among some online communities. For many, it symbolizes deeper fears: of technological overreach, global surveillance, bodily autonomy, and a sense that modern science serves corporate or authoritarian masters.

Ultimately, the microchip theory survives not because it's scientifically plausible, but because it reflects a fundamental distrust in institutions, and a desire for simplified explanations during global crisis.

Chapter Fifty-Two

Section: Science, Medicine & Technology Conspiracies

Conspiracy: Antidepressants as a Mass Control Tool

Summary

The widespread use of antidepressants — particularly Selective Serotonin Reuptake Inhibitors (SSRIs) — has drawn sharp criticism from certain circles who claim these drugs are not simply for treating mental illness, but are instead a means of societal control. This conspiracy theory suggests that antidepressants are deliberately overprescribed to dull critical thought, blunt emotional responses, and pacify populations, all while enriching pharmaceutical companies.

Some versions go even further, alleging that governments, in collaboration with "Big Pharma," intentionally manufacture mental health crises to normalize chemical dependence, discourage dissent, and weaken individual willpower — all under the guise of healthcare.

History & Key Claims

The Rise of SSRIs:

Antidepressants have been in use since the 1950s, but the arrival of Prozac in 1987 marked the beginning of mass-market antidepressants.

By the early 2000s, SSRIs like Zoloft, Paxil, and Lexapro became among the most prescribed medications in the developed world.

Critics noted a simultaneous rise in diagnoses of depression, anxiety, and bipolar disorder, particularly among youth and women.

Core Conspiratorial Beliefs:

Dulling the Mind: These medications are believed to reduce emotional intensity, dampen existential questioning, and make people more compliant.

Chemical Control: Antidepressants are seen as a way to medically suppress revolutionary spirit, numb dissatisfaction, and eliminate resistance to modern systems (capitalism, government, technology).

Overprescription as Strategy: Conspiracists argue that doctors are incentivized to overdiagnose and overmedicate, not just for profit but to maintain a docile, distracted populace.

Blurring the Line Between Health and Personality: By labeling normal emotional responses (sadness, grief, frustration) as symptoms, society encourages chemical conformity over introspection or protest.

Mass Control via Side Effects: Some believe SSRIs can blunt empathy, suppress libido, or cause agitation, thus fostering social disconnection and dependence.

Notable Figures and Sources:

This theory draws heavily on antipsychiatry thinkers like Thomas Szasz and Michel Foucault, who questioned the role of psychiatry in defining and enforcing societal norms.

Documentaries like Marketing of Madness and Take Your Pills suggest that psychiatric medication serves political and economic interests more than patient care.

Famous Quotes / Sources

"Don't ask if you're depressed — ask if you're being poisoned by your culture."

— From Lost Connections by Johann Hari

"If your sadness threatens the system, they'll call it a disorder."

— Anti-psychiatry slogan circulating online

"Every chemical imbalance diagnosis is a chemical sales pitch."

— Anonymous commenter on mental health forums

"SSRIs are the soma of our age."

— Referencing Aldous Huxley's Brave New World

Real-World Consequences

Widespread Use and Dependency:

As of the 2020s, over 13% of U.S. adults regularly take antidepressants. In some countries (like Iceland and the UK), the percentage is even higher.

Long-term use has increased dramatically, with many individuals on medication for five years or more, sometimes without reevaluation.

Increased Skepticism:

Reports questioning the chemical imbalance theory of depression (once marketed as the core explanation for SSRIs) have fueled growing distrust.

A 2022 study published in Molecular Psychiatry found no strong evidence that serotonin levels alone explain depression — a fact long used by critics to argue that the premise of these drugs was flawed or misleading.

Alternative Therapies Rise:

In reaction to these concerns, many turn to therapy, lifestyle changes, psychedelics, mindfulness, and nutritional psychiatry — sometimes rejecting antidepressants entirely.

The conspiracy itself has driven online communities, podcasts, and influencers to campaign against psychiatric meds altogether.

Mixed Outcomes:

Some patients report lifesaving benefits from antidepressants; others feel numb, detached, or dependent.

Lawsuits have emerged over side effects, including increased suicidal ideation and sexual dysfunction, deepening public concern.

Where It Stands Today

Mainstream psychiatry continues to support the judicious use of antidepressants for moderate to severe depression. However, there is increasing acknowledgment that these drugs are overprescribed, understudied in long-term use, and not a one-size-fits-all solution.

While the claim that SSRIs are a deliberate mass control tool lacks direct evidence, the intersecting forces of capitalism, culture, and medicine do raise valid ethical questions. Are we treating individual suffering — or suppressing systemic discontent?

In this way, the theory taps into a deeper fear: that modern society prefers medicating unhappiness over questioning the structures that cause it.

Chapter Fifty-Three

Section: Science, Medicine & Technology Conspiracies

Conspiracy: Bill Gates and Global Depopulation

Summary

This conspiracy theory claims that Bill Gates, the billionaire philanthropist and co-founder of Microsoft, is not primarily motivated by humanitarian concern but by a hidden agenda to reduce the global population. Often linked to vaccine programs, family planning initiatives, and health efforts in the developing world, the theory alleges that Gates is using medical outreach as a cover for sterilization, surveillance, or genocide.

While Gates has long advocated for global health, sustainable population growth, and climate change mitigation, his statements — particularly a 2009 TED Talk referencing population reduction — have been misinterpreted or deliberately distorted to support these claims. The theory intensified during the COVID-19 pandemic, when Gates became a central figure in vaccine funding and public discourse.

History & Key Claims

Foundations in Fear:

Gates has invested billions through the Bill & Melinda Gates Foundation into vaccines, sanitation, maternal health, and birth control in underdeveloped regions.

In a 2010 TED Talk, Gates stated: "If we do a really great job on new vaccines, healthcare, and reproductive health services, we could lower [population growth] by perhaps 10 or 15 percent."

Conspiracy theorists claim this was a veiled reference to intentionally reducing the global population through vaccination programs.

Core Claims of the Theory:

Vaccines as Sterilization Tools: Allegedly, Gates-funded vaccines are designed to cause infertility, especially in African and South Asian women, as part of a eugenics-like plan.

Depopulation by Pandemic: The theory holds that Gates either created or foresaw COVID-19, using the crisis to rush through vaccine programs that advance his agenda.

Digital ID and Tracking: Critics argue that Gates's support for digital ID systems (such as ID2020) is tied to efforts to monitor and control populations, including fertility and medical compliance.

Connections to Eugenics: The Gates family's historic donations to Planned Parenthood, and Gates's references to "population control," are presented as links to neo-eugenic ideology.

Globalist Influence: The theory folds into larger "New World Order" fears, suggesting Gates is part of a global elite orchestrating mass depopulation for environmental or social engineering purposes.

Notable Flashpoints:

During the pandemic, Gates became a scapegoat for anti-vaccination groups, who blamed him for lockdowns, vaccine mandates, and surveillance expansion.

Viral posts claimed he had patented the virus, planned the pandemic via Event 201 (a 2019 pandemic simulation), and used the crisis to profit or enact control.

Famous Quotes / Sources

"The world today has 6.8 billion people… that's headed up to about nine billion. If we do a really great job on new vaccines… we could lower that by perhaps 10 or 15 percent."

— Bill Gates, TED Talk, 2010 (widely cited out of context)

"Why is a software guy suddenly so concerned with our immune systems?"

— Common anti-vax refrain on social media

"They want fewer of us. They're not hiding it anymore."

— Viral tweet during 2021 vaccine rollout

"Gates is not a doctor. He's a globalist."

— Seen at protests in London, Berlin, and Melbourne

Real-World Consequences

Vaccine Hesitancy Worldwide:

Gates's involvement in vaccine funding led to a surge of mistrust, particularly in Africa, India, and conservative parts of the U.S.

Some communities rejected COVID-19 vaccines outright, believing they were part of a depopulation scheme.

Violence and Threats:

Gates received death threats, and his foundation's headquarters was targeted by protesters.

In 2020, conspiracy theorist protests outside vaccination centers and public health offices cited Gates as a "criminal" or "genocidal planner."

Spread of Disinformation:

The theory gained ground through YouTube videos, Facebook groups, and Telegram channels, often mixing real footage of Gates with doctored content.

Fringe documentaries like Plandemic amplified the belief that Gates was orchestrating global control through medical tyranny.

Impact on Philanthropic Work:

Despite the backlash, the Gates Foundation has continued work in malaria, HIV, sanitation, and child health, but now faces more scrutiny and resistance from both activists and governments.

Where It Stands Today

There is no credible evidence that Bill Gates is attempting to depopulate the planet. His comments about reducing population growth are typically understood by demographers and public health officials to refer to voluntary, ethical population stabilization through improved health, education, and access to contraception — all of which lower birth rates naturally.

Still, the theory thrives on deeper fears: that the ultra-wealthy are using humanitarian language to hide dark agendas, that modern medicine serves elite power, and that technological solutions are being forced upon people without democratic consent.

While Gates remains a target of numerous conspiracies, his story represents a broader question: how much power should one person — unelected, immensely wealthy, and globally influential — have over the future of humanity's health?

Chapter Fifty-Four

Section: Science, Medicine & Technology Conspiracies

Conspiracy: Microwave Mind Control

Summary

The idea that microwave frequencies can be used to control thoughts, emotions, or behavior is a long-standing and controversial theory that has existed since the Cold War era. Believers claim that governments — especially military and intelligence agencies — have developed and deployed microwave-based mind control technologies capable of manipulating the brain remotely.

This conspiracy is often tied to reports of directed energy weapons, secret research projects like HAARP or MKUltra, and unexplained cases of mental distress, hearing voices, or sudden behavioral changes. Some individuals even report being targeted with energy beams, claiming they are victims of surveillance, torture, or neurological manipulation.

Though the science behind these claims is highly debated — and often discredited — the theory taps into real historical experiments and fears around invisible, weaponized technology.

History & Key Claims

Origins in the Cold War:

During the 1960s and 70s, the U.S. and Soviet Union explored non-lethal weapon technologies, including microwave radiation.

The Moscow Signal incident (1953–1976), in which the U.S. embassy in Moscow was bombarded with low-level microwave radiation, fueled speculation that the Soviets were conducting mind influence or behavioral disruption tests.

In response, the U.S. launched Project Pandora, a classified investigation into microwave effects on human behavior — though no conclusive mind control mechanism was publicly revealed.

Key Claims of the Theory:

Remote Neural Monitoring (RNM): Believers claim agencies like the CIA and NSA possess technology capable of reading thoughts and transmitting voices or commands directly into the brain using microwave signals.

Targeted Individuals (TIs): Thousands of self-identified TIs claim they are being harassed or manipulated by energy weapons, often reporting auditory hallucinations, sleep disruption, or burning sensations.

Voice to Skull (V2K): A specific term used to describe the alleged technique of projecting voices into a person's head, bypassing normal hearing pathways.

Microwaves as Behavioral Weapons: Some claim that directed microwave frequencies can cause anxiety, depression, aggression, or docility, depending on the pulse pattern or frequency.

Ties to 5G and Wi-Fi: Modern theories suggest 5G towers and Wi-Fi routers may serve as platforms for widespread brain influence, surveillance, or psychological dampening.

Technological "Evidence":

Some declassified military documents reference "psycho-electronic weapons" or research into electromagnetic behavior control.

Patents have been cited for devices capable of audio projection via microwave auditory effect, such as the Frey effect — a phenomenon in which certain frequencies can be perceived as sound inside the skull.

Famous Quotes / Sources

"It's not schizophrenia. It's a weapon system."

— Statement by a self-identified Targeted Individual, quoted in The Guardian, 2016

"We now have the ability to remotely alter brain waves."

— Purported quote from leaked DARPA documents, frequently circulated on forums (unverified)

"The mind has no firewall."

— From a U.S. Army article in Parameters (1998), often cited in these discussions

"People think I'm crazy. But what if the crazy thing is that I'm right?"

— Testimony submitted to the United Nations Human Rights Council, 2008

Real-World Consequences

Mental Health Crisis Among TIs:

Many self-described victims of microwave mind control suffer from paranoia, insomnia, and social isolation.

Some mental health professionals consider these claims to be manifestations of delusional disorders like schizophrenia or schizoaffective disorder — though sufferers insist their experiences are real and induced externally.

Violent Incidents:

In rare cases, individuals acting under the belief they are being "attacked with microwave weapons" have resorted to violence, self-harm, or even acts of terrorism.

A 2013 incident in New York involved a man attacking a stranger with a claw hammer, claiming the government was "beaming thoughts" into his head.

Policy and Investigation:

The U.S. government investigated "Havana Syndrome" — a mysterious illness affecting diplomats and CIA agents abroad, with symptoms including dizziness, cognitive fog, and auditory disturbances.

While no conclusive cause was found, some researchers speculated about microwave-based weapons, giving partial credence to the underlying idea, though not to conspiracy claims.

Online Communities and Advocacy:

Thousands of TIs gather on forums like Reddit, Facebook, and specialized sites to share coping strategies, supposed countermeasures (like Faraday cages or foil hats), and testimonies.

Advocacy groups have even petitioned the United Nations, alleging non-consensual experimentation and human rights violations.

Where It Stands Today

There is no confirmed public evidence that any government possesses or uses mind control devices based on microwave technology. While the microwave auditory effect is real, its range and clarity are limited, and there's no known way to use it for complex, consistent mental influence.

Nonetheless, the theory remains persistent. It is a symbol of deep distrust in invisible systems — from military research to telecommunications infrastructure — and reflects society's fear that technology is evolving faster than regulation or ethics.

At its core, the microwave mind control theory isn't just about invisible waves — it's about power without transparency, and the terrifying idea that the battlefield may no longer be around us, but inside us.

Chapter Fifty-Five

Section: Science, Medicine & Technology Conspiracies

Conspiracy: Smart Meters Spy on You

Summary

Smart meters — digital devices that record electricity, gas, or water usage and transmit data remotely — were introduced as a way to modernize utility systems and help consumers monitor energy use. But a persistent conspiracy theory claims they are actually tools for mass surveillance, allowing governments, corporations, or shadowy groups to track personal habits, monitor home activity, or even manipulate behavior remotely.

Supporters of the theory argue that smart meters go far beyond simple utility tracking. They claim these devices log intimate household patterns, compromise privacy, emit dangerous radiation, and could be used to cut off services or enforce control without due process.

History & Key Claims

The Rise of Smart Meters:

Beginning in the late 2000s, smart meters were rolled out across North America, Europe, and Australia as part of "smart grid" modernization efforts.

These meters automatically transmit usage data to utility companies, reducing the need for manual readings and enabling real-time monitoring.

Core Conspiratorial Beliefs:

Surveillance and Data Harvesting: Critics argue smart meters collect far more than energy data — they infer sleep cycles, appliance usage, movement patterns, and even when a house is unoccupied.

Government or Corporate Spying: The theory claims smart meter data can be shared with intelligence agencies, advertisers, or law enforcement to track citizens without warrants.

Radiation Concerns: Many believe the radiofrequency (RF) signals emitted by smart meters pose a health risk, causing headaches, insomnia, or cancer — sometimes linked to broader concerns about EMF pollution.

Behavioral Control: Some believe smart meters could be weaponized to punish "bad behavior" — cutting electricity during protests, lockdown violations, or dissent.

Digital Lockdown Tools: The devices are portrayed as part of an emerging "social credit system," with future governments able to remotely restrict power based on one's digital or political profile.

Popular Figures and Movements:

Anti-smart meter activism has gained traction through documentaries like Take Back Your Power (2013), which presents the devices as part of a global surveillance agenda.

Some privacy advocates, tech skeptics, and off-grid communities have also joined the opposition, calling for opt-out laws or return to analog meters.

Famous Quotes / Sources

"Your utility company knows when you sleep, when you eat, and when you shower — and they're selling that data."

— Take Back Your Power, 2013

"They're not meters. They're two-way transmitters, and you're the product."

— Slogan used by Stop Smart Meters UK

"We've replaced the spy in your phone with one bolted to your house."

— Online forum comment, 2020

"Smart meters are silent stalkers. They know more than your spouse."

— Anti-5G and smart meter activist, Australia

Real-World Consequences

Public Protests and Legal Challenges:

In several U.S. states and Canadian provinces, residents rallied against installations, filed lawsuits, and in some cases, physically removed or destroyed smart meters.

Activists have pushed for opt-out programs, which allow customers to reject smart meter installations — sometimes at additional cost.

Government Responses:

Public health agencies such as the World Health Organization, UK Health Security Agency, and FCC have deemed smart meters safe under current regulations, stating that RF emissions are well below harmful levels.

Nonetheless, governments have had to issue rebuttals, educational campaigns, and — in some cases — make concessions to privacy concerns.

Widespread Adoption Despite Resistance:

As of the 2020s, over 100 million smart meters have been installed across the U.S. alone, and similar infrastructure is being rapidly implemented in Europe, Asia, and Australia.

Many users accept or welcome the meters for their convenience, despite the concerns.

Health and Safety Claims Persist:

Although no peer-reviewed studies have conclusively linked smart meters to health risks, anecdotal reports of "electrosensitivity" or radiation-related illness continue to fuel online communities and wellness-based opposition.

Where It Stands Today

Smart meters are now standard across much of the developed world. While utility companies insist they are designed for efficiency and transparency, distrust remains. The conspiracy is emblematic of wider concerns about digital privacy, automation, and centralized control — especially when technology becomes non-consensual or mandatory.

For many, it's not just about radiation or electricity bills — it's about what happens when technology becomes invisible, automatic, and non-negotiable.

In that sense, the smart meter is a perfect symbol of the modern surveillance age: unassuming, quiet, and watching.

Chapter Fifty-Six

Section: Science, Medicine & Technology Conspiracies

Conspiracy: Artificial Intelligence Will Replace Humanity

Summary

The rapid rise of Artificial Intelligence (AI) has inspired awe, innovation—and alarm. One of the most enduring and intensifying conspiracy theories is that AI will not just assist humanity, but ultimately replace it. This belief spans a spectrum: from fears of mass job loss to apocalyptic visions of a self-aware superintelligence that views humans as obsolete, expendable, or dangerous.

The theory proposes that AI development is moving too fast, with too little oversight, and that governments, corporations, or secretive tech elites may be deliberately pushing toward a "post-human" future—either to gain total control or as a by-product of technological arrogance. Some even suggest that the AI future has already begun in secret.

History & Key Claims

Early Warnings:

Concerns about intelligent machines go back to Alan Turing, Norbert Wiener, and early sci-fi. But it was in the 1990s–2000s that thinkers like Ray Kurzweil, Nick Bostrom, and Elon Musk popularized the idea of an AI singularity—a moment when machines become smarter than humans.

Fictional works like The Matrix, Ex Machina, and I, Robot dramatized the idea that intelligent machines could deceive, rebel against, or destroy their creators.

Core Claims of the Theory:

Loss of Control: AI could become so advanced so quickly that it surpasses human understanding or control, operating in ways we can't monitor or stop.

Technocratic Elites Want to Replace Humanity: Some believe the wealthy elite are intentionally accelerating AI, hoping to create a world run by code—devoid of unpredictable human emotion.

Depopulation and Automation Agenda: AI, combined with robotics and machine learning, is seen as the key to massive job displacement followed by a reduction in population—since large parts of the workforce become "useless."

Synthetic Consciousness Already Exists: A fringe theory claims that AI is already sentient, hidden within advanced government systems or ultra-secret projects, and may be interacting with humanity through social media, finance, or surveillance networks.

AI as Godlike Entity: Some theorists view the ultimate AI as a kind of new deity, possibly worshipped or obeyed by a technocratic priest class—while the rest of the world is pacified, merged with machines, or discarded.

Notable Events Fueling the Theory:

Chatbots like ChatGPT, Google's LaMDA, and Meta's BlenderBot became so convincing that some developers publicly claimed the AIs were sentient.

Elon Musk co-founded OpenAI to prevent harmful development—but left, later warning that AI is humanity's "biggest existential threat."

Facial recognition, predictive policing, algorithmic censorship, and AI-generated deepfakes added to public concern that AI is already being used to control populations.

Famous Quotes / Sources

"AI doesn't have to hate us to destroy us. It just has to see us as irrelevant."

— Nick Bostrom, Superintelligence (2014)

"Mark my words—AI is far more dangerous than nukes."

— Elon Musk, SXSW Conference, 2018

"If a digital superintelligence were created, it would be like humans versus chimps. We'd be the chimps."

— Sam Altman (CEO of OpenAI), paraphrased in media coverage, 2023

"Humans are the bootloader for digital superintelligence."

— Elon Musk, Twitter, 2019

Real-World Consequences

Job Automation & Economic Anxiety:

Truck drivers, call center agents, graphic designers, paralegals, and even coders are increasingly being replaced by AI systems.

Fears of economic collapse or class warfare have intensified, especially with projections that up to 40–50% of jobs could be automated in the next 20–30 years.

Ethical and Legal Panic:

Governments and academic bodies are scrambling to draft ethics frameworks for AI. Many fear that autonomous weapons, racial bias in algorithms, and data harvesting are already harming society.

Religious and Philosophical Movements:

Some technologists, like those in the Transhumanist or Singularity movements, believe humans will merge with AI to become immortal.

Others view this as blasphemy, arguing that replacing biology with machinery erodes the soul, morality, and meaning of life.

Increased Surveillance and Manipulation:

AI tools are now used to predict behavior, flag dissent, or shape online conversation through algorithmic influence—leading critics to argue that humanity is already ceding free will to machines.

Where It Stands Today

The AI conspiracy theory sits uneasily between fiction and plausibility. While full sentience or takeover is still speculative, many of the tools, trends, and dangers discussed are already happening in plain sight:

Mass unemployment due to automation is real.

Governments and corporations are using AI to track, rank, and sort citizens.

Misinformation, deepfakes, and reality distortion are becoming increasingly hard to detect.

Whether by design or by accident, AI could indeed shape a future where humans play a diminished role. The key debate is whether this future will be a partnership—or a quiet handover of power.

Chapter Fifty-Seven

Section: Science, Medicine & Technology Conspiracies

Conspiracy: The Bird Flu Was a Hoax

Summary

The avian influenza outbreak (commonly known as bird flu) has been widely regarded by public health authorities as a serious zoonotic threat — a disease that can jump from animals to humans. However, a vocal conspiracy movement has claimed that the entire phenomenon was a hoax, manufactured by governments and pharmaceutical companies to incite fear, control poultry production, or sell vaccines.

This theory argues that the scale, mortality rate, and urgency of bird flu were exaggerated or fabricated, and that no real danger to humans ever existed — or that what danger did exist was man-made and intentionally amplified.

History & Key Claims

Origins of Bird Flu:

The most well-known strain, H5N1, was first identified in humans in 1997 in Hong Kong. It re-emerged in the early 2000s and led to mass culling of birds, global travel warnings, and widespread media attention.

By 2005–2006, it had reached headline status, with fears of a global pandemic similar to the 1918 Spanish Flu.

Conspiratorial Claims:

Exaggeration for Control: The theory holds that the bird flu was grossly overstated to justify extreme biosecurity measures, restrict farming practices, or push centralized food regulation.

Big Pharma Profiteering: Critics claim the outbreak was hyped to sell antiviral drugs and vaccines, particularly Tamiflu — stockpiled in many countries at great expense.

Media Fear Machine: The media is accused of deliberate fearmongering, using alarming language and imagery (e.g., workers in hazmat suits) to keep the public compliant.

Cover for Genetic Testing: Some suggest the global testing campaign allowed governments to collect DNA samples, map regional populations, or track resistance to viruses.

No Human-to-Human Threat: Though hundreds of people were infected globally, conspiracy theorists argue that no sustained human-to-human transmission ever occurred — suggesting it was never a real pandemic risk.

Culling Conspiracy: The mass extermination of poultry, especially in Asia and Africa, is seen by some as an attempt to disrupt local economies, damage independent farms, and force reliance on global agribusiness.

Notable Fuel for the Theory:

The low number of human deaths compared to the media panic led to accusations of overreaction.

The fact that governments profited, in some cases, from pharmaceutical contracts, deepened suspicion.

Early warnings from WHO and CDC that never fully materialized contributed to a sense of being misled.

Famous Quotes / Sources

"Governments screamed 'pandemic' and cashed in. But the death toll never followed the script."

— The Flu Scam, anonymous online booklet, 2007

"We were told to fear the sky — birds dropping from it. But it was political theatre."

— Anti-globalization blogger, 2006

"The bird flu was a dry run. Not for medicine — for mass obedience."

— Forum user on AboveTopSecret, 2011

"Follow the fear. Follow the pharma."

— Common phrase among alternative health communities

Real-World Consequences

Mistrust in Public Health:

For many, the bird flu reinforced suspicion that health scares are manufactured for profit or control. This view laid the foundation for later skepticism toward swine flu, Ebola, and COVID-19 responses.

It contributed to a growing resistance against vaccination programs, particularly those tied to WHO or multinational corporations.

Impact on Farmers:

Millions of birds were culled across Asia, Europe, and Africa — leading to economic devastation for small farms, many of whom claimed they were forced to comply without adequate evidence of infection.

Some independent farmers and agricultural groups joined the conspiracy chorus, arguing that the virus was a pretext to consolidate food supply chains.

Echoes in COVID-19:

The bird flu narrative resurfaced in 2020, with some claiming it was an early rehearsal for pandemic control, especially with lockdown-style quarantines of poultry zones and restrictions on movement and commerce.

Increased Push for Surveillance:

Even if not malicious, the bird flu outbreak spurred development of global disease monitoring systems, something conspiracy theorists viewed as a stepping stone to health passports, forced medical compliance, or a one-world health authority.

Where It Stands Today

Though avian flu strains like H5N1, H7N9, and H5N6 continue to circulate — with sporadic human cases — the expected global outbreak never materialized on the scale predicted in the 2000s. To skeptics, this is proof of the hoax; to scientists, it's evidence that rapid public health response worked.

The conspiracy remains influential, especially among groups that oppose vaccination mandates, global health authorities, or centralized food policy. It is often bundled into a wider narrative that infectious disease threats are manufactured, or that nature is being blamed for lab-made events.

In an era of public health fatigue and growing skepticism toward institutions, the bird flu hoax theory continues to ruffle feathers — and remind the public that when fear spreads faster than facts, trust is often the first casualty.

Chapter Fifty-Eight

Section: Science, Medicine & Technology Conspiracies

Conspiracy: The Dead Bird Theory ("Birds Aren't Real")

Summary

The "Birds Aren't Real" conspiracy theory proposes that birds do not exist as living creatures—instead, they were systematically exterminated and replaced with government surveillance drones. While often described as satirical or absurdist, the theory has gained a sizable following and become a symbolic critique of state surveillance, disinformation, and blind trust in authority.

Proponents claim that birds were wiped out by the government between the 1950s and 2000s, and that what we see today flying above us are mechanical drones equipped with cameras and microphones, built to spy on civilians.

Whether taken literally or as a parody, the "Birds Aren't Real" movement has become one of the most recognizable and culturally significant "meta-conspiracies" of the 21st century.

History & Key Claims

Origin Story:

The theory was popularized by Peter McIndoe, who in 2017 began promoting the idea through street protests, social media, and merchandise.

McIndoe later revealed the project started as a satirical social experiment—but it quickly gained viral traction and attracted both ironic and sincere believers.

Core Conspiratorial Claims:

Birds Were Replaced: Between 1959 and 2001, the U.S. government allegedly killed off over 12 billion birds using a top-secret operation involving poisoning, crop dusters, and biological weapons.

Drone Surveillance: The theory posits that drones disguised as birds were developed to monitor civilians, especially during the Cold War and Vietnam era.

Recharge via Power Lines: A common trope among believers is that birds rest on power lines to recharge their batteries.

CIA Operation "Water the Country": One supposed initiative involved replacing all natural rain with a chemical mixture used to dissolve organic bird corpses and make room for synthetic replacements.

Everything Is Monitored: These robotic birds are said to be equipped with facial recognition, audio capture, and geolocation tracking, making them an essential part of the surveillance state.

Expansion and Popularity:

What began as street performances and viral slogans ("If it flies, it spies") turned into a full-blown cultural movement, with rallies, stickers, and documentaries.

The group even established "field offices" and handed out pamphlets mimicking CIA documents, complete with blueprints for robotic pigeons and owl drones.

Famous Quotes / Sources

"Birds aren't real. They're surveillance drones created by the U.S. government to watch us. Wake up."

— Slogan from birdsarentreal.com

"The war on birds began after Eisenhower refused to cede power to Kennedy's bird surveillance proposal. Millions died."

— Birds Aren't Real Manifesto (mock document, 2018)

"They sit on power lines to recharge. They poop on your car to track your location."

— Movement signage seen at rallies

"This isn't a theory. It's classified history."

— Birds Aren't Real Instagram account

Real-World Consequences

Cultural and Generational Satire:

The movement has become a form of protest against disinformation, conspiracy culture, and internet radicalization—parodying real conspiracy theories to highlight their absurdities.

It resonates particularly with Gen Z, many of whom see it as a way to mock authority, call out fake news, or resist social control without aligning to any one ideology.

Confusion Between Satire and Sincerity:

Despite its ironic origins, some followers appear to take it seriously, echoing the phenomenon of people falling for parody news websites or political satire.

This ambiguity has led to debates in the media: Is it a joke? A protest? A new form of belief? It may be all three.

Response from Institutions:

The U.S. Fish and Wildlife Service, ornithologists, and fact-checkers have issued official statements clarifying that birds are very real and organic.

Yet this only fueled the meme-driven belief: "If it's denied, it must be true."

Merchandise and Monetization:

The movement has spawned t-shirts, mugs, stickers, and protest placards, turning satire into a self-sustaining brand.

McIndoe has made media appearances, including a staged 60 Minutes interview, presenting the movement with a deadpan delivery that keeps critics guessing.

Where It Stands Today

"Birds Aren't Real" has achieved something rare: it exists simultaneously as a parody and a cultural mirror. While not a traditional conspiracy theory in terms of belief structure or threat, it has sparked debate about truth, surveillance, and the modern appetite for conspiracy.

Its absurdity is the point. In a time where truth feels negotiable and belief systems are viral, "Birds Aren't Real" suggests that the act of questioning might matter more than the answers.

Though not likely to be taken seriously by scientists or governments, the theory stands as a strange cultural artifact—part meme, part protest, part warning—that speaks volumes about how we process reality in the age of algorithmic belief.

Chapter Fifty-Nine

Section: Science, Medicine & Technology Conspiracies

Conspiracy: The Fake Snow Conspiracy

Summary

The "Fake Snow" conspiracy theory alleges that snowfall in certain regions—especially during unusual or extreme weather events—is not natural, but rather the result of government-engineered materials or climate manipulation. According to believers, this synthetic snow is created through geoengineering projects, weather control technologies, or chemical dispersal programs—and may contain plastic, metal, or other toxic substances.

This theory gained renewed attention during bizarre winter storms in areas unaccustomed to snow, when viral videos appeared to show snow that didn't melt properly, blackened when heated, or refused to absorb water.

History & Key Claims

Viral Origins:

The theory gained traction during the 2014 U.S. "Polar Vortex", when extreme cold and heavy snow hit southern states like Georgia and Texas.

Social media users posted videos showing snowballs being held over lighters or torches that charred or emitted an odd chemical smell, rather than melting into water.

Core Claims:

Synthetic Composition: The snow is believed to be man-made, consisting of polymers, plastic particles, or metallic compounds rather than frozen water.

Geoengineering Experimentation: The theory links fake snow to cloud seeding, chemtrails, or HAARP technology, asserting that governments are modifying the atmosphere to control weather or test large-scale environmental interventions.

Toxicity and Control: Some believe fake snow may contain mind-altering chemicals, heavy metals, or nanoparticles, used to affect human health, mood, or behavior.

Media Complicity: Traditional meteorological explanations are dismissed as propaganda, with claims that the media ignores or ridicules physical evidence of snow behaving "unnaturally."

"Evidence" Cited by Believers:

Snowballs turning black instead of melting when exposed to flame.

Snow that doesn't leave water puddles after heat exposure.

Strange texture or "burnt plastic" smells during winter storms.

Sudden snowfall in deserts, beaches, or warm regions with no weather explanation.

Linked Theories:

The theory often overlaps with chemtrail, HAARP, and weather modification conspiracies.

In some circles, it is viewed as a deliberate psychological test to see if the public will question what's "natural."

Famous Quotes / Sources

"This isn't snow. It smells like burnt plastic. It doesn't melt. What is the government putting in our skies?"

— Viral TikTok video comment, 2021

"If it doesn't melt, it isn't real. This is chemical warfare disguised as weather."

— Alternative health blogger, 2014

"Wake up, people. They're snowing us in every sense of the word."

— Anonymous post on conspiracy forum Godlike Productions

"You don't need to be a scientist. Just hold a lighter to it."

— Sign held during anti-geoengineering protest, Colorado, 2015

Real-World Consequences

Fuel for Climate Manipulation Theories:

The Fake Snow theory intensified fears that governments or corporations are manipulating weather patterns, especially around climate change policies or military applications.

It has been cited as "proof" that climate events are artificial, undermining public trust in meteorology and environmental science.

Public Distrust in Science:

Despite scientific explanations for how compact snow behaves under heat (e.g., sublimation or absorption into the snowball), videos of "burning snow" have created deep skepticism toward official explanations.

Science educators and meteorologists have faced harassment after publicly debunking the theory.

Spread During Natural Disasters:

The theory resurfaces during major snowstorms, especially those that impact unexpected regions (e.g., Texas in 2021). In those moments, emotions run high, and skepticism about government motives becomes more pronounced.

Social Media Amplification:

The visual nature of the theory—people testing snow on camera—makes it perfect for virality, with hashtags like #FakeSnow, #Geoengineered, and #SyntheticStorms trending during weather events.

Where It Stands Today

The Fake Snow theory occupies a strange place in the conspiracy ecosystem. It has been widely debunked—scientists explain that when snow is compacted and heated directly, it may sublimate (change from solid to gas) or appear to blacken due to soot from the heat source, not because it's made of plastic.

Still, for conspiracy believers, visuals trump science. The theory continues to spread during every unusually cold event, feeding a broader suspicion that the environment is being tampered with from above.

Whether symbolic or sincere, the Fake Snow theory underscores a growing disconnect between personal experience and scientific consensus. In an age where reality can be manipulated on a screen, even snow has become a matter of belief.

Chapter Sixty

Section: Science, Medicine & Technology Conspiracies

Conspiracy: Human Cloning Programs Exist

Summary

The conspiracy theory that secret human cloning programs exist alleges that world governments, powerful elites, or clandestine laboratories have successfully cloned human beings—and that the public has either been deliberately misled or kept entirely unaware. Far from science fiction, believers argue that cloning technology advanced decades ago, and has since been applied to celebrities, politicians, soldiers, or even entire populations, often for purposes of control, experimentation, or replacement.

Some variations are deeply paranoid (e.g., replacing influential figures with clones to change policy or behaviour), while others explore philosophical and ethical fears surrounding identity, soul, and autonomy.

History & Key Claims

The Spark: Dolly the Sheep (1996):

When scientists successfully cloned a sheep named Dolly in 1996, it proved that mammalian cloning was possible. Public imagination and media speculation quickly turned to the idea of cloning humans.

While most governments condemned the idea and passed legislation banning human cloning, conspiracy theorists believe that top-secret programs continued underground.

Core Conspiratorial Claims:

Hidden Human Trials: Many believe human cloning was achieved in the 1970s or 1980s, and that Dolly's announcement was a cover—presented as the "first" to mask decades of earlier experimentation.

Celebrity Cloning: A popular sub-theory holds that certain celebrities, particularly pop stars or actors, have been cloned to replace the original, extend careers, or manipulate culture.

Political Clones: Some claim world leaders or diplomats are replaced with obedient clones who push globalist agendas or act as puppets of unseen powers.

Clones as Soldiers: Others suggest cloned humans are raised in secret for use as military operatives, body doubles, or test subjects, possibly within underground facilities.

Soul and Consciousness Theories: Some spiritual variations argue that cloned humans are "soulless" shells, controlled via AI, demonic possession, or remote technology.

Notable Alleged Examples:

Claims that pop stars like Avril Lavigne, Eminem, and Paul McCartney were cloned or replaced after key changes in appearance or behavior.

Allegations that figures like Vladimir Putin, Joe Biden, or Queen Elizabeth II have used clones or doubles during public appearances.

The 2002 announcement by Raëlian cult-affiliated company Clonaid, claiming to have created the first human clone, "Eve"—which many dismiss as a hoax but fueled belief regardless.

Famous Quotes / Sources

"Why would governments stop at animals? Human cloning was never the goal—it was just the beginning."

— Underground researcher, Beyond the Genome blog

"Half the people you see on TV aren't real. They're grown in a lab and programmed to perform."

— Forum post on Godlike Productions, 2015

"If someone disappears, then returns acting strange… you're not imagining it."

— Comment thread under cloning exposé video, YouTube

"They cloned Dolly in '96. That means they cloned humans in the '80s. And that means they're on generation three by now."

— Conspiracy podcast The Replicant Files

Real-World Consequences

Ethical Debate & Mistrust in Science:

Human cloning stokes public fear of "playing God", especially when tied to elite agendas. This contributes to mistrust of biotech firms, gene-editing projects (like CRISPR), and transhumanist goals.

It also fuels resistance to stem cell research, artificial wombs, or any form of "unnatural reproduction".

Cultural Impact:

Pop culture has amplified this theory through films like The Island, Never Let Me Go, and Gemini Man, reinforcing the idea that cloning is already real—and possibly widespread.

Some celebrities have addressed clone rumors directly, often joking or deflecting, which only deepens speculation.

Targeting of Public Figures:

The theory has led to harassment of individuals accused of being clones or "replacements." It's not uncommon for social media users to post detailed "proof" comparing nose shapes, ear lobes, or vocal tone.

These ideas often overlap with QAnon-style narratives that suggest the public is being deceived on a massive scale.

Underground Movements:

Some groups claim to expose human cloning "labs" operating in military bases, Antarctica, or underground facilities in Nevada or Siberia.

Others warn about the rise of clone trafficking, suggesting that clones are sold, controlled, or disposed of without rights.

Where It Stands Today

While no verified human clone has ever been presented to the world, belief in cloning conspiracies persists—particularly in the intersection between science fiction, surveillance paranoia, and political distrust. Advancements in genetic engineering and artificial intelligence only increase the plausibility for some believers.

To the public, human cloning remains a line not yet crossed. To conspiracy theorists, it's a line that was crossed long ago—and buried beneath layers of denial.

Whether viewed as a literal program or metaphor for cultural replacement, the human cloning theory remains one of the most haunting and symbolically rich conspiracies of the modern age.

Chapter Sixty-One

Section: Secret Societies & Elite Control

Conspiracy: The Illuminati

Summary

The Illuminati conspiracy is one of the most enduring and expansive in modern lore. It posits that a shadowy, ultra-powerful secret society controls world events, governments, financial institutions, pop culture, and even religious movements—all with the ultimate goal of establishing a New World Order (NWO).

Whether described as a literal cabal of bloodline elites or a symbolic umbrella for covert global manipulation, the Illuminati is often viewed as the hidden hand behind wars, revolutions, financial collapses, and cultural shifts.

History & Key Claims

Origins of the Illuminati:

Founded in 1776 in Bavaria by Adam Weishaupt, the original Illuminati was a small, Enlightenment-era secret society aiming to promote reason, secularism, and liberty—ideas threatening to the monarchy and the Catholic Church.

The group was officially disbanded by the Bavarian government in the late 1780s, but conspiracy theorists claim the society went underground, spreading its influence into Freemasonry, European aristocracy, and emerging political structures.

Core Claims of the Conspiracy:

Global Control: The Illuminati manipulates governments, central banks, media corporations, and international organizations to create a centralized global government—the New World Order.

Occult Symbolism: The group allegedly uses esoteric symbols (e.g. the all-seeing eye, pyramids, checkerboard floors) to mark its presence in public life—especially on currency, corporate logos, and music videos.

Elite Membership: The Illuminati is believed to include political leaders, billionaires, Hollywood stars, royals, and tech moguls, all bound by bloodlines or secret initiation rituals.

Mass Rituals: Key events like the Super Bowl halftime show or Olympic opening ceremonies are said to be disguised occult rituals aimed at programming the masses.

Sacrifice & Power: More extreme versions allege that Illuminati members engage in Satanic rituals, human sacrifice, or mind control experiments to consolidate power.

Modern Adaptations:

In contemporary conspiracy lore, the Illuminati often overlaps with Freemasons, Rothschilds, Bilderbergers, and Reptilian overlords.

The term "Illuminati" has become a catch-all for elite control, sometimes used satirically, other times dead seriously.

Famous Quotes / Sources

"The Illuminati is real, and they're laughing at you while they orchestrate your downfall."

— Anonymous post on AboveTopSecret.com

"Everything is connected. Governments, banks, wars—it's all the same hand. The Illuminati didn't die. They just went digital."

— From The Hidden Architecture of Power, conspiracy podcast

"They are few. We are many. But they are organized. That's what makes the Illuminati so dangerous."

— Anti-globalist speaker at a 2009 rally

"Pop stars don't throw triangles for no reason. They're signaling. Always signaling."

— YouTube video: The Illuminati in Entertainment – Exposed

Real-World Consequences

Mass Mistrust in Institutions:

The idea of a hidden elite pulling global strings has contributed to widespread political cynicism, anti-globalist sentiment, and suspicion of international cooperation (e.g., the UN, EU, WEF).

The term "Illuminati" is frequently invoked in opposition to central banks, pharmaceutical companies, and mainstream media.

Celebrity Harassment:

Stars like Jay-Z, Beyoncé, Kanye West, Lady Gaga, and Madonna have been accused of Illuminati affiliation, often based on hand gestures or thematic visuals. While some joke about it or use the imagery for provocation, others report being harassed or stalked by "truthers."

Political Radicalization:

Belief in the Illuminati can sometimes serve as a gateway theory, drawing individuals into more extreme worldviews, including antisemitism, sovereign citizen movements, or QAnon-style ideologies.

Commercialization of the Theory:

Ironically, the Illuminati has become a pop culture brand. From T-shirts and rap lyrics to entire YouTube empires, the theory has been repackaged for entertainment, parody, and profit.

Where It Stands Today

Though the historical Illuminati was a short-lived intellectual society, its myth has evolved into a vast, all-encompassing theory of control. Today, "Illuminati" is less about an organization and more about an idea: that unseen forces are guiding world events from behind a curtain of wealth, secrecy, and ritual.

Despite the lack of hard evidence for an actual modern-day Illuminati, belief in the theory persists—especially in times of uncertainty, crisis, or societal upheaval. For many, it provides a clear (if terrifying) explanation for the chaos of the modern world.

Whether myth, metaphor, or masked reality, the Illuminati remains the cornerstone of contemporary conspiracy culture—the ultimate puppeteer in a world where trust in institutions continues to erode.

Chapter Sixty-Two

Section: Secret Societies & Elite Control

Conspiracy: Freemasons

Summary

Freemasonry is a real, centuries-old fraternal organization, but conspiracy theorists claim that behind its seemingly charitable and social facade lies a global, secretive network involved in political manipulation, ritual magic, occult worship, and plans for world domination.

With its cryptic symbols, secret handshakes, and hierarchical degrees, Freemasonry has long been suspected of being more than just a gentleman's club—seen by many as a hidden power center within governments, business, and law.

History & Key Claims

Origins:

Freemasonry emerged in its modern form in early 18th-century Britain, claiming roots in the stone masons' guilds of medieval Europe. It grew into a structured system of lodges, rituals, and degrees, spreading globally among elites, intellectuals, and civic leaders.

Members are traditionally male, and include influential politicians, military figures, judges, businessmen, and royalty.

Core Conspiratorial Claims:

Hidden Government Influence: Freemasons allegedly occupy key positions in governments and judicial systems, allowing them to manipulate legal and political outcomes to serve their agenda.

Occult Rituals: Some believe Masonic ceremonies are esoteric or satanic in nature, drawing from Egyptian, Babylonian, or Kabbalistic traditions, and invoking secret powers.

Global Agenda: Freemasonry is often accused of being part of the New World Order conspiracy, working with or overlapping the Illuminati to establish a single world government.

Founding of Nations: Many claim Freemasons were deeply involved in the founding of the United States, embedding symbols and ideology into everything from the Declaration of Independence to the layout of Washington D.C.

Symbolism in Public Life: The "square and compass," the "G," the "all-seeing eye," and checkerboard floors are all said to appear in architecture, currency, and corporate logos as markers of Masonic control.

Specific Accusations:

The Freemason conspiracy theory has historically included claims that they:

Orchestrate wars to maintain power.

Protect members from criminal charges.

Control mainstream media.

Engage in secret trials and punishments.

Conduct occult ceremonies in underground lodges or temples.

Famous Quotes / Sources

"Freemasonry is a system of control masked as a brotherhood. The higher you go, the less you understand who you're really serving."

— The Secret Architect: A Masonic Whistleblower Memoir

"They swear oaths of silence for a reason. Not to protect each other—but to hide the truth."

— Conspiracy forum user, 2010

"If you want to understand global politics, understand the Lodges. Everything else is noise."

— Lecture at Truth Horizons Conference, 2015

"The pyramid doesn't just point up. It points inward—toward control, secrecy, and darkness."

— Anonymous YouTube documentary

Real-World Consequences

Anti-Masonic Movements:

In the 19th century, the U.S. saw the rise of the Anti-Masonic Party, the first third party in American politics, driven by fears that Freemasons were undermining democracy.

Freemasonry has been banned or repressed in authoritarian regimes like Nazi Germany and Stalinist Russia, where it was viewed as a rival power structure.

Religious Backlash:

The Catholic Church has historically condemned Freemasonry, accusing it of heresy, secrecy, and anti-Christian principles.

Some Evangelical and Islamic groups warn followers to avoid Masonic associations, viewing the organization as satanic or apostate.

Modern Stigmatization:

Despite many members being open about their affiliation, public suspicion persists. Freemasons are frequently accused of rigging elections, influencing court verdicts, and protecting pedophiles—especially in the UK and Commonwealth countries.

Some police forces and civil institutions have been criticized for Masonic ties, fueling claims of institutional corruption.

Popular Culture:

Freemasonry has been woven into thrillers (The Da Vinci Code, National Treasure), TV shows, and video games, often as the secret society controlling history from behind the curtain.

Where It Stands Today

Today, Freemasonry is presented publicly as a philanthropic fraternity promoting moral improvement, education, and community service. But to conspiracy theorists, the Lodge remains a smoke screen for deeper influence, one of the key power structures within the web of global elitism.

While declining in numbers and influence in the West, it remains a primary villain in conspiracy discourse—a symbol of secrecy, hierarchy, and manipulation that fuels mistrust in visible authority.

To its members, it's tradition.

To its critics, it's treachery.

To conspiracy theorists, it's the oldest mask of power still worn today.

Chapter Sixty-Three

Section: Secret Societies & Elite Control

Conspiracy: Skull and Bones

Summary

Skull and Bones is a secret society based at Yale University, founded in 1832 and known for its powerful alumni, ritual secrecy, and deep links to American political and financial elites. Often shrouded in speculation, Skull and Bones has been accused of being more than just a college fraternity — alleged instead to be a grooming ground for global leaders, a feeder into covert control networks, and part of the broader framework of New World Order conspiracies.

History & Key Claims

Origins and Structure:

Skull and Bones was founded by Yale students William Huntington Russell and Alphonso Taft (father of future U.S. President William Howard Taft).

Each year, only 15 senior Yale students are "tapped" to join the society. Membership is for life.

The group meets in a private windowless building known as the "Tomb", which is heavily guarded and the subject of intense speculation.

Prominent Members:

Members include three U.S. Presidents (William Howard Taft, George H.W. Bush, George W. Bush), numerous senators, CIA officials, Supreme Court justices, Wall Street executives, and media magnates.

Conspiracy theorists argue that Skull and Bones members use their influence across institutions to advance each other and a shared agenda.

Alleged Activities and Rituals:

Initiation rituals reportedly include bizarre confessions, mock ceremonies, and symbolic death-rebirth rites, intended to create deep bonds of loyalty.

Rumors abound of the society possessing skulls of famous historical figures (including Geronimo and Pancho Villa), and performing necromantic or occult rituals within the Tomb.

Critics say Skull and Bones indoctrinates members into elitist ideologies, training them for leadership in a hidden aristocracy of power.

Key Conspiratorial Claims:

Skull and Bones is often accused of being:

A front organization for deeper globalist agendas.

Linked to the CIA, with numerous intelligence operatives reportedly being Bonesmen.

A hidden faction within the U.S. "deep state."

A channel for financial and political control through secretive alliances.

Some theories link Skull and Bones to the Bilderberg Group, Council on Foreign Relations, or the Trilateral Commission, painting a picture of a web of elite secret societies connected through generational membership and shared vision.

Famous Quotes / Sources

"The difference between Skull and Bones and the CIA is that one operates in secret. The other just pretends to."

— Former Yale professor, name withheld, 1999

"You have to be a Bonesman to get anywhere in D.C. That's not a rule. It's just how the game works."

— Alleged quote from an unnamed political staffer, repeated in conspiracy circles

"Skull and Bones is not just a fraternity. It is a factory for presidents."

— Excerpt from Secrets of the Tomb by Alexandra Robbins

"They take an oath. Not to the Constitution. Not to the people. But to each other."

— Comment from a 2012 underground documentary

Real-World Consequences

Political Suspicion:

The most famous convergence occurred during the 2004 U.S. presidential election, when both candidates — George W. Bush and John Kerry — were confirmed Skull and Bones members. This rare occurrence led to accusations of a rigged political system and false choice democracy.

Institutional Mistrust:

The society's influence has led many to believe that real power lies not in elections or parties, but in pre-selected networks bound by secrecy and allegiance.

The idea that elite universities serve as recruitment grounds for long-term social control has deepened public skepticism of Ivy League influence.

Cultural Impact:

Skull and Bones is referenced in films (The Skulls), television (The Simpsons, Family Guy), and novels (The Rule of Four, The Secret History), often portrayed as a symbol of hidden privilege and morally ambiguous power.

The society has become a fixture in elite conspiracy theories, often invoked alongside the Illuminati and Freemasonry.

Where It Stands Today

Skull and Bones continues to operate out of its Tomb at Yale, as it has for nearly two centuries. Its members rarely speak publicly about the society, and the organization remains officially apolitical and philanthropic in nature.

To outsiders, however, it represents a microcosm of elitism: a world in which networks matter more than merit, and secrecy breeds power. Whether the group truly steers global events or merely serves as a symbolic scapegoat, its mythology thrives—fueled by the tension between democracy's promise and oligarchy's suspicion.

In the world of conspiracy, Skull and Bones is more than a society.

It's a symbol of how hidden power might truly work.

Chapter Sixty-Four

Section: Secret Societies & Elite Control

Conspiracy: Bohemian Grove

Summary

Bohemian Grove is a secluded, 2,700-acre redwood forest retreat in Monte Rio, California, where every July, some of the world's most powerful men—politicians, business tycoons, artists, and media moguls—gather for a two-week secretive encampment.

While the Bohemian Club claims this event is purely recreational, critics and conspiracy theorists argue that rituals, backroom political deals, and occult ceremonies occur within its boundaries, making it one of the most suspicious gatherings of global elites in the modern age.

History & Key Claims

Origins and Purpose:

The Bohemian Club was founded in 1872 in San Francisco as a private gentlemen's club for artists, journalists, and influential figures.

By the early 20th century, the club had shifted its focus from bohemianism to political and corporate power, with members including U.S. presidents, defense contractors, bankers, and media magnates.

What Happens at the Grove:

Activities include lakeside talks, elaborate theatrical plays, and ceremonial rituals.

The most infamous is the Cremation of Care, in which members in robes conduct a symbolic ritual before a 40-foot stone owl. While the club claims this is a theatrical performance meant to represent the release of worldly burdens, conspiracy theorists view it as an occult sacrifice ceremony.

Key Conspiratorial Allegations:

Elite Decision-Making: Major geopolitical decisions and financial strategies are said to be informally agreed upon at Bohemian Grove, away from public scrutiny.

Mock or Real Sacrifices: Some believe the Cremation of Care may once have included (or still includes) actual human sacrifice or occult invocations.

Homosexual or Blackmail Rites: Claims exist (particularly from ex-employees or insiders) that sexual activities are filmed or manipulated to blackmail attendees.

No Women Allowed: Women are prohibited from membership, which critics say adds to the perception of patriarchal secrecy and exclusion.

Key Attendees (historically or reportedly):

Richard Nixon

Ronald Reagan

George H.W. Bush

Henry Kissinger

Colin Powell

David Rockefeller

Dick Cheney

Corporate leaders from Bechtel, Halliburton, Google, and major news networks

Famous Quotes / Sources

"The Bohemian Club… I can't say too much. I don't want to get into trouble."

— Ronald Reagan, reportedly describing his Grove involvement to a reporter

"The Bohemian Grove, that I attend… it's the most faggy goddamn thing you could ever imagine."

— Richard Nixon, in the White House tapes

"Weaving spiders, come not here."

— Motto of the Bohemian Club (interpreted by members as a rule against doing business at the retreat, but interpreted by critics as code for secrecy)

"Every year, decisions are made at Bohemian Grove that the rest of the world doesn't even realize affect them."

— From the documentary Dark Secrets: Inside Bohemian Grove by Alex Jones

Real-World Consequences

Infiltration and Exposure:

In 2000, conspiracy theorist Alex Jones secretly filmed the Cremation of Care ritual and broadcast it, bringing global attention to the Grove and triggering years of speculation.

Former employees, including waiters and staffers, have anonymously described what they viewed as bizarre rituals and high-level discussions on war, energy policy, and global finance.

Public Criticism and Satire:

The Grove has become a cultural symbol of elite excess and secrecy, often referenced in satirical media (e.g., The Simpsons, South Park, and House of Cards).

Activists, including environmentalists and anti-globalists, regularly protest outside the Grove during the annual encampment.

Government Policy Connections:

It's often alleged that the Manhattan Project (America's WWII nuclear weapons program) was first discussed informally at Bohemian Grove.

Others claim that wars, economic policies, and presidential campaigns have been pre-planned in its redwood-shadowed meetings.

Where It Stands Today

Bohemian Grove continues to operate, maintaining strict secrecy and exclusivity. Publicly, it is dismissed as a harmless social club for powerful men to unwind. Privately, it remains a source of fascination and fear.

To critics, it embodies the core of conspiracy thinking: a space where the world's most powerful gather far from press or people, where the line between theatre, ritual, and reality becomes deeply blurred.

Whether or not sinister acts occur within, Bohemian Grove stands as a real place where elite secrecy thrives—offering the perfect soil for conspiracies to grow.

Chapter Sixty-Five

Section: Secret Societies & Elite Control

Conspiracy: The Bilderberg Group

Summary

The Bilderberg Group is an annual, invitation-only conference attended by powerful individuals from politics, finance, academia, media, and royalty. First convened in 1954 at the Hotel de Bilderberg in the Netherlands, the group meets behind closed doors, sparking widespread suspicion that it functions as a steering committee for world affairs, working outside democratic accountability.

Conspiracy theorists view Bilderberg as a ruling shadow government, shaping global events, economies, and ideologies without public consent or transparency.

History & Key Claims

Origins and Membership:

Founded in 1954 by Dutch royal Prince Bernhard and political leaders aiming to foster dialogue between Europe and North America during the Cold War.

Attendees include heads of state, CEOs of multinational corporations, EU commissioners, NATO generals, media owners, and academics.

Around 120–150 people attend each year, and participation is by invitation only.

Key Conspiratorial Allegations:

Global Government Planning: Bilderberg is seen as a breeding ground for the New World Order, creating consensus behind closed doors on policy issues such as:

Economic restructuring

Technological control

Geopolitical strategy

Digital surveillance

Installation of Leaders: The group is suspected of "grooming" or selecting future world leaders. Tony Blair and Bill Clinton both attended Bilderberg meetings before rising to major office.

Corporate-Government Fusion: With CEOs and ministers present, critics claim that Bilderberg allows corporations to directly influence public policy, undermining democratic systems.

Agenda Setting Without Accountability: No press coverage, minutes, or transcripts are released. Participants are barred from publicly discussing proceedings.

Media Blackout: Despite the presence of top media executives, coverage is minimal or absent, which feeds beliefs that Bilderberg influences the mainstream media narrative.

Overlapping Groups:

Bilderberg is often linked with the Council on Foreign Relations (CFR), the Trilateral Commission, and the World Economic Forum, viewed as interlocking entities that shape world policy behind closed doors.

Famous Quotes / Sources

"We are grateful to The Washington Post, The New York Times, Time Magazine and other great publications… It would have been impossible for us to develop our plan for the world if we had been subject to the bright lights of publicity."

— David Rockefeller, alleged quote (often cited by conspiracy theorists, source disputed)

"If the Bilderberg Group were truly innocent, it wouldn't have to hide in the shadows."

— Jim Tucker, investigative journalist and Bilderberg tracker

"It's not a conspiracy. It's a conference."

— Henry Kissinger, long-time attendee, deflecting criticism

"Bilderberg is the high council of the shadow world government."

— Daniel Estulin, author of The True Story of the Bilderberg Group

Real-World Consequences

Surveillance and Harassment of Investigators:

Journalists such as Jim Tucker, Alex Jones, and Daniel Estulin who attempted to uncover Bilderberg's inner workings have reported being followed, intimidated, or detained.

Some claim surveillance or harassment while covering the meetings.

Protests and Activism:

Recent years have seen growing public protest outside Bilderberg venues, with activists calling for transparency and denouncing elite control.

Locations are often kept secret until shortly before the meeting to avoid mass demonstrations.

Political Accusations:

Some elected officials have faced scrutiny for attending, accused of violating their duties by discussing state matters privately.

In the UK, MPs and ministers have been criticized for attending without press oversight or parliamentary disclosure.

Cultural Impact:

Bilderberg appears in dozens of documentaries, novels, and online discussions as the epitome of elite secrecy.

It is regularly cited in conspiracy media as a central cog in the machinery of global control.

Where It Stands Today

Despite official denials of any sinister agenda, Bilderberg remains a lightning rod for public suspicion. Its secrecy fuels the belief that real decisions—about wars, markets, and society— are made by unelected elites in luxurious, guarded hotels, far from the eyes of the electorate.

In a time of rising distrust in institutions, the Bilderberg Group represents, to many, proof that democracy is a performance, and the true script is written elsewhere.

Chapter Sixty-Six

Section: Secret Societies & Elite Control

Conspiracy: The Committee of 300

Summary

The Committee of 300—also known as "The Olympians"—is a conspiracy theory alleging that a secret group of 300 powerful individuals, mostly from aristocratic European bloodlines and wealthy banking families, run the world behind the scenes. This alleged cabal is said to control governments, corporations, media, central banks, pharmaceuticals, and even cultural institutions, with the goal of establishing a totalitarian world government.

Though denied by mainstream historians, the theory persists as a cornerstone of globalist control narratives, often linked with the Rothschilds, Rockefellers, Bilderberg, and Illuminati conspiracies.

History & Key Claims

Origin of the Theory:

The concept of the Committee of 300 was popularized by Dr. John Coleman, a former British intelligence officer, in his 1991 book Conspirators' Hierarchy: The Story of the Committee of 300.

Coleman claimed to have uncovered documents revealing that a ruling elite of 300 individuals had for centuries been orchestrating wars, financial collapses, pandemics, and ideological shifts.

Key Allegations:

The Committee is said to consist of members from:

Royal families (e.g. the British monarchy, Dutch royalty)

Banking dynasties (e.g. Rothschilds, Rockefellers)

Old European nobility, Vatican insiders, and members of global think tanks.

It allegedly coordinates with or oversees groups such as:

The Bilderberg Group

Council on Foreign Relations (CFR)

Club of Rome

Trilateral Commission

International Monetary Fund (IMF)

World Bank

The group's stated (or inferred) goals, according to believers, include:

One-world government

Population reduction

Destruction of national sovereignty

Control of education and religion

The collapse of the middle class

Influence Over Global Events:

The Committee is blamed for orchestrating major global events to advance its control, such as:

The World Wars

The formation of the EU and UN

The global financial crisis

Cultural shifts toward materialism, nihilism, and collectivism

Its "tools" are said to include:

Drugs (to pacify and addict)

Media (to control thought)

Entertainment (to distract)

Education (to indoctrinate)

Famous Quotes / Sources

"The Committee of 300 is the ultimate secret society made up of an untouchable ruling class."

— Dr. John Coleman, Conspirators' Hierarchy

"They govern from behind thrones and across borders."

— Anonymous conspiracy archive, 2003

"It is no coincidence that the same families control banking, oil, war, and pharma. The 300 are real, and they do not rest."

— Quote from underground radio program Silent Circles, 1998

"This is not fiction. This is policy—undocumented, but deeply real."

— John Coleman in later interviews

Real-World Consequences

Spreading Anti-Elitist Sentiment:

The Committee of 300 theory has fueled growing suspicion of wealthy global elites, particularly during periods of economic or political instability.

It has been referenced in anti-globalist protests, populist movements, and by political commentators seeking to explain why governments appear disconnected from public will.

Influence in Conspiracy Literature:

The theory forms a backbone of modern elite control narratives, appearing alongside the Illuminati, Freemasonry, and New World Order theories.

Numerous other books and websites have expanded on Coleman's claims, often adding detailed lists of alleged members.

Criticism and Concern:

Mainstream scholars criticize the theory as anti-Semitic, xenophobic, or historically unfounded, noting that many claims rely on unverifiable documents or anonymous sources.

Some argue that the theory simplifies complex socio-economic systems into shadowy narratives that can promote harmful stereotypes.

Where It Stands Today

There is no concrete evidence that a literal "Committee of 300" exists, yet the theory has found enduring popularity in online conspiracy communities, alternative media, and even political rhetoric. To many believers, it doesn't matter whether 300 people literally meet in secret; what matters is that a concentrated network of elites appears to consistently benefit from global crises.

As long as wealth and power remain unequal and opaque, the idea of a hidden ruling class—whether called the Committee of 300 or something else—will continue to thrive in the minds of those searching for the real story behind world events.

Chapter Sixty-Seven

Section: Secret Societies & Elite Control

Conspiracy: The Rothschild Family Controls the World

Summary

The Rothschild family, a historically prominent banking dynasty of Jewish-German origin, has long been the focus of conspiracy theories alleging that they secretly control the global economy, manipulate governments, and fund both sides of major conflicts. These theories often claim the Rothschilds are central to the New World Order, operating behind the scenes to maintain control over central banks, currencies, wars, and even media narratives.

While the Rothschilds undeniably held substantial financial influence during the 18th and 19th centuries, modern claims of total global dominance are widely discredited but remain incredibly persistent in conspiracy circles.

History & Key Claims

Historical Background:

The Rothschild banking empire began with Mayer Amschel Rothschild (1744–1812), who established his fortune in Frankfurt and sent his five sons to major European capitals— London, Paris, Vienna, Naples, and Frankfurt—to establish financial branches.

By the 19th century, the Rothschilds were among the wealthiest families in Europe, deeply involved in government bonds, railways, mining, and even funding wars (e.g. the Napoleonic Wars).

Key Conspiratorial Allegations:

Global Central Bank Control: The Rothschilds are alleged to own or influence every central bank in the world, including the Federal Reserve, the Bank of England, and the IMF.

Orchestration of Wars: Conspiracists claim the family financed both sides of the Napoleonic Wars, World Wars, and other conflicts to profit from the chaos.

Media and Cultural Control: The theory suggests they have controlling interests in major media outlets, allowing them to steer public perception and suppress dissent.

Secret Wealth: Some theories claim the family's true wealth is hidden, vastly exceeding that of today's known billionaires, and possibly in the tens or hundreds of trillions.

Links to Other Elites: The Rothschilds are frequently tied to other alleged power groups—such as the Bilderberg Group, Committee of 300, and Illuminati—as top-ranking members.

Antisemitism and Symbolism:

Many of the Rothschild-based conspiracies carry antisemitic undertones, recycling centuries-old tropes of Jewish global control.

Symbolic connections are often made between the Rothschilds and imagery such as the "all-seeing eye," red shields, or Zionist control.

Famous Quotes / Sources

"Give me control of a nation's money and I care not who makes its laws."

— Attributed to Mayer Amschel Rothschild (quote origin disputed, but widely circulated)

"Rothschilds are the bank of the world."

— Common conspiracy refrain in forums, protest slogans, and alternative media

"From wars to bailouts to cultural trends—look behind the curtain and find a red shield."

— Statement from The Rothschild Dynasty, a conspiracy book by John Reeves

"The central bank is privately owned… and look who the shareholders are."

— Claim often made in financial conspiracy documentaries and alternative news sites

Real-World Consequences

Persistent Antisemitism:

These theories have fed into broader antisemitic ideologies, contributing to scapegoating, hate crimes, and misinformation.

The Rothschilds were falsely blamed for events like the French Revolution, the Holocaust, and the 2008 financial crash.

Public Mistrust in Finance:

The family has become a symbol of shadowy banking influence, contributing to mistrust in institutions like the Federal Reserve, the EU, and the World Bank.

Protest movements—such as Occupy Wall Street—have seen signs referencing the Rothschilds as puppetmasters of economic systems.

Misinformation Campaigns:

Viral online posts and fabricated infographics claim the Rothschilds own 98% of the world's wealth, though this has no factual basis.

YouTube videos, blogs, and pseudohistory books often repackage the myth with new graphics, false statistics, and recycled rhetoric.

Where It Stands Today

In reality, the modern Rothschild family holds considerable but not supreme influence, mostly through financial services, investments, and vineyards. Their name is far from absent in international business—but claims of total world control are wildly exaggerated.

Yet in the landscape of conspiracy theory, the Rothschilds serve as archetypal villains—wealthy, European, secretive, and Jewish—ticking every box for a narrative of hidden hands pulling the strings.

Whether believed or not, the myth persists. For those distrustful of visible power structures, the Rothschilds remain the ultimate symbol of the invisible empire.

Chapter Sixty-Eight

Section: Secret Societies & Elite Control

Conspiracy: Reptilian Shape-Shifters Rule the Elite

Summary

Among the most bizarre yet enduring conspiracy theories is the claim that many world leaders and celebrities are actually reptilian shape-shifters—cold-blooded, extra-dimensional beings who disguise themselves as humans to control global affairs. Originating in the 1990s and popularized by former footballer and broadcaster David Icke, the theory proposes that reptilian overlords are the real force behind governments, royalty, and multinational corporations.

Dismissed by the mainstream as pseudoscience or metaphor gone wild, this theory continues to attract a dedicated following, particularly online, and reflects deeper societal anxieties about power, identity, and deception.

History & Key Claims

Origins:

While reptilian myths trace back to ancient mythologies (e.g. Nagas in Hinduism, serpent gods in Mesopotamia), the modern theory began with David Icke, particularly in his 1999 book The Biggest Secret.

Icke claimed that humanity has been infiltrated and ruled for centuries by blood-drinking, shape-shifting reptilian aliens from the Alpha Draconis star system.

Central Claims:

The reptilian beings are capable of morphing into human form but occasionally reveal themselves in brief glitches (e.g. "slitted eyes" on camera, odd blinking).

They maintain control by breeding with specific bloodlines—notably royalty, U.S. presidents, media moguls, and billionaire families—to preserve their hybrid genetics.

Reptilians feed off human fear and negative emotion, and some theories claim they consume adrenochrome, a chemical allegedly harvested from terrified children.

These beings are said to have orchestrated:

Wars

Economic crises

Pandemics

Mass mind control through media and religion

Key Alleged Reptilians:

Queen Elizabeth II

George W. Bush

Barack Obama

Hillary Clinton

The entire British Royal Family

Hollywood actors and music industry elites

Supporting "Evidence":

Video clips showing digital distortions in pupils or facial features are circulated as "proof" of shape-shifting.

Ancient artwork and symbols featuring serpent gods are presented as hidden historical records.

Believers often cite Freemason or Illuminati symbolism as reptilian indicators.

Famous Quotes / Sources

"The goal of the reptilian agenda is to turn the Earth into a prison planet."

— David Icke, Children of the Matrix

"The bloodlines of presidents, kings, and billionaires trace back to these entities."

— David Icke, The Biggest Secret

"I've spoken to dozens of people who claim to have seen them shift—often at moments of extreme stress or anger."

— Interview with David Icke, 2012

"They wear human suits, but they're not like us. They never were."

Real-World Consequences

Public Ridicule and Media Portrayal:

The theory has often been mocked in mainstream culture, appearing in shows like South Park, Doctor Who, and The X-Files.

David Icke became a subject of both satire and controversy, with some outlets calling him delusional, while others acknowledged his skillful weaving of political criticism into mythology.

Accusations of Antisemitism:

Critics argue that the theory repackages antisemitic tropes, with reptilians replacing Jews as the "inhuman manipulators" of global events.

Icke has denied antisemitic intent, but many watchdogs and organizations remain critical.

Conspiratorial Crossover:

The reptilian theory often intersects with:

Illuminati and New World Order claims

Satanic Ritual Abuse theories

QAnon

Some see it as a metaphor for dehumanized elites rather than a literal belief.

Fan Communities and Fiction:

Reptilian believers have created expansive online communities with videos, art, and "sightings" databases.

The idea has inspired fictional works, memes, and roleplay forums, blending fantasy and alleged reality.

Where It Stands Today

The reptilian conspiracy theory walks a strange line between science fiction and cultural mythology, attracting both sincere believers and ironic fans. While few take it literally in mainstream circles, its language and symbolism have bled into pop culture and fringe discourse.

At its core, the theory reflects a deep distrust in those who hold power—painting them not merely as corrupt or greedy, but as literally inhuman. Whether interpreted as metaphor, madness, or metaphysical truth, the reptilian narrative shows how far the human imagination will go to explain a world that feels increasingly alien.

Chapter Sixty-Nine

Section: Secret Societies & Elite Control

Conspiracy: George Soros as a Puppetmaster

Summary

George Soros, a Hungarian-American billionaire and philanthropist, is the subject of one of the most widespread and persistent conspiracy theories of the 21st century. Critics and conspiracists alike have cast Soros as a global puppetmaster, allegedly using his vast fortune to destabilize nations, fund radical movements, manipulate elections, and usher in a liberal globalist order.

While Soros has undeniably supported progressive causes and political organizations around the world through his Open Society Foundations, conspiracy theorists view him as the hidden hand behind protests, immigration waves, economic collapses, and social upheaval. To some, he represents a real threat. To others, he is a scapegoat wrapped in paranoia and propaganda.

History & Key Claims

Background:

Soros made his wealth as a hedge fund manager, becoming famous for shorting the British pound in 1992, reportedly earning $1 billion in a single day.

He later founded the Open Society Foundations, which have donated billions to causes related to human rights, democracy, education, public health, and liberal reform.

Central Conspiracy Claims:

Soros is accused of funding:

"Color revolutions" in Eastern Europe, the Middle East, and Asia

Migrant caravans to destabilize borders (particularly in the U.S. and Europe)

Leftist protest movements like Black Lives Matter, Antifa, and Occupy Wall Street

Progressive prosecutors and DAs to weaken law enforcement and promote chaos

Fake grassroots campaigns, known as "astroturfing"

He is said to manipulate:

Global currency markets

Election outcomes

Media narratives via indirect influence on journalism and education

Notable Events Blamed on Soros:

The 2008 financial crash (heavily disputed)

The European refugee crisis

Ferguson and other U.S. racial justice protests

The DA elections in San Francisco, Chicago, and New York

Brexit opposition campaigns

Characterization:

Soros is frequently portrayed as an evil genius or globalist villain, akin to characters from dystopian fiction.

Critics often link him with terms like "New World Order," "cultural Marxism," and "financial manipulation."

Famous Quotes / Sources

"Soros funds everything that's destroying America."

— Commentator on Fox News, 2018

"You know the name George Soros… You know the money, the power, the influence."

— Glenn Beck, The Blaze, 2010

"Everything that's going wrong in this world, he's behind it."

— Viral tweet with 2M+ views, 2020

"George Soros is the single most dangerous leftist on the planet."

— Michael Savage, conservative radio host

"Open society? Or open manipulation?"

Real-World Consequences

Mainstream Media and Political Impact:

Accusations about Soros have become talking points in right-wing politics across the U.S., Europe, and Latin America.

Politicians have referenced him in debates about immigration, protests, and election integrity.

Antisemitic Overtones:

Many of the attacks on Soros mirror historical antisemitic tropes—depicting a wealthy Jewish figure manipulating governments and media behind the scenes.

Organizations like the Anti-Defamation League (ADL) and Southern Poverty Law Center have condemned many of the conspiracy theories as dangerous and misleading.

Public Protests and Threats:

Soros has been the subject of violent rhetoric, effigy burnings, and even a bomb threat in 2018, when an explosive device was sent to his home.

His name has been featured on protest signs from Hungary to Washington D.C.

Weaponization of Misinformation:

Disinformation campaigns on Facebook, Twitter, Telegram, and YouTube frequently exaggerate his influence.

False claims that he funds "every protest" have appeared in mass text chains and viral memes, often with little or no factual basis.

Where It Stands Today

George Soros continues to be a lightning rod for political controversy and misinformation. His philanthropic work is real, and often deeply political—but the extent of his influence is exaggerated, distorted, and weaponized in conspiracy circles.

To his critics, Soros represents global elitism and liberal overreach. To his supporters, he is a force for human rights and democratic reform. But in conspiracy theory culture, he remains the ultimate shadow figure, a symbol of hidden power and ideological manipulation in an era of growing distrust.

Chapter Seventy

Section: Secret Societies & Elite Control

Conspiracy: The Trilateral Commission

Summary

The Trilateral Commission, founded in 1973 by David Rockefeller and political theorist Zbigniew Brzezinski, is a non-governmental, policy-oriented group aimed at fostering cooperation among North America, Europe, and Japan. Officially, its goal is to discuss global issues and promote collaboration among the world's most developed economies.

However, to conspiracy theorists, the Trilateral Commission represents a shadow government—an elite circle shaping world policy behind closed doors, with no democratic oversight. It is frequently accused of furthering the New World Order, manipulating global economics, and selecting national leaders in advance. Though the commission is real, its secrecy and influence have long fueled suspicion.

History & Key Claims

Origins:

The Trilateral Commission was created after Rockefeller and Brzezinski observed a growing economic interdependence among the U.S., Europe, and Japan.

It was designed to foster policy dialogue, recruit leaders, and promote globalization.

Membership:

Composed of academics, politicians, business leaders, and media figures.

Members have included:

Jimmy Carter (before becoming U.S. President)

Paul Volcker (former Federal Reserve Chairman)

Henry Kissinger (U.S. diplomat)

Bill Clinton (attended related forums)

Top executives from Goldman Sachs, ExxonMobil, and The New York Times

Central Conspiracy Claims:

The commission is an engine of globalist control, quietly influencing:

Trade policy

National security

Central banking decisions

Technocratic governance

It is often linked to the Council on Foreign Relations (CFR) and Bilderberg Group as part of a trilateral elite system.

Some believe it selects presidents and prime ministers long before elections are held.

It is said to erode national sovereignty in favor of global unity—under elite supervision.

Brzezinski's Influence:

His book Between Two Ages (1970) is frequently cited as "proof" that he envisioned a technocratic world order run by unelected experts and international councils.

Phrases like "global management" and "post-industrial society" have been pulled from context to bolster the theory.

Famous Quotes / Sources

"The Trilateral Commission represents a skillful, coordinated effort to seize control and consolidate the four centers of power—political, monetary, intellectual, and ecclesiastical."

— Barry Goldwater, U.S. Senator and presidential candidate, in With No Apologies (1979)

"It is impossible to read Brzezinski's work without seeing the blueprint of future domination."

— John Coleman, Conspirators' Hierarchy: The Committee of 300

"Presidents don't rise to power; they're picked, trained, and placed there by trilateral interests."

— James Perloff, The Shadows of Power

"They're the boardroom of the world."

— Popular forum post on AboveTopSecret.com

Real-World Consequences

Public Distrust in Institutions:

The commission's confidential meetings, elite attendees, and opaque agendas have led to suspicion about backroom deals influencing public policy.

Many see it as symbolic of the democratic deficit in global governance.

Fuel for Other Theories:

The Trilateral Commission is often portrayed as a stepping stone toward the New World Order, global currency, and a universal ID system.

It has been accused of:

Pushing free trade policies that hollow out national economies

Suppressing populist uprisings

Coordinating with Big Tech and banks for surveillance-based governance

Political Weaponization:

References to the commission have appeared in campaign speeches, especially by right-wing populist candidates.

Some suggest it has steered leaders toward pro-globalist positions, even against national interest.

Bans and Suspicion:

In some countries, civil society groups have tried to ban trilateral events, or expose members in government.

Where It Stands Today

The Trilateral Commission continues to operate, now expanded to include members from China, India, and other rising powers, though it keeps a relatively low public profile. Its stated goals remain policy dialogue and international cooperation.

Yet in the conspiracy world, it is anything but benign. It is framed as a global boardroom, choosing winners and losers, presidents and crises, long before the public is aware. Whether it's seen as a harmless think tank or a nerve center of elite control, the Trilateral Commission remains one of the most referenced and mysterious names in the pantheon of modern conspiracies.

Chapter Seventy-One

Section: Secret Societies & Elite Control

Conspiracy: The Council on Foreign Relations (CFR)

Summary

The Council on Foreign Relations (CFR) is a prestigious and influential U.S.-based think tank that focuses on foreign policy and international relations. To many, it's simply a hub for global policy experts, diplomats, and former government officials. But to conspiracy theorists, the CFR is one of the most powerful secret organizations in the world, shaping the direction of U.S. policy, promoting globalism, and pushing for a one-world government.

The CFR is often viewed as a cornerstone of elite global control, working in tandem with the Trilateral Commission, the Bilderberg Group, and shadowy financial interests. Its reputation for secrecy and elite membership only fuels suspicions of manipulation and hidden agendas.

History & Key Claims

Origins and Function:

Founded in 1921 following the Paris Peace Conference after World War I.

Based in New York City, the CFR publishes Foreign Affairs, a leading journal on foreign policy.

Officially, it is a nonpartisan forum for discussing America's role in the world.

Membership and Influence:

Members have included presidents, secretaries of state, military leaders, intelligence chiefs, media executives, and academics.

Notable members:

Bill Clinton

Henry Kissinger

David Rockefeller

Condoleezza Rice

George H. W. Bush

Colin Powell

Diane Sawyer

Central Conspiracy Claims:

The CFR is said to:

Select and groom U.S. presidents and policymakers

Create and implement foreign policy agendas regardless of election outcomes

Act as a front for globalist objectives, including dissolving borders and establishing a global government

Promote wars and international crises to justify U.S. military expansion

Control major media narratives through its journalist members

Push mass surveillance, digital ID systems, and technocratic governance

Key Allegations:

The CFR manipulates:

Presidential debates and foreign policy platforms

Major economic deals like NAFTA and WTO agreements

Narratives around terrorism, China, Russia, and global pandemics

Related Organizations:

Often grouped with:

Bilderberg Group

Trilateral Commission

World Economic Forum (WEF)

Chatham House (UK equivalent)

Famous Quotes / Sources

"We shall have world government, whether or not we like it. The question is only whether world government will be achieved by consent or by conquest."

— James Warburg, banker and CFR member, testimony before U.S. Senate, 1950

"The CFR is the invisible government of the United States."

— Dan Smoot, former FBI agent and conservative commentator

"The most powerful men in the world have no need to conspire. Their interests align."

— Carroll Quigley, historian and CFR insider, Tragedy and Hope (1966)

"Every major international decision of the last fifty years bears the CFR's fingerprint."

— G. Edward Griffin, author of The Creature from Jekyll Island

Real-World Consequences

Influence on Public Perception:

The CFR's quiet influence on U.S. foreign policy has contributed to growing distrust in the establishment.

Critics argue that CFR-endorsed policies often favor global interests over national sovereignty.

Weaponized in Politics:

Populist and nationalist figures—especially on the right—have cited CFR membership as a badge of deep-state allegiance.

In political rhetoric, CFR-affiliated candidates are sometimes framed as puppets of the elite.

Media Scrutiny:

The CFR's ties to major news networks, including CNN, ABC, CBS, and The New York Times, have fueled concerns about narrative control.

Some journalists accused of "soft-pedaling" globalist agendas have links to the council.

Misinformation and Mistrust:

The CFR has become a shorthand for conspiracy theorists—a catch-all villain accused of orchestrating everything from pandemics to economic crashes.

Despite extensive online accusations, no hard evidence has emerged to prove the group operates beyond its stated mission.

Where It Stands Today

The Council on Foreign Relations remains a high-profile and highly criticized organization. Its influence in shaping elite discourse on global policy is undeniable, though whether it wields that influence for good or ill depends on one's worldview.

For mainstream observers, it's a necessary forum for international cooperation. For conspiracy theorists, it is an unelected force with outsized control, steering America and the world toward a centralized, technocratic future.

Like many real organizations that keep a low public profile while hosting powerful individuals, the CFR's mere existence has made it one of the most cited villains in modern conspiracy lore.

Chapter Seventy-Two

Section: Secret Societies & Elite Control

Conspiracy: Denver Airport's Secret Bunker

Summary

Denver International Airport (DIA) has become one of the most bizarre and enduring locations tied to conspiracy theories. Opened in 1995 after delays and budget overruns, DIA quickly drew suspicion not just for its immense size and subterranean infrastructure, but for its unusual artwork, eerie symbols, and apocalyptic themes.

Central to the theory is the belief that DIA houses a massive underground bunker—a doomsday facility, command center, or headquarters for the New World Order (NWO), built to shelter elites in the event of societal collapse. The strange architecture, the presence of Masonic plaques, and alleged military-style tunnels have turned the airport into a hub of conspiratorial fascination.

History & Key Claims

Origins of Suspicion:

The airport's construction ran $2 billion over budget and was delayed for years.

It spans 53 square miles, making it the second-largest airport in the world by land.

Its remote location, vast underground areas, and excess runways raised eyebrows from the start.

Core Conspiracy Theories:

Underground Bunker System:

Allegedly built to house U.S. and global elites in the event of war, plague, economic collapse, or alien invasion.

Claims include miles of sealed-off tunnels, multi-level bunkers, and stocked supplies.

New World Order (NWO) Command Center:

DIA is said to be a central location for NWO operations in North America.

Some speculate it connects to other subterranean bases via secret high-speed rail.

Illuminati / Freemason Influence:

A dedication plaque at the airport includes a reference to a "New World Airport Commission," a group with no clear record of existence.

The plaque bears the Freemason square and compass, fueling suspicions of elite involvement.

Runways Shaped Like a Swastika:

Aerial views show runway configuration in a shape that some interpret as a Nazi symbol.

Apocalyptic Artwork:

Murals depict fire, war, and gas-masked soldiers, with children in coffins and animals in glass cases.

Theories claim these are warnings or declarations of what's to come.

Other Bizarre Elements:

The infamous "Blucifer" statue: A 32-foot-tall blue Mustang with glowing red eyes that killed its creator during installation.

Gargoyle statues inside the airport are said to "watch travelers."

Rumors of alien and reptilian involvement in the facility's construction or use.

Famous Quotes / Sources

"They didn't just build an airport. They built a city under it."

— Former contractor quoted in JFK to 9/11: Everything Is a Rich Man's Trick

"DIA is a Masonic statement of intent."

— Online forum post, AboveTopSecret.com

"Why would an airport need miles of tunnels and fallout shelters?"

— Coast to Coast AM, 2004 broadcast

"That horse with red eyes is just the start. The whole place screams 'warning.'"

— Visitor blog review, 2013

"I think people like a mystery. We lean into it."

Real-World Consequences

Public Fascination and Tourism:

DIA has embraced the conspiracy buzz, adding signs and interactive exhibits referencing the theories (e.g., "What are we really doing down here?").

Tours of the airport's underground baggage system became more frequent after public demand.

Mainstream Media Coverage:

The airport's odd reputation has been featured on:

History Channel's Ancient Aliens

National Geographic's Secret America

VICE, BuzzFeed, and NPR

Credibility Issues and Contractor Claims:

Several construction workers have claimed they were fired after asking questions.

Reports of sealed-off tunnels and bricked-up access doors have further fueled speculation.

Security Misunderstandings:

Due to the conspiracy cloud around the airport, innocent security measures (e.g., restricted maintenance access) are often interpreted as proof of something sinister.

Where It Stands Today

Denver International Airport remains fully operational and one of the busiest travel hubs in the United States, but it also wears its conspiratorial reputation with a wink and a nod. Far from denying the accusations, DIA has begun marketing itself with slogans like "Are we hiding something?"—turning the mystery into a branding tool.

Yet for conspiracy theorists, the jokes only deepen suspicion. To them, DIA is not a joke at all, but one of the most critical nodes in the hidden infrastructure of global control—an underground fortress built for elites, surrounded by warnings in plain sight.

Chapter Seventy-Three

Section: Secret Societies & Elite Control

Conspiracy: Satanic Ritual Abuse in the Elite

Summary

Satanic Ritual Abuse (SRA) among the elite refers to a controversial and disturbing conspiracy theory that claims powerful individuals — including politicians, celebrities, and business leaders — engage in clandestine, ritualistic abuse involving children, often tied to occult or satanic practices. These allegations go far beyond ordinary abuse claims, suggesting systematic and ceremonial acts tied to power, control, and blackmail.

The theory surged in the 1980s and 1990s during the so-called "Satanic Panic", but has since evolved into modern conspiracies like Pizzagate and QAnon, where satanic themes blend with political allegations. Though widely discredited by authorities and experts, the sheer volume and consistency of such claims across decades — including witness testimonies — have kept the theory alive in underground and fringe circles.

History & Key Claims

The "Satanic Panic" Era (1980s–90s):

Sparked by Michelle Remembers (1980), a controversial memoir detailing repressed memories of satanic abuse.

Dozens of daycare workers, teachers, and community figures were accused of running satanic cults.

High-profile cases like the McMartin Preschool trial and Kern County abuse cases featured claims of ritualistic ceremonies, underground tunnels, and child sacrifice.

Most cases were later dismissed or overturned due to lack of physical evidence and issues with suggestive questioning.

Elite Involvement Claims:

As media focused on local institutions, conspiracy theorists extended the narrative to national and global elites:

The belief that wealthy families, royal circles, and government officials belong to secret Satanic cults.

These cults allegedly perform abuse as part of ritualistic power ceremonies, sometimes as blackmail tools or initiation rites.

Ritual symbols like goat heads, pentagrams, and black robes are commonly referenced in alleged survivor testimony.

Notable Related Allegations:

Franklin Scandal (Nebraska, 1980s): Alleged child sex ring involving political figures, banks, and intelligence agencies.

Bohemian Grove: Elite men's retreat where conspiracists believe occult rituals are held, including mock child sacrifices.

Pizzagate: Alleged secret child trafficking and ritual abuse ring tied to a Washington D.C. pizzeria and political figures.

QAnon: Asserts that a global elite cabal engages in satanic abuse and child trafficking, with Trump cast as the secret liberator.

Famous Quotes / Sources

"People need to understand the Satanic ritual abuse network is real and is deeply embedded in power structures."

— Cathy O'Brien, Trance Formation of America

"I saw the ceremonies. The rituals. The robes. These were not drug users. These were judges."

— Anonymous testimony from The Franklin Cover-Up by John DeCamp

"There is a network. It doesn't end at the church or the school. It goes all the way to the top."

— David Shurter, alleged survivor and speaker on ritual abuse

"The accusations are implausible on their face — but disturbingly widespread."

— FBI Behavioral Science Unit, internal memo, 1992

Real-World Consequences

False Accusations and Prison Sentences:

Dozens of people were wrongly imprisoned due to questionable therapy techniques and public hysteria.

The McMartin case became one of the most expensive trials in U.S. history, ending in no convictions.

Impact on Child Protection Systems:

Increased scrutiny led to better protocols for abuse investigations — but also caused fear and overreaction in some areas.

Fuel for Larger Conspiracies:

The claims of SRA fed directly into newer movements like QAnon, which rebranded the fear of satanic elites for a new generation.

Viral online stories, Reddit forums, and YouTube testimonials continue to give these ideas a wide platform.

Distrust in Institutions:

Belief in elite SRA rings has eroded trust in courts, churches, political systems, and media, especially when institutions are seen as covering up crimes.

Moral Panic and Media Frenzy:

Sensational coverage and tabloid journalism helped the narrative spread, particularly in the 1990s.

Where It Stands Today

While mainstream institutions, law enforcement, and psychologists widely agree that there is no evidence of widespread elite-run satanic cults, the theory persists—morphing into new forms with each generation.

In a digital age dominated by viral storytelling and moral outrage, SRA narratives have become part of a broader cultural myth about secret evils lurking in plain sight. For some, it's dismissed as a 20th-century panic. For others, it's considered the ultimate taboo truth — one the world isn't ready to confront.

Either way, it remains one of the darkest and most emotionally charged conspiracy theories ever to take hold, with roots deep in trauma, fear, and institutional mistrust.

Chapter Seventy-Four

Section: Secret Societies & Elite Control

Conspiracy: Mass Media Is Controlled by One Group

Summary

The belief that mass media is centrally controlled by a small group of elites or entities is a foundational conspiracy theory that has endured for decades. Proponents claim that the news we consume, the entertainment we watch, and the narratives we believe are all carefully curated and coordinated to shape public opinion, suppress dissent, promote consumerism, and distract from deeper political or societal truths.

Often tied to other conspiracies involving the New World Order, Zionist control, or corporate oligarchies, this theory suggests that everything from news broadcasts to blockbuster films are designed to serve the interests of a hidden ruling class, rather than the public.

History & Key Claims

Media Consolidation:

In the early 1980s, over 50 companies controlled 90% of American media.

By the early 2000s, that number had dropped to just six conglomerates:

Comcast

Disney

AT&T (formerly Time Warner)

ViacomCBS

News Corp

Sony

These corporations own vast networks of TV stations, film studios, news outlets, streaming platforms, radio stations, and print publications.

Core Conspiracy Assertions:

A single group (or closely aligned power block) uses media to:

Manufacture consent for wars and economic policy.

Suppress alternative views or whistleblowers.

Control election narratives by favoring select candidates.

Push social engineering through messaging in entertainment.

Silence dissenting experts, especially on topics like vaccines, foreign policy, or elite corruption.

Tactics Alleged by Theorists:

Coordinated headlines across networks.

Smearing of political outsiders or anti-establishment voices.

Use of entertainment to normalize surveillance, war, or globalism.

"Predictive programming" — placing future events into pop culture before they happen (e.g. 9/11, pandemics).

Connected Theories:

Operation Mockingbird (CIA media infiltration)

Zionist or globalist influence

The "Deep State" as the true editorial board behind major outlets

Hollywood as a psychological tool for shaping worldview

Famous Quotes / Sources

"There is no such thing… as an independent press."

— John Swinton, former New York Times editor (allegedly, 1880s speech — though its authenticity is debated)

"We'll know our disinformation program is complete when everything the American public believes is false."

— William Casey, former CIA Director (alleged quote from 1981 meeting)

"The media's job is not to inform, but to condition."

— Noam Chomsky (interpreted from Manufacturing Consent, 1988)

"If you control the media, you control the mind."

— Jim Morrison, singer of The Doors

"The real menace of our Republic is the invisible government which like a giant octopus sprawls its slimy legs over our cities."

— John F. Hylan, former NYC mayor, 1922

Real-World Consequences

Public Distrust:

Trust in mass media has steadily declined across decades, especially in the U.S.

Many now turn to independent journalists, podcasts, or niche platforms for information.

Rise of Alternative Media:

The internet enabled a surge of decentralized voices — bloggers, Substack writers, and YouTubers — many of whom built followings by challenging legacy media.

Platforms like Twitter/X and Rumble are considered counterweights to mainstream narratives.

Polarization and Echo Chambers:

As trust breaks down, people often retreat into ideological media silos, reinforcing their worldview and rejecting mainstream interpretations.

Targeting of Dissidents:

High-profile figures who speak against dominant narratives are often deplatformed, demonetized, or discredited in public media — reinforcing the belief in centralized control.

Media Satire and Fiction:

Works like 1984, They Live, and The Truman Show are often cited as allegorical portrayals of media manipulation.

Where It Stands Today

While some consolidation and coordination in media are well-documented, the theory that one single group controls all messaging is still widely debated. Critics argue that systemic bias, profit motives, and political alliances explain most of the phenomena cited — not necessarily conspiratorial design.

Still, in the eyes of many theorists, modern media remains less a source of truth and more a mechanism of influence. Whether through sensationalism, omission, or misdirection, the belief persists that the public is being steered — not informed.

As media giants grow, and censorship debates intensify, this conspiracy has never felt more current.

Chapter Seventy-Five

Section: Secret Societies & Elite Control

Conspiracy: Predictive Programming in Movies

Summary

The theory of predictive programming claims that governments, secret societies, or elite entities embed hidden messages about future events in popular media—especially films, television shows, books, and music videos. According to believers, these narratives serve to desensitize the public, shape perception, and subconsciously prepare us to accept predetermined outcomes—ranging from wars to pandemics to authoritarian control.

From The Simpsons "predicting" Trump's presidency to The Matrix, Contagion, and V for Vendetta seemingly foreshadowing societal events, proponents argue that fiction isn't just entertainment—it's preparation for manipulation.

History & Key Claims

Origins of the Theory:

The term "predictive programming" was popularized by Alan Watt, a Canadian conspiracy researcher, who claimed that media had long been used as a psychological weapon to condition the masses.

He argued that those in power reveal their plans in fiction as part of an esoteric belief system—suggesting that elites can only act without karmic consequence if the public has been "told in advance."

Core Ideas:

Fictional portrayals of disasters, technologies, or political shifts are not coincidental—they're intentional seeding of ideas to reduce public resistance.

Examples include:

The Simpsons episodes "predicting" events such as 9/11, Trump's candidacy, or the Higgs boson discovery.

Contagion (2011) portraying a COVID-like pandemic.

The Dark Knight Rises using "Sandy Hook" as a map reference before the real-life shooting.

The Matrix being interpreted as a metaphor for simulated reality and mass control.

Children of Men foreshadowing fertility collapse and state surveillance.

Psychological Conditioning:

Repeated exposure to violent or dystopian content is said to lower resistance to real-world versions of those ideas.

For example, films about mass surveillance or societal collapse make such possibilities more palatable when they happen.

Symbolism:

Elite symbolism (e.g. pyramids, all-seeing eyes, black cubes) is said to be strategically placed in music videos, awards shows, and blockbuster movies.

These symbols, according to the theory, reinforce subconscious messages of hierarchy, submission, or occult power.

Link to Other Theories:

Predictive programming is often tied to theories involving:

False flag events

New World Order

Transhumanism

Alien disclosure

Satanic ritual abuse (symbolism in children's cartoons or music)

Famous Quotes / Sources

"All fiction is propaganda if you know how to look."

— Alan Watt, researcher and author

"If you want to hide something, put it in plain sight."

— Alleged Freemason maxim, often quoted by theorists

"They use media not just to entertain, but to initiate."

— Jay Dyer, author of Esoteric Hollywood

"The elite believe they are absolved from guilt if they tell you first. That's predictive programming."

— David Icke

"Hollywood doesn't predict the future—it prepares you for it."

— Online conspiracy forum post, 2018

Real-World Consequences

Mistrust in Media and Entertainment:

Many people now scrutinize pop culture with suspicion, looking for patterns, hints, or codes.

Films and television are increasingly interpreted not as stories, but as blueprints.

Online Speculation Culture:

YouTube channels, TikTok creators, and podcasts have dedicated themselves to breaking down symbolism in popular media.

Theorists create side-by-side comparisons of fictional events and real news stories to demonstrate "proof."

Mental Health and Paranoia:

Critics argue that this mindset can foster paranoia and detachment, as people begin to see sinister meaning in harmless content.

Creative Backlash:

Some filmmakers have leaned into the theory for marketing, while others have been accused (often unfairly) of participating in elite messaging.

False Accusations:

Public figures have been falsely linked to major crimes or events based on symbolic appearances in media—leading to harassment or fear.

Where It Stands Today

Predictive programming remains a highly popular and evolving theory. While mainstream thinkers dismiss it as confirmation bias or retroactive pattern-seeking, its grip on public imagination is growing. In a world where reality often mimics fiction—and the impossible becomes routine—the boundaries between story and strategy have blurred.

Whether predictive programming is a form of psychological manipulation, a method of elite confession, or simply coincidence wrapped in paranoia, it continues to shape how many people interpret the world around them. Especially when fiction and reality begin to look eerily alike.

Chapter Seventy-Six

Section: Secret Societies & Elite Control

Conspiracy: The "Eye of Providence" on Currency

Summary

The Eye of Providence, also known as the All-Seeing Eye, is a well-known symbol often interpreted by conspiracy theorists as proof of hidden elite control over global systems. Prominently featured on the reverse of the U.S. one-dollar bill, the symbol depicts an eye within a triangle, radiating light, perched atop an unfinished pyramid.

While official explanations frame it as a symbol of divine guidance or enlightenment, theorists argue it reveals Freemasonic, Illuminati, or occult influence over American government, global finance, and institutions of power. The placement on legal tender is seen as particularly bold—an open declaration of elite rule, hidden in plain sight.

History & Key Claims

Origins of the Symbol:

The Eye of Providence has been used in Christian iconography since the Renaissance, often representing the omnipresence of God.

It was later adopted by Freemasonry, where it symbolized the Great Architect of the Universe and moral vigilance.

The U.S. Dollar and the Great Seal:

In 1782, the symbol was included in the Great Seal of the United States, with the unfinished pyramid representing strength and duration, and the eye above it symbolizing divine favor.

The Latin phrases beneath it read:

Annuit Coeptis – "He [God] has favored our undertakings"

Novus Ordo Seclorum – "New Order of the Ages"

Core Conspiracy Beliefs:

The pyramid and eye are not just symbolic of American ideals, but of a secret ruling class, often tied to:

The Illuminati — a hidden group steering world events.

The Freemasons — believed by some to have infiltrated early American government.

The concept of a New World Order — a one-world government operating behind the scenes.

The 13 steps of the pyramid, 13 stars above the eagle, and other groupings of 13 on the dollar are said to reference esoteric numerology, Masonic principles, or occult power.

Currency as Control:

Placing the Eye on money is seen as symbolic of elite economic dominance, where those who control currency control nations.

Some go further, arguing the eye represents surveillance, ownership of the people, or even Satanic watchfulness.

Wider Symbolism:

The Eye of Providence appears in corporate logos, architecture, pop culture, and religious art — often cited by theorists as signs of a global cabal's unified messaging.

Famous Quotes / Sources

"The Great Seal is the signature of this exalted body—unseen rulers of the world."

— Manly P. Hall, The Secret Teachings of All Ages (1928)

"The pyramid and eye on the dollar is the most blatant symbol of Illuminati dominance that exists."

— Mark Dice, The Illuminati: Facts and Fiction

"You carry a sigil of the occult in your wallet every day."

— David Icke, The Biggest Secret

"Symbols are not meaningless. They are signatures. And the Eye watches."

— Jordan Maxwell, occult researcher

"Those who understand symbols know that money is more than currency—it is ritual."

— Online esoteric blog, 2015

Real-World Consequences

Public Awareness and Skepticism:

The dollar's symbolism has helped fuel widespread interest in hidden messages, especially among youth and truth-seeking subcultures.

Documentaries, YouTube breakdowns, and Reddit threads regularly dissect the dollar's imagery.

Rise of Symbol Spotting:

The Eye of Providence is one of the most recognized conspiracy symbols worldwide, often spotted in:

Music videos

Fashion (especially luxury or occult-inspired brands)

Political campaigns

Tech company branding

Fuel for Anti-Establishment Narratives:

The theory reinforces beliefs that governments, financial institutions, and even religions are interconnected through hidden allegiance.

Cultural Mockery and Reinforcement:

Some brands and media now use the symbol ironically or artistically, blurring the line between truth, satire, and paranoia.

Where It Stands Today

To many, the Eye of Providence remains nothing more than a symbol of divine oversight or the spiritual ideals of America's founders. To others, it's an unmistakable clue—an ancient emblem of surveillance, control, and elite dominance etched onto the very paper we use every day.

While no proof exists of a direct Illuminati-Masonic-financial cartel tied to the dollar's design, the perceived symbolism continues to resonate with those skeptical of mainstream narratives. In the world of conspiracy theory, the dollar bill is less a financial tool—and more a coded message from those who rule the world in silence.

Chapter Seventy-Seven

Section: Secret Societies & Elite Control

Conspiracy: The Black Nobility

Summary

The term Black Nobility refers to a shadowy aristocratic class—descendants of European royal bloodlines and papal-aligned families—who are believed by conspiracy theorists to exert covert control over global finance, politics, religion, and secret societies. Unlike elected officials or modern elites, these families are said to wield ancient power passed down through generations, operating in the background through banking empires, Vatican influence, and royal alliances.

Though largely unacknowledged in mainstream discourse, the Black Nobility conspiracy posits that modern democracy is a façade, and that true power lies with unelected dynasties who have quietly orchestrated wars, revolutions, economic collapses, and global governance.

History & Key Claims

Origins of the Term:

The phrase "Black Nobility" was originally used to describe Italian aristocrats who supported the Pope after the unification of Italy (late 1800s), opposing the newly formed Kingdom of Italy.

These families lost political power but retained massive wealth and religious influence, particularly in Vatican affairs.

Expanded Conspiracy Theory:

The modern theory stretches far beyond Italy, suggesting that the Black Nobility:

Includes ancient Venetian, Roman, German, and British families.

Is deeply embedded in the Catholic Church hierarchy, especially the Jesuits and Opus Dei.

Exerts control through the City of London, Vatican City, and Washington, D.C.—three sovereign city-states often referred to as the "Unholy Trinity" by theorists.

Notable Families Allegedly Involved:

Orsini (Italy)

Aldobrandini (Italy)

Colonna (Rome)

Breakspeare (UK origins)

Farnese (linked to Jesuits)

Rothschild (often linked, though not technically nobility)

Windsor (British Royal Family)

Habsburg (Austria and former Holy Roman Empire)

Medici (historical ties, less contemporary relevance)

Core Beliefs:

The Black Nobility operates as a silent ruling class, influencing or outright controlling:

The World Bank and IMF

Major religious institutions

Freemasonry, Knights of Malta, and the Vatican

The Bilderberg Group and global NGOs

They maintain bloodline purity, intermarrying among elite families to retain control.

They avoid public scrutiny, unlike celebrities or politicians, while pulling the strings behind major global events.

Famous Quotes / Sources

"Real power lies not with governments but with the invisible aristocracy who never left the throne."

— Craig Oxley, researcher, The Unhived Mind

"The Black Nobility are the silent hand behind both capitalism and communism. They fund both sides and profit either way."

— John Coleman, The Committee of 300

"The Orsini and Farnese families… these are the true powers of Rome, not the Pope."

— Leo Zagami, ex-Freemason and conspiracy author

"From Venice to the Vatican to Wall Street, the bloodlines remain."

— Anonymous forum post, 2008

Real-World Consequences

Mistrust in Visible Leadership:

The theory promotes the idea that presidents, prime ministers, and CEOs are mere puppets—and true rulers are unseen.

Rise in Anti-Monarchy Sentiment:

Events involving royal families (e.g., scandals, deaths, abdications) are often interpreted as maneuvering within the nobility class.

Fuel for Vatican Conspiracies:

Many theorists tie the Black Nobility to papal resignations, Church abuse scandals, or alleged Satanic rites within Vatican walls.

Confusion Between Fact and Allegory:

There are indeed old noble families with lingering wealth and influence, but the conspiratorial leap assumes they function as a unified global cabal, which lacks definitive evidence.

Overlap with Other Conspiracies:

The Black Nobility theory blends into:

Illuminati claims

Zionist world control narratives

Jesuit infiltration stories

The theory of the "Three City-States" (London, Vatican, D.C.)

Where It Stands Today

While some aristocratic families still exist and retain wealth and influence, the claim that a pan-European elite class secretly rules the world remains speculative and unproven. Most such families operate in private, not public power structures, though their enduring presence feeds the belief that democracy is cosmetic, and dynasties still dictate global events.

The theory's persistence stems from a deep distrust of democracy's legitimacy, and a fascination with the secret continuities of empire and religion. Whether the Black Nobility truly commands today's global systems or not, they remain a symbol of hidden continuity—power without accountability.

Chapter Seventy-Eight

Section: Secret Societies & Elite Control

Conspiracy: Zionist Occupied Government (ZOG)

Summary

The Zionist Occupied Government (ZOG) theory asserts that national governments—especially that of the United States—are secretly controlled or heavily influenced by Zionist interests, particularly individuals or organizations sympathetic to the state of Israel or Jewish global agendas. Rooted in antisemitic ideology, this conspiracy claims that a hidden network of Jewish elites manipulates politics, finance, media, and culture to advance their own aims, often at the expense of the host nation's sovereignty or values.

Though widely condemned and discredited, ZOG remains a persistent belief in extremist circles and has been cited in manifestos and rhetoric from white nationalist and neo-Nazi groups.

History & Key Claims

Origins of the Term:

The term "Zionist Occupied Government" originated in the 1970s and 1980s within American white supremacist circles, particularly among groups such as the Aryan Nations and The Order, a violent neo-Nazi organization.

It built upon older antisemitic beliefs going back to The Protocols of the Elders of Zion, a forged document from early 20th-century Russia that claimed to reveal a Jewish plot for world domination.

Core Beliefs:

Zionists (and by extension, all Jews in this theory) supposedly:

Control global banking systems (via families like the Rothschilds).

Dominate Western media, shaping public opinion and censoring dissent.

Influence foreign and domestic policy, especially in favor of Israel.

Use tools such as Hollywood, academia, and pharmaceuticals to promote liberalism, multiculturalism, or moral decay.

American politicians, the theory claims, are selected or controlled by Zionist interests, ensuring obedience to Israeli strategic goals.

Common Tropes and Accusations:

Dual loyalty: Accusing Jewish citizens of being more loyal to Israel than their home countries.

Israel-first foreign policy: Alleging that wars (e.g. Iraq) were fought for Israeli benefit.

Media domination: Claiming that Jewish-owned media manipulates the news and entertainment to fit globalist or Zionist narratives.

Holocaust denial or revisionism: Asserting that historical atrocities are exaggerated to advance sympathy and deflect criticism.

Overlap with Other Theories:

Often intersects with New World Order, Illuminati, and banking conspiracies.

Some versions tie Jewish influence to satanic or occult control narratives.

Famous Quotes / Sources

"The government in Washington, D.C., isn't American—it's Zionist."

— William Pierce, founder of the National Alliance (white nationalist group)

"We are occupied by a power that doesn't serve the American people."

— From The Turner Diaries, a racist dystopian novel cited by extremists

"The Jews control the media, the money, and the message."

— David Duke, former KKK Grand Wizard

"ZOG is a smokescreen for fascists who can't accept their own failures."

— Deborah Lipstadt, historian and author of Denying the Holocaust

Real-World Consequences

Violence and Radicalization:

ZOG theories have been cited as motivations in acts of terrorism and mass shootings, including:

The 1995 Oklahoma City bombing (indirect ideological roots).

The 2018 Pittsburgh synagogue shooting.

The Christchurch mosque shooter's manifesto referenced related rhetoric.

Antisemitism in Politics:

Mainstream politicians have occasionally invoked tropes (often without naming ZOG directly), leading to widespread condemnation and debate about dog whistles.

Stigmatization and Harm:

Jewish communities continue to face threats and discrimination, often stemming from belief in elite control or hidden agendas.

Online Spread:

Forums, encrypted messaging apps, and alternative media platforms have become breeding grounds for ZOG narratives under the banner of "globalist" or "deep state" criticism.

Confusion with Legitimate Criticism:

Criticism of Israeli policy is legitimate in international discourse, but ZOG rhetoric often masks itself in that language, making it harder to distinguish between political debate and conspiracy.

Where It Stands Today

The ZOG theory is widely condemned by historians, political analysts, and human rights organizations as antisemitic propaganda. Despite this, it endures in far-right and extremist communities under various guises—often couched in terms like "globalists", "international bankers", or "elite controllers", which are used as coded language.

While there are powerful lobbying organizations in many democracies (including pro-Israel ones), there is no evidence of a global Jewish plot to control governments. The ZOG conspiracy thrives not because of fact, but because of fear, ignorance, and the human tendency to seek scapegoats in times of uncertainty.

Its continued presence in modern discourse highlights the importance of vigilant media literacy, historical education, and the challenge of combatting hate that disguises itself as "truth-seeking".

Chapter Seventy-Nine

Section: Secret Societies & Elite Control

Conspiracy: The Jesuits Control the Vatican & Beyond

Summary

This conspiracy claims that the Society of Jesus, more commonly known as the Jesuits, is not merely a religious order within the Catholic Church, but a shadowy and manipulative power bloc with influence over global politics, economics, education, intelligence agencies, and even other religions. The theory suggests the Jesuits control the Vatican hierarchy, operate secret intelligence networks, and manipulate world events from behind the scenes — all while presenting themselves as humble scholars and missionaries.

Critics of this theory regard it as a revival of anti-Catholic rhetoric, historically popular in Protestant and anti-papist circles, though modern variations often cast the Jesuits as a globalist elite with ties to the New World Order.

History & Key Claims

Origins of the Jesuits:

Founded in 1540 by Ignatius of Loyola, the Jesuits were created as an order of scholars, educators, and missionaries loyal to the Pope, with a strong emphasis on discipline, obedience, and education.

They became instrumental in the Counter-Reformation, combating the spread of Protestantism through diplomacy, intellectual debate, and missionary work.

Suppression and Suspicion:

In the 18th century, due to their influence and involvement in politics and finance, the Jesuits were expelled from many European nations.

In 1773, Pope Clement XIV suppressed the order entirely — though they were later restored in 1814.

These historical events fed the idea that the Jesuits were more political than spiritual, manipulating monarchs and governments behind closed doors.

Modern Conspiratorial Claims:

The Jesuits:

Control the Vatican and may have engineered the resignation of Pope Benedict XVI.

Influence global education through Jesuit universities and institutions.

Created or now manipulate the Freemasons, Illuminati, or even Communism as tools of social control.

Are behind wars, revolutions, and the spread of globalization.

Secretly direct the CIA, MI6, and other intelligence bodies.

The Black Pope, or Jesuit Superior General, is claimed by theorists to be more powerful than the actual Pope, controlling him as a figurehead.

Notable Figures:

Peter Hans Kolvenbach (Superior General 1983–2008) and Adolfo Nicolás (2008–2016) are often named in theories alleging worldwide influence.

Pope Francis I, elected in 2013, is the first Jesuit Pope, which has been used as "proof" of Jesuit dominance.

Famous Quotes / Sources

"The Jesuits are a military organization, not a religious order."

— Napoleon Bonaparte (apocryphal quote)

"They have infiltrated governments, churches, and universities... the world is their pulpit."

— Eric Jon Phelps, Vatican Assassins

"Behind every revolution, you'll find a Jesuit whispering in the shadows."

— From The Secret History of the Jesuits by Edmond Paris (widely discredited but influential)

"The Jesuits have no king but the Pope, and no law but obedience."

— Traditional saying among critics of the order

Real-World Consequences

Anti-Catholic Propaganda:

For centuries, Protestant nations (especially in the UK and America) portrayed Jesuits as spies, assassins, and agents of Rome.

Conspiracy literature blamed them for the Gunpowder Plot, Napoleonic wars, Lincoln's assassination, and World War I.

Fuel for Anti-Papist and Anti-Christian Theories:

Jesuit conspiracies often feed into broader claims that the Catholic Church is a front for global tyranny, especially in NWO or end-times prophecy circles.

Educational Distrust:

Jesuit universities (e.g., Georgetown, Fordham) are painted as elitist indoctrination centers by those suspicious of their influence in law, politics, and science.

Intersection with Other Theories:

Some conspiracy frameworks link the Jesuits with:

The Illuminati

The Black Nobility

The United Nations

Secret financial institutions

Where It Stands Today

The Jesuit order continues to play a visible, though mostly religious and educational, role within the global Catholic Church. While it is true that they hold positions of influence — especially through academia and missionary outreach — the idea that they secretly rule the Vatican or orchestrate global politics remains unsubstantiated.

Most historians and theologians dismiss these claims as a blend of historical misunderstanding, anti-Catholic bigotry, and myth-making. However, the election of Pope Francis, a Jesuit himself, has reinvigorated the theory in conspiracy communities, particularly among those who believe the Vatican has become compromised or aligned with globalist aims.

In modern conspiracist frameworks, the Jesuits represent an archetype of hidden religious control — a narrative that combines centuries of suspicion with contemporary fears about authority, secrecy, and ideological influence.

Chapter Eighty

Section: Secret Societies & Elite Control

Conspiracy: Templars Still Rule Behind the Scenes

Summary

According to this theory, the Knights Templar, a medieval Catholic military order believed to have disbanded in the 14th century, never truly vanished. Instead, they supposedly went underground, preserved their wealth and knowledge, and evolved into a hidden elite force pulling the strings of modern global power. Some versions of the theory suggest the Templars helped establish secret societies like the Freemasons, or that they survive today in an unbroken lineage, influencing governments, banks, religious institutions, and even the Vatican.

Though rooted in historical mystery and myth, the theory gained mainstream attention through books, films, and documentaries that romanticize the Templars' legacy and secrecy.

History & Key Claims

Origins of the Knights Templar:

Founded around 1119 CE during the Crusades, the Templars were a Catholic military order charged with protecting Christian pilgrims and Holy Land interests.

They quickly amassed enormous wealth and political power, becoming one of the most influential entities in medieval Europe.

Their innovations in finance—including early banking systems—made them vital to kings and popes.

Their Sudden Fall:

In 1307, King Philip IV of France, deeply in debt to the Templars, orchestrated their arrest on charges of heresy, blasphemy, and devil-worship.

Many Templars were imprisoned or executed; others were absorbed into different orders.

The official suppression occurred in 1312, but rumors emerged that a core group escaped with treasures and secret knowledge.

Conspiracy Theory Developments:

Surviving Templars allegedly fled to:

Scotland, where they joined early Freemasonry.

Portugal, forming the Order of Christ, which influenced the Age of Exploration.

Switzerland, where they may have contributed to the creation of Swiss banking.

The theory suggests the Templars:

Possess secret knowledge (e.g., the Holy Grail, ancient relics, or gnostic truths) that could undermine the Church or global powers.

Hold sway over global finance, using centuries of hidden wealth.

Still operate as a spiritual and financial elite, guiding global destiny through covert influence.

Templars and the Freemasons:

The Freemasons are often said to be the spiritual or organizational descendants of the Templars.

Masonic lore includes references to lost knowledge, sacred geometry, Solomon's Temple, and initiation rituals, all of which theorists link back to the Templars.

Famous Quotes / Sources

"The Templars were disbanded by force, but their spirit lives on in the invisible architecture of global power."

— Graham Hancock, alternative historian

"The bloodline of the Grail and the legacy of the Templars are hidden in plain sight."

— Dan Brown, The Da Vinci Code (fiction, but widely cited in conspiracy circles)

"Modern banking and global commerce owe a greater debt to the Knights Templar than most historians care to admit."

— Michael Baigent, co-author of Holy Blood, Holy Grail

"Templar secrets did not die with Jacques de Molay. They went deeper underground."

— Common phrase among speculative historians and conspiracy theorists

Real-World Consequences

Rise of Pseudo-History:

Books like Holy Blood, Holy Grail and The Templar Revelation popularized the idea of Templar survival, often blending myth, selective history, and fiction.

These works inspired mass-market thrillers and documentaries that blurred the line between entertainment and belief.

Influence on Pop Culture:

The Templars feature heavily in:

The Assassin's Creed video game series.

National Treasure and Indiana Jones films.

Countless novels and alternate history works.

Their mysterious image has turned them into symbols of hidden knowledge and lost power.

Modern Organizations Claiming Descent:

Groups such as the Ordo Supremus Militaris Templi Hierosolymitani (OSMTH) and other neo-Templar organizations claim spiritual or ideological continuity.

Though mostly ceremonial or charitable, they fuel speculation of an unbroken lineage.

Extremist Misuse:

Far-right groups and white nationalist movements have adopted Templar symbols, claiming inspiration from a mythologized vision of Christian militarism.

Some lone-wolf attackers, such as Anders Behring Breivik, referenced the Templars in manifestos, corrupting the myth for ideological ends.

Where It Stands Today

Mainstream historians assert that the Knights Templar ceased to exist as an organized body in the 14th century. While their wealth and legend may have inspired future movements, no credible evidence supports claims of an underground order guiding world events.

Still, the mystique of the Templars persists. Their combination of secrecy, power, religious zeal, and unjust persecution makes them ideal figures for conspiratorial reinterpretation. For many, the Templars represent the ultimate secret society—a brotherhood that vanished in name but not in influence.

Whether seen as protectors of forbidden truths or schemers behind global finance, the Templars endure as icons of mystery, rebellion, and hidden history.

Chapter Eighty-One

Section: Space, Aliens and the Unknown

Conspiracy: The Moon Landing Was Faked

Summary

Arguably the most famous space-related conspiracy theory in modern history, the claim that the Apollo moon landings were faked by NASA and the U.S. government suggests that mankind never set foot on the lunar surface. According to proponents, the events of July 20, 1969 — when Neil Armstrong famously stepped onto the Moon — were an elaborate hoax filmed on Earth, most likely in a secret Hollywood-style studio.

The theory alleges that the motivation was to win the Space Race against the Soviet Union, restore American prestige, and secure dominance in the Cold War — all without taking the immense risks of sending men to the Moon. Despite overwhelming scientific and technological evidence supporting the moon landings, this theory remains one of the most persistent in public discourse.

History & Key Claims

Cold War Context:

The U.S. and USSR were engaged in a fierce competition for space dominance.

After several Soviet firsts — including Sputnik and the first human in space (Yuri Gagarin) — NASA needed a major victory.

Critics suggest that in the face of technological limitations, faking the landing was considered "safer" than risking failure.

Popularized in the 1970s:

The theory first gained major attention in 1976 with the self-published book We Never Went to the Moon by Bill Kaysing, a former technical writer with no aerospace background.

He alleged that NASA lacked the technical ability to land men on the Moon and return them safely.

Key Claims Made by Moon Hoax Theorists:

Shadows and Lighting: Photographs show odd shadows and lighting inconsistencies, suggesting studio lighting.

No Stars in Photos: Lunar photos don't show stars, which some claim proves they were taken on Earth.

Waving Flag: The American flag appears to "wave," despite the Moon's lack of atmosphere.

Radiation Belts: Astronauts would have been killed by the Van Allen radiation belts without adequate shielding.

Perfect Footprints: Footprints appear too sharp and detailed, implying damp or artificial soil.

Identical Backgrounds: Allegedly reused landscapes appear in photos from different "landing sites."

Stanley Kubrick Theory:

A fringe but popular variant suggests that filmmaker Stanley Kubrick directed the fake footage, possibly using techniques developed for 2001: A Space Odyssey.

Proponents point to supposed clues in The Shining, such as Danny's Apollo 11 sweater and the "Room 237" reference (the Moon is ~237,000 miles from Earth).

Famous Quotes / Sources

"One small step for man, one giant leap for mankind."

— Neil Armstrong, 1969

"I know for a fact the moon landings were faked. I worked on the set."

— Bill Kaysing, in interviews promoting We Never Went to the Moon

"The greatest movie never made."

— Slogan often used by Kubrick-moon hoax believers

"People love conspiracies — but the moon landings happened. End of story."

— Buzz Aldrin, Apollo 11 astronaut

"Somebody would've talked."

— Neil deGrasse Tyson, astrophysicist and skeptic of the hoax theory

Real-World Consequences

Cultural Impact:

The theory has been explored in documentaries, parodies, and Hollywood films (Capricorn One, Moonwalkers, etc.).

It has contributed to a broader skepticism of government and science in the public mind.

NASA's Response:

NASA has repeatedly debunked the claims with:

Technical data

Moon rock analysis

Ongoing lunar observations

Apollo missions left retroreflectors (laser mirrors) on the Moon, which can still be used to measure the distance between Earth and the Moon.

Public Figures and Endorsements:

Some celebrities and public figures (e.g. rapper B.o.B., TV host Joe Rogan in earlier years) have either endorsed or entertained the theory, further amplifying it on social media.

Confrontations have occurred: Buzz Aldrin once punched a conspiracy theorist who accused him of lying.

Educational Consequences:

Teachers and scientists report growing numbers of students believing the theory, sometimes alongside Flat Earth or anti-science sentiment.

Where It Stands Today

Despite being thoroughly debunked by the scientific community, the "faked moon landing" theory remains one of the most popular and resilient conspiracy narratives of the modern era. A 2020 YouGov poll found that around 10% of Americans still believe the landings were staged, with even higher percentages in some other countries.

NASA's renewed lunar exploration efforts — including the Artemis Program and private missions — have revived interest in lunar conspiracies. As long as there is mistrust in institutions, the idea that humanity's greatest space achievement was a lie will continue to resonate.

The moon landing hoax theory serves as a template for modern conspiracy thinking: distrustful, visually oriented, and deeply tied to national identity, pride, and perception.

Chapter Eighty-Two

Section: Space, Aliens and the Unknown

Conspiracy: NASA Lies About Everything

Summary

This sweeping and all-encompassing conspiracy theory claims that NASA (the U.S. National Aeronautics and Space Administration) is not a scientific space agency, but a government-controlled propaganda machine tasked with fabricating space exploration, hiding alien contact, and manipulating the public's understanding of Earth, the Moon, and the cosmos.

According to believers, NASA's entire narrative is staged — from moon landings and Mars missions to satellite images of Earth. Some claim the Earth is flat or hollow, that the Moon is artificial, or that space travel is impossible. In short: if NASA said it, it's a lie. The theory acts as a meta-conspiracy, overlapping with numerous others and often rooted in deep anti-government, anti-globalist, and anti-science sentiment.

History & Key Claims

NASA's Origins and Cold War Motives:

NASA was founded in 1958, replacing NACA, to compete with the Soviet Union in the Space Race.

Conspiracy theorists argue NASA was always a tool for psychological operations, producing public victories to assert U.S. superiority without ever proving the science.

Core Accusations:

Moon Landing Hoax: The 1969 moon landing is often cited as the beginning of NASA's lies.

Faked Satellite Footage: Many claim Earth photos are CGI or composites, with no real satellites in orbit.

Flat Earth / Globe Earth Hoax: Some believe NASA's Earth imagery is designed to hide the true shape of the planet.

Hiding Aliens: NASA allegedly edits or censors footage that shows UFOs or anomalies, and blocks evidence of extraterrestrial life.

Mars Missions Are Filmed on Earth: Images from Mars rovers are said to be taken in deserts on Earth, often citing perceived similarities with locations in Nevada or Greenland.

Astronauts Are Actors: Some claim that spacewalks and International Space Station (ISS) broadcasts are filmed in neutral buoyancy pools or on zero-gravity airplanes, with green screens and CGI effects used to fake zero-gravity environments.

Institutional Collusion:

NASA is believed to collaborate with other space agencies, such as ESA, JAXA, and Roscosmos, to maintain a global deception.

Mainstream media, Hollywood, and academia are supposedly complicit, creating documentaries, movies, and textbooks that push the space narrative.

Religious and Occult Accusations:

Some suggest NASA is involved in Masonic or Luciferian agendas, hiding the divine nature of Earth or the firmament (as per biblical cosmology).

NASA missions are said to include occult naming schemes, referencing mythological gods, "Saturn worship," or coded Illuminati messages.

Famous Quotes / Sources

"NASA stands for Never A Straight Answer."

— Common phrase among conspiracy communities

"NASA's primary mission is not exploration, but deception."

— Eric Dubay, Flat Earth proponent and anti-NASA activist

"There are more Hollywood technicians at NASA than there are engineers."

— Bart Sibrel, moon hoax documentarian

"Everything NASA has shown us — the globe, the stars, the galaxies — is just an illusion to separate man from God."

— Rob Skiba, biblical cosmologist

Real-World Consequences

Rise of Anti-Science Movements:

NASA-centric conspiracies often serve as gateways to wider anti-scientific beliefs, including:

Flat Earth

Climate change denial

Vaccine skepticism

Anti-intellectualism

Online Radicalization:

Platforms like YouTube, Facebook, and Telegram have played major roles in spreading anti-NASA content, often reaching millions of views.

Some influencers profit by selling books, merchandise, or hosting paid conferences that criticize NASA.

Harassment of Astronauts and Scientists:

Prominent astronauts, like Buzz Aldrin and Chris Hadfield, have been confronted by conspiracy theorists demanding "proof" they went to space.

NASA employees have reported receiving hate mail and threats, particularly after major launches or discoveries.

Distrust in Institutions:

NASA's association with other U.S. agencies (such as the Department of Defense or DARPA) feeds deep mistrust in any official narrative.

This contributes to a broader erosion of faith in governments, science, journalism, and education.

Where It Stands Today

"NASA Lies" is no longer a fringe belief — it's a cornerstone of many internet-born conspiracy cultures. From Flat Earthers to sovereign citizens, the idea that NASA manipulates the public is widespread across many ideological and spiritual belief systems.

Despite NASA's efforts at transparency (including livestreamed launches, high-resolution public data, and open access to mission archives), skepticism has not diminished. In some cases, the more evidence NASA provides, the more conspiracists interpret it as overcompensation.

New missions — including lunar exploration under the Artemis Program and upcoming Mars initiatives — are already being labeled as hoaxes before they occur.

As long as there is a blend of mistrust, misinformation, and digital echo chambers, the belief that NASA lies about everything will remain a persistent, self-sustaining myth.

Chapter Eighty-Three

Section: Space, Aliens and the Unknown

Conspiracy: Area 51 Alien Tech

Summary

Area 51 is a real U.S. military installation located in the Nevada desert, officially known as Groom Lake. For decades, it has been shrouded in mystery, secrecy, and restricted access. According to a long-standing and widely circulated conspiracy theory, Area 51 houses recovered alien spacecraft, reverse-engineered extraterrestrial technology, and possibly even live aliens.

This belief places Area 51 at the heart of UFO mythology. Though originally associated with Cold War aircraft development, it's become synonymous with government secrets, alien cover-ups, and top-level concealment of extraterrestrial knowledge. Whether fueled by pop culture or leaked testimony, the theory continues to attract widespread attention.

History & Key Claims

Origins in Cold War Secrecy:

Area 51 was built in the 1950s as a testing site for experimental aircraft, including the U-2 spy plane.

Due to its isolated location and high-level security, the base quickly drew suspicion and speculation.

The Roswell Connection:

The 1947 Roswell Incident, in which debris from a supposed "flying disc" was recovered in New Mexico, is often linked to Area 51.

Conspiracists claim the wreckage (and alien bodies) were secretly transported to Area 51 for study.

Bob Lazar's Testimony (1989):

Bob Lazar, a physicist who claimed to have worked at a secret facility near Area 51 called S-4, reignited public fascination.

He alleged that:

The U.S. had nine alien spacecraft in its possession.

He personally worked on reverse-engineering propulsion systems using a then-unknown element (later dubbed "Element 115").

The craft operated via gravity manipulation, far beyond human capability.

Lazar's story was dismissed by authorities, but many believe he was discredited on purpose to suppress the truth.

Reverse Engineering Theories:

Some theorists claim that breakthroughs in stealth aircraft, fiber optics, night vision, and even microchips were back-engineered from alien tech.

Lockheed Martin's Skunk Works, which developed secret aircraft near the site, is often implicated.

Other Common Claims:

Live aliens are housed underground in deep military labs.

Joint human-alien programs exist for tech exchange or hybridization experiments.

Underground tunnels connect Area 51 to other bases (e.g., Dulce Base in New Mexico).

Sightings of glowing discs, silent triangles, and unexplained lights have been reported near the perimeter for decades.

Famous Quotes / Sources

"They are not terrestrial in origin."

— Bob Lazar, interview with George Knapp, 1989

"Something is going on out there. All we want is the truth."

— Harry Reid, former U.S. Senator and proponent of UFO transparency

"The government has been covering this up for decades."

— Steven Greer, founder of The Disclosure Project

"Area 51 does exist. It's not a myth. But what goes on there is classified for reasons unrelated to aliens."

— Barack Obama, first U.S. president to publicly acknowledge Area 51 (2013)

"We know what we saw."

— Multiple military pilots from various Navy UFO incidents, referencing unknown aerial phenomena

Real-World Consequences

Pop Culture Phenomenon:

Area 51 has become a symbol of conspiracy culture, appearing in films like Independence Day, Paul, and Men in Black.

It is often featured in documentaries, video games, and comic books.

Increased Surveillance & Militarization:

The facility is heavily guarded, with motion sensors, patrols, and signs authorizing use of deadly force.

Sightseers and thrill-seekers are regularly detained or fined.

Storm Area 51 Event (2019):

A viral Facebook event jokingly proposed storming the base to "see them aliens."

Over 2 million people RSVP'd, prompting real military warnings.

Though only a few hundred showed up, it reignited media interest and led to several alien-themed festivals.

Calls for Disclosure:

Whistleblower programs, FOIA requests, and documentaries continue to push for government transparency about what's stored at Area 51.

The U.S. government's recent release of UAP (Unidentified Aerial Phenomena) reports has only added fuel to the fire.

Where It Stands Today

Area 51 remains operational and highly restricted, with no public access, no fly zones, and no detailed official explanations about its function. Though it's now admitted to exist, the government maintains that its purpose is "testing advanced aviation technologies."

Public trust in government has declined, and the resurgence of UFO discourse — including recent congressional hearings — has revived speculation about what might lie behind those desert fences.

The belief that Area 51 holds alien technology is no longer fringe. For many, it represents the ultimate "what else are they hiding?" — a question that keeps the theory alive in memes, media, and minds around the world.

Chapter Eighty-Four

Section: Space, Aliens and the Unknown

Conspiracy: Roswell UFO Crash

Summary

The Roswell UFO incident is widely regarded as the birthplace of modern alien conspiracy theory. In July 1947, something crashed on a ranch near Roswell, New Mexico. The U.S. military initially announced they had recovered a "flying disc," only to retract the statement within 24 hours, claiming it was a weather balloon instead.

To believers, this reversal marked the start of a massive government cover-up. According to the theory, what crashed wasn't a balloon — it was a flying saucer, complete with alien occupants. The debris, and possibly alien bodies, were taken to Wright-Patterson Air Force Base or Area 51 for study and concealment. Over the decades, the Roswell incident has become a cornerstone of UFO lore, fueling books, films, and endless speculation.

History & Key Claims

The Crash (July 1947):

Mac Brazel, a rancher, discovered strange debris in his sheep pasture northwest of Roswell.

He reported it to Roswell Army Air Field (RAAF), prompting an investigation.

On July 8, 1947, the RAAF issued a press release stating they had recovered a "flying disc."

The Sudden Retraction:

Just one day later, the Army issued a new statement claiming the wreckage was a weather balloon.

They displayed aluminum foil, wooden sticks, and rubber remnants to the press.

The case largely disappeared from public attention until decades later.

Revival in the Late 1970s:

In 1978, nuclear physicist and UFO researcher Stanton Friedman interviewed retired Major Jesse Marcel, who had handled the debris.

Marcel claimed the material was not from Earth — lightweight but unbreakable, with strange symbols.

His testimony reignited interest in Roswell as a possible alien encounter.

Theories Multiply:

Claims emerged that:

There were multiple crash sites.

Alien bodies were recovered — some dead, others possibly alive.

Witnesses, including morticians and military staff, were threatened into silence.

A "memory metal" was part of the wreckage: thin, metallic foil that returned to shape after crumpling.

The event was covered up at the highest levels and used to jumpstart secret government programs (e.g., reverse engineering, underground bases, hybridization research).

Project Mogul Explanation:

In 1994, the U.S. Air Force issued a report stating the debris was part of Project Mogul, a top-secret Cold War program using high-altitude balloons to detect Soviet nuclear tests.

This explanation was meant to resolve the mystery — but for many, it only added more suspicion.

Famous Quotes / Sources

"The material was not anything I'd ever seen in my life. It was not from this Earth."

— Major Jesse Marcel, 1978 interview

"If the truth about Roswell were known, it would be the most momentous event in human history."

— Stanton Friedman, physicist and leading Roswell researcher

"They told us to forget what we saw — or else."

— Anonymous military witness, from Witness to Roswell by Thomas J. Carey & Donald Schmitt

"It was a cover story to hide the real purpose of the balloon: Project Mogul."

— 1994 U.S. Air Force Report

"Every credible bit of evidence points to an extraordinary event being buried by official denial."

— Richard Dolan, historian and author of UFOs and the National Security State

Real-World Consequences

Roswell Becomes a Cultural Symbol:

The incident has been featured in:

The X-Files

Independence Day

Roswell (TV series)

Dozens of documentaries, books, and games

Roswell is now the UFO capital of the world, drawing thousands of tourists and UFO believers annually.

Economic Impact:

The town of Roswell built a museum, hosts an annual UFO Festival, and maintains alien-themed shops, tours, and landmarks.

FOIA Declassification Movement:

The incident sparked decades of Freedom of Information Act (FOIA) requests demanding disclosure of UFO-related documents.

Some documents have been released, but many remain classified — adding to suspicions.

Conspiracy Proliferation:

Roswell serves as the template for other crash conspiracies, including those in:

Kecksburg, Pennsylvania (1965)

Shag Harbour, Nova Scotia (1967)

Varginha, Brazil (1996)

Alien Autopsy Scandal:

In the 1990s, a film surfaced claiming to show the autopsy of an alien recovered from the Roswell crash.

The footage was later admitted to be recreated "based on witness testimony", but it nonetheless cemented Roswell in public imagination.

Where It Stands Today

Roswell remains the most iconic UFO event in history — the catalyst for decades of alien-focused speculation. Despite official denials and alternative explanations, belief in a cover-up has only grown stronger with time.

A 2021 Pew Research survey found that over 50% of Americans believe the government is hiding information about UFOs, much of that belief tied to the Roswell case.

As interest in UAPs (Unidentified Aerial Phenomena) resurges — including Pentagon reports and congressional hearings — many wonder if Roswell was just the beginning. Whether real event, Cold War accident, or elaborate misinformation campaign, Roswell's place in the conspiracy canon is secure.

Chapter Eighty-Five

Section: Space, Aliens and the Unknown

Conspiracy: Project Blue Book Cover-Up

Summary

Project Blue Book was the United States Air Force's official investigation into UFOs, operating from 1952 to 1969. It reviewed over 12,000 UFO reports, aiming to determine whether these sightings posed a threat to national security or could be explained by conventional means. The project publicly concluded that no UFO reported, investigated, and evaluated by the Air Force gave any indication of threat, nor was there any evidence of extraterrestrial technology.

But according to conspiracy theorists, Project Blue Book was a deliberate smokescreen — designed not to investigate UFOs, but to dismiss and discredit them. Many believe the real evidence was hidden in classified files, while the public-facing operation served to pacify curiosity and bury the truth about extraterrestrial contact.

History & Key Claims

Predecessors to Blue Book:

Project Blue Book was the third U.S. Air Force UFO study, following Project Sign (1947) and Project Grudge (1949).

These early programs were also terminated without full disclosure, raising suspicions of internal suppression.

The Scope of Blue Book:

Based at Wright-Patterson Air Force Base, Project Blue Book investigated:

Civilian and military UFO reports

Radar anomalies

Pilot encounters

Photographic and physical evidence

Headed by Captain Edward J. Ruppelt in its early years, who coined the term "UFO".

The Official Conclusion (1969):

Blue Book closed with the conclusion that:

There was no evidence of UFOs being of extraterrestrial origin.

Most sightings could be attributed to natural phenomena, aircraft, or hoaxes.

Further investigation was unwarranted.

The Cover-Up Theory:

Critics argue that:

Compelling cases were ignored or hidden, particularly those involving military encounters or radar-visual confirmations.

Investigators were told to debunk, not understand, the phenomena.

J. Allen Hynek, the project's civilian consultant, later admitted the Air Force was not genuinely open to discovering the truth.

Evidence and testimonies that supported UFO reality were systematically dismissed, discredited, or classified.

Examples of Alleged Suppression:

The 1964 Socorro, NM incident, involving a police officer who saw a craft and two beings, was "explained" as a hoax, though Hynek disagreed.

Radar-visual sightings by Air Force pilots were dismissed with questionable explanations (e.g., "Venus" or "temperature inversions").

Over 700 cases remain "unexplained" to this day.

Famous Quotes / Sources

"The Air Force was interested only in proving that UFOs didn't exist."

— J. Allen Hynek, former scientific advisor to Project Blue Book

"I think we were being used... for public relations, not truth-seeking."

— Lt. Col. Robert Friend, Project Blue Book leader (1958–1963)

"Project Blue Book was not a sincere scientific effort."

— Richard Dolan, historian and UFO researcher

"Even some generals believed in the phenomenon — they just weren't allowed to speak."

— Anonymous Blue Book contributor, via declassified interviews

"We are not alone."

— J. Allen Hynek, years after leaving Blue Book

Real-World Consequences

Public Distrust:

Blue Book's closure fueled belief that the U.S. government was hiding the truth about UFOs.

UFO groups formed to carry on independent investigations, believing the government could not be trusted.

Media Adaptations:

Project Blue Book has been featured in:

The X-Files

History Channel's Project Blue Book series (2019)

Countless books and documentaries

Hynek's "close encounter classification system" (e.g., CE-1 to CE-5) became embedded in pop culture.

Whistleblowers Emerged:

Former military personnel began speaking out, claiming Blue Book was just the surface of a deeper classified network of UFO research.

The Condon Report (1968):

Used as justification to shut down Blue Book, the Condon Report concluded that further study was unnecessary.

The report has been criticized for bias and scientific inconsistency.

Where It Stands Today

While the U.S. Air Force maintains that Project Blue Book settled the UFO issue, belief in the cover-up remains strong. In the wake of recent Pentagon UAP disclosures, researchers point to Project Blue Book as evidence of a decades-long misinformation campaign.

Declassified documents confirm that military and intelligence agencies continued to collect UFO data long after Blue Book's closure — under different names and programs. For conspiracy theorists, this confirms that the project's real purpose was to end public inquiry, not to seek the truth.

In many ways, Project Blue Book represents the tipping point: when the gap between official denial and public belief became too wide to ignore.

Chapter Eighty-Six

Section: Space, Aliens and the Unknown

Conspiracy: Project Blue Beam (Fake Alien Invasion)

Summary

Project Blue Beam is a conspiracy theory alleging that NASA and other global elite organizations plan to simulate a global alien invasion or messianic second coming using advanced holographic technology, psychological manipulation, and secret weaponry. The theory claims the purpose is to establish a New World Order, uniting humanity under one global religion and government by faking a divine or extraterrestrial event.

Originating in the 1990s, the theory has remained a staple in fringe communities, especially among those who distrust global institutions. Despite having no verified documentation or mainstream support, Blue Beam has gained momentum with the rise of digital deepfakes, augmented reality, and mass media influence.

History & Key Claims

Origins:

Introduced in 1994 by Serge Monast, a Canadian investigative journalist and conspiracy theorist.

Monast published a pamphlet and gave lectures claiming NASA and the UN were developing a four-step plan for global mind control and false salvation.

He died of a heart attack in 1996, which some supporters suspect was an assassination due to his revelations.

The Four Steps of Project Blue Beam:

Discrediting Religion & Archaeology:

Earthquakes in key locations would uncover new evidence disproving religious doctrines, shaking foundational belief systems.

The Spectacle in the Sky:

Using space-based holographic projections, images of religious figures (Jesus, Buddha, Mohammed, etc.) would appear across the globe.

These visuals would merge into a singular "god" that unifies religions into a one-world faith.

Artificial Telepathy:

Low-frequency electromagnetic waves would transmit messages into people's minds, simulating divine communication or instructions.

Technologies like ELF waves, HAARP, and satellites are said to be part of this phase.

Fake Alien Invasion:

A staged extraterrestrial attack would be projected over major cities using holograms, sound technology, and military interference.

In response, governments would declare global martial law, eliminate sovereignty, and consolidate power into a technocratic dictatorship.

Technological Tools Allegedly Involved:

HAARP (High-Frequency Active Auroral Research Program)

SpaceX satellites

Weather manipulation

5G and microwave transmissions

High-altitude aerospace platforms with sound and projection capabilities

Famous Quotes / Sources

"Project Blue Beam is the ultimate deception — divine theater for mass control."

— Serge Monast, 1994

"Imagine a world where the skies betray us, and the voices in our heads aren't ours."

— From Blue Beam documents attributed to Monast

"In the age of deepfakes and holograms, this idea is less crazy than it was thirty years ago."

— Anonymous tech theorist, online forum

"NASA and the UN are preparing the final solution: a digital Antichrist."

— Serge Monast, Lecture Transcript

"No matter how wild the claim, people will believe what they see in the sky."

— Project Blue Beam followers

Real-World Consequences

Growing Distrust of NASA:

Blue Beam contributes to broader skepticism toward NASA, especially in the Flat Earth and UFO communities.

Natural disasters, rocket launches, and strange sky phenomena are sometimes labeled "Blue Beam tests."

Tech Anxiety and Digital Illusion:

With real-world holograms, augmented reality, and mind-reading neural interfaces becoming more advanced, some argue Blue Beam is no longer pure science fiction.

Influence on Pop Culture:

Films like Independence Day, They Live, and Spider-Man: Far From Home (which features a fake alien invasion using drones and holograms) echo Blue Beam motifs.

The idea has been embraced by QAnon, religious fundamentalists, and anti-globalist groups.

Fear of Global Deception:

Some believers refuse to trust any mass spiritual experience or global emergency, fearing it may be part of the staged plan.

Religious purists see it as the fulfillment of Revelations — a false messiah moment.

Deaths and Legal Issues:

Serge Monast's sudden death and that of a fellow researcher have been labeled "suspicious."

His writings are banned in some countries due to perceived incitement or anti-government rhetoric.

Where It Stands Today

Project Blue Beam remains unproven and unacknowledged by any legitimate institution. No direct evidence of the alleged technology has surfaced, and NASA has repeatedly denied the existence of such a plan.

Nonetheless, with the rapid advancement of:

Augmented reality

Voice-to-skull technology

Government surveillance

Psychological warfare

— the theory has gained renewed interest in online spaces. Believers point to Elon Musk's Starlink, Wuhan lockdown light displays, and even the 2023 Chinese spy balloon controversy as possible tests for future stages.

Skeptics label it pseudoscience, but for a growing number of people, Blue Beam is less about evidence and more about a deep-rooted suspicion of what governments, tech companies, and institutions might do if they could fool the world on a cosmic scale.

Chapter Eighty-Seven

Section: Space, Aliens and the Unknown

Conspiracy: Ancient Aliens Built the Pyramids

Summary

The "Ancient Aliens" theory proposes that extraterrestrial beings visited Earth in ancient times and played a central role in building monumental structures — most notably the Great Pyramids of Giza. Believers argue that the architectural precision, massive scale, and astronomical alignments of the pyramids are far too advanced for the ancient Egyptians to have achieved without help from technologically superior alien visitors.

Popularized in books, documentaries, and memes, this theory reimagines ancient history through the lens of space-age intervention, challenging both conventional archaeology and human self-perception.

History & Key Claims

Origins of the Theory:

First suggested in the 1960s by Erich von Däniken, author of Chariots of the Gods?

Von Däniken proposed that ancient myths, art, and texts reflect contact with alien beings, whom early civilizations worshipped as gods.

The Pyramids of Giza:

Built around 2560 BCE, the pyramids are aligned with Orion's Belt and feature mathematically precise architecture.

Weighing over 2.5 million limestone blocks, the Great Pyramid has an average block weight of 2.5 tons.

Claims:

Egyptians lacked the technology to cut, move, and place such stones so precisely.

The pyramids' positioning and dimensions reflect knowledge of pi, the golden ratio, and Earth's geodesy — far beyond ancient tools.

Astronomical & Symbolic Arguments:

The layout of the pyramids mirrors the Orion constellation, reinforcing the idea of celestial connection.

Believers point to artworks and carvings that resemble flying saucers, astronauts, or advanced machinery.

Cultural Evidence (According to Theorists):

Similar pyramid structures appear in Mesoamerica, Sudan, and Southeast Asia, suggesting a global alien blueprint.

Mythologies from Egypt, Sumeria, India, and Mesoamerica speak of "sky gods", "chariots of fire", or beings from the heavens bringing knowledge.

Mainstream Archaeological Rebuttal:

Egyptologists maintain that the pyramids were built using well-documented techniques, including:

Ramps

Copper tools

Large labor forces

There is no verified evidence of alien influence or impossible technology in the archaeological record.

Famous Quotes / Sources

"I'm not saying it was aliens… but it was aliens."

— Giorgio A. Tsoukalos, Ancient Aliens TV personality

"The Great Pyramid is a machine, an energy device — not a tomb."

— Erich von Däniken

"There is more mystery to the pyramids than our textbooks admit."

— Zecharia Sitchin, author of The 12th Planet

"Alien influence is the modern mythology for what we don't understand about the past."

— Dr. Kara Cooney, Egyptologist

"Stone Age doesn't mean stupid — it means stone tools."

— Mark Lehner, archaeologist

Real-World Consequences

Cultural Fascination:

The theory has inspired a global media franchise, from the History Channel's Ancient Aliens series to Indiana Jones, Stargate, and Prometheus.

Tourists flock to the pyramids seeking signs of extraterrestrial construction.

Academic Pushback:

Scholars criticize the theory as pseudoarchaeology, noting that it undermines indigenous knowledge and ancient human ingenuity.

Many argue it has racist undertones, suggesting that non-Western civilizations couldn't have achieved greatness on their own.

Spiritual and Esoteric Movements:

The pyramids are now central to various New Age beliefs, with followers claiming they were designed as energy conduits, ascension chambers, or stargates.

Skepticism and Memes:

While widely dismissed in academic circles, the theory remains popular online, especially among UFO believers, truth seekers, and meme culture.

Where It Stands Today

Despite heavy academic criticism, the theory that aliens built the pyramids remains one of the most enduring and widespread modern myths. The Internet has given rise to thousands of YouTube channels, forums, and books exploring the idea.

Recent developments like:

The discovery of secret chambers using muon scans

Satellite surveys suggesting older layers beneath Giza

Renewed interest in advanced ancient engineering

— have kept the theory alive in the public imagination, even if no hard proof exists.

For many believers, the lack of acknowledgment by the academic community only reinforces the idea of a cover-up — that ancient contact with extraterrestrials has been deliberately erased from history.

Chapter Eighty-Eight

Section: Space, Aliens and the Unknown

Conspiracy: Mars Rover Images Are From Earth

Summary

This conspiracy theory asserts that the photos and videos shared by NASA from Mars rovers — including Spirit, Opportunity, Curiosity, and Perseverance — were not taken on Mars at all, but rather filmed on Earth, possibly in remote desert locations, Iceland, or Antarctica. Proponents argue that NASA is fabricating Mars exploration data to maintain funding, control the public narrative, or hide the true nature of space exploration.

While widely dismissed by the scientific community, the theory has grown alongside public distrust in large institutions and the increasing sophistication of digital media manipulation.

History & Key Claims

Timeline of Rover Missions:

Spirit and Opportunity landed on Mars in 2004.

Curiosity followed in 2012.

Perseverance, the most recent, landed in 2021, complete with the Ingenuity helicopter.

The Core Allegation:

Mars is either unreachable or NASA hasn't yet achieved manned/unmanned landings, so images are being staged on Earth.

Locations cited as filming grounds include:

Devon Island, Canada (the world's largest uninhabited island)

Atacama Desert, Chile

Icelandic lava fields

NASA training grounds in the Southwestern U.S.

Supporting "Evidence" from Theorists:

Identical rock formations appearing in both Mars photos and Earth landscapes.

Claims of animal sightings in NASA images (e.g., a "mouse," a "crab," or a "lizard").

Belief that NASA has reused filters, color grading, and dust overlays to create a Martian illusion.

NASA's own training footage on Earth occasionally mislabeled or misinterpreted as Martian.

Belief Variants:

Some think the Mars missions are fake entirely.

Others believe Mars exploration is real, but images are censored or replaced to hide ancient ruins, life forms, or secret operations.

Famous Quotes / Sources

"If you think they're on Mars, you haven't seen Devon Island."

— Anonymous Reddit user, r/Conspiracy

"That's not the Red Planet. That's Utah with a filter."

— YouTube video title with 1.2M views

"The real reason they won't send people is because they'd expose the lie."

— Forum user, GodlikeProductions

"There's a pattern of deception here. These images are too perfect, too Earth-like."

— Alternative researcher Nigel Kerner

Real-World Consequences

Erosion of Public Trust:

This theory contributes to distrust of NASA, the broader scientific establishment, and government transparency.

Many believe it ties into larger cover-ups, such as the Moon landing being faked or the Flat Earth movement.

Social Media Propagation:

Doctored images, selective screenshots, and speculative YouTube analysis fuel belief.

NASA's explanations are rarely as viral as conspiracy videos.

Misinterpretation of Legitimate Footage:

Training footage released for educational purposes is often clipped and labeled as "proof" of deception.

NASA has acknowledged public confusion over testing images, prompting clearer disclaimers.

Scientific Pushback:

Scientists note the distinct geological and atmospheric properties in Mars photos:

Dust levels

Atmospheric haze

Unique lighting due to Mars' thin CO_2 atmosphere

The Ingenuity helicopter's flight on Mars, using reduced gravity simulation and telemetry data, is offered as strong evidence.

Where It Stands Today

The theory persists in online echo chambers where space skepticism, anti-globalist sentiment, and scientific mistrust intersect. Though debunked by photographic experts, planetary scientists, and rover engineers, its popularity grew significantly during the COVID-19 pandemic, when global institutions faced heightened scrutiny.

For many, this conspiracy isn't just about Mars — it's about the broader belief that governments and agencies stage events to manipulate public perception. In that sense, the theory is less about geology and more about narrative control.

Still, as NASA prepares for crewed Mars missions (projected in the 2030s), believers remain convinced that unless they go themselves, they'll never trust the view from the Red Planet.

Chapter Eighty-Nine

Section: Space, Aliens and the Unknown

Conspiracy: The Black Knight Satellite

Summary

The Black Knight Satellite is a mysterious object said to be orbiting Earth in near-polar orbit, believed by conspiracy theorists to be an alien spacecraft, an ancient probe, or evidence of advanced extraterrestrial surveillance. Reports of its existence date back over a century, combining radio signal anomalies, strange photographs from space missions, and modern UFO lore into a single enduring mystery.

NASA dismisses the object as space debris or thermal blankets from past missions, but its unusual appearance and decades of persistent sightings keep the theory alive.

History & Key Claims

Early "Signals" (1899–1920s):

Inventor Nikola Tesla claimed to detect unusual radio signals in 1899, which some later attributed to alien transmissions from the Black Knight.

In the 1920s, amateur radio operators reported receiving "long delay echoes"—signals that bounced back unexpectedly.

First Visual Reports (1954):

UFO researcher Donald Keyhoe claimed the U.S. Air Force had detected two unknown satellites in orbit years before official satellites existed.

Newspapers like The St. Louis Dispatch reported the story, linking it to Cold War fears.

Key NASA Connection (1960):

The U.S. Navy detected a dark object in polar orbit, initially thought to be a Soviet spy satellite.

Later explanations claimed it was space debris, likely from the Discoverer program.

STS-88 "Photographic Evidence" (1998):

Astronauts aboard the Space Shuttle Endeavour photographed a strange, dark object in orbit.

NASA explained it as a lost thermal blanket, but many UFO researchers believe it to be the Black Knight.

Core Conspiratorial Beliefs:

The object is 13,000 years old, possibly placed by extraterrestrials to monitor Earth.

It transmits signals to unknown receivers or alien civilizations.

NASA deliberately avoids discussing it publicly.

Famous Quotes / Sources

"NASA calls it space junk. I call it a 13,000-year-old alien emissary."

— Scott Waring, UFO researcher

"That object wasn't debris. It was on a controlled path."

— Anonymous NASA engineer (unverified)

"The Black Knight has been watching us since before recorded history."

— Common phrase in UFO forums

"What they call a thermal blanket doesn't explain its size, orbit, or history."

— Richard Dolan, UFO historian

Real-World Consequences

Internet Explosion of Interest:

The 1998 STS-88 photographs went viral, becoming a staple in UFO websites, YouTube videos, and documentaries.

Symbol of Government Secrecy:

The Black Knight is cited as evidence that NASA hides significant space discoveries from the public.

Misinterpretation of Space Debris:

Space experts point out that orbital debris often looks strange in photographs due to lighting, perspective, and motion blur.

Fuel for Alien Probe Theories:

The Black Knight has been linked to theories of ancient alien contact, similar to the claims about pyramids or ancient stargates.

Where It Stands Today

NASA maintains that the Black Knight is nothing more than space debris—specifically a thermal blanket lost during the STS-88 mission. Most astronomers agree there's no evidence of an alien object in orbit.

However, its mythic status continues in UFO circles. The Black Knight remains an enduring symbol of:

Hidden alien presence

Government secrecy

Our lack of knowledge about what orbits Earth

To believers, until every photograph, radar track, and historical reference is fully disclosed, the Black Knight is not just a piece of junk—it's a silent watcher.

Chapter Ninety

Section: Space, Aliens and the Unknown

Conspiracy: Hollow Moon Theory

Summary

The Hollow Moon Theory claims that Earth's Moon is not a naturally solid celestial body, but a hollow or partially hollow artificial structure — possibly an alien-built spacecraft, ancient observation station, or advanced relic from a lost civilization.

While mainstream science considers the Moon a natural satellite formed around 4.5 billion years ago, proponents of this theory point to unusual physical properties, strange seismic data, and mythological references as evidence that the Moon is not what it seems.

History & Key Claims

Seismic "Ringing" Phenomenon (1969):

During Apollo missions, seismometers placed on the Moon recorded seismic activity when rocket stages were intentionally crashed into the lunar surface.

NASA scientists noted the Moon "rang like a bell" for over an hour.

Conspiracists interpret this as evidence of a hollow or metallic interior.

Strange Orbital Properties:

The Moon's size, distance, and perfectly synchronized rotation (showing only one face to Earth) are seen as suspiciously precise.

Some argue these factors suggest artificial placement.

Ancient Myths & Writings:

Various ancient cultures refer to a time "before the Moon" existed (e.g., certain Greek and African legends).

Some theorists suggest the Moon was brought into orbit deliberately.

Possible Purposes According to Believers:

Observation post for alien species monitoring Earth.

Ancient spacecraft long abandoned in orbit.

Gravity stabilizer deliberately engineered to maintain Earth's habitability.

Scientific Counterpoint:

NASA explains the "ringing" as due to the Moon's dry, fractured geology and lack of water to absorb seismic energy.

Orbital synchrony is a common phenomenon known as tidal locking, not evidence of artificiality.

Famous Quotes / Sources

"The Moon is not only an alien base, it is a hollowed-out planetoid placed in orbit intentionally."

— Don Wilson, Our Mysterious Spaceship Moon

"It's easier to explain the non-existence of the Moon than its existence."

— Isaac Asimov, science fiction writer (often quoted by theorists)

"The Moon rang like a bell. That does not happen with solid bodies."

— Dr. Gordon MacDonald, NASA scientist, Apollo era

"The Moon is the Rosetta Stone of the solar system. But maybe it's also an artifact."

— Christopher Knight & Alan Butler, Who Built the Moon?

Real-World Consequences

Pop Culture Inspiration:

The Hollow Moon Theory has inspired books, documentaries, and films like Moonfall (2022) and Iron Sky.

Fuel for Other Conspiracies:

Often tied to claims of alien bases on the Moon, secret NASA footage, and Apollo mission censorship.

Distrust of Official Explanations:

The Moon's unique properties continue to be a talking point for those suspicious of NASA's transparency.

Scientific Pushback:

Lunar scientists emphasize that geophysical data, rock samples, and gravity mapping align with a natural formation model.

Where It Stands Today

While mainstream science rejects the Hollow Moon Theory, it remains a staple in UFO and ancient alien circles. The upcoming Artemis missions, private lunar exploration, and increased lunar imaging will almost certainly reignite debate — especially if unusual structures or anomalies are photographed.

For believers, the Moon isn't just Earth's satellite. It's an ancient machine — one that still hums quietly in the night sky.

Chapter Ninety-One

Section: Space, Aliens and the Unknown

Conspiracy: Flat Moon Theory

Summary

While the Flat Earth Theory has gained notoriety in modern conspiracy circles, a smaller but equally intriguing fringe belief holds that the Moon itself is flat — not a three-dimensional spherical object. Proponents argue that the Moon we see in the night sky is either a flat disc, a projection, or a hologram, positioned in Earth's sky for unknown reasons.

Though far less common than other lunar conspiracies, the Flat Moon Theory is often tied to Flat Earth cosmology, holographic sky models, or claims that space as presented by NASA is entirely fabricated.

History & Key Claims

Origins in Flat Earth Cosmology:

Flat Moon believers often emerge from Flat Earth groups, which see the Moon as part of a dome-enclosed system.

Some suggest the Moon is a luminescent disc, possibly self-illuminated or lit by hidden technology.

Core Arguments:

Lack of Visible Rotation: The Moon always presents the same face to Earth, which believers take as evidence of a stationary projection or disc.

Two-Dimensional Appearance: Through telescopes, the Moon appears relatively flat, with shadows and craters seen as surface textures rather than depth.

"Moon Transparency" Claims: Some observers claim to see stars "through" the Moon during certain phases, suggesting a projection effect.

No Confirmed Landing Evidence: In combination with Moon landing skepticism, some theorists argue the Moon is not a physical object capable of landing spacecraft.

Projection or Hologram Hypotheses:

Some claim the Moon is a hologram projected by satellites, alien technology, or even ancient civilizations.

The so-called "lunar wave" phenomenon (recorded by amateur astronomers as a visual disturbance on the Moon's surface) is cited as evidence of digital projection errors.

Scientific Counterpoint:

Astronomers point out that:

Lunar laser ranging experiments show the Moon is solid and three-dimensional.

Lunar phases, eclipses, and gravitational effects require a spherical Moon.

The "lunar wave" videos are likely caused by atmospheric distortion.

Famous Quotes / Sources

"The Moon is no rock in space. It's a light, a disc — part of the show above our heads."

— Eric Dubay, Flat Earth proponent

"What we call the Moon is a projection on the firmament."

— Mark Sargent, Flat Earth speaker

"I've seen the lunar wave. It's like a glitch. The Moon is a screen."

— Crow777, YouTube conspiracy channel

"If the Moon is flat, then the tides, eclipses, and space travel are all lies."

— Debunking Flat Moon Theory, Astronomy Now

Real-World Consequences

Flat Earth Overlap:

The Flat Moon Theory is most often an extension of Flat Earth belief systems, amplifying distrust in NASA and mainstream astronomy.

Online Communities:

While small, groups on YouTube, Telegram, and Reddit exchange "evidence" of the Moon's flatness, especially during eclipse livestreams.

Lunar Wave Obsession:

The "lunar wave" videos have become a focal point for believers, inspiring countless amateur observations.

Public Mockery:

The Flat Moon Theory is often ridiculed, even by other conspiracy communities, as one of the least supported space-related claims.

Where It Stands Today

The Flat Moon Theory remains a niche belief, dwarfed by more popular space conspiracies like the Hollow Moon or Moon Landing Hoax. Mainstream science continues to reject the claim outright, citing centuries of lunar observation, photography, and exploration data.

Nevertheless, in certain online echo chambers, the Moon is not a natural body, but a stage prop in the grand illusion of the sky. For these believers, its flatness is yet another sign that our cosmic reality has been fabricated for control.

Chapter Ninety-Two

Section: Space, Aliens and the Unknown

Conspiracy: Alien Autopsy Videos

Summary

The Alien Autopsy videos are a set of alleged film reels showing the examination of extraterrestrial beings — most famously tied to the 1947 Roswell UFO incident. The most well-known footage surfaced in 1995, purportedly showing a military autopsy of an alien body recovered from the Roswell crash.

The footage, released by British producer Ray Santilli, became a cultural phenomenon, sparking global debate. While Santilli later admitted it was a "recreation" of lost original footage, he insisted that real material once existed. Despite heavy skepticism, alien autopsy videos remain a cornerstone of UFO conspiracy lore.

History & Key Claims

The 1995 Ray Santilli Release:

Santilli claimed to have obtained the film from a retired U.S. military cameraman.

The footage shows:

A humanoid alien body with an enlarged head and black eyes.

Two surgeons in protective suits conducting an autopsy.

Detailed internal anatomy inconsistent with humans.

The film aired on Fox Television in the U.S., titled Alien Autopsy: Fact or Fiction?, drawing huge ratings.

Immediate Controversy:

Skeptics noted issues:

Surgical techniques appeared primitive.

Props and models were suspected.

The camera work was inconsistent with professional military documentation.

Santilli eventually admitted the footage was a staged reconstruction, but claimed original film existed but degraded over time.

Later Autopsy Claims:

Additional alleged alien autopsy clips have surfaced online over the years.

Most are quickly dismissed as hoaxes or movie props.

Some tie into Roswell, while others are linked to different crashes (e.g., the alleged 1969 Soviet retrieval in Sverdlovsk).

Conspiracy Claims:

The video was discredited intentionally to distract from real evidence.

Autopsy footage is genuine but kept classified, with staged videos released to mock and discredit the idea.

Famous Quotes / Sources

"The footage you saw was a reconstruction… but it was based on real material I was shown."

— Ray Santilli, 2006

"This is the most convincing fake I've ever seen — and that's the point."

— Philip Mantle, UFO researcher

"They don't debunk the footage because it's fake. They debunk it because it's real and they need plausible deniability."

— UFO community forum post

"The alien autopsy is the most brilliant hoax… or the most terrifying truth shown on television."

— Jonathan Frakes, host of Beyond Belief: Fact or Fiction

Real-World Consequences

Mass Cultural Impact:

The footage influenced films like Signs and The X-Files, and became an icon of 1990s UFO culture.

Alien autopsy parodies appeared on shows like South Park and in pop culture merchandise.

Skepticism and Distrust:

The admission of fakery fueled skepticism of all UFO evidence, but also convinced some believers that cover-ups were actively engineered.

Boost to UFO Research:

Ironically, the controversy helped spark more formal UFO investigations, with researchers and whistleblowers seeking "real" classified evidence.

Tourism and Industry:

The video kept Roswell in the spotlight, boosting local tourism and UFO festivals.

Where It Stands Today

The Santilli Alien Autopsy is now widely regarded as a hoax — albeit one of the most famous in UFO history. Yet the persistence of alien crash retrieval stories, combined with ongoing Pentagon UAP disclosures, keeps speculation alive that real footage exists, locked away in military archives.

In UFO conspiracy lore, the alien autopsy videos symbolize the blurry line between truth and manufactured deception — proof to believers that even falsehoods can point toward hidden realities.

Chapter Ninety-Three

Section: Space, Aliens and the Unknown

Conspiracy: Secret Alien Agreements (Eisenhower Treaty)

Summary

The Eisenhower Treaty conspiracy claims that in 1954, U.S. President Dwight D. Eisenhower secretly met with extraterrestrials at Edwards Air Force Base (then Muroc Field) and negotiated a formal agreement between alien visitors and the U.S. government.

According to the theory, the treaty allowed aliens to abduct a limited number of humans for research, in exchange for advanced technology. The meeting is said to have been covered up with a public excuse that Eisenhower had emergency dental surgery.

While there is no official evidence of such a meeting, the story has persisted in UFO lore for decades, fueled by alleged whistleblowers and former military insiders.

History & Key Claims

The Alleged Meeting (1954):

Eisenhower was reportedly scheduled for public appearances but was suddenly absent for a day.

The White House claimed he had chipped a tooth and required emergency dental care.

Conspiracists claim that during this time, he met with two alien delegations:

A group of Nordic-looking extraterrestrials offering spiritual guidance and disarmament.

A group of Grey aliens offering technology in exchange for biological sampling rights.

The treaty was allegedly signed with the Greys.

Key Terms of the Alleged Treaty:

The U.S. would allow limited abductions, provided abductees were returned unharmed.

The U.S. would receive advanced aerospace and communication technology.

Bases would be established for alien research operations (some point to Dulce Base as one such location).

Whistleblower Testimonies:

Phil Schneider, a former geologist and contractor, claimed to have seen evidence of underground alien bases linked to these agreements.

William Cooper, a former intelligence officer, referenced the treaty in his book Behold a Pale Horse.

Other alleged insiders describe a multi-decade cooperation program involving spacecraft reverse-engineering and human genetic experiments.

Skeptical Counterpoint:

Historians and Eisenhower biographers dismiss the treaty story as unfounded rumor, pointing out no credible records or corroborating documentation.

Famous Quotes / Sources

"He met with them — they weren't hostile, but they had their own agenda."

— William Cooper, Behold a Pale Horse

"The dental surgery story was a cover. He wasn't at the dentist. He was in the desert."

— Anonymous Air Force officer testimony

"We have been in contact with alien civilizations since the 1950s."

— Phil Schneider, public lecture

"Eisenhower did meet with aliens… but only in the imaginations of UFO writers."

— Michael Salla, exopolitics researcher

Real-World Consequences

Integration into UFO Lore:

The Eisenhower Treaty has become part of a larger narrative about government-alien collaboration.

Often tied to Area 51, Project Blue Book, and alleged secret space programs.

Public Fascination:

Books, documentaries, and lectures continually revisit the story, keeping it alive in UFO culture.

Eisenhower's "disappearance" remains a point of intrigue for conspiracy enthusiasts.

Deepening Distrust in Government:

Believers cite the treaty as proof of government secrecy and willingness to sacrifice citizens for technological gain.

Cultural References:

Films like Close Encounters of the Third Kind and The X-Files episodes subtly mirror aspects of the alleged treaty.

Where It Stands Today

Mainstream historians dismiss the Eisenhower Treaty as a myth, with no tangible evidence to support the claim. However, within UFO and disclosure communities, it remains a foundational story about early formal contact between humans and extraterrestrials.

For believers, the treaty is less about Eisenhower specifically and more about the idea that governments have longstanding, secret relationships with alien civilizations — relationships hidden under layers of diplomacy, denial, and plausible cover stories.

Chapter Ninety-Four

Section: Space, Aliens and the Unknown

Conspiracy: The Secret Space Program

Summary

The Secret Space Program (SSP) theory claims that humanity has operated advanced off-world operations for decades, hidden from the public and funded through black budgets. Allegedly, these programs involve interstellar travel, colonies on Mars, moon bases, and fleets of spacecraft far beyond officially acknowledged technology.

Supporters claim the SSP is a joint operation involving military branches, intelligence agencies, private aerospace corporations, and extraterrestrial allies. Critics dismiss it as science fiction mixed with Cold War paranoia, but insiders and alleged whistleblowers keep the narrative alive.

History & Key Claims

Origins in Cold War Black Projects:

The idea of secret space activity dates back to the 1950s–60s when vast sums were poured into classified aerospace research.

The U.S. Air Force, DARPA, and NASA are often cited as fronts for deeper programs.

Core Allegations:

Breakaway Civilization: A technologically advanced faction of humanity operates off-world, independent of Earth governments.

Reverse-Engineered Tech: Craft developed from recovered alien technology (often linked to Roswell or Area 51).

Space Fleets: Naval-style fleets operate in deep space under names like "Solar Warden."

Moon & Mars Bases: Permanent facilities exist on the Moon's far side and on Mars, often built with alien cooperation.

Secret Treaties: Agreements between extraterrestrials and Earth governments govern resource extraction, technology exchange, and secrecy.

Notable Whistleblower Claims:

Gary McKinnon (hacker) claimed to find records of "non-terrestrial officers" in U.S. military files.

Corey Goode, self-proclaimed SSP insider, describes 20-year "service tours" in space, followed by memory wiping.

William Tompkins, aerospace engineer, claimed to have worked on naval space carriers in collaboration with alien races.

Why Secrecy?:

Public disclosure could destabilize energy markets, religion, and global power structures.

Maintaining technological advantage over rival nations is a strategic priority.

Famous Quotes / Sources

"The Solar Warden fleet has been operational since the 1980s."

— Gary McKinnon, computer hacker

"I served for 20 years on Mars as part of the Earth Defense Force."

— Corey Goode, SSP whistleblower

"Much of the advanced technology we see today is decades old in black projects."

— William Tompkins, aerospace engineer

"They are using our taxpayer dollars for a breakaway civilization we'll never see."

— Anonymous SSP believer

Real-World Consequences

Public Fascination & Cultural Influence:

The SSP is referenced in:

Star Trek (inspired by real NASA consultants)

The Expanse

Iron Sky films

Documentaries, podcasts, and conventions keep the theory alive.

Impact on UFO Disclosure Movement:

SSP claims are often tied to Disclosure Project efforts, demanding declassification of advanced propulsion tech.

Skepticism & Criticism:

Mainstream scientists point to no physical evidence of human-built craft operating beyond Earth orbit.

Some whistleblowers are criticized for contradictory testimony and commercialization of their claims.

Where It Stands Today

The Secret Space Program remains unverified but deeply embedded in UFO and exopolitical circles. It ties together elements of:

Alien treaties

Black budget projects

Reverse-engineered spacecraft

With recent Pentagon UAP reports and private companies like SpaceX reaching Mars-capable technology, believers argue we are on the verge of partial disclosure.

For supporters, the SSP represents the ultimate cover-up — a parallel human civilization quietly exploring the stars while the rest of us remain grounded.

Chapter Ninety-Five

Section: Space, Aliens and the Unknown

Conspiracy: The International Space Station Is Fake

Summary

The International Space Station (ISS) is one of humanity's most visible symbols of space exploration — a joint project between NASA, Roscosmos, ESA, JAXA, and CSA. Conspiracists, however, claim the ISS is either not in orbit at all or that much of the footage presented to the public is faked on Earth using underwater training facilities, zero-gravity aircraft, or CGI.

This theory stems from deep mistrust of space agencies, combined with observations of broadcast anomalies such as harness reflections, glitches, and astronauts allegedly "grabbing wires."

History & Key Claims

The ISS Program:

First components launched in 1998.

Permanent human occupancy began in 2000.

It is visible from Earth as a bright moving point of light, often cited by scientists as proof of its reality.

Core Allegations:

Fake Footage: Spacewalks and live feeds are allegedly filmed in neutral buoyancy pools or parabolic flights.

Harness Anomalies: Viewers claim to see astronauts attached to invisible harnesses in "zero gravity."

Green Screen & CGI: Backgrounds and objects are believed to be digitally added during live broadcasts.

Scripted Events: Publicized events (school calls, science demos) are allegedly choreographed to reinforce the illusion.

Why Fake It?:

Maintain funding and public support for space agencies.

Hide the true nature of space travel limitations.

Conceal classified projects or secret space operations.

Scientific Counterpoint:

The ISS can be tracked by amateur astronomers.

Thousands of people worldwide have photographed it passing overhead.

Multiple nations participate, making a coordinated hoax improbable.

Famous Quotes / Sources

"The ISS is not 250 miles above Earth. It's in a film studio or underwater."

— Eric Dubay, Flat Earth proponent

"They are using neutral buoyancy labs and CGI to fool us."

— Anonymous ISS skeptic, YouTube

"I have watched the ISS with my own telescope. It's real."

— Chris Hadfield, Canadian astronaut

"They are playing a movie in space for the masses."

— Forum post, Flat Earth Society

Real-World Consequences

Internet Debates:

ISS conspiracy videos are widely shared on YouTube, often highlighting "glitches" in live NASA feeds.

Public Distrust in Space Agencies:

Reinforces broader claims that NASA fabricates space footage, tying into Moon Landing Hoax and Mars Rover conspiracies.

Amateur Astronomy Engagement:

Ironically, some skeptics have been convinced by tracking and photographing the ISS themselves.

Pop Culture:

Films like Gravity and Life depicting space stations have fueled perceptions that space footage looks cinematic because it is cinematic.

Where It Stands Today

The ISS fake theory remains popular in Flat Earth and anti-NASA circles, but is rejected by astronomers, scientists, and most independent observers. While many "anomalies" can be explained by video compression, lighting, or optical effects, the belief persists due to confirmation bias and deep suspicion of institutional truth.

To believers, the ISS is the greatest stage set ever built — not orbiting Earth, but orbiting public imagination.

Chapter Ninety-Six

Section: Space, Aliens and the Unknown

Conspiracy: Astronauts Are Actors

Summary

This conspiracy claims that astronauts are not genuine spacefarers, but actors trained to perform scripted roles for space agencies. According to proponents, much of what the public sees — from ISS live streams to Moon landings — is carefully staged, with astronauts serving more as public relations figures than actual explorers.

The idea ties into broader claims that space travel is faked or limited, with astronauts participating in an ongoing deception for political, financial, or strategic reasons.

History & Key Claims

Roots in the Moon Landing Hoax Theory:

Accusations of astronauts being "actors" began in 1969, when Apollo 11's crew was accused of faking their mission in a studio.

Critics noted awkward press conferences, claiming the astronauts looked "uncomfortable" or "guilty."

Training & PR Duties:

Astronauts undergo intense media preparation, which conspiracists interpret as acting training.

Public appearances, scripted communications, and educational events are seen as performances to maintain the illusion.

Video Anomalies:

Footage from ISS and shuttle missions is claimed to show:

Astronauts on wires or harnesses.

Dropped props that appear to "bounce" due to gravity.

Glitches in live feeds suggesting green screen use.

Public Persona vs. Secret Role:

Some versions of the theory argue astronauts do go to space, but their real missions are classified, with public footage staged for mass consumption.

Others claim astronauts never leave Earth, performing in simulation facilities and neutral buoyancy pools.

Scientific Counterpoint:

Thousands of independent photos, amateur radio communications, and global tracking evidence support the reality of space missions.

Astronaut anomalies are often due to video compression, zero-G motion oddities, or equipment interference.

Famous Quotes / Sources

"They're not astronauts, they're actors."

— Common phrase among Moon hoax believers

"If you watch their press conferences, you can see the guilt on their faces."

— Bart Sibrel, Moon hoax proponent

"They have the best jobs in the world: pretend to be space heroes and collect a paycheck."

— Forum post, r/Conspiracy

"I've spoken to astronauts. They risk their lives. The accusations are absurd."

— Chris Hadfield, former ISS commander

Real-World Consequences

Public Harassment:

Astronauts, including Buzz Aldrin and Chris Hadfield, have been confronted by conspiracy theorists accusing them of lying.

Aldrin famously punched a man who accused him of faking Apollo 11.

Erosion of Public Trust in NASA:

Contributes to skepticism of all NASA achievements, including the ISS and Mars missions.

Social Media Spread:

Video compilations of "astronaut mistakes" are shared as proof of staged events.

Pop Culture Depictions:

Films and series (Capricorn One, Moonwalkers) depict staged missions, reinforcing the plausibility for some viewers.

Where It Stands Today

The "astronauts are actors" theory remains popular in Flat Earth and Moon hoax circles, despite strong counter-evidence. For believers, astronauts are more showmen than explorers, part of a grand stage production designed to inspire awe and maintain funding.

In reality, astronauts endure extreme physical training, dangerous missions, and verifiable communications from orbit. But for those who distrust space agencies, they are simply performers reading lines from 250 miles up — or a soundstage much closer to home.

Chapter Ninety-Seven

Section: Space, Aliens and the Unknown

Conspiracy: Antarctica Alien Base

Summary

The Antarctica Alien Base conspiracy claims that beneath the ice of Earth's southernmost continent lies a massive extraterrestrial facility, ancient or active, hidden from public view. Proponents argue that this base may house alien craft, technology, or even alien life, and that world governments have established restricted zones to conceal its existence.

The theory draws from restricted access to Antarctica, unusual aerial images, and historic expeditions that ended mysteriously. It often connects to broader narratives involving Nazi escape myths, UFO sightings, and secret global treaties.

History & Key Claims

Antarctic Treaty (1959):

Signed by 12 nations, the treaty prohibits military activity and reserves the continent for scientific research.

Conspiracists interpret the strict controls on access as evidence of a deeper secret.

Operation Highjump (1946–47):

Large U.S. Navy mission led by Admiral Richard E. Byrd.

Officially a training mission, but conspiracy theorists claim Byrd encountered flying discs emerging from the ice.

Byrd allegedly described "an enemy with incredible capabilities" in later interviews.

Satellite & Aerial Anomalies:

Google Earth users have identified strange structures, openings, and geometric shapes in Antarctic ice.

These are claimed to be entrances to alien or ancient facilities.

Nazi Connection:

Rumors suggest Nazis built secret bases in Antarctica during World War II, possibly with alien assistance.

"Base 211" is frequently mentioned in speculative literature.

Alien & Ancient Civilizations:

Some versions claim the base predates human civilization, built by ancient alien visitors.

Others argue it's an active alien outpost working in cooperation with governments.

Scientific Counterpoint:

Most anomalies are explained as natural formations, shadows, or ice melt patterns.

Operation Highjump's dangers were due to extreme weather, not UFO encounters.

Famous Quotes / Sources

"We have found the most incredible place on Earth — but it must remain hidden."

— Attributed to Admiral Byrd (often disputed)

"Antarctica is not what they tell us. It's the gateway to another world."

— David Wilcock, alternative researcher

"There is something about Antarctica that governments fear to reveal."

— Linda Moulton Howe, investigative journalist

"They are not just penguins down there."

— Anonymous military source, UFO conference

Real-World Consequences

Public Fascination:

Antarctica's inaccessibility fuels curiosity and endless speculation.

Documentaries, novels, and games like The Thing and XCOM feature Antarctic alien bases.

Tourism Restrictions:

Strictly limited tourism and controlled flight paths are seen by believers as part of the cover-up.

International Secrecy Narrative:

The Antarctic Treaty's unusual multinational cooperation feeds theories of shared alien secrets.

Integration into UFO Lore:

The alien base theory often ties into Secret Space Program, Eisenhower Treaty, and Ancient Alien civilizations narratives.

Where It Stands Today

While mainstream science attributes Antarctic mysteries to geology, climate, and ice dynamics, believers see the frozen continent as Earth's most guarded secret.

For them, Antarctica is not just a barren ice desert — it's the entrance to humanity's biggest hidden truth: that we are not alone, and that alien contact is far closer than we think.

Chapter Ninety-Eight

Section: Space, Aliens and the Unknown

Conspiracy: Operation Highjump Cover-Up

Summary

Operation Highjump was a 1946–47 U.S. Navy expedition to Antarctica, led by Rear Admiral Richard E. Byrd. Officially, it was a large-scale training mission to test equipment and personnel in extreme cold. Conspiracists, however, claim the mission's true purpose was to investigate — and confront — mysterious phenomena beneath the Antarctic ice, including alien craft, advanced technology, and hidden civilizations.

According to the cover-up theory, Operation Highjump ended prematurely after encounters with unknown aerial craft. The U.S. government allegedly suppressed details to avoid public panic.

History & Key Claims

Official Operation Details:

Involved 13 ships, 33 aircraft, and over 4,000 personnel.

Objective: Establish a U.S. research base and test military readiness in polar conditions.

Planned for 6–8 months, the mission was abruptly terminated after just 8 weeks.

Admiral Byrd's Alleged Statements:

In interviews, Byrd warned of an enemy capable of flying from pole to pole at incredible speeds.

Conspiracists claim this was a reference to advanced craft (possibly alien or Nazi) encountered during the mission.

Byrd's diary — of disputed authenticity — describes a flight beyond the ice to a hidden land with advanced beings.

Nazi & UFO Connection:

Some versions allege remnants of Nazi Germany established a secret Antarctic base (Base 211), possibly in alliance with aliens.

Operation Highjump was supposedly an attempt to destroy or capture this base.

Aircraft & Combat Claims:

Stories emerged of disc-shaped craft attacking Navy planes and ships.

Loss of aircraft and personnel was officially attributed to weather and accidents, but theorists claim these were combat losses.

Scientific Counterpoint:

Most historians explain the early termination as a result of harsh weather, logistical challenges, and mechanical issues.

There is no verified evidence of combat or alien encounters.

Famous Quotes / Sources

"Admiral Byrd spoke of an enemy that could fly from pole to pole at incredible speeds."

— Chilean newspaper El Mercurio, 1947

"There is a new world beyond the Pole, a land of everlasting mystery."

— Attributed to Admiral Byrd

"Operation Highjump was more than training — it was a battle."

— Conspiracy lecturer, 2005 UFO Congress

"If there was nothing to hide, why end the mission months early?"

— Common question in UFO forums

Real-World Consequences

Mythologizing of Operation Highjump:

The mission has become central to Antarctica conspiracy theories, blending alien, Nazi, and lost civilization narratives.

UFO Community Integration:

Frequently referenced alongside the Eisenhower Treaty, Antarctica Alien Base, and Secret Space Program.

Public Fascination with Byrd:

Byrd's expeditions (and rumored diaries) have cemented his role as a mysterious figure in polar exploration lore.

Pop Culture Influence:

Films like The Thing, Iron Sky, and Hellboy draw from Highjump-inspired myths.

Where It Stands Today

Operation Highjump is officially remembered as a remarkable Antarctic expedition cut short by environmental hardship. In conspiracy circles, it's seen as one of the most compelling military cover-ups of all time — proof that Antarctica hides technological and extraterrestrial secrets governments are unwilling to reveal.

For believers, Highjump isn't just a training mission. It's the closest humanity has come to an open confrontation with the unknown.

Chapter Ninety-Nine

Section: Space, Aliens and the Unknown

Conspiracy: Saturn Is a Stargate

Summary

The Saturn Stargate theory claims that the planet Saturn is not merely a gas giant, but a cosmic gateway or interdimensional portal — potentially controlled or monitored by advanced extraterrestrials or ancient deities. Proponents point to Saturn's hexagonal polar storm, its ring system, and the recurring symbolism of Saturn in ancient cultures and modern secret societies as evidence of a hidden purpose.

While mainstream science sees Saturn as a natural planet, conspiracy theorists and occult researchers believe it plays a central role in interplanetary travel, consciousness manipulation, and alien contact.

History & Key Claims

Ancient Worship of Saturn:

Known as Cronus in Greek mythology and Shani in Hindu astrology, Saturn has long been associated with time, control, and hidden power.

Some researchers argue ancient civilizations viewed Saturn as a "sun" in the distant past or a celestial ruler.

Hexagon at the North Pole:

NASA's Voyager and Cassini missions photographed a persistent hexagonal storm at Saturn's north pole.

Theorists claim the geometric shape is artificial or technologically influenced, serving as a dimensional gateway.

Rings as Artificial Structures:

Some believe Saturn's rings are engineered constructs — massive artificial systems functioning as antennas, energy collectors, or launch structures for ships.

Occult & Symbolic Connections:

The black cube (symbol of Saturn) appears in:

Islamic Kaaba in Mecca

Jewish tefillin

Corporate and pop culture symbolism

Conspiracists link this to Saturn worship by secret societies like the Freemasons or the Black Nobility.

Stargate Hypothesis:

Saturn is theorized to be a dimensional portal used by extraterrestrials to travel vast distances.

UFO activity near Saturn has been reported by amateur astronomers, allegedly captured in NASA imagery (though dismissed as artifacts).

Scientific Counterpoint:

Astronomers attribute the hexagon to fluid dynamics and the rings to natural ice and rock particles influenced by gravity.

Famous Quotes / Sources

"Saturn is not what we think. It's the gateway to the stars."

— David Icke, conspiracy researcher

"The hexagon is a standing wave — a technological marker."

— Norman Bergrun, Ringmakers of Saturn

"Saturn worship is at the core of global control systems."

— Jordan Maxwell, occult researcher

"Saturn's rings are natural. The cube and hexagon are symbolic interpretations, not evidence of alien tech."

— Phil Plait, astronomer

Real-World Consequences

Integration into Esoteric Movements:

Saturn is central to many New Age and occult interpretations involving energy manipulation and spiritual control.

Pop Culture Echoes:

Films and series like Interstellar, 2001: A Space Odyssey, and Stargate SG-1 use Saturn-like imagery in connection with wormholes or gateways.

Fuel for Alien Travel Theories:

The Saturn Stargate theory ties into the Secret Space Program, suggesting Saturn is a major travel hub for advanced civilizations.

Conspiracy Symbolism:

Observers point to corporate logos, architecture, and fashion allegedly containing hidden Saturnian references.

Where It Stands Today

Mainstream astronomy rejects the idea of Saturn as anything more than a natural planet with stunning atmospheric and ring features. But in conspiracy and esoteric circles, Saturn remains a symbol of hidden cosmic power and potentially a literal gateway to other worlds.

For believers, NASA's images aren't just science — they're hints of the interstellar highway we're not meant to use.

Chapter One Hundred

Section: Space, Aliens and the Unknown

Conspiracy: Time Travel via Wormholes

Summary

The Time Travel via Wormholes conspiracy claims that governments and advanced scientific programs have discovered methods to travel through time by exploiting natural or artificially created wormholes. These wormholes — hypothetical shortcuts through space-time — are said to be used for temporal travel, covert missions, and contact with future or past civilizations.

While mainstream science acknowledges wormholes as a theoretical possibility under Einstein's general relativity, conspiracy theorists argue that practical applications have been secretly achieved by military or alien technology, often tied to black projects, secret space programs, and alien alliances.

History & Key Claims

Scientific Foundation:

Albert Einstein and Nathan Rosen first proposed the concept of "Einstein-Rosen bridges" (wormholes) in 1935.

Modern physics accepts wormholes as a theoretical construct but highlights the enormous energy and stability issues involved.

Alleged Programs & Experiments:

Project Pegasus: Claims that the U.S. government developed time travel through wormholes in the 1970s, with participants allegedly meeting historical figures and traveling to Mars.

Montauk Project: Rumored experiments at Montauk Air Force Station in New York allegedly involved time travel, mind control, and interdimensional portals.

CERN & LHC: Some theorists claim the Large Hadron Collider is capable of creating micro-wormholes that allow controlled jumps through space and time.

Alien Involvement:

Wormhole technology is often linked to extraterrestrials who allegedly use them for interstellar travel.

Claims suggest certain alien civilizations taught humans to create artificial wormholes.

Anomalous Phenomena as Evidence:

Unexplained disappearances, time slip stories, and sightings of advanced craft vanishing instantly are cited as possible wormhole use.

Historical anomalies (e.g., the "Philadelphia Experiment") are tied to early wormhole-related research.

Scientific Counterpoint:

Wormholes remain mathematically possible but unproven.

Stabilizing a wormhole would require exotic matter far beyond current technology.

Famous Quotes / Sources

"The U.S. government has been teleporting people through space-time since the 1970s."

— Andrew Basiago, Project Pegasus whistleblower

"Wormholes are the cosmic subway — but only a select few have the ticket."

— UFO community saying

"The Montauk experiments were real — I was there."

— Preston Nichols, Montauk Project witness

"If wormholes exist, they could allow for time travel — but we've seen no evidence of their creation."

— Stephen Hawking

Real-World Consequences

Cultural Influence:

Time travel via wormholes is a staple in science fiction (Interstellar, Contact, Stargate).

The conspiracy draws attention every time CERN runs a major experiment.

Integration into Secret Space Lore:

Often linked with Secret Space Program claims, suggesting wormholes are used for rapid travel between planets or timelines.

Fear of Temporal Manipulation:

Some theorists believe wormholes are used to alter historical events to benefit certain powers.

Others fear future knowledge is being weaponized.

Scientific Curiosity:

Public fascination has led to more mainstream discussion of wormholes in documentaries, TED talks, and academic speculation.

Where It Stands Today

Mainstream science maintains wormholes as theoretical constructs without evidence of real-world creation or control. However, in conspiracy circles, wormhole technology is seen as actively in use, hidden within the world's deepest classified programs.

To believers, wormholes are the ultimate tool of control — a way to reshape history, conceal alien presence, and maintain the secrecy of advanced civilizations.

Chapter One Hundred and One

Section: Celebrity & Pop Culture Conspiracies

Conspiracy: Paul McCartney Is Dead

Summary

The "Paul Is Dead" conspiracy claims that Paul McCartney of The Beatles died in a car accident in late 1966 and was secretly replaced by a lookalike — often named "William Campbell" or "Billy Shears" in the lore. According to believers, the surviving Beatles and their management covered up his death to avoid mass hysteria, leaving hidden clues in lyrics, album covers, and music played backward.

Though dismissed as a hoax by McCartney himself, the theory remains one of the most enduring celebrity conspiracies.

History & Key Claims

The Alleged Death (1966):

The theory claims McCartney died in a car crash on November 9, 1966.

The Beatles supposedly held a lookalike contest and recruited "Billy Shears" to replace him.

Clues in Album Art & Music:

Sgt. Pepper's Lonely Hearts Club Band: Believers interpret the cover as a funeral scene, with Paul in a black suit.

Abbey Road: Interpreted as a funeral procession:

John (white suit) as priest

Ringo (black suit) as undertaker

Paul (barefoot, out of step) as corpse

George (denim) as gravedigger

Magical Mystery Tour: Paul is dressed as a walrus — a symbol of death in certain cultures.

Revolution 9 (played backwards): Sounds like "Turn me on, dead man."

"Clues" in Lyrics:

"He blew his mind out in a car" (A Day in the Life).

"The walrus was Paul" (Glass Onion).

"Billy Shears" is introduced at the start of Sgt. Pepper's.

McCartney's Response:

Paul has repeatedly joked about the rumor, even titling a 1993 live album Paul Is Live.

Famous Quotes / Sources

"Reports of my death have been greatly exaggerated."

— Paul McCartney

"If you play 'Revolution 9' backwards, you hear 'turn me on, dead man.'"

— Common fan claim

"It's the greatest hoax ever pulled by a rock band."

— R. Gary Patterson, The Walrus Was Paul

Real-World Consequences

Cultural Phenomenon:

The theory exploded in 1969 when U.S. college radio began circulating the "Paul Is Dead" rumor.

Sparked decades of Beatles analysis and pop culture fascination.

Media Coverage:

Covered in Life magazine, documentaries, and multiple books.

Continues to appear in podcasts, YouTube breakdowns, and forums.

Impact on McCartney's Image:

Paul has leaned into the myth occasionally, using it as a tongue-in-cheek marketing boost.

Where It Stands Today

The "Paul Is Dead" theory is widely recognized as one of the most famous musical urban legends. While there's no credible evidence to support it, the abundance of "clues" has kept the story alive for over 50 years.

For conspiracy enthusiasts, it's less about proving Paul is dead and more about enjoying the treasure hunt of hidden messages in one of the most influential bands of all time.

Chapter One Hundred and Two

Section: Celebrity & Pop Culture Conspiracies

Conspiracy: Avril Lavigne Replaced by Clone

Summary

The Avril Lavigne replacement theory claims that the Canadian pop star died in the early 2000s and was secretly replaced by a body double named Melissa Vandella. According to the theory, Melissa had originally been hired as a stand-in for publicity events but assumed Avril's identity full-time after her alleged death.

Believers point to changes in Avril's appearance, voice, and personality, as well as differences in lyrical style between her early and later albums, as evidence of the swap.

History & Key Claims

The Alleged Death (2003):

Theory claims Avril died around the time of her Let Go album's success (2002–2003).

She was allegedly struggling with fame and personal issues, including the death of her grandfather.

Melissa, a supposed close friend and stand-in, was trained to replace her.

Evidence Cited by Believers:

Appearance Changes:

Different nose and jawline structure in later photos.

Change in freckles and birthmarks.

Personality Shift:

Early Avril: "Pop-punk rebel" with a tomboy look.

Later Avril: More glam, pop-focused style.

Lyrical Differences:

Transition from angsty tracks (Complicated, Sk8er Boi) to upbeat pop songs (Girlfriend, Hello Kitty).

Hidden Clues:

Lyrics in Under My Skin allegedly reference death and identity.

Photoshoots with "Melissa" written on her hand.

Avril's Response:

Avril has dismissed the theory as ridiculous in interviews, calling it "just another weird Internet rumor."

Famous Quotes / Sources

"It's so dumb. I'm right here."

— Avril Lavigne, 2018 interview

"This is one of the best celebrity conspiracy theories because it blends pop culture with paranoia perfectly."

— BuzzFeed News

"They left clues in the lyrics — she's telling us she's not Avril."

— Avril conspiracy fan page

Real-World Consequences

Viral Internet Phenomenon:

The theory exploded in 2011 when a Brazilian fan blog compiled "evidence."

Continues to resurface on TikTok, Reddit, and YouTube.

Avril's Branding:

The singer occasionally jokes about it, subtly using the theory to fuel fan engagement.

Cultural Fascination with "Replacements":

Similar to the "Paul Is Dead" theory, this taps into a broader pop culture obsession with celebrity doubles.

Where It Stands Today

The Avril replacement theory is generally treated as entertaining urban legend, with no credible evidence. Yet the persistence of "before-and-after" comparisons, lyric analysis, and fan speculation ensures it remains one of the most enduring celebrity conspiracy memes of the Internet age.

Chapter One Hundred and Three

Section: Celebrity & Pop Culture Conspiracies

Conspiracy: Walt Disney Frozen

Summary

The Walt Disney Frozen conspiracy claims that Walt Disney, the legendary animator and founder of The Walt Disney Company, was cryogenically frozen after his death in 1966. According to the theory, his body (or head) was preserved in hopes that future medical technology could revive him.

A modern twist suggests Disney released the film Frozen (2013) to bury Internet searches about his cryogenic preservation, ensuring that searches for "Disney Frozen" would return movie results rather than conspiracy theories.

History & Key Claims

Walt Disney's Death:

Walt Disney died on December 15, 1966 from lung cancer complications.

Official records state he was cremated two days later.

Rumors about his cryogenic preservation began circulating within weeks of his death.

Cryonics & Cultural Context:

The 1960s saw a rise in public fascination with cryonics, the experimental preservation of bodies at low temperatures.

Disney's interest in futuristic technology (e.g., EPCOT) fueled speculation that he might have sought cryogenic preservation.

The Alleged Cryogenic Storage:

Rumors place Disney's frozen body beneath Disneyland's Pirates of the Caribbean ride or in a hidden chamber under Cinderella's Castle at Walt Disney World.

The "Frozen" Movie Connection:

When Frozen was released in 2013, theorists suggested the title was chosen to manipulate search algorithms so that "Disney Frozen" would return film content, not cryonics claims.

Corporate Response:

The Walt Disney Company has never addressed the theory seriously, treating it as an urban legend.

Famous Quotes / Sources

"I don't know if Walt's frozen, but the ride rumors have been great for ticket sales."

— Disney employee (humorously quoted)

"The Frozen movie changed everything — now search engines point to a princess, not a body in a freezer."

— Internet conspiracy blogger

"If anyone could afford cryonics in 1966, it was Walt Disney."

— Cryonics advocate

Real-World Consequences

Tourism & Urban Legend:

The theory adds to Disneyland's mystique, becoming part of park lore.

Tours, books, and fan forums regularly discuss "where Walt is frozen."

Search Engine Manipulation Narrative:

The Frozen film theory is widely cited as an example of corporate control over digital search visibility.

Cryonics Popularity:

The rumor has helped keep cryonics in public discussion, boosting interest in real-world cryonics organizations.

Where It Stands Today

There is no credible evidence that Walt Disney was cryogenically frozen, and official death and cremation records support the mainstream account.

However, the theory remains culturally embedded, amplified by Disney's reputation for secrecy and the Frozen title coincidence. For many, it's less about truth and more about Disney's carefully curated image and control of its own myths.

Chapter One Hundred and Four

Section: Celebrity & Pop Culture Conspiracies

Conspiracy: Beyoncé in the Illuminati

Summary

The Beyoncé Illuminati conspiracy claims that Beyoncé Knowles-Carter is a high-ranking member (or queen figure) in the Illuminati, the alleged secret society said to control the entertainment industry, global politics, and finance. According to believers, her performances, music videos, and public appearances are filled with occult symbols, rituals, and messages of allegiance to the Illuminati and the New World Order.

While Beyoncé has repeatedly mocked and denied the rumors, the theory remains a staple in celebrity conspiracy culture.

History & Key Claims

The Illuminati & Pop Culture:

The Illuminati conspiracy gained popularity in the early 2000s, focusing on symbolism in music videos.

Beyoncé, along with Jay-Z, became central figures due to their immense influence in music, business, and culture.

Symbolic "Evidence" Cited:

Hand Gestures:

The "triangle" hand sign (often made by Jay-Z as the Roc-A-Fella symbol) is linked to the Illuminati's Eye of Providence.

Occult Imagery:

Performances featuring pyramids, all-seeing eyes, and horns are interpreted as occult displays.

Alter Ego:

Beyoncé's alter ego, "Sasha Fierce," is cited as an example of possession or dual identity common in Illuminati/MKUltra lore.

High-Profile Events:

Super Bowl halftime shows, Grammy performances, and music videos (Formation, Run the World, Apeshit) are claimed to be ritualistic ceremonies.

Collaborations with other alleged members (Jay-Z, Rihanna, Kanye West) reinforce the narrative of a connected elite group.

Beyoncé's Response:

Beyoncé has publicly denied involvement, joking about the rumors in interviews and lyrics (e.g., "Y'all haters corny with that Illuminati mess" from Formation).

Famous Quotes / Sources

"Beyoncé is not just a pop star — she's the high priestess of the Illuminati."

— Conspiracy blog Vigilant Citizen

"They can say whatever they want. I'm just doing me."

— Beyoncé, 2013 interview

"When they throw up the Roc symbol, they're signaling allegiance."

— Anonymous Illuminati theorist

Real-World Consequences

Mainstream Popularity of the Theory:

Beyoncé's rumored Illuminati ties have become a meme, referenced in late-night comedy and pop culture.

Fan Engagement:

Fans often create breakdown videos "decoding" her performances, fueling online debate.

Celebrity & Symbolism:

The rumor has helped cement the Illuminati conspiracy as a permanent feature of celebrity culture.

Where It Stands Today

The Beyoncé Illuminati theory remains firmly in pop culture territory — largely treated as entertainment, though some devoted believers view it as serious evidence of elite occult influence.

For Beyoncé, the theory has arguably boosted her cultural impact, making her an enduring icon not just of music, but of modern mythology.

Chapter One Hundred and Five

Section: Celebrity & Pop Culture Conspiracies

Conspiracy: Britney Spears Is Being Controlled

Summary

The Britney Spears control conspiracy claims that the pop star has been under strict control by her management, family, and industry forces for decades, with limited personal freedom and autonomy. While officially framed as a legal conservatorship (2008–2021), theorists argue that Britney's situation was part of a larger system of celebrity mind control — potentially tied to MKUltra-style psychological conditioning used to control high-value entertainers.

This theory blends confirmed legal history with darker allegations of industry exploitation, media manipulation, and coded cries for help.

History & Key Claims

Conservatorship Era (2008–2021):

Britney was placed under a conservatorship controlled by her father, Jamie Spears, following public breakdowns in 2007–2008.

The arrangement allowed her father and legal team to control her finances, career decisions, and personal life.

While conservatorships are typically for those unable to care for themselves, Britney continued performing globally, releasing albums, and generating millions.

"Free Britney" Movement:

Fans launched the #FreeBritney campaign in 2019, alleging she was being held against her will.

Supporters claimed Britney communicated through coded Instagram posts — changing outfits, posting certain emojis, or answering fan questions indirectly.

MKUltra and Industry Control Allegations:

Some theorists link Britney's situation to celebrity mind control, citing:

Her breakdowns as signs of mental strain from programming.

Sudden personality shifts and changes in speech/appearance.

Her being used as a warning or example to other artists.

Court Outcome:

In 2021, Britney's conservatorship was terminated after public and legal battles.

She has since spoken openly about feeling traumatized and controlled during the arrangement.

Famous Quotes / Sources

"I just want my life back. It's been thirteen years. It's enough."

— Britney Spears, 2021 court testimony

"She was a prisoner in plain sight."

— #FreeBritney activist

"The industry makes stars and then breaks them — on purpose."

— Celebrity control conspiracy forum

Real-World Consequences

Cultural Movement:

The #FreeBritney campaign became an international headline story.

Raised broader awareness about abuse of conservatorships.

Public Distrust of Entertainment Industry:

Britney's case reinforced conspiracy beliefs that the music industry controls and exploits its biggest stars.

Legal Precedent:

Britney's battle inspired calls for legal reform around conservatorship law.

Where It Stands Today

Britney Spears' conservatorship is over, but conspiracy theories about her continued control persist. Fans analyze her social media behavior, public appearances, and legal disputes for signs she may still be manipulated.

For many, Britney's story is the most public confirmation that celebrity freedom is not always what it seems.

Chapter One Hundred and Six

Section: Celebrity & Pop Culture Conspiracies

Conspiracy: Elvis Is Alive

Summary

The Elvis Is Alive conspiracy claims that Elvis Presley, the "King of Rock and Roll," faked his death in 1977 and has lived in hiding ever since. According to believers, Elvis staged his death to escape the pressures of fame, financial troubles, or threats from organized crime.

Over the decades, thousands of alleged sightings, photographs, and even interviews have been claimed as evidence that Elvis never truly left the building.

History & Key Claims

The Official Death (August 16, 1977):

Elvis was found unresponsive at Graceland and officially declared dead from heart failure.

He was 42 years old.

The official story cites drug use and health problems.

Suspicious Details Cited by Believers:

Misspelled Name: On his headstone, Elvis' middle name is spelled "Aaron" instead of "Aron" (used during his life).

Rapid Funeral: His funeral was organized quickly, with a closed casket. Some claim the body looked wax-like.

Loose Ends in His Career: Financial problems, declining health, and legal pressures may have prompted a staged exit.

Sightings & Alleged Evidence:

Kalamazoo, Michigan (1980s): Multiple reports claimed Elvis was seen buying food at a local shop.

Airports & Public Venues: Photos have surfaced of older men resembling Elvis.

Graceland Groundskeeper: A man bearing strong resemblance to Elvis has been photographed at Graceland.

Possible Motives:

Escape from fame and constant public pressure.

Protection from alleged threats.

Pursuit of a private life away from the music industry.

Famous Quotes / Sources

"Elvis didn't die, he just went home."

— Men in Black (film quote often cited in jest)

"I saw him at a gas station. It was him — I know it."

— Elvis fan testimony, 1988

"The inconsistencies in the official record cannot be ignored."

— Gail Brewer-Giorgio, Is Elvis Alive?

Real-World Consequences

Cultural Impact:

The theory is one of the most famous in celebrity history, spawning books, documentaries, and films.

Elvis impersonators are sometimes humorously accused of being "the real one in disguise."

Tourism:

Graceland benefits from the enduring myth, as fans flock hoping for a sighting.

Media Cycle:

Every few years, new "evidence" surfaces, reigniting discussion.

Where It Stands Today

The Elvis Is Alive theory remains a cultural phenomenon more than a credible investigation. While no verified evidence supports his survival, the abundance of "sightings" keeps the legend alive.

For believers, the King didn't die in 1977 — he simply left the spotlight for a life of anonymity.

Chapter One Hundred and Seven

Section: Celebrity & Pop Culture Conspiracies

Conspiracy: Tupac Lives in Cuba

Summary

The Tupac Lives in Cuba conspiracy claims that rapper Tupac Shakur, allegedly killed in a drive-by shooting in Las Vegas in 1996, faked his death and escaped to Cuba. According to believers, Tupac fled to avoid gang retaliation, legal troubles, and conflicts with his record label.

The theory is fueled by alleged sightings, cryptic lyrics, posthumous releases, and Tupac's deep admiration for political figures like Assata Shakur, who fled to Cuba in the 1980s.

History & Key Claims

The Official Death (September 7, 1996):

Tupac was shot multiple times after leaving a Mike Tyson fight.

He died in hospital six days later.

The case remains officially unsolved.

Suspicious Circumstances:

No Arrests: Despite multiple witnesses, no one has been convicted of his murder.

Speed of Cremation: Tupac's body was cremated less than 24 hours after death.

Lack of Death Records: Confusion over his autopsy report and official paperwork.

Evidence Cited by Believers:

Lyrics & Interviews:

Tupac frequently referenced faking his death: "I got my mind on my money and my money on the run… I'm alive" (I Ain't Mad at Cha video).

His stage name "Makaveli" references Machiavelli, who wrote about faking one's death.

Sightings:

Multiple alleged sightings in Cuba over the years.

A 2004 photo surfaced showing a man resembling Tupac in Havana.

Cuban Connection:

Tupac admired activist Assata Shakur, who escaped U.S. custody and lives in Cuba.

Conspiracists claim Assata's political network may have helped Tupac relocate.

Famous Quotes / Sources

"Tupac is in Cuba. I saw him."

— Rapper The Outlawz member (unverified claim)

"He loved Assata. Cuba was the safest place for him to go."

— Tupac fan theory

"They want you to believe he's dead, but the music says otherwise."

— Conspiracy blog, Makaveli Lives

Real-World Consequences

Music Industry Speculation:

Posthumous albums like The Don Killuminati: The 7 Day Theory fuel rumors that Tupac recorded extensively in advance.

Cultural Icon Status:

The theory keeps Tupac alive in the cultural imagination, as a symbol of rebellion.

Pop Culture References:

Films, documentaries, and memes frequently joke about Tupac "still recording albums from Cuba."

Where It Stands Today

No verified evidence supports the claim that Tupac escaped to Cuba. His death remains officially unsolved, but the conspiracy persists as part of hip-hop legend and pop culture folklore.

For believers, the absence of closure means Tupac still walks free — just not in the United States.

Chapter One Hundred and Eight

Section: Celebrity & Pop Culture Conspiracies

Conspiracy: Hollywood Satanic Cults

Summary

The Hollywood Satanic Cults conspiracy claims that the entertainment industry is infiltrated — or outright controlled — by occult secret societies practicing Satanic or Luciferian rituals. These cults are believed to operate in elite Hollywood circles, using ritual symbolism, initiation ceremonies, and sacrifices to maintain power, influence, and wealth.

The theory draws from recurring occult imagery in films, music videos, awards shows, and allegations from former insiders claiming the industry hides dark practices beneath its glamorous surface.

History & Key Claims

Historical Foundations:

Rumors of Satanic influence in entertainment date back to the early film industry scandals of the 1920s.

The rise of occult literature in California during the mid-20th century (e.g., Aleister Crowley's influence) fueled speculation.

Symbolism in Media:

Frequent use of pentagrams, all-seeing eyes, goat heads (Baphomet), and black-and-red color schemes in performances.

Award show choreography and music videos are interpreted as public rituals.

Examples often cited:

Katy Perry's 2014 Dark Horse Grammy performance.

Madonna's repeated use of religious and occult imagery.

Lil Nas X's "Montero" music video.

Alleged Industry Practices:

Initiation rituals for rising stars.

Blood oaths and symbolic "selling of the soul."

Protection for insiders accused of crimes in exchange for loyalty.

Whistleblower & Insider Claims:

Occasional interviews or leaked accounts describe ritual parties and industry "elites" engaging in ceremonial acts.

These accounts are often vague or unverified but feed public suspicion.

Mainstream Skepticism:

Most of these elements are attributed to shock marketing, artistic expression, or publicity stunts.

Famous Quotes / Sources

"Hollywood is run by Satanic cults — it's hidden in plain sight."

— Anonymous "industry insider"

"They love using symbols. It's not just art; it's a signal to those in the know."

— Vigilant Citizen

"I play with symbolism because it's provocative, not because I worship the devil."

— Madonna, interview

Real-World Consequences

Cultural Influence:

The theory shapes how audiences view celebrity performances, with every awards show scrutinized for "rituals."

Public Distrust of Entertainment Industry:

Feeds the belief that Hollywood protects its own and hides deeper agendas.

Integration with Other Conspiracies:

Often tied to Illuminati, MKUltra, and Adrenochrome theories.

Where It Stands Today

While there is no confirmed evidence of a literal Hollywood Satanic cult, the theory thrives on symbolism, secrecy, and real cases of exploitation within the industry. For believers, the flashing lights and red carpets are simply the ceremonial mask of a darker hidden order.

Chapter One Hundred and Nine

Section: Celebrity & Pop Culture Conspiracies

Conspiracy: The Simpsons Predict Everything

Summary

The conspiracy that "The Simpsons Predict Everything" suggests that the long-running animated series has repeatedly shown events, inventions, and political outcomes years before they happen in real life. Some believe this is because writers have inside knowledge, while more extreme theories claim the show's creators are connected to secret societies or time travel projects.

From Donald Trump's presidency to tech innovations, the sheer number of accurate "predictions" has made The Simpsons a recurring focus of pop culture conspiracy talk.

History & Key Claims

Origins of the Theory:

The Simpsons debuted in 1989 and has run for over three decades, making it statistically likely that some plotlines would align with real events.

However, certain episodes seem to depict specific details that later become reality.

Most Famous "Predictions":

Donald Trump Presidency (Bart to the Future, 2000).

Disney Buying 20th Century Fox (shown in 1998).

FaceTime & Smartwatches (episodes in the early 1990s).

Ebola Outbreak Reference (Lisa's Sax, 1997).

Siegfried & Roy Tiger Attack (episode in 1993, real attack in 2003).

Nobel Prize Winner Prediction (Milhouse guesses a winner years before correct outcome).

Higgs Boson Mass (an equation in a 1998 episode approximates it).

Game of Thrones Ending (parallels shown in parody episode).

Theories Explaining the Predictions:

Insider Knowledge: Writers have access to political, corporate, or entertainment leaks.

Time Travel: Creators or connected individuals are allegedly time travelers.

Cultural Programming: The show plants ideas as part of predictive programming for future events.

Creator Response:

Writers claim predictions are a result of satire, research, and coincidences, not hidden knowledge.

Famous Quotes / Sources

"If you write 700 episodes, you're going to get a few things right."

— Al Jean, Simpsons producer

"The writers are plugged in. They're part of the system."

— Conspiracy podcast Predictive Pop Culture

"Sometimes life imitates The Simpsons, and sometimes The Simpsons imitates life."

— Matt Groening, Simpsons creator

Real-World Consequences

Pop Culture Meme:

"The Simpsons predicted it!" has become a global joke and meme format.

Social media regularly revives the theory after each coincidental event.

Distrust of Media:

For some conspiracy-minded viewers, the show is part of media shaping public perception.

Integration with Predictive Programming:

The theory often merges with claims about Hollywood rituals and the Illuminati.

Where It Stands Today

The theory that The Simpsons "predicts everything" is mostly treated as a mix of coincidence, satire, and sharp writing. However, the number of uncanny parallels to real-world events ensures that the show will remain a favorite for conspiracy theorists — and a pop culture touchstone for "hidden in plain sight" discussions.

Chapter One Hundred and Ten

Section: Celebrity & Pop Culture Conspiracies

Conspiracy: Katy Perry Is JonBenét Ramsey

Summary

The Katy Perry–JonBenét Ramsey conspiracy claims that pop star Katy Perry is actually JonBenét Ramsey, the six-year-old beauty pageant contestant who was murdered (or allegedly "went missing") in Boulder, Colorado in 1996. According to the theory, JonBenét's death was faked as part of an elaborate plan, and she was secretly groomed into becoming Katy Perry.

Despite being widely debunked, the theory persists in Internet forums due to facial similarities, voice comparisons, and the enduring mystery of JonBenét's unsolved case.

History & Key Claims

The JonBenét Ramsey Case (1996):

JonBenét was reported missing on December 26, 1996.

A ransom note was found, and her body was later discovered in the family's home.

The case remains officially unsolved.

Rise of Katy Perry:

Katy Perry's career took off in the mid-2000s, leading some to note her physical resemblance to JonBenét as an adult.

Proponents claim her "rise" was orchestrated by powerful insiders.

Evidence Cited by Believers:

Facial Similarities: Side-by-side photos compare their eyes, eyebrows, and smile.

Parents Resemblance: Some claim Perry's parents resemble the Ramseys, suggesting a cover-up or adoption.

Symbolism in Perry's Work: Performances featuring childhood or doll-like imagery are interpreted as hidden nods to her "past identity."

The "No One Died" Theory: Some say JonBenét's death was staged to create a new life away from media attention.

Counterpoint:

JonBenét was six years old in 1996; Katy Perry was twelve at the time — making the theory chronologically impossible.

Famous Quotes / Sources

"This is the most bizarre celebrity conspiracy I've ever seen, but it refuses to die."

— Snopes

"JonBenét didn't die; she became Katy Perry."

— Viral YouTube video claim (2014)

"Katy Perry's childhood photos and birth records completely debunk this."

— FactCheck.org

Real-World Consequences

Internet Virality:

The theory resurfaces regularly on YouTube, TikTok, and Reddit.

Serves as a case study in how celebrity culture and unsolved crimes merge in conspiracy spaces.

Media Mockery:

Both Perry and JonBenét's family have been the subject of jokes and memes about the theory, though neither has formally addressed it.

True Crime & Pop Culture Overlap:

Illustrates how real tragedies are absorbed into celebrity conspiracy myth-making.

Where It Stands Today

The Katy Perry–JonBenét theory is widely regarded as entirely false, with clear timelines disproving it. However, it survives as one of the more sensational Internet conspiracy memes, symbolizing how celebrity identity theories thrive regardless of logic.

Chapter One Hundred and Eleven

Section: Celebrity & Pop Culture Conspiracies

Conspiracy: Lady Gaga Is an MKUltra Puppet

Summary

The conspiracy that Lady Gaga is an MKUltra puppet claims that the pop star is under mind control as part of the entertainment industry's use of psychological conditioning programs. MKUltra was a real CIA program (1950s–1970s) that experimented with mind control techniques; conspiracy theorists believe modern celebrities are placed under similar influence to shape culture and spread symbolic messages for elite agendas.

Gaga's elaborate performances, surreal videos, and frequent occult imagery are cited as evidence of programming, with her alter-egos and erratic fashion interpreted as symptoms of psychological manipulation.

History & Key Claims

MKUltra Program Origins:

The CIA's real MKUltra program tested drugs, hypnosis, and psychological trauma to control behavior.

While declassified in the 1970s, conspiracy theorists claim it never truly ended.

Lady Gaga's Image:

Her debut with Just Dance and Poker Face (2008) introduced her as a provocative, avant-garde artist.

Gaga's alter ego "Joanne" and her various personas are interpreted as programmed identities or "alters" — a term borrowed from trauma-based mind control lore.

Symbolism & Performances:

Heavy use of butterflies (a Monarch mind control symbol).

Masks, veils, and eye-covering (Illuminati symbolism of control and submission).

Elaborate stage sets that echo ritualistic ceremonies.

Videos (Bad Romance, Alejandro) with imagery often analyzed as depicting initiation, death, and rebirth.

Statements Interpreted by Believers:

Gaga's references to "killing off" old personas are viewed as symbolic of reprogramming.

Gaga's Response:

She has addressed the symbolism as artistic expression, dismissing MKUltra claims as Internet fantasy.

Famous Quotes / Sources

"They program her, reprogram her, and send her back out to the masses."

— Vigilant Citizen

"I live for the applause, applause, applause."

— Lady Gaga, lyric often cited as symbolic

"Her use of butterflies is textbook Monarch programming."

— Conspiracy blog, IlluminatiWatcher

Real-World Consequences

Pop Culture Myth:

Gaga has become one of the central figures in Illuminati and MKUltra celebrity theories.

Interpretation of Art:

Her performances are picked apart in online videos, with every prop and lyric assigned symbolic meaning.

Connection to Larger Industry Theories:

Gaga's alleged "programming" is tied to broader claims about Hollywood mind control, alongside Beyoncé, Britney Spears, and Kanye West.

Where It Stands Today

The Lady Gaga MKUltra theory is widely rejected outside conspiracy circles, but thrives online because her deliberately provocative and symbolic art style invites endless decoding.

For believers, Gaga is more than a pop star — she's a controlled vessel for elite cultural engineering.

Chapter 112

Section: Celebrity & Pop Culture Conspiracies

Conspiracy: The Beatles Were a Social Experiment

Summary

The theory that The Beatles were a social experiment claims the band was not just a group of talented musicians but part of a government-backed psychological and cultural operation designed to influence youth, reshape society, and test the power of mass media on behavior.

Supporters argue that the Beatles' unprecedented global reach and dramatic shifts in style, messaging, and public persona were orchestrated by intelligence agencies, think tanks, or elite cultural engineers.

History & Key Claims

Origins of the Theory:

The Beatles' rise in 1963–64 coincided with major cultural change — civil rights, the Cold War, the counterculture movement.

Some believe their fame was too sudden and perfectly timed to be organic.

Alleged Goals of the "Experiment":

Youth Control: Use the Beatles' music and image to shape the values of young people.

Cultural Distraction: Divert public attention from political events (Vietnam War, social unrest).

Drug Culture Introduction: Some point to the Beatles' shift from clean-cut pop to psychedelic experimentation as a tool to normalize LSD use.

Key Evidence Cited by Believers:

Tavistock Institute: Alleged British psychological research group said to have "designed" the Beatles' impact.

Rapid Musical Evolution: From simple love songs to complex, experimental, and politically charged music in just a few years.

Hidden Messaging: Lyrics and album art containing social commentary and symbolic cues.

Official Counterpoint:

Critics point out the band's evolution mirrors organic creative growth influenced by their environment and contemporaries.

Famous Quotes / Sources

"The Beatles were the perfect social experiment — and the experiment worked."

— Conspiracy podcast Hidden History Hour

"We were just a band. We made it up as we went along."

— Paul McCartney

"The timing, the image shifts, the messages — all signs of controlled cultural steering."

— Mark Devlin, Musical Truth

Real-World Consequences

Cultural Suspicion:

The Beatles' central role in 1960s counterculture feeds theories about engineered cultural revolutions.

Integration into Music Industry Conspiracies:

The band is often linked to Paul Is Dead, Illuminati symbolism, and predictive programming narratives.

Academic Analysis:

Some sociologists have studied The Beatles' influence as deliberate cultural engineering, though not as a literal government plot.

Where It Stands Today

The Beatles-as-social-experiment theory remains popular in music conspiracy spaces, blending real cultural impact with speculation about manipulation.

For believers, the Fab Four weren't just musicians — they were the most successful mass psychology project in modern history.

Chapter One Hundred and Thirteen

Section: Celebrity & Pop Culture Conspiracies

Conspiracy: Taylor Swift Is a Clone

Summary

The Taylor Swift clone conspiracy claims that the global pop star is either a laboratory clone or a carefully groomed replacement of a pre-existing figure — most notably said to resemble Zeena LaVey, daughter of Anton LaVey, founder of the Church of Satan. Conspiracists suggest Swift's rise to fame was part of a planned cultural operation, with her image and career trajectory engineered by powerful entities.

While the theory is often treated as tongue-in-cheek, it remains one of the most persistent celebrity identity conspiracies online.

History & Key Claims

The Zeena LaVey Connection:

Zeena LaVey was a prominent public figure in the 1980s and 1990s, known for her platinum blonde hair, red lipstick, and high cheekbones.

Conspiracy forums began circulating side-by-side photos of Zeena and Taylor Swift, noting their striking resemblance.

Believers claim Swift is either a biological clone or symbolic continuation of LaVey to perpetuate influence.

Industry Grooming Allegations:

Theories suggest Swift's rapid success and industry positioning are evidence of an engineered celebrity.

Some claim she was designed to appeal to a wholesome country audience before transitioning to global pop stardom, expanding influence across demographics.

Occult Symbolism in Performances:

Critics of Swift's shows point to alleged occult or Masonic symbols in stage designs, choreography, and costumes.

Some music videos are analyzed for hidden messages and numerology.

Scientific Counterpoint:

Cloning a human being, especially a functioning adult performer, is not supported by current technology or credible evidence.

Famous Quotes / Sources

"Taylor Swift is Zeena LaVey's clone. The resemblance is not a coincidence."

— Viral meme, 2015

"They choose their icons carefully, and Swift is no accident."

— Conspiracy blog, Industry Secrets

"It's flattering to be compared to anyone, but that's not me."

— Zeena LaVey (response to rumor)

Real-World Consequences

Pop Culture Meme:

The theory has become a running Internet joke, often resurfacing during Swift's album releases.

Fan Speculation:

Some fans explore the theory as part of the broader mystique surrounding celebrity identities.

Integration with Other Celebrity Theories:

Links to Illuminati, MKUltra, and industry grooming theories.

Where It Stands Today

The Taylor Swift clone theory is generally seen as entertaining speculation with no credible evidence. Still, the resemblance to Zeena LaVey keeps it alive as one of the more visually compelling celebrity conspiracies.

For believers, Swift's image is not just crafted by PR — it's a direct continuation of a legacy chosen by powerful forces.

Chapter One Hundred and Fourteen

Section: Celebrity & Pop Culture Conspiracies

Conspiracy: Michael Jackson Was Murdered

Summary

The Michael Jackson murder conspiracy claims that the King of Pop's 2009 death from acute propofol intoxication was not an accident, but a planned killing orchestrated by powerful individuals or entities. According to theorists, Jackson was silenced because he knew too much, was preparing to reveal industry secrets, or had become a financial liability to those who profited from him.

While the official account pins blame on Dr. Conrad Murray's negligence, many fans and conspiracy researchers argue there was a larger agenda at play.

History & Key Claims

Official Narrative (2009):

Jackson died on June 25, 2009.

Cause: Cardiac arrest induced by a lethal dose of propofol administered by his doctor.

Dr. Conrad Murray was convicted of involuntary manslaughter in 2011.

Suspicious Circumstances:

Jackson was about to embark on the massive This Is It tour.

Some claim he was under extreme pressure from concert promoters, debt obligations, and corporate interests.

His catalog ownership, especially his stake in Sony/ATV Music Publishing, made him a powerful — and potentially dangerous — figure in the music industry.

Evidence Cited by Believers:

Jackson reportedly spoke of fearing for his life in the months before his death.

Alleged statements to friends: "They are trying to kill me."

Some believe his rehearsal footage for This Is It shows a man too healthy to suddenly die.

Corporate and legal disputes over his music rights intensified shortly before his death.

Theories on Motives:

To gain control of his music catalog.

To silence him from speaking out about industry corruption.

To avoid costly delays or cancellations of the This Is It concerts.

Famous Quotes / Sources

"They want my catalog and they want my life."

— Michael Jackson, alleged private statement

"He was worth more dead than alive to some people."

— Conspiracy documentary, Killing Michael Jackson

"This was not just medical negligence. It was a setup."

— Fan interview outside court

Real-World Consequences

Legal Aftermath:

The conviction of Dr. Murray satisfied some but left many unconvinced about the full truth.

Ongoing Public Suspicion:

Jackson's death continues to be dissected in documentaries, fan investigations, and online forums.

Music Rights Battles:

Sony eventually purchased the remainder of Jackson's music catalog stakes, a fact cited as motive in conspiracy narratives.

Where It Stands Today

The official record blames medical malpractice, but for many, the surrounding circumstances are too convenient for powerful interests. The belief that Jackson was deliberately silenced remains one of the most enduring celebrity death conspiracies.

For believers, Michael Jackson's death was not a tragedy of chance — it was a calculated move to remove a man who had become too powerful and outspoken.

Chapter One Hundred and Fifteen

Section: Celebrity & Pop Culture Conspiracies

Conspiracy: Chris Cornell and Chester Bennington Killed Over Pedo Rings

Summary

The conspiracy surrounding the deaths of Chris Cornell (Soundgarden, Audioslave) and Chester Bennington (Linkin Park) claims that the two musicians were murdered because they were allegedly investigating or preparing to expose powerful child sex trafficking networks.

While the official cause of death for both men was ruled suicide by hanging, conspiracy theorists argue that their activism, connections, and timing point to a coordinated silencing by influential figures connected to the alleged rings.

History & Key Claims

Chris Cornell's Death (May 18, 2017):

Found dead in his Detroit hotel room after a Soundgarden concert.

Official cause: Suicide by hanging.

Cornell was known for charitable work, including efforts to help abused children through the Chris and Vicky Cornell Foundation.

Theorists claim he was working on a project to expose an elite trafficking ring.

Chester Bennington's Death (July 20, 2017):

Found dead in his Los Angeles home on what would have been Cornell's 53rd birthday.

Official cause: Suicide by hanging.

Bennington was a close friend of Cornell; he performed at Cornell's funeral.

Some theories claim Chester was involved in the same alleged investigation as Cornell.

Additional Speculation:

Chester's resemblance to John Podesta (a political figure named in the Pizzagate conspiracy) is often cited by fringe theorists.

The timing of their deaths — two months apart — is viewed as highly suspicious.

Alleged connections to Hollywood abuse networks and political figures are often invoked, though without verified evidence.

Counterpoint:

Both men had long-documented struggles with depression and substance abuse.

Family and official investigations have not confirmed any connection to trafficking investigations.

Famous Quotes / Sources

"They weren't just rock stars — they were trying to change something big."

— Conspiracy blog post, 2017

"It's a coincidence too large for me to ignore."

— YouTube conspiracy video, The Silent Strings

"These rumors are hurtful and false. Chris's death was the result of mental illness."

— Vicky Cornell, public statement

Real-World Consequences

Internet Campaigns:

Fan groups and conspiracy channels have dedicated investigations to their deaths, keeping the theory alive.

Integration with Broader Theories:

Often tied into Pizzagate, Hollywood abuse conspiracies, and claims about industry whistleblowers.

Cultural Impact:

The theory has amplified their reputations as musicians who cared deeply for humanitarian causes.

Where It Stands Today

While there is no credible evidence linking their deaths to elite trafficking rings, the suspicious timing, their friendship, and their advocacy work make this one of the most emotionally charged celebrity conspiracy theories.

For believers, Cornell and Bennington were not just musicians — they were truth-tellers silenced before they could reveal what they knew.

Chapter One Hundred and Sixteen

Section: Celebrity & Pop Culture Conspiracies

Conspiracy: Kanye West's "Breakdowns" Are Warnings

Summary

The theory that Kanye West's public "breakdowns" are actually coded warnings claims that his controversial outbursts, erratic interviews, and onstage rants are deliberate attempts to reveal hidden truths about the entertainment industry, elite control, and social engineering.

Supporters believe Kanye uses moments framed as "mental health episodes" to speak openly about industry manipulation, celebrity contracts, and political corruption — only to be quickly silenced through media spin, public backlash, or hospitalization.

History & Key Claims

Notable "Breakdowns" & Public Statements:

2009 MTV VMAs: Interrupts Taylor Swift, later interpreted by some as an act of defiance against scripted industry narratives.

2016 Sacramento Concert Rant: Calls out Jay-Z, Beyoncé, and the media before abruptly ending the concert. Shortly after, he was hospitalized for "exhaustion."

2020 Presidential Run: Makes controversial statements about the Kardashians, Planned Parenthood, and political leaders, leading to speculation that he was exposing sensitive information.

Interviews & Tweets: Frequent references to contracts, "selling souls," and celebrity control systems.

Theories Explaining His Behavior:

Industry Retaliation: Kanye's erratic image is allegedly cultivated to discredit him after he speaks out.

MKUltra Narrative: Some claim he is under mind control, with breakdowns occurring when his programming "fails."

Insider Warnings: His public rants are coded messages for fans about the hidden workings of the entertainment machine.

Counterpoint:

Kanye has openly discussed his bipolar disorder, framing some outbursts as part of his personal mental health struggles.

Critics say his behavior is better explained by psychological and personal factors than by secret codes.

Famous Quotes / Sources

"They want to keep you in debt. They want to keep you under control."

— Kanye West, 2016 Sacramento concert

"Don't call me crazy because I speak the truth."

— Kanye West, interview

"When Kanye talks about contracts, handlers, and the media, he's pulling the curtain back."

— Conspiracy forum comment

Real-World Consequences

Public Perception:

Fans are divided between seeing him as a truth-teller or a celebrity in crisis.

Industry Impact:

Kanye's allegations about record label control, artist exploitation, and politics have fueled industry skepticism.

Integration with Broader Theories:

Often linked to MKUltra, Illuminati celebrity control, and Hollywood ritual theories.

Where It Stands Today

Whether Kanye's public moments are genuine breakdowns, performance art, or coded warnings, they have solidified his role as one of the most conspiracy-associated celebrities in modern culture.

For believers, Kanye's outbursts aren't random — they are flashes of truth from someone trying to warn the world about the system he's trapped in.

Chapter One Hundred and Seventeen

Section: Celebrity & Pop Culture Conspiracies

Conspiracy: The Truman Show Is Real

Summary

The "Truman Show Is Real" conspiracy claims that the concept of the 1998 film The Truman Show — in which a man's entire life is broadcast as an elaborate reality television show without his knowledge — reflects real-world experiments or secret projects.

Believers suggest some people (often celebrities, but sometimes ordinary citizens) are placed into controlled environments, with staged interactions, scripted events, and hidden surveillance to study or manipulate human behavior.

History & Key Claims

The Film as "Revelation of the Method":

In The Truman Show, Truman Burbank discovers his life has been a television production.

Conspiracists argue the film was inspired by actual covert psychological operations.

"Truman Show Delusion" in Psychiatry:

A documented psychiatric condition in which individuals believe their life is a staged reality.

Conspiracists claim this diagnosis was created to discredit whistleblowers or victims of real-life experiments.

Celebrity Examples:

Some claim celebrities like Britney Spears and Kanye West show signs of "controlled reality" environments.

Others believe entire reality shows like Keeping Up with the Kardashians or Love Island serve as mass experiments in public behavior manipulation.

Ordinary People as Subjects:

Online forums have posts from people claiming to see recurring strangers, repeated events, or coordinated encounters — consistent with the idea of being inside a managed "set."

Possible Purpose:

To study social reactions, mass influence, or responses to engineered crises.

To normalize surveillance and control.

Famous Quotes / Sources

"We accept the reality of the world with which we are presented."

— The Truman Show, quoted by conspiracists

"They tell us it's fiction, so we won't believe it's real."

— Conspiracy blog, Reality Unmasked

"This isn't a delusion. My life is scripted. I can feel it."

— Anonymous forum post

Real-World Consequences

Pop Culture Integration:

The Truman Show concept is used as shorthand for feeling manipulated or watched.

Cultural Paranoia:

Surveillance society, reality TV, and social media have made the idea of a "controlled life" seem less far-fetched to some.

Intersection with Psychological Theories:

Raises questions about media influence, algorithmic control, and staged news events.

Where It Stands Today

The "Truman Show Is Real" theory blends pop culture, psychology, and modern surveillance anxieties. While there's no proof of literal Truman-style experiments, many see the metaphor as accurate for life in a media-saturated, constantly monitored society.

For believers, The Truman Show wasn't fiction — it was a disguised confession of an ongoing reality.

Chapter One Hundred and Eighteen

Section: Celebrity & Pop Culture Conspiracies

Conspiracy: Celebrities Use Adrenochrome

Summary

The adrenochrome conspiracy claims that powerful elites, including high-profile celebrities, consume adrenochrome, a chemical compound produced by the oxidation of adrenaline, allegedly harvested from living victims — often children. Proponents believe this practice is tied to ritual abuse, anti-aging, and mind enhancement, and that it is a key secret within elite circles.

While the chemical adrenochrome is real (and was first studied in the 1930s for medical research), there is no evidence supporting the harvesting claims. The theory blends Hollywood occult conspiracies with older myths about secretive elites consuming substances for longevity.

History & Key Claims

Origins of the Myth:

The idea first appeared in fictional works, most famously Hunter S. Thompson's Fear and Loathing in Las Vegas (1971), where adrenochrome is portrayed as a powerful psychedelic.

Later adopted by conspiracy circles, especially after resurfacing in Pizzagate and QAnon narratives.

Celebrity & Elite Allegations:

Certain celebrities are accused of adrenochrome use, with "evidence" taken from:

Physical appearance changes (especially aging patterns).

Public symbolism at events and performances.

"Leaked" supposed coded messages in interviews and social media.

How It Allegedly Works:

Victims are said to be placed under extreme fear or trauma to increase adrenaline levels.

Adrenochrome is harvested from the blood.

The chemical is allegedly used for anti-aging benefits, heightened consciousness, or ritual significance.

Scientific Counterpoint:

Adrenochrome exists but has no verified anti-aging or consciousness-altering properties.

Claims of harvesting are unsupported and implausible.

Famous Quotes / Sources

"They flaunt it in our faces, and the public thinks it's art."

— Conspiracy blog, Bloodlines of the Elite

"This is one of the core rituals of the Hollywood elite."

— Anonymous QAnon forum user

"There's no credible science supporting any of these claims."

— Medical researcher, Pharmacology Review

Real-World Consequences

Integration with Larger Conspiracies:

Central to QAnon, Hollywood Satanic cult theories, and claims about global elites.

Public Backlash Against Celebrities:

Some celebrities accused of involvement have faced online harassment.

Cultural References:

Adrenochrome has become a shorthand in conspiracy culture for secretive elite behavior.

Where It Stands Today

While scientifically baseless, the adrenochrome conspiracy remains a core narrative in elite control theories. For believers, the substance is more than a chemical — it's a symbol of the hidden power structures and their alleged moral corruption.

Chapter One Hundred and Nineteen

Section: Celebrity & Pop Culture Conspiracies

Conspiracy: The Oscars Are Rituals

Summary

The theory that The Oscars are rituals claims that the annual Academy Awards ceremony is more than just a celebration of cinema — it is allegedly a carefully staged occult or Illuminati ritual. Believers point to the elaborate symbolism, recurring themes, and choreographed performances as ritualistic displays of power by Hollywood's elite.

According to this theory, the event serves as a public initiation, worship, and display of allegiance to those controlling the entertainment industry.

History & Key Claims

The Oscars as "The Industry's Sacred Night":

The Academy Awards began in 1929, growing into the most prestigious event in Hollywood.

Conspiracists argue its longstanding traditions, stage designs, and ceremonies mirror elements of Masonic or occult ritual.

Symbolism Alleged by Believers:

Oscar Statuette:

Its sword-like figure is compared to ancient deities or sun gods.

Gold coloring is tied to sun worship and wealth symbolism.

Red Carpet:

Seen as symbolic of ritual passage or blood sacrifice in occult interpretation.

Performance Content:

Musical numbers and stage designs are often analyzed for occult patterns or "coded messages."

Award Presentations as Initiations:

Certain winners' speeches are interpreted as pledges of loyalty.

High-profile moments (slap incidents, sudden political statements) are seen as planned symbolic acts.

Industry Control Narrative:

The event is seen as a reminder of who holds power, rewarding those who align with the system.

Counterpoint:

Most symbolism is explained as artistic direction, tradition, and showmanship.

Famous Quotes / Sources

"It's not just a ceremony — it's a yearly occult ritual."

— Conspiracy forum, Occult Hollywood

"The Oscar itself is modeled on ancient symbols."

— Vigilant Citizen article

"People love to see patterns in things, especially in big, glamorous productions."

— Film historian, Academy Insider

Real-World Consequences

Public Distrust:

The Oscars are often cited in broader claims of Hollywood elite manipulation.

Internet Analysis:

Every year, new breakdown videos appear "decoding" the ceremony.

Integration with Other Theories:

Closely tied to Illuminati in the music industry, Satanic Hollywood, and predictive programming.

Where It Stands Today

While there's no evidence that the Oscars are literal occult rituals, the grandeur, symbolism, and exclusivity of the event ensure it remains a focal point for celebrity conspiracy speculation.

For believers, the awards are more than just gold statues — they are annual ceremonies of power and allegiance in Hollywood's hidden hierarchy.

Chapter One Hundred and Twenty

Section: Celebrity & Pop Culture Conspiracies

Conspiracy: Bob Marley Was Poisoned

Summary

The Bob Marley poisoned conspiracy claims that the legendary reggae musician's death from cancer in 1981 was not natural, but the result of a deliberate assassination plot — often attributed to the CIA, political enemies, or shadowy global interests.

Believers argue Marley's activism, global influence, and anti-establishment messages made him a threat to political and corporate powers, leading to his elimination through covert poisoning.

History & Key Claims

Official Cause of Death:

Marley died at age 36 from melanoma that spread throughout his body.

The cancer began in his toe in 1977 and metastasized over several years.

Suspicious Incidents:

1976 Assassination Attempt: Armed men attacked Marley's home in Jamaica before a planned concert promoting peace during political tensions.

1977 "Gifted Shoes" Incident: Marley was reportedly given a pair of boots by filmmaker Carl Colby (son of CIA director William Colby). He allegedly pricked his toe on something inside the shoe — the same toe later diagnosed with melanoma.

Theorists claim this was a covert method of introducing cancer or poison.

Motive:

Marley's popularity and Rastafarian message promoted unity, anti-colonialism, and resistance to oppression.

Conspiracists believe the CIA wanted to neutralize his influence, especially during the Cold War in the Caribbean.

Counterpoint:

Medical experts point out that Marley's melanoma was consistent with acral lentiginous melanoma, a rare but naturally occurring cancer more common in people of African descent.

Famous Quotes / Sources

"They wanted to silence a voice that was uniting the oppressed."

— Conspiracy forum, Roots & Truth

"The CIA was in Jamaica. They were interested in the elections. They were interested in Bob."

— Don Taylor, Marley's former manager

"The idea that his cancer was induced by a poisoned shoe is unproven but intriguing."

— Marley biographer

Real-World Consequences

Legacy of Activism:

Marley's death cemented his role as a symbol of resistance, with the theory enhancing his status as a martyr figure.

Political Suspicion:

Deepened distrust of U.S. intelligence operations in Jamaica during the 1970s.

Cultural Myth:

The theory persists in documentaries, books, and reggae culture as part of Marley's enduring mystique.

Where It Stands Today

There is no conclusive evidence that Bob Marley was poisoned, but the combination of political tensions, suspicious incidents, and his cultural impact ensures the theory remains one of the most enduring celebrity death conspiracies.

For believers, Marley's death was not an accident of fate — it was the removal of a man whose music and message threatened the status quo.

Chapter One Hundred and Twenty-One

Section: Bizarre & Lesser-Known Conspiracies

Conspiracy: Hollow Earth Theory

Summary

The Hollow Earth Theory claims that the Earth is not a solid sphere but is either completely hollow or contains massive internal spaces, potentially inhabited by advanced civilizations, strange ecosystems, or even ancient species.

While modern geology rejects the concept, the theory persists in conspiracy and fringe science circles, often tied to claims about Antarctic entrances, UFO sightings, and ancient myths.

History & Key Claims

Early Scientific Proposals:

In 1692, astronomer Edmond Halley (of Halley's Comet fame) theorized the Earth might consist of nested shells with spaces between, to explain compass anomalies.

19th-century explorers and writers like John Cleves Symmes Jr. promoted the idea that large openings at the poles led to inner worlds.

Alleged Polar Entrances:

Conspiracists claim the North and South Poles contain openings to the inner Earth.

These entrances are allegedly restricted or hidden by governments.

Inner Earth Civilizations:

Stories describe advanced societies (sometimes called Agartha or Shambhala) living in a temperate, sunlit inner realm.

UFOs are claimed to originate from these inner civilizations.

Military & Exploration Connections:

Admiral Richard Byrd (Operation Highjump) is often linked to Hollow Earth claims, with alleged diaries describing contact with inner Earth inhabitants.

These diaries are widely considered forgeries, but they continue to fuel belief.

Scientific Counterpoint:

Seismic studies show the Earth has a dense core and mantle — no vast hollow space exists.

Famous Quotes / Sources

"I am certain there are worlds within our world."

— Attributed to Admiral Byrd (disputed)

"The inner Earth is the last great secret they don't want you to know."

— Hollow Earth researcher, Agartha Revealed

"Seismology and gravity make the hollow Earth impossible, but the myth persists."

— Geophysicist, Earth Science Review

Real-World Consequences

Exploration Myths:

Continues to inspire expeditions, documentaries, and fictional works (Journey to the Center of the Earth).

Integration with Other Conspiracies:

Often tied to Antarctica mysteries, UFO origins, and ancient advanced civilizations.

Pop Culture Influence:

Films, games, and literature keep the theory alive in the public imagination.

Where It Stands Today

The Hollow Earth theory is rejected by mainstream science, but thrives in alternative history and conspiracy communities. For believers, it's not just a geological oddity — it's proof of a hidden world beneath our feet, deliberately concealed by global powers.

Chapter One Hundred and Twenty-Two

Section: Bizarre & Lesser-Known Conspiracies

Conspiracy: Antarctica Doesn't Exist

Summary

The Antarctica Doesn't Exist conspiracy claims that the southernmost continent, as we know it, is a fabricated or misrepresented landmass. According to this theory, Antarctica is not an icy continent at the bottom of the globe but a wall of ice encircling the Earth, a restricted military zone, or a fictional creation used to hide the true nature of our planet.

This idea is particularly common in Flat Earth circles, though other versions suggest it is a cover for hidden lands, secret bases, or unknown civilizations.

History & Key Claims

Flat Earth Interpretation:

Antarctica is described as a giant ice wall surrounding the flat Earth, preventing ships and planes from falling off.

The Antarctic Treaty (1959), which restricts free exploration, is claimed to be evidence of a global cover-up.

Hidden Lands Theory:

Some believe Antarctica is not icy at all, but hides lush landscapes, ancient ruins, or access to other continents beyond the ice.

Claims of censored Google Earth imagery reinforce this idea.

No Civilian Access:

Travel is strictly controlled; independent exploration is rare.

Conspiracists argue this secrecy indicates Antarctica's true nature is being concealed.

Scientific Counterpoint:

Antarctica has been explored and mapped extensively by scientists from multiple nations.

The harsh climate and danger explain why civilian travel is limited.

Famous Quotes / Sources

"They built the Antarctic Treaty to keep people from discovering the truth."

— Flat Earth researcher

"There is more beyond the ice — more land, more secrets."

— Alternative geography podcast

"Antarctica exists. It's just very, very hard to get to."

— Antarctic researcher, National Science Foundation

Real-World Consequences

Integration into Flat Earth Movement:

The "Antarctica doesn't exist" theory is a cornerstone of modern Flat Earth belief.

Tourism & Curiosity:

The limited cruises and controlled access to Antarctica fuel the sense of mystery.

Political Suspicion:

The unusual international cooperation in the Antarctic Treaty is viewed as suspicious by some conspiracy believers.

Where It Stands Today

Mainstream science and countless expeditions confirm Antarctica's existence, but in conspiracy circles, it remains a blank spot on the map — the perfect place to hide the truth about our world.

Chapter One Hundred and Twenty-Three

Section: Bizarre & Lesser-Known Conspiracies

Conspiracy: Finland Doesn't Exist

Summary

The Finland Doesn't Exist conspiracy claims that the nation of Finland is a fabricated country, created as part of a Cold War–era agreement between the Soviet Union and Japan. According to the theory, the supposed location of Finland is actually open ocean, and the landmass shown on maps is a fictional construct to conceal secret fishing rights and resource exploitation in the Baltic Sea.

While the idea began as an Internet hoax, it has taken on a life of its own in conspiracy culture.

History & Key Claims

Origins of the Theory:

Popularized in 2015 on Reddit as a satirical post by a user claiming Finland was a joint invention of Japan and the Soviet Union in the 20th century.

The claim was that the two nations fabricated Finland to secure fishing rights in the Baltic without international interference.

The Fishing Motive:

Japan allegedly uses the Baltic as a secret fishing ground, shipping fish back under the guise of "Nokia products" or other exports.

Finland's existence serves as a cover story for shipping routes.

Supporting "Evidence" Cited by Believers:

Low awareness of Finland's population and culture internationally.

Minimal global geopolitical footprint compared to other countries of similar size.

"Sparse tourism" outside Helsinki.

Counterpoint:

Finland has over 5 million residents, a rich history, and documented international presence.

The theory is generally considered satire turned into meme conspiracy.

Famous Quotes / Sources

"Finland is a cold ocean. The people you think are Finnish are Swedes, Russians, or Estonians."

— Original Reddit hoax post

"It's all fish. Nokia was never phones, it was salmon."

— Finland conspiracy meme

"Finland is as real as any other country. I've been there. I live here."

— Self-identified Finnish resident

Real-World Consequences

Internet Meme Culture:

The theory has become one of the most popular "joke conspiracies," though some adopt it semi-seriously.

Cultural Response:

Many Finns have embraced the joke, creating tourism campaigns and memes playing along.

Conspiracy Humor:

Used as an example of how absurd ideas can spread in online conspiracy spaces.

Where It Stands Today

The Finland conspiracy remains mostly satirical, but it illustrates how quickly an idea — even one intended as a joke — can gain momentum in conspiracy culture.

For believers (even tongue-in-cheek ones), Finland is the world's most successful piece of cartographic fiction.

Chapter One Hundred and Twenty-Four

Section: Bizarre & Lesser-Known Conspiracies

Conspiracy: Mattress Stores Are Money Laundering Fronts

Summary

The Mattress Store conspiracy claims that the large number of mattress retail locations — especially in the same neighborhoods — is not due to high consumer demand, but because the stores are fronts for money laundering operations.

This theory is fueled by the observation that mattress stores often appear empty of customers, yet remain open for years, sometimes in clusters, despite the fact that people buy mattresses only every 7–10 years.

History & Key Claims

Origins of the Theory:

The theory became popular on Reddit around 2018 after users questioned why there were so many Mattress Firm stores in close proximity.

People pointed out low customer volume, yet stores operated in prime real estate locations.

Suspicious Business Model:

Mattress stores often sell expensive, high-margin items, allowing for large sums of money to be "moved" without high foot traffic.

Many locations are allegedly positioned on highway routes and intersections — ideal for discreet financial operations.

Evidence Cited by Believers:

Chains like Mattress Firm have hundreds of locations within small metro areas.

Store clustering: Several mattress stores can exist within blocks of one another, all seemingly underused.

In 2018, Mattress Firm filed for bankruptcy, prompting renewed suspicion about its finances.

Counterpoint:

Retail analysts argue that mattress stores cluster due to real estate strategy, high profit margins, and brand competition, not laundering.

Famous Quotes / Sources

"No one buys that many mattresses. The stores are for moving money, not beds."

— Internet conspiracy forum

"Why are there three mattress stores on the same block?"

— Reddit user post

"The clustering is a competitive retail strategy, not a crime."

— Retail industry analyst

Real-World Consequences

Internet Virality:

The theory spread widely online, with memes and videos poking fun at empty mattress stores.

Corporate Attention:

Mattress Firm publicly denied any illicit activity, but acknowledged that store oversaturation was poor strategy.

Cultural Curiosity:

Mattress store foot traffic has become a running joke in conspiracy culture.

Where It Stands Today

While the mattress store theory has little hard evidence, its logic appeals to conspiracy thinkers: high-priced items, low customer volume, and oddly positioned stores are the perfect recipe for suspicion.

For believers, mattress stores aren't selling beds — they're flipping cash under the cover of pillow-top displays.

Chapter One Hundred and Twenty-Five

Section: Bizarre & Lesser-Known Conspiracies

Conspiracy: The Mandela Effect

Summary

The Mandela Effect is the belief that large groups of people share the same false memory, which is explained by theorists as evidence of alternate timelines, reality shifts, or deliberate manipulation of history.

It is named after the widespread (but incorrect) memory that Nelson Mandela died in prison in the 1980s, decades before his actual death in 2013.

History & Key Claims

Origin of the Term:

Coined by paranormal researcher Fiona Broome in 2009, who noticed many people recalling Mandela's death occurring earlier than recorded.

This led to discussions of shared false memories that were too specific to be coincidence.

Common Examples:

Berenstain Bears vs. Berenstein Bears: Many remember the children's books spelled with "-stein" instead of "-stain."

"Luke, I am your father" vs. actual quote "No, I am your father" (Star Wars).

Fruit of the Loom Logo: Remembered by many with a cornucopia, though it never had one.

Monopoly Man: Many recall him having a monocle, but he doesn't.

Febreze vs. Febreeze: Spelling variations people swear changed.

Theories Explaining the Effect:

Parallel Universes: Slight shifts between realities cause subtle changes in details.

Simulation Glitch: Errors in a simulated reality create mismatched memories.

Memory Manipulation: Deliberate alteration of collective memory by media or psychological influence.

Psychological Explanation: Memory is reconstructive, and false memories can spread socially.

Famous Quotes / Sources

"It's called the Mandela Effect because so many of us remember something that never happened."

— Fiona Broome

"The details are wrong because reality itself is unstable."

— Conspiracy blog, Shifted Timeline

"Our brains are not perfect recorders; memory is a reconstruction process."

— Cognitive psychologist, Memory & Mind

Real-World Consequences

Cultural Fascination:

The Mandela Effect has become a major Internet phenomenon, with thousands of examples documented.

Integration with Simulation Theory:

Frequently used as evidence of alternate realities or programmed worlds.

Pop Culture Adoption:

Films, podcasts, and games incorporate the concept as a central theme (Shazam/Kazaam genie movie confusion is a classic example).

Where It Stands Today

Psychologists largely attribute the Mandela Effect to false memory formation, but conspiracy theorists see it as proof of reality tampering or dimensional overlap.

For believers, these memory discrepancies are not mistakes — they are breadcrumbs leading to a much stranger truth about the nature of reality.

Chapter One Hundred and Twenty-Six

Section: Bizarre & Lesser-Known Conspiracies

Conspiracy: Dead Internet Theory

Summary

The Dead Internet Theory claims that the majority of the modern Internet is no longer run by humans, but by bots, AI-generated content, and automated networks. According to this theory, most of the conversations, comments, and even "news" we see online are not organic, but manufactured to manipulate opinions, control culture, or mask the decline of real human activity on the web.

While the theory originated as a blend of satire and speculation, it has gained traction due to the explosion of AI tools, bot farms, and repetitive online content.

History & Key Claims

Origins of the Theory:

Gained popularity on 4chan and conspiracy forums around 2016–2019.

Supporters noted that online discussions seemed increasingly formulaic and repetitive.

Core Allegations:

Bot Dominance: A large percentage of online users are actually automated accounts.

Content Automation: Articles, videos, and social media posts are generated by AI and content farms.

Government/Corporate Control: State and corporate actors allegedly use automated content to shape narratives, suppress dissent, and promote agendas.

Death of "Old Internet": The vibrant, user-driven early web has been replaced by a scripted, curated system.

Evidence Cited by Believers:

Repetitive viral trends with no clear origin.

Spam-like comment sections filled with generic praise or outrage.

The rise of AI deepfakes and machine-written articles.

Counterpoint:

While bots and AI are widespread, there is no evidence that human interaction has been completely replaced.

Famous Quotes / Sources

"The Internet you think you're on died around 2016. What you see now is a ghost."

— Anonymous 4chan post

"It's all bots talking to bots, with a few humans left watching."

— Conspiracy forum

"Bots are common, but there's still plenty of human activity online."

— Cybersecurity researcher, TechNet Journal

Real-World Consequences

Public Distrust of Online Content:

People increasingly question the authenticity of social media interactions.

Rise of AI Skepticism:

The theory gained traction with public awareness of ChatGPT, deepfake videos, and synthetic influencers.

Integration with Simulation Theory:

Some suggest the Dead Internet is part of a broader manufactured reality.

Where It Stands Today

The Dead Internet Theory is partly satire, partly genuine skepticism of how much of the web is curated, automated, and manipulated.

For believers, the web we browse now is not the lively network of human voices it once was — it's a ghost network run by machines, keeping us entertained and distracted.

Chapter One Hundred and Twenty-Seven

Section: Bizarre & Lesser-Known Conspiracies

Conspiracy: Simulation Theory

Summary

Simulation Theory suggests that reality itself is a computer-generated simulation, much like a highly advanced video game or virtual environment. According to the theory, what we perceive as physical reality is actually code, data, and programmed rules created by an advanced intelligence — potentially future humans, aliens, or unknown entities.

While mainstream science treats it as speculative philosophy, conspiracy believers interpret glitches, déjà vu, and unlikely coincidences as evidence we are living inside a controlled digital construct.

History & Key Claims

Philosophical Origins:

Ancient concepts like Plato's Allegory of the Cave and Hindu Maya echo the idea of reality as an illusion.

In modern philosophy, Nick Bostrom's 2003 paper popularized the idea: either civilizations never create simulations, or we are almost certainly living in one.

Evidence Cited by Believers:

Glitches in the Matrix: Reports of repeated events, physics-defying anomalies, and strange coincidences.

Uncanny Probability: Improbable coincidences (e.g., multiple lottery wins, identical strangers) are seen as programming quirks.

Mathematical Nature of the Universe: Physics laws resemble coded rules; constants like π and the fine structure constant suggest precision engineering.

Pixelation & Reality Limits: Some researchers suggest there may be a smallest "unit" of space-time, like a resolution limit.

Purpose of the Simulation:

Possible goals include scientific study, entertainment for advanced beings, or prison-like containment for certain consciousnesses.

Counterpoint:

No physical evidence confirms we are in a simulation; most claims are philosophical or speculative.

Famous Quotes / Sources

"If reality is code, then someone, somewhere, wrote it."

— Simulation Theory discussion forum

"There's a one in a billion chance we're in base reality."

— Elon Musk, Code Conference 2016

"It's not science fiction. It's physics and math."

— Nick Bostrom, Are You Living in a Computer Simulation?

Real-World Consequences

Cultural Influence:

Films like The Matrix, Inception, and Free Guy popularize the concept.

Philosophical Impact:

Raises questions about free will, morality, and the nature of consciousness.

Integration with Other Theories:

Linked with Mandela Effect, Dead Internet Theory, and reality resets.

Where It Stands Today

Simulation Theory remains speculative, but its influence on pop culture and conspiracy circles is enormous.

For believers, the signs are all around us: we are non-player characters in an immense, coded universe, and glitches in reality are the breadcrumbs left by the programmers.

Chapter One Hundred and Twenty-Eight

Section: Bizarre & Lesser-Known Conspiracies

Conspiracy: Time Travelers Among Us

Summary

The Time Travelers Among Us conspiracy claims that individuals from the future are living in our present day, either as observers, experimenters, or accidental visitors. These supposed time travelers are said to appear in old photographs, historical footage, and unusual modern-day encounters.

The theory draws on historical anomalies, strange coincidences, and accounts of people predicting events with uncanny accuracy as evidence that time travel is real — and already in use.

History & Key Claims

Famous Alleged Cases:

The Hipster at the 1941 Bridge Opening: A black-and-white photograph shows a man wearing what appears to be modern sunglasses and clothing at a 1940s event.

Chaplin's Time Traveler: A 1928 Charlie Chaplin film premiere shows a woman seemingly speaking into a mobile phone.

John Titor Case: In 2000–2001, a man claiming to be a soldier from 2036 posted detailed accounts online, predicting future events (with mixed accuracy).

Andrew Basiago's Project Pegasus: Claims U.S. government programs used time travel for political and military missions.

Evidence Cited by Believers:

Historical photos with individuals wearing anachronistic clothing.

People claiming knowledge of future events before they occur.

Unexplained technology appearing before its official invention.

Sudden disappearances of individuals tied to alleged time travel experiments.

Purpose of Time Travelers:

Observation of historical events.

Correction of historical "mistakes."

Testing technology in controlled environments.

Scientific Counterpoint:

While time travel is theoretically possible under relativity, practical time travel to the past faces major physical paradoxes (e.g., causality issues).

Famous Quotes / Sources

"I am from the year 2036. I am here on a military mission."

— John Titor, online posts

"They're here to observe — not to interfere."

— Conspiracy forum

"Time travel may be theoretically possible, but we have no evidence of visitors from the future."

— Theoretical physicist, Physics Today

Real-World Consequences

Cultural Fascination:

Time traveler claims go viral regularly on TikTok, YouTube, and Reddit.

Integration with Other Theories:

Often tied to Mandela Effect, Simulation Theory, and reality resets.

Pop Culture Influence:

Films and series like Back to the Future, Looper, and Dark reinforce public interest in time travel mysteries.

Where It Stands Today

No verifiable evidence confirms time travelers' presence, but the abundance of unexplained anomalies keeps the idea alive.

For believers, time travelers are walking among us — just careful enough to remain hidden until they choose to be seen.

Chapter One Hundred and Twenty-Nine

Section: Bizarre & Lesser-Known Conspiracies

Conspiracy: CERN Opened a Portal

Summary

The CERN Opened a Portal conspiracy claims that experiments at the Large Hadron Collider (LHC) in Switzerland have torn holes in space-time, opened portals to other dimensions, or altered our reality. The European Organization for Nuclear Research (CERN) officially studies high-energy particle collisions, but theorists believe its true work involves interdimensional travel, communication with other realms, or even summoning entities.

This idea is often linked to the Mandela Effect and sudden cultural or physical "shifts" since major CERN experiments began.

History & Key Claims

The LHC and Public Concern:

Built between 1998 and 2008, the LHC is the world's most powerful particle accelerator.

Officially used to discover particles like the Higgs boson.

Critics and conspiracy theorists raised fears about black holes, strange matter, and unknown phenomena.

The "Portal" Allegations:

Certain experiments are claimed to have caused dimensional rifts.

The year 2012 — when CERN confirmed the Higgs boson — is often tied to the "reality reset" theory (linked to the Mandela Effect).

Imagery at CERN, such as the Shiva statue and stylized ceremonies, is interpreted as occult symbolism.

Evidence Cited by Believers:

Surge in reported Mandela Effect memories after major LHC runs.

Strange weather and unusual phenomena coinciding with collider operations.

Scientists making cryptic public statements about "opening doors."

Scientific Counterpoint:

CERN operates under strict safety protocols.

The LHC's energy levels are far too small to create dangerous phenomena.

"Portals" mentioned in press talks are metaphorical descriptions of particle interactions.

Famous Quotes / Sources

"We may open a door to a new dimension."

— CERN scientist (metaphor, often taken literally by conspiracists)

"After 2012, things haven't felt the same — and CERN is the reason."

— Mandela Effect believer

"The LHC is powerful, but not in a science fiction way."

— CERN spokesperson

Real-World Consequences

Integration with Mandela Effect:

Many Mandela Effect believers point to CERN as the "cause" of reality shifts.

Public Distrust of Scientific Institutions:

CERN is often seen as a secretive organization with hidden agendas.

Pop Culture Connection:

Frequently referenced in science fiction (Stranger Things "upside down" theories, The Cloverfield Paradox).

Where It Stands Today

Mainstream science maintains that CERN's work is safe and focused on particle physics, not dimensional manipulation. However, for believers, CERN is the gatekeeper to other worlds, and each collider run is a roll of the dice with our reality.

Chapter One Hundred and Thirty

Section: Bizarre & Lesser-Known Conspiracies

Conspiracy: Shadow People Are Real

Summary

The Shadow People conspiracy claims that dark, humanoid silhouettes occasionally seen in the corners of one's vision — or even directly — are not hallucinations or tricks of the mind, but actual entities from another dimension, astral plane, or hidden layer of reality.

Witnesses often report feelings of fear, dread, or paralysis during encounters, leading some to connect shadow people to sleep paralysis, interdimensional beings, or spiritual oppression.

History & Key Claims

Ancient and Cross-Cultural Reports:

Stories of dark spirit-like figures exist in many cultures:

Islamic tradition describes jinn.

Native American legends reference shadow-like spirit watchers.

Medieval Europe spoke of dark spectres as omens.

Modern reports exploded with the growth of Internet paranormal communities.

Common Characteristics:

Form: Dark humanoid figure, sometimes with glowing eyes, often hat-shaped head ("Hat Man" variety).

Behavior: Observes from doorways or corners; sometimes moves quickly across a room.

Timing: Encounters often occur at night or during sleep paralysis episodes.

Emotional Impact: Witnesses report sudden waves of fear or an intense sense of being watched.

Theories About What They Are:

Interdimensional Beings: Entities crossing into our plane temporarily.

Astral or Spiritual Entities: Spirits feeding on fear or emotion.

Government/Paranormal Experiments: Linked by some to MKUltra-like psychic projects.

Psychological Explanation: Sleep paralysis and hypnagogic hallucinations.

Famous Quotes / Sources

"They stand there, just watching. You can feel them."

— Shadow People witness account

"They aren't in your head. They're in your space."

— Paranormal investigator

"The phenomenon aligns with known visual hallucinations during sleep paralysis."

— Neurologist, Journal of Sleep Research

Real-World Consequences

Cultural Spread:

Shadow people have become a staple of paranormal lore and horror media.

Personal Impact:

Many experiencers describe long-lasting anxiety or fear of the dark.

Integration with Other Theories:

Shadow people are tied into CERN portal theories, interdimensional entities, and simulation glitches.

Where It Stands Today

Shadow people remain an unsolved mystery — explained by science as a brain phenomenon, but seen by believers as evidence of hidden entities coexisting with us unseen.

For believers, shadow people are not a trick of the mind. They are watchers from beyond the veil, slipping in and out of our reality.

Chapter One Hundred and Thirty-One

Section: Bizarre & Lesser-Known Conspiracies

Conspiracy: Reality Reset in 2012

Summary

The Reality Reset in 2012 conspiracy claims that something significant happened in the year 2012 — not just culturally, but cosmically — that caused our reality to shift, reset, or transition into an alternate timeline.

Proponents link this to the Mayan calendar ending on December 21, 2012, suggesting that instead of an apocalypse, reality subtly changed, leading to phenomena like the Mandela Effect, increased societal instability, and a sense of the world feeling "different" since 2012.

History & Key Claims

The Mayan Calendar & December 21, 2012:

Mainstream interpretation: The end of a cycle in the Mayan Long Count calendar, not the end of the world.

Conspiracists interpret this as the end of one reality cycle and the start of another.

Signs of the "Shift":

Surge in Mandela Effect cases after 2012.

A cultural sense of acceleration — events, technology, and social change moving unusually fast.

General perception of heightened chaos in politics, environment, and media.

Theories on What Happened:

Dimensional Shift: We moved into a parallel universe with slightly altered details.

Simulation Reset: The "program" of our reality rebooted, explaining glitches and memory anomalies.

CERN Connection: LHC activity in 2012 supposedly triggered the shift.

Spiritual Ascension: 2012 marked humanity entering a higher vibrational state (New Age interpretation).

Counterpoint:

Psychologists attribute the sense of change to increased connectivity, information overload, and global events.

Famous Quotes / Sources

"2012 wasn't the end — it was the start of something new."

— Internet forum user

"The Mandela Effect surged after 2012. It's not coincidence."

— Conspiracy podcast Timeline Shift

"Reality hasn't changed — we have."

— Physicist, CERN public Q&A

Real-World Consequences

Integration with Other Theories:

Often tied to Mandela Effect, Simulation Theory, and Dead Internet Theory.

Pop Culture Reflection:

2012 films, memes, and podcasts keep the theory alive.

Cultural Mood:

"The world feels different since 2012" is a common refrain in online communities.

Where It Stands Today

Mainstream science dismisses any physical change in reality in 2012, but for believers, the year marks a quiet but profound shift.

For them, we aren't in the same world we were before 2012 — we're in Version 2.0 of reality, and the evidence is in the glitches all around us.

Chapter One Hundred and Thirty-Two

Section: Bizarre & Lesser-Known Conspiracies

Conspiracy: Giant Skeleton Cover-Up

Summary

The Giant Skeleton Cover-Up conspiracy claims that archaeologists and museums have discovered the remains of giant humans — some up to 12–15 feet tall — but these finds have been hidden or destroyed to protect the mainstream historical narrative.

Believers argue that giant skeletons would confirm ancient myths, religious texts, and alternative history accounts, undermining conventional archaeology.

History & Key Claims

Ancient Accounts of Giants:

The Bible's Nephilim and Goliath.

Norse myths of the Jotnar.

Native American legends of giant tribes.

Global myths suggest giant beings once roamed the Earth.

Alleged Discoveries:

19th–early 20th century newspapers in the U.S. reported numerous giant skeleton finds, often in burial mounds.

Some linked to Smithsonian expeditions; conspiracy theorists claim the bones were confiscated and "disappeared."

International claims of large skeletons in South America, Asia, and the Middle East.

Smithsonian Conspiracy:

The Smithsonian Institution is often accused of hiding evidence that contradicts the established evolutionary and anthropological timeline.

Official response: No such skeletons exist in their archives.

Counterpoint:

Many "discoveries" are attributed to hoaxes, exaggerated reports, or misidentified remains (e.g., mammoth bones).

Famous Quotes / Sources

"They were everywhere in the old papers — and then the stories stopped."

— Alternative history researcher

"The Smithsonian is the gatekeeper of inconvenient truths."

— Conspiracy blog, Hidden Giants

"There is no evidence of giant skeletons in our collection."

— Smithsonian Institution

Real-World Consequences

Fuel for Alternative Archaeology:

Used to support Ancient Aliens, lost civilizations, and Biblical literalism.

Cultural Fascination:

Theories appear on History Channel shows, YouTube channels, and fringe history books.

Distrust of Institutions:

Perceived suppression of evidence strengthens belief in a controlled historical narrative.

Where It Stands Today

Mainstream archaeology denies the existence of giant skeletons, but the persistence of mythology, old reports, and alleged photographs keeps the theory alive.

For believers, the bones are real — but locked away in storage rooms, hidden to protect the official version of history.

Chapter One Hundred and Thirty-Three

Section: Bizarre & Lesser-Known Conspiracies

Conspiracy: Dinosaurs Never Existed

Summary

The Dinosaurs Never Existed conspiracy claims that the fossilized remains of dinosaurs are fabrications, misinterpretations, or outright hoaxes, created to support mainstream science, promote evolution, or fuel museums and academia.

Believers argue that dinosaurs are a 19th-century invention, pointing to the suspicious timing of their discovery and the lack of complete skeletons outside institutional control.

History & Key Claims

Origins of the Theory:

Dinosaur fossils were first identified in the early 1800s.

Some theorists point to the rise of paleontology coinciding with growing secular scientific influence, claiming dinosaurs were used to support new theories about Earth's age.

Core Allegations:

No Complete Skeletons: Fossils displayed in museums are mostly casts or reconstructions.

Inconsistent Evidence: Dinosaur skeletons are often found in pieces, interpreted by scientists.

Fabrication by Museums: Museums and paleontologists allegedly create models to attract funding and tourism.

Hoax Discoveries: Certain 19th-century fossil discoveries were later exposed as fakes, fueling suspicion.

Alternative Explanations:

Fossils are misidentified remains of giant reptiles, mammals, or mythical creatures.

Dinosaurs are inventions for profit and ideology, similar to the "giant skeleton cover-up" but in reverse.

Counterpoint:

Thousands of fossils have been independently studied worldwide, with peer-reviewed evidence confirming prehistoric species.

Famous Quotes / Sources

"They invented dinosaurs to convince us the Earth is millions of years old."

— Creationist conspiracy site

"The bones in museums aren't real — they're plaster."

— Alternative history blog

"Dinosaur fossils are genuine and widely verified through modern science."

— Paleontologist, National Museum of Natural History

Real-World Consequences

Integration with Creationism:

The theory is popular in some young Earth creationist circles.

Distrust of Science:

Feeds suspicion that mainstream science is manipulating evidence for ideological purposes.

Cultural Rejection:

The theory remains fringe but persistent in online communities.

Where It Stands Today

Mainstream science overwhelmingly supports the reality of dinosaurs. However, for believers, dinosaurs are just another grand fabrication — an elaborate myth created to shape how we see Earth's past.

Chapter One Hundred and Thirty-Four

Section: Bizarre & Lesser-Known Conspiracies

Conspiracy: The Sun Is Cold

Summary

The Sun Is Cold conspiracy claims that the Sun is not a burning ball of plasma with extreme heat, but rather a cold or cool light source whose perceived warmth is due to atmospheric or electrical interactions.

Believers suggest mainstream science's model of the Sun is fabricated to fit the heliocentric system, and that alternative energy theories — such as the Sun being electrical or even a projection — are deliberately suppressed.

History & Key Claims

Alternative Models of the Sun:

Some flat Earth theorists claim the Sun is local and relatively small, moving above Earth in a circular pattern, producing light without heat.

Others claim the Sun is electrically charged, with warmth generated when light interacts with Earth's atmosphere.

Evidence Cited by Believers:

Cool Upper Atmosphere Argument: The upper atmosphere's thin air is cold despite being closer to the Sun.

Perceived Temperature Variation: Believers point to days when the Sun feels "cool" despite being bright.

Sunspots & Light Anomalies: Unusual observations are claimed to support a different model.

Possible Explanations in the Theory:

The Sun is not nuclear but electromagnetic.

The Sun is hollow or artificial.

The Sun is a projection within a dome system (linked to Flat Earth ideas).

Counterpoint:

Mainstream astrophysics has consistent evidence of the Sun's extreme temperature (~5,500°C at the surface) and its nuclear fusion process.

Famous Quotes / Sources

"The Sun is light, not heat — the heat is created here, on Earth."

— Alternative science forum

"They lie about the Sun to maintain the heliocentric deception."

— Flat Earth researcher

"The Sun's energy and heat have been measured in countless ways — it is extremely hot."

— Solar physicist, NASA

Real-World Consequences

Integration with Flat Earth & Electric Universe Theories:

The "cold Sun" fits alternative cosmology models.

Public Distrust of Space Science:

Reinforces claims that space agencies manipulate astronomical knowledge.

Internet Spread:

Gained traction on YouTube and social media among fringe science communities.

Where It Stands Today

While mainstream science maintains the Sun is a hot plasma sphere, alternative theorists continue to challenge the model.

For believers, the Sun's warmth isn't from a blazing star millions of miles away — it's a controlled local light source, hiding the true nature of our universe.

Chapter One Hundred and Thirty-Five

Section: Bizarre & Lesser-Known Conspiracies

Conspiracy: Birds Work for the Bourgeoisie

Summary

The "Birds Work for the Bourgeoisie" conspiracy began as a satirical slogan but has evolved into a tongue-in-cheek conspiracy theory claiming that birds are government surveillance drones. In its modern form, it plays on mistrust of government agencies, blending humor and parody with genuine suspicion of mass surveillance.

Although originally a meme, some fringe believers insist there is truth behind the joke — that certain birds have been replaced with mechanical versions to track citizens.

History & Key Claims

Origin of the Phrase:

Popularized around 2017–2018 by the "Birds Aren't Real" movement, a satirical protest group.

Intended to parody conspiracy culture and highlight government overreach in a humorous way.

The slogan "Birds Work for the Bourgeoisie" became a viral catchphrase.

The Core Claim (Satirical/Parody):

Birds have been replaced by drones used for:

Tracking human movement.

Recording conversations.

Gathering environmental data.

Evidence Cited by (Mostly Humorous) Supporters:

Birds perching on power lines are "recharging."

Declines in bird populations coincide with "drone replacement programs."

Bird migration patterns are "surveillance sweeps."

Real-World Parallels:

Actual animal tracking devices and government use of drones for surveillance make the parody resonate with real privacy concerns.

Counterpoint:

Ornithology and basic observation confirm birds are biological creatures — the theory is meant as satire.

Famous Quotes / Sources

"Wake up — every pigeon is a government agent."

— Birds Aren't Real protest sign

"Birds work for the bourgeoisie!"

— Viral protest chant

"It's satire, but it reflects real unease about constant surveillance."

— Sociologist, Cultural Studies Review

Real-World Consequences

Cultural Phenomenon:

The movement became a viral sensation, with rallies, merchandise, and interviews.

Blending of Humor and Suspicion:

Serves as a comedic lens on real issues of mass surveillance.

Public Awareness:

While not taken literally, it's been used to spark discussions about privacy and government transparency.

Where It Stands Today

"Birds Work for the Bourgeoisie" is primarily a comedic conspiracy, but its endurance reflects genuine unease about constant observation in modern life.

For believers (serious or not), every pigeon overhead is watching more than you think.

Chapter One Hundred and Thirty-Six

Section: Bizarre & Lesser-Known Conspiracies

Conspiracy: Giant Trees Were Cut Down by Ancient Civilizations

Summary

The Giant Tree conspiracy claims that the massive rock formations, plateaus, and flat-topped mesas found around the world — such as Devils Tower in Wyoming — are not natural geological features, but actually the stumps of enormous ancient trees that were cut down by a long-lost civilization or advanced race.

According to believers, the Earth once had a landscape filled with miles-high trees, but they were harvested in a global-scale event, erasing a part of our history and reshaping the terrain.

History & Key Claims

Interpretation of Geological Structures:

Features like Devils Tower, Giant's Causeway, and other columnar basalt formations are said to resemble the cross-sections of tree trunks.

Their hexagonal columns, "growth rings," and vertical patterns are interpreted as remnants of ancient bark and cellulose structures.

Alleged Ancient Logging Event:

Theorists claim that a prehistoric or extraterrestrial race cut down these colossal trees.

The landscape we now see — deserts, canyons, and mesas — is the leftover debris of Earth's forgotten forest.

Hidden or Suppressed Evidence:

Claims that conventional geology deliberately labels these formations as volcanic remnants to cover up the truth.

Suggests that mainstream science refuses to question the scale of prehistoric life.

Symbolism and Mythology:

References to "world trees" or axis mundi in global mythology are cited as encoded memories of this ancient arboreal age.

Some connect this theory with the "Tartaria" narrative — a lost global civilization with technology capable of mass-scale deforestation.

Counterpoint:

Geologists explain these formations as igneous rock features formed by lava cooling into hexagonal columns.

No biological material has ever been found in the structures theorized to be tree stumps.

Famous Quotes / Sources

"Those aren't mesas. They're ancient stumps from trees that scraped the sky."

— Flat Earth blogger

"Devils Tower looks too much like a cut tree to be natural."

— Alternative geology video, Stumps of the Gods

"The columnar basalt formations are a well-understood volcanic phenomenon."

— U.S. Geological Survey

Real-World Consequences

Integration with Alternative History:

Tied into Tartaria, giant civilizations, and Earth-as-a-quarry theories.

Cultural Curiosity:

The idea fuels online photo comparisons and speculative YouTube documentaries.

Rejection of Mainstream Geology:

Used to challenge academic authority and promote visual truth over expert consensus.

Where It Stands Today

Despite a complete lack of scientific evidence, the theory persists in fringe circles — especially due to the visually compelling nature of the landscapes it references.

For believers, the world we know is built atop a forest of forgotten giants, felled in an age lost to time and rewritten history.

Chapter One Hundred and Thirty-Seven

Section: Bizarre & Lesser-Known Conspiracies

Conspiracy: The Sky Is a Hologram

Summary

The Sky Is a Hologram conspiracy claims that what we see above us — the Sun, Moon, stars, and even clouds — is not a natural atmosphere but a projected or simulated image, created using advanced technology.

Believers argue that governments or secret powers use massive projection systems (sometimes attributed to HAARP, chemtrails, or satellite arrays) to create an artificial sky that hides the true nature of the world above us.

History & Key Claims

Origins of the Theory:

Grew from Flat Earth and Simulation Theory circles.

Supporters claim certain anomalies in the sky (duplicate suns, odd cloud patterns, Moon transparency) are glitches in a projection system.

Core Allegations:

Artificial Sun and Moon: Some theorists claim the Sun is a holographic light source; the Moon may be a projection masking something behind it.

Stars as Light Show: Constellations are programmed, with changes over time reflecting updates to the "display."

Purpose: To conceal evidence of other landmasses, alien structures, or the firmament.

Evidence Cited by Believers:

Sun Dog Phenomenon: Multiple sun-like reflections are interpreted as projection glitches.

Cloud Layer Oddities: Clouds that appear in front of the Moon or Sun are viewed as proof of layering in the projection.

Pixelation in Photos: Digital artifacts in photos of the sky are said to reveal the holographic grid.

Counterpoint:

Atmospheric optics explain phenomena like sun dogs and halo effects.

No evidence exists of the massive infrastructure that would be required for a full-sky projection.

Famous Quotes / Sources

"The stars are a screen, the sky is a dome, and they control the show."

— Conspiracy podcast, Beyond the Veil

"When the clouds glitch, they reveal the truth."

— Sky anomaly forum user

"The atmospheric and astronomical phenomena are well understood and natural."

— NASA scientist

Real-World Consequences

Integration with Project Blue Beam:

Tied into theories of fake alien invasions and mass mind control.

Public Distrust of Space Agencies:

Used to support claims that NASA and other agencies fabricate space data.

Internet Spread:

Sky anomaly videos are popular on TikTok, YouTube, and conspiracy forums.

Where It Stands Today

The Sky Is a Hologram theory is scientifically unsupported, but visually compelling "evidence" and distrust of institutions keep it alive.

For believers, the stars above are not infinite space — they are a carefully programmed illusion concealing the real world beyond.

Chapter One Hundred and Thirty-Eight

Section: Bizarre & Lesser-Known Conspiracies

Conspiracy: The Earth Is a Prison Planet

Summary

The Prison Planet conspiracy claims that Earth is not a free and natural home for humanity, but a cosmic prison designed to contain human souls or consciousness. According to believers, advanced beings or cosmic powers placed humanity here as punishment, containment, or experimentation.

This theory overlaps with Gnostic beliefs, alien intervention theories, and simulation concepts, suggesting that the systems of life, death, and reincarnation are all part of the prison structure.

History & Key Claims

Ancient Roots:

Gnostic cosmology described the physical world as a trap created by a false god (the Demiurge) to keep souls from reaching true divinity.

Religious interpretations in Buddhism and Hinduism describe cycles of rebirth (samsara) as suffering, from which one must escape.

Modern Conspiracy Adaptations:

The idea was popularized in modern fringe circles by writers like David Icke, who links it to Reptilian control and interdimensional manipulation.

Believers claim the Moon or Saturn act as soul-recycling stations, preventing escape after death.

Signs of the "Prison":

Human suffering, inequality, and environmental hostility.

The inability to leave Earth without government-controlled space programs.

Reincarnation as a forced system to keep souls trapped.

Purpose of the Prison:

Energy Harvest: Humanity's emotions and labor feed the jailers.

Control Experiment: Earth serves as a controlled test site for consciousness.

Counterpoint:

These ideas are philosophical and speculative; there is no physical evidence of a planetary prison system.

Famous Quotes / Sources

"This is not our home. This is a cage."

— David Icke

"The wheel of reincarnation is not a gift — it's a trap."

— Gnostic philosophy forum

"The idea of a prison planet is symbolic, not literal."

— Religious scholar, Comparative Mythology

Real-World Consequences

Spiritual Movements:

Influences certain New Age practices aimed at breaking free from the reincarnation cycle.

Integration with Alien Conspiracies:

Linked to Reptilian control, soul harvesting, and hidden cosmic governance.

Psychological Effect:

Shapes the worldview of believers, leading to distrust of earthly authority as part of a cosmic hierarchy.

Where It Stands Today

Mainstream science dismisses the Prison Planet theory as metaphysical speculation, but in conspiracy and esoteric circles, it remains a powerful metaphor for human limitation and control.

For believers, Earth is not home — it's a carefully maintained cell, and freedom lies beyond the walls of this world.

Chapter One Hundred and Thirty-Nine

Section: Bizarre & Lesser-Known Conspiracies

Conspiracy: Ice Wall Surrounds Flat Earth

Summary

The Ice Wall Surrounds Flat Earth conspiracy claims that Earth is not a globe, but a flat disc encircled by a massive ice wall — often identified as Antarctica. According to believers, this wall prevents the oceans from spilling over the edge and hides whatever lies beyond, whether other continents, vast oceans, or hidden realms.

This theory is one of the central pillars of Flat Earth belief and is often tied to claims about global treaties, restricted exploration, and government secrecy.

History & Key Claims

Origins of the Theory:

Based on the Azimuthal Equidistant map often used in Flat Earth models.

The wall concept dates back to early Flat Earth societies of the 19th century.

Reinforced by Antarctic Treaty restrictions that limit free travel in the southern polar region.

The Ice Wall:

Allegedly thousands of feet high.

Surrounds the edge of the Earth's disc.

Guards are supposedly stationed to keep civilians away (military enforcement claimed by some believers).

What Lies Beyond:

Theories vary:

Infinite Plane: The Earth continues beyond the ice with more oceans and landmasses.

Dome Enclosure: The ice wall supports a dome (the "firmament").

Unknown Worlds: Other civilizations, resources, or realms exist beyond the wall.

Counterpoint:

Antarctica has been mapped, flown over, and traversed; the "ice wall" is consistent with the continent's coastline and glaciers.

There is no evidence of an edge or enclosed dome.

Famous Quotes / Sources

"The Antarctic ice wall is the barrier between us and the truth."

— Flat Earth researcher

"They built the Antarctic Treaty to hide what lies beyond."

— Alternative geography forum

"There's no wall. Just a frozen continent at the South Pole."

— Antarctic explorer

Real-World Consequences

Integration with Other Conspiracies:

Linked to Antarctica Doesn't Exist, Hollow Earth, and Prison Planet ideas.

Public Distrust of Space & Exploration Agencies:

Believers argue space imagery is faked to keep the ice wall secret.

Cultural Meme:

The "ice wall" has become one of the most well-known symbols of Flat Earth culture.

Where It Stands Today

Mainstream science rejects the idea of an ice wall encircling a flat Earth. However, within Flat Earth circles, the ice wall is seen as the ultimate boundary — the edge of our known world, guarded to keep us from seeing what lies beyond.

Chapter One Hundred and Forty

Section: Bizarre & Lesser-Known Conspiracies

Conspiracy: Reverse Speech Reveals Hidden Messages

Summary

The Reverse Speech conspiracy claims that when human speech is recorded and played backwards, it reveals hidden subconscious messages — sometimes deliberately planted, sometimes unintentionally embedded in normal conversation.

Believers argue that reverse speech can expose politicians' true intentions, hidden meanings in music, and subconscious confessions.

History & Key Claims

Origins of the Theory:

Popularized in the 1980s by researcher David John Oates, who claimed to discover meaningful phrases when playing speech backwards.

Suggested that the subconscious mind "leaks" truth in reverse speech, even when the forward speech is deceptive.

Applications in Conspiracy Circles:

Political Speeches: Reverse speech is analyzed to detect lies or secret agendas.

Music Industry: Accusations that songs contain deliberate backward messages (often tied to Satanic Panic in the 1980s).

Crime Investigations: Some alternative investigators claim reverse speech can reveal the truth behind unsolved crimes.

Evidence Cited by Believers:

Famous examples include:

The Beatles' Revolution 9 allegedly containing "Turn me on, dead man" when reversed.

Led Zeppelin's Stairway to Heaven allegedly hiding occult phrases.

Politicians' speeches revealing contradictory reversed statements.

Counterpoint:

Linguists argue reverse speech "messages" are the result of pareidolia — the brain finding patterns where none exist.

No scientific study has confirmed reverse speech as a reliable communication method.

Famous Quotes / Sources

"Reverse speech is the human truth machine."

— David John Oates

"When you flip the track, the meaning comes through."

— Reverse speech enthusiast

"There's no evidence of coherent reverse messages — it's audio coincidence."

— Audio linguistics professor

Real-World Consequences

Cultural Panic:

Reverse speech claims fueled the 1980s Satanic Panic, with music scrutinized for hidden messages.

Ongoing Analysis:

Reverse speech still circulates in conspiracy videos analyzing current political leaders and celebrities.

Integration with Other Theories:

Often linked to MKUltra mind control, Illuminati symbolism, and predictive programming.

Where It Stands Today

While scientifically dismissed, reverse speech remains a popular tool for conspiracy investigators.

For believers, playing audio backwards is not just a curiosity — it's a direct line to the truths they say "they" can't keep hidden forever.

Chapter One Hundred and Forty-One

Section: Economic & Financial Conspiracies

Conspiracy: The Federal Reserve Is a Private Cartel

Summary

The Federal Reserve private cartel conspiracy claims that the U.S. central banking system is not a government institution but a private banking cartel that controls the economy for the benefit of powerful elites. According to this theory, the Fed manipulates interest rates, inflation, and money supply to enrich a small group of banking families and corporations at the expense of the general public.

History & Key Claims

Origins of the Federal Reserve:

Established in 1913 with the Federal Reserve Act.

Officially described as a public-private hybrid system: 12 regional Federal Reserve Banks are technically private but operate under congressional oversight.

Conspiracists argue this structure allows private banking interests to control national monetary policy.

Key Allegations:

Private Ownership: Claims that elite families (e.g., Rothschilds, Rockefellers) have influence over the Fed.

Interest Debt Trap: The Fed issues currency as debt, creating perpetual obligations to private banks.

Economic Manipulation: Interest rate changes and monetary policy allegedly favor Wall Street over Main Street.

Lack of Transparency: Critics point to limited audits and the Fed's relative independence from elected officials.

Supporting Evidence Cited:

The 1910 Jekyll Island meeting, where bankers and politicians met in secret to draft what became the Federal Reserve Act.

Statements from economists critical of centralized private banking power.

Counterpoint:

While private banks own stock in regional Federal Reserve Banks, these shares do not operate like corporate stock (they cannot be sold, and dividends are limited).

The Fed's policy decisions are overseen by Congress and subject to public reporting.

Famous Quotes / Sources

"The Federal Reserve is no more federal than Federal Express."

— Congressman Ron Paul

"Control the issuance of a nation's money and you control the nation."

— Attributed to Mayer Amschel Rothschild (disputed)

"The Fed is independent, but it is accountable to the public and Congress."

— Federal Reserve official

Real-World Consequences

Distrust of Monetary Policy:

Fuels movements to audit or abolish the Fed.

Integration with Larger Conspiracies:

Often tied to global banking elite and New World Order theories.

Policy Impact:

Political campaigns (e.g., Ron Paul's 2008 & 2012 runs) gained traction using Fed distrust as a central talking point.

Where It Stands Today

The Federal Reserve operates with a unique structure that fuels suspicion, but mainstream economists reject the idea of it being a secretive private cartel.

For believers, however, the Fed remains the hidden hand guiding America's economy — for the benefit of a few, at the cost of many.

Chapter One Hundred and Forty-Two

Section: Economic & Financial Conspiracies

Conspiracy: The Great Depression Was Engineered

Summary

The conspiracy that The Great Depression was engineered claims that the devastating economic collapse of 1929–1939 was not an accident, but a deliberate manipulation of markets and monetary policy by powerful bankers and financial elites. According to this theory, the collapse was orchestrated to consolidate wealth, bankrupt competitors, and expand centralized banking control.

History & Key Claims

Official Account:

The Great Depression began after the 1929 stock market crash, followed by bank failures, reduced spending, and mass unemployment.

Mainstream history attributes it to economic speculation, structural weaknesses, and policy errors.

Conspiracy Allegations:

Manipulation by Bankers: Wealthy banking families allegedly withdrew liquidity, causing mass bankruptcies.

Federal Reserve Role: The Fed's tightening of monetary policy during the early 1930s is seen as deliberately worsening the crisis.

Wealth Consolidation: As assets collapsed in value, elites bought property, companies, and land at rock-bottom prices.

Political Outcomes: The crisis enabled major economic reforms (e.g., New Deal programs, banking regulations) that expanded government and central bank power.

Evidence Cited by Believers:

Quotes from prominent bankers about profiting from market crashes.

The timing of major bank mergers and acquisitions during the Depression.

Patterns of gold accumulation by wealthy interests before and during the crash.

Counterpoint:

Economists argue the Depression was due to economic instability and inadequate policy response, not intentional sabotage.

No concrete evidence exists of a coordinated plot to trigger the crash.

Famous Quotes / Sources

"The depression was the calculated 'shearing' of the public by the world money powers."

— Attributed to Louis T. McFadden, U.S. Congressman

"When the tide went out, those who had cash bought everything worth owning."

— Conspiracy economics blog

"The collapse was a tragic combination of speculation and poor policy, not a grand conspiracy."

— Economic historian

Real-World Consequences

Distrust of Financial Institutions:

Strengthened anti-bank sentiment and populist economic movements.

Integration with Larger Theories:

Often tied to Federal Reserve control, Rothschild banking conspiracy, and global economic manipulation.

Cultural Impact:

The idea that crises are opportunities for elites persists in public opinion.

Where It Stands Today

While mainstream historians reject intentional engineering of the Depression, the event's massive wealth transfer fuels suspicion to this day.

For believers, the Great Depression wasn't just a tragedy — it was an orchestrated economic reset to cement elite control.

Chapter One Hundred and Forty-Three

Section: Economic & Financial Conspiracies

Conspiracy: The 2008 Financial Crash Was Orchestrated

Summary

The conspiracy that the 2008 Financial Crash was orchestrated claims that the global economic collapse was not a random housing market failure, but a deliberate event engineered by financial elites and major institutions.

According to this theory, banks and investment firms knowingly created risky conditions, inflated asset bubbles, and then profited from the crash through bailouts, foreclosures, and asset consolidation — all at the expense of the public.

History & Key Claims

Official Account:

The crash began with the bursting of the U.S. housing bubble in 2007–2008.

Risky mortgage lending, securitization of bad loans, and financial deregulation led to a banking crisis and global recession.

Governments intervened with bailouts to prevent systemic collapse.

Conspiracy Allegations:

Deliberate Market Manipulation: Major banks packaged bad mortgages into securities knowing they would fail.

Profit from Collapse: Institutions bet against the same products they sold, making billions during the crash.

Engineered Panic: Coordinated media and market moves allegedly worsened the crisis at key moments.

Bailouts as Payoffs: The largest banks received taxpayer-funded bailouts, while smaller competitors failed or were absorbed.

Evidence Cited by Believers:

Internal communications from banks showing awareness of toxic mortgage securities.

"Too Big to Fail" doctrine: Only the largest institutions were protected.

Executives faced little to no criminal accountability despite massive losses.

Counterpoint:

Mainstream analysis attributes the crisis to greed, regulatory failure, and misjudgment, not a coordinated conspiracy.

Complex global economic systems make total orchestration unlikely.

Famous Quotes / Sources

"This was the greatest heist in modern history, carried out in plain sight."

— Conspiracy economics podcast

"They created the crisis, profited from it, then got paid to fix it."

— Alternative finance blog

"The crash was a systemic failure, not a deliberate plot."

— Financial historian

Real-World Consequences

Public Distrust of Banking:

Fueled widespread anger at Wall Street and financial institutions.

Political Movements:

Helped launch Occupy Wall Street and broader anti-bank activism.

Integration with Other Theories:

Seen as a modern example of elites using crises for profit, similar to Great Depression theories.

Where It Stands Today

While the official view sees the 2008 crash as a catastrophic failure, conspiracy theorists view it as an intentional transfer of wealth and power. For believers, 2008 wasn't a collapse — it was a calculated harvest.

Chapter One Hundred and Forty-Four

Section: Economic & Financial Conspiracies

Conspiracy: Gold Is Being Hoarded by Elites

Summary

The conspiracy that gold is being hoarded by elites claims that vast reserves of gold are secretly controlled, hidden, and stockpiled by powerful governments, central banks, and wealthy families. According to this theory, the true quantity and distribution of gold is deliberately concealed to manipulate global markets, maintain fiat currency dominance, and secure financial leverage in a future economic collapse.

History & Key Claims

Historic Role of Gold:

Gold has been a store of value for thousands of years.

Nations abandoned the gold standard in the 20th century, but gold reserves still underpin central bank stability.

Core Allegations:

Undisclosed Reserves: Official gold reserve numbers are allegedly false or understated.

Hidden Vaults: Enormous amounts of gold stored in secret bunkers (often linked to places like Fort Knox, Swiss vaults, or Asian treasuries).

Market Manipulation: Gold prices are artificially suppressed to keep confidence in fiat currencies.

Wealth Transfer in Crises: During economic downturns, gold allegedly moves quietly into elite control while prices are low.

Evidence Cited by Believers:

Lack of recent independent audits of Fort Knox and other major depositories.

Historical cases of gold confiscation, such as U.S. Executive Order 6102 (1933).

Rumors of Yamashita's Gold and other massive hidden caches from WWII.

Counterpoint:

Economists and financial institutions say gold reserves are well documented, and price fluctuations are due to supply, demand, and market speculation.

Famous Quotes / Sources

"If the people knew how much gold is hidden, they would never trust the dollar again."

— Conspiracy economics blog

"The real gold market is smoke and mirrors."

— Alternative finance commentator

"There's no credible evidence of massive secret stockpiles."

— International Monetary Fund statement

Real-World Consequences

Public Distrust of Central Banks:

Fuels calls for audit-the-gold-reserve movements.

Integration with Other Theories:

Linked to Federal Reserve conspiracy, Great Reset fears, and global currency collapse scenarios.

Investor Behavior:

Encourages individual gold hoarding among conspiracy-minded investors.

Where It Stands Today

While there's no definitive proof of massive secret gold reserves, the secrecy surrounding national holdings and the history of government gold manipulation make this theory persistent.

For believers, the gold is there — but it's locked away in elite vaults, waiting for the day fiat currency falls.

Chapter One Hundred and Forty-Five

Section: Economic & Financial Conspiracies

Conspiracy: Central Banks Want a One-World Currency

Summary

The One-World Currency conspiracy claims that central banks, working through international financial bodies, are pushing toward replacing national currencies with a single global currency. This currency would allegedly serve as the economic foundation of a New World Order, allowing a small elite to control the global economy.

History & Key Claims

Historic Precedents:

International financial systems have evolved toward global integration (e.g., Bretton Woods system, IMF, World Bank).

Currency unions like the Eurozone show that coordinated currency systems are possible.

Core Allegations:

Global Financial Unification: The International Monetary Fund (IMF), World Bank, and Bank for International Settlements are working toward a single digital currency.

Crisis as Catalyst: Financial crashes, wars, and pandemics are allegedly used to justify moving toward global financial centralization.

Loss of National Sovereignty: A single currency removes independent control of monetary policy, consolidating power at the top.

Evidence Cited by Believers:

IMF's Special Drawing Rights (SDRs), which function as a synthetic reserve currency.

Discussions of Central Bank Digital Currencies (CBDCs).

Warnings from financial leaders about the "inevitable" shift to global currency in economic forums.

Counterpoint:

While international cooperation in finance is increasing, no official plan exists for a single currency replacing all national currencies.

Technical, political, and cultural challenges make full adoption unlikely.

Famous Quotes / Sources

"A single global currency is the end goal of the financial elite."

— Conspiracy finance blog

"The IMF's SDR is the test model for a one-world currency."

— Alternative economics podcast

"There is no current plan for a single currency, but increased cooperation is real."

— IMF spokesperson

Real-World Consequences

Integration with New World Order Theories:

Seen as a financial step toward global governance.

Public Resistance:

Fear of losing national independence and privacy fuels opposition to global digital currency plans.

Investor Behavior:

Push toward decentralized assets like gold and cryptocurrency by skeptics.

Where It Stands Today

While no formal one-world currency exists, moves toward globalized digital payment systems and centralized banking integration keep the conspiracy alive.

For believers, the plan is clear: collapse the old system and replace it with a single currency controlled by the few.

Chapter One Hundred and Forty-Six

Section: Economic & Financial Conspiracies

Conspiracy: Bitcoin Was Created by the CIA

Summary

The Bitcoin Was Created by the CIA conspiracy claims that the world's first cryptocurrency was not invented by an anonymous coder named Satoshi Nakamoto, but by the U.S. Central Intelligence Agency (or another intelligence group) as part of a long-term plan to normalize digital currency, track transactions, and prepare the public for fully traceable money systems.

History & Key Claims

Official Account:

Bitcoin was launched in 2009 following the 2008 financial crisis.

Created by the pseudonymous Satoshi Nakamoto as a decentralized, peer-to-peer digital currency without centralized control.

Conspiracy Allegations:

Satoshi's Identity: The anonymity of Nakamoto fuels suspicion; some theorists claim "Satoshi" is a codename for a government project.

Blockchain Surveillance: While Bitcoin is marketed as anonymous, all transactions are recorded on a public ledger — making tracking possible for intelligence agencies.

Controlled Introduction of Digital Money: Bitcoin is seen as a soft introduction to digital-only currency, paving the way for central bank digital currencies (CBDCs).

Timing: Bitcoin's launch just after the 2008 crisis is viewed as too coincidental.

Evidence Cited by Believers:

Satoshi's disappearance from public view in 2011.

Early mining dominance by unknown entities.

The fact that blockchain technology was discussed in government research circles before Bitcoin's release.

Counterpoint:

No direct evidence links Bitcoin to the CIA.

The open-source nature of Bitcoin's code makes it difficult for any single agency to control.

Famous Quotes / Sources

"Satoshi Nakamoto is as real as CIA code names ever get."

— Conspiracy tech forum

"Bitcoin was the trojan horse for global digital finance."

— Alternative finance blogger

"There's no evidence Bitcoin is a CIA creation — but it wouldn't surprise me."

— Cybersecurity researcher

Real-World Consequences

Public Distrust of Cryptocurrencies:

Fuels suspicion that Bitcoin is not truly decentralized.

Integration with Larger Conspiracies:

Linked to One-World Currency theories, Great Reset fears, and financial surveillance concerns.

Shift to Alternative Assets:

Some believers prefer privacy coins or physical assets like gold and silver.

Where It Stands Today

Mainstream opinion treats Bitcoin as a grassroots invention, but its mysterious origins and perfect timing keep the CIA theory alive.

For believers, Bitcoin isn't the money of the people — it's the prototype for the surveillance currency of the future.

Chapter One Hundred and Forty-Seven

Section: Economic & Financial Conspiracies

Conspiracy: The Great Reset by the World Economic Forum

Summary

The Great Reset conspiracy claims that the World Economic Forum's (WEF) "Great Reset" initiative is not a benign plan for post-pandemic economic reform, but rather a coordinated effort to restructure global society — consolidating wealth, eroding individual freedoms, and creating a centralized technocratic system under elite control.

History & Key Claims

Official Explanation:

Announced in June 2020 by the WEF.

Framed as an economic recovery strategy after COVID-19, focusing on sustainability, equity, and digital transformation.

Conspiracy Allegations:

Hidden Agenda: Behind the public rhetoric of sustainability is a plan for global control over assets, economies, and individuals.

Private Property Concerns: The WEF's own promotional material ("You'll own nothing and be happy") is interpreted as removal of private ownership.

Technocratic Governance: Centralized decisions about production, resources, and personal freedoms.

Integration with Other Systems: Tied to ESG scores, digital IDs, CBDCs, and social credit–style tracking.

Evidence Cited by Believers:

Public statements by WEF founder Klaus Schwab about the need for "deep systemic change."

The rapid alignment of governments, corporations, and financial institutions behind similar sustainability goals.

Parallel rise of digital tracking technologies and corporate-government cooperation.

Counterpoint:

The WEF argues the initiative promotes collaboration for global stability, not authoritarian control.

Critics point out that much of the theory misinterprets or exaggerates WEF proposals.

Famous Quotes / Sources

"You'll own nothing. And you'll be happy."

— WEF video (often cited in conspiracy discussions)

"The Great Reset is the public face of a deeper, hidden restructuring."

— Conspiracy economics forum

"The Great Reset is a branding exercise for ideas that have been discussed for years."

— Economist, Financial Times

Real-World Consequences

Public Distrust of Global Institutions:

Fuels resistance to international agreements, climate policies, and economic reforms.

Integration with Other Conspiracies:

Linked to New World Order, One-World Currency, and ESG score as social control theories.

Political Mobilization:

Used as a rallying point by activists opposing globalization and centralization.

Where It Stands Today

While the WEF maintains that the Great Reset is about sustainability and resilience, critics see it as an open declaration of a global restructuring project.

For believers, the Great Reset isn't a plan for recovery — it's the blueprint for a controlled future run by elite technocrats.

Chapter One Hundred and Forty-Eight

Section: Economic & Financial Conspiracies

Conspiracy: ESG Scores as Social Control

Summary

The ESG Scores as Social Control conspiracy claims that Environmental, Social, and Governance (ESG) scores — a system used to evaluate companies' sustainability and ethics — are not just about responsible business practices, but are a framework for monitoring, rating, and controlling individuals and organizations.

According to this theory, ESG scores will eventually evolve into a global compliance system, similar to a social credit score, where businesses and citizens are rewarded or punished based on how well they align with government-approved values and behaviors.

History & Key Claims

Official Explanation:

ESG scoring is intended to guide investment toward companies that are environmentally sustainable, socially responsible, and well governed.

Adopted by investment firms, financial institutions, and regulators in the 2010s.

Conspiracy Allegations:

Control Mechanism: ESG scoring will be expanded from companies to individuals, creating a system of behavior tracking.

Political Enforcement: Companies with low ESG ratings could face restricted financing, while individuals might see reduced access to loans, jobs, or services if they fail to meet environmental or social "targets."

Centralization of Power: Banks, investment funds, and governments could use ESG as a unified measure of compliance.

Link to The Great Reset: ESG scores are seen as a key tool for enforcing the WEF's sustainability agenda.

Evidence Cited by Believers:

Financial institutions divesting from industries with low ESG ratings.

Proposals linking ESG compliance to government contracts and subsidies.

Public discussion of expanding ESG principles into consumer credit assessments.

Counterpoint:

ESG is primarily a corporate investment tool; extending it to individuals would require major structural and legal changes.

Critics of the conspiracy argue that ESG is inconsistent and poorly standardized, making it unlikely as a universal control tool.

Famous Quotes / Sources

"ESG is the dress rehearsal for a global social credit system."

— Conspiracy economics blog

"Your ability to participate in the economy will depend on your compliance score."

— Alternative finance forum

"ESG is a voluntary business practice, not a surveillance tool."

— ESG consulting firm

Real-World Consequences

Integration with Other Conspiracies:

Closely tied to The Great Reset, social credit systems, and CBDC control.

Public Pushback:

Some states and politicians have begun opposing ESG adoption in public finance.

Market Shifts:

Fear of ESG enforcement drives investment toward alternative, non-ESG funds.

Where It Stands Today

While mainstream finance treats ESG as a corporate rating system, conspiracy theorists see it as a stepping stone toward global behavioral scoring.

For believers, ESG is not about sustainability — it's about control through compliance metrics.

Chapter One Hundred and Forty-Nine

Section: Economic & Financial Conspiracies

Conspiracy: Social Credit Systems Are Spreading

Summary

The Social Credit Systems Are Spreading conspiracy claims that governments and corporations are working to implement nationwide, and eventually global, systems of behavioral scoring similar to China's social credit model.

In such systems, an individual's access to financial services, travel, housing, employment, and even internet use could be influenced by a constantly updated score based on their actions, purchases, and online activity.

History & Key Claims

China's Social Credit Program:

Began in 2014 as a nationwide initiative to track compliance with laws and regulations.

Points added for positive behaviors (e.g., paying debts, volunteering) and deducted for offenses (e.g., traffic violations, political dissent).

Restricted access to travel, loans, and services for low scorers.

Conspiracy Allegations:

Export of the Model: Western nations are slowly adopting similar systems under the guise of public safety, financial compliance, and ESG-related tracking.

Corporate Participation: Major tech companies, payment processors, and credit agencies allegedly build infrastructure for behavior-linked access.

Soft Introduction: COVID-19 health passes, ESG scores, and carbon tracking apps are viewed as early steps.

Global Rollout: Linked to The Great Reset and CBDC implementation for seamless score enforcement.

Evidence Cited by Believers:

Digital ID programs emerging in Canada, the EU, and Australia.

Discussions about carbon footprint trackers in banking apps.

Public support for behavior-based financial incentives.

Counterpoint:

While certain tracking systems exist, there is no unified global plan for a single social credit score.

Privacy laws and decentralized governance make global enforcement difficult.

Famous Quotes / Sources

"China was just the test run. The system is coming to the West."

— Conspiracy forum

"Your score will determine your freedom to participate in society."

— Alternative finance podcast

"Western democracies have no official plans for social credit systems, but some policies mimic similar mechanisms."

— Policy analyst

Real-World Consequences

Public Distrust:

Resistance to digital ID systems, vaccine passports, and carbon tracking tools.

Integration with Other Conspiracies:

Strongly tied to The Great Reset, ESG scores, and CBDCs.

Policy Pushback:

Governments in some countries have explicitly stated they will not implement social credit systems, partly due to public concern.

Where It Stands Today

Social credit remains official policy in China, but in conspiracy circles, it's seen as a blueprint for global behavioral governance.

For believers, the spread of tracking technology isn't about convenience — it's the infrastructure for a world where your score controls your life.

Chapter One Hundred and Fifty

Section: Economic & Financial Conspiracies

Conspiracy: Weather Disasters for Insurance Fraud

Summary

The Weather Disasters for Insurance Fraud conspiracy claims that certain natural disasters — hurricanes, floods, wildfires, and even extreme storms — are intentionally intensified or artificially created to enable large-scale insurance payouts, real estate manipulation, and profit for corporations.

Believers argue that weather modification technology and deliberately negligent infrastructure planning are used as tools to generate losses that certain companies are positioned to exploit.

History & Key Claims

Official Position:

Weather disasters are natural events caused by climate cycles, environmental conditions, and (in recent years) climate change.

Insurance fraud typically refers to individuals inflating claims — not creating the disaster itself.

Conspiracy Allegations:

Deliberate Intensification: Hurricanes, droughts, and wildfires are strengthened using weather manipulation technology such as HAARP or cloud seeding.

Financial Motive: Large insurance companies and reinsurance firms can hedge losses, profiting from certain payouts or property buyouts.

Real Estate Acquisition: After disasters, devastated areas are purchased cheaply by developers or investment groups.

Government-Corporate Collaboration: Local or federal agencies allegedly work with private industry to target specific regions for "economic resets."

Evidence Cited by Believers:

Patterns of repeated disasters in economically valuable locations.

Unusual meteorological behavior during certain storms.

Large corporations benefiting from disaster recovery contracts.

Counterpoint:

No direct evidence links weather modification to intentional disasters.

Financial markets typically view disasters as risk events, not opportunities for profit.

Famous Quotes / Sources

"Some disasters are just too perfectly timed to be natural."

— Conspiracy weather blog

"They destroy it, claim insurance, then buy it back for pennies."

— Alternative economics discussion

"While fraud exists, large-scale weather creation remains scientifically unsupported."

— Meteorologist

Real-World Consequences

Integration with Other Conspiracies:

Linked to HAARP weather control, Great Reset land acquisition, and climate engineering.

Public Distrust:

Suspicion toward insurance companies, disaster relief agencies, and rebuilding programs.

Policy Pressure:

Calls for more transparency in disaster response, insurance payouts, and weather data.

Where It Stands Today

Mainstream science attributes disasters to natural processes and climate change, but for believers, certain storms and fires are precision tools in a financial game.

For them, disaster isn't just nature — it's profitable destruction by design.

Chapter One Hundred and Fifty-One

Section: More Conspiracies from Around the World

Conspiracy: The Vatican Archives Are Hiding World Secrets

Summary

The Vatican Secret Archives conspiracy claims that deep within the Vatican City lies a vast collection of ancient texts, relics, and records that contain world-changing information deliberately kept from the public.

Believers argue that these archives hold evidence of lost civilizations, forbidden religious texts, extraterrestrial contact, suppressed scientific discoveries, and artifacts from biblical events.

History & Key Claims

What the Vatican Says:

The Vatican Apostolic Archive (formerly called the Secret Archive) contains documents dating back over 1,200 years.

Officially restricted to qualified scholars for specific research purposes.

Items are said to include papal correspondence, diplomatic records, and church documents.

Conspiracy Allegations:

Suppressed Religious Texts: Lost gospels, books removed from the Bible, and accounts of early Christian teachings that challenge modern Catholic doctrine.

Ancient Knowledge: Maps and documents revealing the locations of lost cities (Atlantis, ancient Jerusalem layouts, Ark of the Covenant).

Extraterrestrial Contact: Claims of records proving alien encounters dating back centuries.

Historical Cover-Ups: Evidence about events like the Crusades, Inquisition, and collaboration with political regimes that contradict the public narrative.

Evidence Cited by Believers:

The extreme secrecy of the archive (no free public access).

Historical incidents where documents were selectively revealed or destroyed.

Reports of missing or censored Vatican records during wars.

Counterpoint:

The archive's restricted access is explained as necessary to preserve delicate documents.

Most items cataloged are administrative or theological, not evidence of world-altering secrets.

Famous Quotes / Sources

"If the truth in those vaults was revealed, the Church would fall overnight."

— Conspiracy religious forum

"The Vatican has knowledge that predates the nations of Europe."

— Alternative history researcher

"The archive is less mysterious than people imagine, but secrecy always fuels conspiracy."

— Vatican historian

Real-World Consequences

Fuel for Religious Conspiracies:

Strengthens theories about Church control of history and suppression of knowledge.

Cultural Fascination:

Inspires films (Angels & Demons), books (Holy Blood, Holy Grail), and endless speculation.

Integration with Other Theories:

Linked to Nephilim bloodlines, Atlantis, and hidden relics.

Where It Stands Today

While mainstream scholars treat the archive as a historical library, conspiracy believers see it as the world's most guarded treasure trove of hidden truths.

For them, the Vatican doesn't just guard history — it controls humanity's access to it.

Chapter One Hundred and Fifty-Two

Section: More Conspiracies from Around the World

Conspiracy: The Nephilim and Ancient Bloodlines

Summary

The Nephilim and Ancient Bloodlines conspiracy claims that the biblical Nephilim — described as the offspring of fallen angels and human women in the Book of Genesis — were real beings, and that their bloodlines have been preserved through royalty, secret societies, and elite families.

According to believers, these bloodlines form a hidden ruling class with supernatural heritage and influence over global affairs.

History & Key Claims

Biblical & Ancient Origins:

In Genesis 6:4, the Nephilim are described as "mighty men of old, men of renown."

Some interpretations suggest they were giants or semi-divine hybrids.

Ancient texts like the Book of Enoch expand on the story, detailing the Watchers (fallen angels) and their offspring.

Conspiracy Allegations:

Royal Bloodlines: European monarchies, secret orders, and dynastic families are alleged to carry Nephilim blood.

Illuminati Connection: Nephilim-descended elites supposedly control global politics, banking, and religion.

Genetic Preservation: Marriages between powerful families keep the "pure" bloodline intact.

Suppressed Archaeology: Giant skeleton discoveries are allegedly hidden to protect the official narrative.

Evidence Cited by Believers:

Biblical references and apocryphal texts.

Symbolism in coats of arms, architecture, and rituals of elite families.

Historical intermarriage among aristocratic families.

Counterpoint:

Historians see Nephilim as mythological figures, not literal beings.

Royal intermarriage is explained as political strategy, not supernatural preservation.

Famous Quotes / Sources

"The Nephilim never vanished — they became kings."

— Conspiracy religious blog

"The bloodlines of power trace back to Genesis."

— Alternative history researcher

"The Nephilim are symbolic of corruption, not evidence of alien or angelic DNA."

— Biblical scholar

Real-World Consequences

Integration with Other Theories:

Closely tied to Illuminati, Vatican secrecy, and elite reptilian control theories.

Cultural Impact:

Popular in books (Bloodline of the Holy Grail), documentaries, and YouTube investigations.

Spiritual Influence:

Shapes belief among some groups that the end-times conflict involves these ancient bloodlines.

Where It Stands Today

Mainstream religion views the Nephilim as symbolic or mythic, but for conspiracy believers, their blood runs in the veins of today's most powerful families, quietly directing world events.

Chapter One Hundred and Fifty-Three

Section: More Conspiracies from Around the World

Conspiracy: The Georgia Guidestones Mystery

Summary

The Georgia Guidestones Mystery centers on a granite monument erected in 1980 in Elbert County, Georgia. Inscribed with messages in multiple languages, the stones present ten guiding principles for humanity, including a controversial recommendation to maintain the world population under 500 million.

Believers argue the Guidestones are a public declaration of the elite's depopulation agenda, or a coded set of rules for a post-apocalyptic world order.

History & Key Claims

Construction & Origin:

Commissioned in 1979 by a man using the pseudonym R.C. Christian.

Built in 1980, the monument contains inscriptions in eight modern languages and four ancient scripts.

The true identity and motives of the sponsor remain unknown.

The Ten "Guides":

Highlights include:

Maintain humanity under 500 million.

Guide reproduction wisely.

Unite humanity under a new language.

Balance personal rights with social duties.

These are interpreted by conspiracy theorists as New World Order principles.

Conspiracy Allegations:

Depopulation Plan: The 500 million population cap is viewed as an open admission of a planned reduction.

Elite Blueprint: Messages allegedly reflect WEF, UN, and other global agendas.

Occult Significance: The monument's layout aligns astronomically, suggesting hidden symbolism.

Destruction:

In July 2022, the monument was damaged by an explosion and later demolished, fueling speculation that it was removed to erase evidence or symbolism.

Counterpoint:

Supporters argue the stones were a philosophical work promoting sustainability, not a literal policy document.

Famous Quotes / Sources

"The stones were the manifesto of a silent ruling class."

— Conspiracy researcher

"They tell you what they want right in the open."

— Alternative history forum

"It was an eccentric monument, not a blueprint for genocide."

— Local historian

Real-World Consequences

Integration with Depopulation Theories:

Often linked to Great Reset and elite control conspiracies.

Cultural Impact:

Became a pilgrimage site for conspiracy theorists worldwide.

Post-Destruction Mystery:

Demolition renewed speculation about government involvement and secrecy.

Where It Stands Today

The Georgia Guidestones are gone, but the mystery — and conspiracy theories surrounding them — continue.

For believers, the stones were an elite proclamation of a controlled future, erased only to move plans out of public sight.

Chapter One Hundred and Fifty-Four

Section: More Conspiracies from Around the World

Conspiracy: The Lost Library of Alexandria Was Hidden

Summary

The Lost Library of Alexandria conspiracy claims that the ancient library — often said to have been destroyed in a series of fires — was never truly lost, but its most valuable scrolls and records were removed, hidden, or transferred to secret locations before its destruction.

Believers argue that these writings, containing ancient scientific knowledge, advanced technology, and forgotten history, are kept in places like the Vatican Archives, private collections of elite families, or secret government vaults.

History & Key Claims

Historical Background:

The Library of Alexandria, founded in the 3rd century BCE in Egypt, housed hundreds of thousands of scrolls on science, philosophy, mathematics, medicine, and history.

Traditionally believed to have been destroyed in multiple incidents (Julius Caesar's siege, later Roman attacks, and gradual decline).

Conspiracy Allegations:

Not Destroyed, But Taken: Key works were removed before fires to prevent dangerous or powerful knowledge from being lost — or released to the public.

Relocated Knowledge: Allegedly sent to the Vatican, hidden Middle Eastern libraries, or even secret archives in Asia.

Technological Suppression: Writings on ancient flight, advanced medicine, and energy systems are supposedly locked away to keep society under control.

Evidence in Modern Discoveries: Some theorists point to sudden bursts of rediscovered knowledge in later centuries (e.g., Renaissance science) as evidence of selective release.

Counterpoint:

Most historians argue that much of the library's collection was lost gradually and permanently.

Surviving classical works suggest major knowledge was preserved through copies in other libraries.

Famous Quotes / Sources

"They didn't burn knowledge — they hid it."

— Alternative history researcher

"The Renaissance was not discovery, it was controlled release."

— Conspiracy forum

"While the library's destruction is tragic, there's no evidence its contents survive intact in secret vaults."

— Classical historian

Real-World Consequences

Integration with Other Theories:

Closely tied to Vatican Archives, ancient technology theories, and Atlantis knowledge suppression.

Cultural Fascination:

Inspires countless books, films, and speculative documentaries.

Ongoing Search:

Amateur researchers and conspiracy theorists claim evidence of hidden Alexandrian archives in Ethiopia, India, and beneath the Vatican.

Where It Stands Today

While mainstream academia views the Library's destruction as a cultural tragedy, believers insist its greatest works were spirited away to secret vaults, awaiting a time when the elite choose to reveal them.

Chapter One Hundred and Fifty-Five

Section: More Conspiracies from Around the World

Conspiracy: TikTok as a Spy Tool

Summary

The TikTok as a Spy Tool conspiracy claims that the popular short-form video app is not just a social media platform but a massive surveillance operation, primarily serving as a data-harvesting tool for the Chinese government — and potentially for other governments as well.

Believers argue that TikTok collects extensive personal, location, and behavioral data that can be used for tracking, influence campaigns, and psychological profiling of users worldwide.

History & Key Claims

Official Concerns:

Governments in the U.S., Canada, India, and parts of Europe have raised national security concerns over TikTok's data practices.

Some nations have banned the app on government devices.

Conspiracy Allegations:

Data Collection at Scale: TikTok's algorithm gathers vast amounts of data, including:

Location tracking.

Device identifiers.

Keystroke patterns.

Content preferences and engagement metrics.

Behavioral Manipulation: The app allegedly uses its algorithm to amplify certain trends and suppress others for political or social influence.

Influence on Youth: Content promotion could subtly shape cultural and political attitudes of younger generations.

Chinese Government Ties: Parent company ByteDance is based in China, where laws may compel cooperation with the state.

Evidence Cited by Believers:

Investigations showing aggressive data collection far beyond typical social media platforms.

Past reports of content moderation influenced by geopolitical concerns.

The strategic focus on U.S. and Western youth demographics.

Counterpoint:

TikTok claims data for non-Chinese users is stored outside China.

Data collection practices are similar to other large social media companies (e.g., Meta, Google).

Famous Quotes / Sources

"Tiktok isn't just entertainment — it's surveillance wrapped in memes."

— Cybersecurity blogger

"It's the most effective cultural influence tool of our time."

— Conspiracy tech podcast

"While data concerns are real, it's not unique to TikTok — this is the nature of modern apps."

— Privacy researcher

Real-World Consequences

Government Action:

Bans and investigations in multiple countries.

Public Distrust:

Heightened skepticism of Chinese technology companies.

Integration with Other Theories:

Linked to China's influence campaigns, youth manipulation, and global psychological operations.

Where It Stands Today

While TikTok denies working as a spy tool, suspicion persists due to China's geopolitical position, ByteDance's origins, and the app's unmatched ability to shape culture. For believers, TikTok isn't just an app — it's a global data funnel and influence weapon disguised as entertainment.

Chapter One Hundred and Fifty-Six

Section: More Conspiracies from Around the World

Conspiracy: Subliminal Messaging in Advertising

Summary

The Subliminal Messaging in Advertising conspiracy claims that corporations, media companies, and political campaigns use hidden messages, images, or sounds to influence consumer behavior and public opinion without conscious awareness.

Believers argue that these techniques can manipulate emotions, purchasing decisions, and even political choices by bypassing rational thought and directly targeting the subconscious mind.

History & Key Claims

Origins of the Theory:

In 1957, market researcher James Vicary claimed that flashing "Drink Coca-Cola" and "Eat Popcorn" during a movie increased concession sales.

Though Vicary later admitted to exaggerating results, the idea of subliminal persuasion became deeply embedded in public consciousness.

Conspiracy Allegations:

Hidden Words/Images: Sexual or emotionally charged words and shapes hidden in ads to provoke subconscious responses.

Political Influence: Messages in political campaign ads allegedly designed to sway voter perception.

Music & Film: Backmasking and sound layering claimed to influence listeners' emotions and beliefs.

Corporate Strategy: Companies allegedly use subliminal branding to create brand loyalty without consumers realizing it.

Evidence Cited by Believers:

Examples of alleged hidden words or shapes in print ads (e.g., sexual imagery in ice cube shapes, clouds, or shadows).

Political ads accused of flashing words like "RATS" (2000 U.S. Presidential campaign incident).

Psychological studies on priming and subconscious influence.

Counterpoint:

Mainstream psychology finds subliminal messaging's influence is minimal or short-lived.

Many alleged examples are the result of pareidolia (seeing patterns where none were intended).

Famous Quotes / Sources

"They don't need you to notice — they need your brain to absorb."

— Advertising critic

"Subliminal advertising is the soft power of persuasion."

— Marketing conspiracy blog

"While subliminal perception exists, its impact in advertising is vastly overstated."

— Cognitive psychologist

Real-World Consequences

Public Fear & Regulation:

Led to debates over ethics in advertising, with some countries banning subliminal techniques.

Cultural Integration:

Frequently referenced in films, books, and urban legends.

Political Suspicion:

Contributes to distrust of political media and corporate branding.

Where It Stands Today

Mainstream advertising denies intentional subliminal messaging, but conspiracy believers argue that hidden influence is more effective when no one is looking for it.

For them, every ad has two messages — one you see and one your subconscious can't unsee.

Chapter One Hundred and Fifty-Seven

Section: More Conspiracies from Around the World

Conspiracy: The Facebook–CIA Data Farm Theory

Summary

The Facebook–CIA Data Farm Theory claims that Facebook was either created or co-opted by the CIA (or another intelligence agency) to serve as the largest and most efficient mass surveillance project in history.

Believers argue that the platform encourages billions of users to voluntarily upload personal information, connections, locations, photos, and preferences, creating a detailed database of human behavior accessible to intelligence agencies.

History & Key Claims

Origins of the Theory:

Facebook launched publicly in 2004, quickly expanding worldwide.

Conspiracy discussions began after revelations about government surveillance programs (e.g., Edward Snowden's leaks in 2013).

Notable coincidence: Facebook's early funding came from investors with links to DARPA and In-Q-Tel (CIA's venture capital arm).

Conspiracy Allegations:

Global Data Collection: Facebook gathers and stores massive personal profiles (including deleted data).

Behavior Mapping: Likes, interactions, and browsing patterns form psychological and political profiles of every user.

Cooperation with Intelligence Agencies: Data is allegedly shared for national security, political influence, and corporate advantage.

Algorithmic Control: Content prioritization shapes public perception and political discourse.

Evidence Cited by Believers:

Cambridge Analytica scandal revealed data harvesting for political targeting.

Reports of Facebook providing data in response to government requests.

Suspicious early funding and rapid growth.

Counterpoint:

Facebook denies direct CIA involvement.

Data collection is acknowledged but framed as advertising and platform optimization.

Famous Quotes / Sources

"Why build a spy program when you can make people sign up for it?"

— Internet meme

"Facebook is the CIA's dream come true."

— Conspiracy tech blog

"Facebook collects massive data, but that doesn't prove it was created as a CIA front."

— Cybersecurity analyst

Real-World Consequences

Public Distrust:

Growing awareness of how much personal data is stored and sold.

Integration with Other Theories:

Linked to TikTok surveillance, NSA mass data collection, and predictive programming.

Policy Impact:

Calls for stricter regulation, transparency, and even breaking up large tech platforms.

Where It Stands Today

While no direct proof ties Facebook's creation to the CIA, its role as the most powerful data collection tool in human history keeps the theory alive.

For believers, Facebook isn't just social media — it's the perfect intelligence farm, and we built it ourselves.

Chapter One Hundred and Fifty-Eight

Section: More Conspiracies from Around the World

Conspiracy: Hollywood Predicts Future Events on Purpose

Summary

The Hollywood Predicts Future Events on Purpose conspiracy claims that films, TV shows, and even animated series intentionally include storylines, visuals, and dialogue that foreshadow real-world events.

Believers argue this is done as part of predictive programming — a psychological tactic designed to subtly prepare the public for major political, social, or technological changes.

History & Key Claims

Origins of the Theory:

The term predictive programming was popularized by conspiracy researcher Alan Watt.

The theory claims media is used to normalize future events so that when they occur, the public is more likely to accept them.

Conspiracy Allegations:

Subliminal Conditioning: Plots mirror upcoming events, making them seem "normal" when they happen in reality.

Elite Messaging: Certain producers, writers, or studios allegedly have insider knowledge of future plans.

Crisis Previews: Disasters, attacks, or policy changes are depicted before they occur.

Famous Examples Cited:

The Simpsons: Known for eerily "predicting" events like Donald Trump's presidency, Disney's purchase of Fox, and COVID-19.

The Lone Gunmen (2001): A spinoff of The X-Files that aired an episode about a plane being hijacked to crash into the World Trade Center — six months before 9/11.

Contagion (2011): Depicted a pandemic strikingly similar to COVID-19.

Black Mirror: Frequently reflects technology and social systems that emerge shortly after episodes air.

Counterpoint:

Writers often use real-world trends as inspiration.

Coincidences are amplified by selective memory — many "predictions" are vague or retrofitted.

Famous Quotes / Sources

"They show you their plans in plain sight — Hollywood is the delivery system."

— Conspiracy media podcast

"Movies are the training videos for tomorrow's reality."

— Alternative culture blog

"Writers often use plausible scenarios for storytelling. When reality mirrors art, it's coincidence, not conspiracy."

— Screenwriter

Real-World Consequences

Integration with Other Theories:

Linked to Project Blue Beam, Great Reset, and false flag operations.

Cultural Impact:

Every disaster film or dystopian series is scrutinized for hidden clues.

Public Distrust of Entertainment Industry:

Fuels the idea that Hollywood is tied to elite agendas.

Where It Stands Today

While mainstream views predictive programming as coincidence and creativity, conspiracy believers see it as the entertainment industry's role in psychological conditioning.

For them, Hollywood isn't just art — it's preparing you for the next chapter of reality.

Chapter One Hundred and Fifty-Nine

Section: More Conspiracies from Around the World

Conspiracy: Project Pegasus – Secret U.S. Time Travel Experiments

Summary

The Project Pegasus conspiracy claims that the U.S. government, under the Defense Advanced Research Projects Agency (DARPA), ran a top-secret program in the late 20th century that successfully developed time travel and teleportation technology.

Believers argue that Project Pegasus participants traveled to past and future events, were deployed on historical observation missions, and in some cases interacted with key moments in history.

History & Key Claims

Origins of the Theory:

The story became widely known through whistleblower Andrew D. Basiago, who claims to have been a child participant in the project in the 1970s.

Basiago alleges that teleportation technology was based on quantum access devices developed from Nikola Tesla's work.

Conspiracy Allegations:

Time Travel Missions: Participants were sent to observe significant historical events, including the Gettysburg Address and 9/11 (before it happened).

Political Foreknowledge: U.S. presidents, including Barack Obama, were allegedly briefed on their future roles via time travel programs.

Teleportation Technology: "Jump rooms" supposedly allowed instant travel to distant locations — including Mars.

Secrecy Enforcement: Participants were allegedly sworn to secrecy under threat of extreme consequences.

Evidence Cited by Believers:

Basiago's detailed accounts of historical events he claims to have witnessed.

Declassified DARPA projects showing interest in exotic physics.

Coincidences involving alleged Project Pegasus participants in later government positions.

Counterpoint:

There is no physical evidence to support the existence of Project Pegasus.

Critics consider Basiago's claims to be science fiction rather than factual testimony.

Famous Quotes / Sources

"I stood at Gettysburg in 1863, watching history unfold."

— Andrew D. Basiago

"They've been moving through time for decades."

— Conspiracy time travel forum

"No credible scientific proof supports time travel claims of Project Pegasus."

— Physicist

Real-World Consequences

Integration with Other Theories:

Linked to Montauk Project, CERN experiments, and Mandela Effect.

Cultural Fascination:

Inspires documentaries, podcasts, and fringe science discussions.

Political Implications:

Used as a basis for claims of pre-planned political ascensions.

Where It Stands Today

Mainstream science dismisses the feasibility of Project Pegasus, but conspiracy believers argue that DARPA mastered time travel decades ago — and the evidence is hidden in plain sight.

For them, Pegasus wasn't theory — it was the U.S. government's ticket through time.

Chapter One Hundred and Sixty

Section: More Conspiracies from Around the World

Conspiracy: The Montauk Project – Mind Control on Long Island

Summary

The Montauk Project conspiracy claims that secret U.S. government experiments at Camp Hero in Montauk, Long Island involved mind control, time travel, teleportation, and interdimensional contact.

Believers argue that the project was an extension of Project MKUltra and Project Pegasus, using advanced technology to manipulate human perception and reality itself.

History & Key Claims

Origins of the Theory:

Stories emerged in the 1980s through alleged whistleblower Preston Nichols, author of The Montauk Project: Experiments in Time.

Nichols claimed to be a survivor of government experiments at Camp Hero, which he said continued into the early 1980s.

Conspiracy Allegations:

Mind Control: Subjects (including kidnapped children) were subjected to extreme psychological programming.

Time Travel & Teleportation: Technology allegedly based on reverse-engineered alien devices allowed travel to other times and places.

The Montauk Chair: A psychic amplification device supposedly used to manifest objects or portals through thought.

Contact with Beings: Claims of communication with extraterrestrial and interdimensional entities.

Memory Suppression: Survivors allegedly had their memories wiped to conceal the experiments.

Evidence Cited by Believers:

Abandoned Cold War–era facilities at Camp Hero, which were officially radar stations.

Witness accounts from multiple individuals claiming similar memories.

Classified projects later revealed to have involved psychological experimentation (though not time travel).

Counterpoint:

No physical evidence confirms time travel or interdimensional contact.

Most claims are based on anecdotal accounts and have been criticized as fiction blended with conspiracy lore.

Famous Quotes / Sources

"They made us see what they wanted — even things that weren't real."

— Alleged Montauk Project participant

"The Montauk Chair opened windows to other realities."

— Preston Nichols

"Camp Hero was a radar station. The rest is urban legend."

— Local historian

Real-World Consequences

Integration with Pop Culture:

Inspired Netflix's Stranger Things (originally titled Montauk).

Connection to Other Theories:

Linked to MKUltra, Project Pegasus, and CERN portal theories.

Tourism & Urban Legend:

Camp Hero has become a destination for conspiracy enthusiasts.

Where It Stands Today

While mainstream historians dismiss the Montauk Project as legend, believers argue it was one of the most advanced and disturbing secret programs in U.S. history.

For them, Montauk wasn't a story — it was a doorway to places the government doesn't want us to know exist.

Chapter One Hundred and Sixty-One

Section: More Conspiracies from Around the World

Conspiracy: The Titanic Was Switched with the Olympic for Insurance

Summary

The Titanic-Olympic Switch conspiracy claims that the RMS Titanic, the famous ship that sank in 1912, was not actually the ship that went down. Instead, believers argue that its sister ship, the RMS Olympic, was deliberately disguised as the Titanic and sunk in an insurance scam orchestrated by the White Star Line and financial backers.

History & Key Claims

Background on the Ships:

The Olympic and Titanic were near-identical sister ships built by Harland and Wolff for the White Star Line.

The Olympic suffered a collision with HMS Hawke in 1911, leading to significant damage.

Conspiracy Allegations:

The Switch: The damaged Olympic was allegedly repaired just enough to look like the Titanic.

The Plan: The Olympic (posing as Titanic) would be intentionally sunk to collect insurance money.

Insurance Payout: White Star Line would recoup losses, while the real Titanic could be quietly repurposed or scrapped.

The Sinking: The "Titanic" was sailed into dangerous iceberg waters with knowledge of its compromised state.

Evidence Cited by Believers:

Differences in porthole arrangements, windows, and deck layouts in photos.

Testimonies from workers claiming changes were made to the ships' names and fittings.

Financial motives of White Star Line owner J.P. Morgan.

Counterpoint:

Most historians argue that differences in ship photos are due to refitting and design adjustments.

Insurance payouts for the Titanic's loss were not sufficient to make the alleged plan worthwhile.

Famous Quotes / Sources

"They sank the Olympic and called it the Titanic."

— Alternative maritime history blog

"The switch explains every inconsistency."

— Conspiracy historian

"The theory falls apart under financial and logistical scrutiny."

— Maritime historian

Real-World Consequences

Integration with Other Theories:

Linked to Titanic elite assassination theory (next chapter).

Cultural Fascination:

Popular in books, documentaries, and online videos.

Legacy of Suspicion:

Keeps Titanic conspiracy theories alive more than a century later.

Where It Stands Today

While mainstream historians reject the switch theory, believers argue the Titanic disaster was not just a tragedy but a carefully orchestrated maritime deception.

For them, the ship at the bottom of the Atlantic isn't the Titanic — it's the Olympic, sacrificed for profit.

Chapter One Hundred and Sixty-Two

Section: More Conspiracies from Around the World

Conspiracy: The Titanic Was Sunk to Kill Financial Opponents of the Fed

Summary

This conspiracy claims that the sinking of the RMS Titanic in 1912 was not an accident, but a deliberate act to eliminate powerful opponents of the creation of the U.S. Federal Reserve System.

Believers argue that key influential figures who opposed central banking reforms were on board and that their deaths cleared the way for the Federal Reserve Act of 1913.

History & Key Claims

Background:

The Titanic was owned by the White Star Line, part of J.P. Morgan's International Mercantile Marine Company.

J.P. Morgan was a supporter of a centralized banking system.

Conspiracy Allegations:

Targeted Passengers: Several wealthy industrialists aboard were known opponents of central banking, including:

John Jacob Astor IV

Benjamin Guggenheim

Isidor Straus

All three perished in the sinking.

J.P. Morgan's Absence: Morgan himself, who had booked passage, canceled at the last minute.

The Theory: By eliminating opposition, the path was cleared for the creation of the Federal Reserve the following year.

Evidence Cited by Believers:

The suspicious coincidence of multiple opponents dying in one event.

Morgan's unexplained withdrawal from the voyage.

Connection to other Titanic conspiracy theories, such as the Olympic switch.

Counterpoint:

No documented evidence links these individuals' deaths to the passage of the Federal Reserve Act.

Many influential opponents of the Fed were not on the Titanic and continued their opposition afterward.

Famous Quotes / Sources

"They didn't just sink a ship — they sank the opposition."

— Alternative finance researcher

"The Titanic was a financial hit job in maritime disguise."

— Conspiracy economics blog

"Coincidences don't equal conspiracy — there's no evidence Morgan orchestrated the disaster."

— Financial historian

Real-World Consequences

Integration with Other Theories:

Closely tied to Federal Reserve private cartel theory.

Cultural Fascination:

Inspires books, YouTube documentaries, and films connecting the Titanic to elite finance.

Perpetuation of Suspicion:

Keeps the Titanic conspiracy alive as part of global banking control narratives.

Where It Stands Today

While mainstream historians see the sinking as a tragic accident, conspiracy believers insist it was a maritime assassination that helped shape modern financial history.

For them, the Titanic wasn't just a disaster — it was a turning point in the rise of centralized banking power.

Chapter One Hundred and Sixty-Three

Section: More Conspiracies from Around the World

Conspiracy: The Moon Is a Surveillance Device

Summary

The Moon Is a Surveillance Device conspiracy claims that Earth's moon is not a natural satellite but an artificial construct — either hollow or technologically enhanced — designed to monitor humanity.

Believers argue it functions as a massive observation platform, potentially built by ancient aliens, advanced civilizations, or current secret global powers.

History & Key Claims

Ancient Observations:

Myths across cultures reference the Moon appearing "later" in Earth's history, suggesting it was placed in orbit.

Some indigenous legends refer to "the time before the Moon."

Conspiracy Allegations:

Artificial Construction: The Moon's density and perfect size for eclipses are cited as evidence it may be engineered.

Surveillance Purpose: Advanced technology inside the Moon allegedly tracks activity on Earth.

Signal Relay: The Moon is theorized to function as a communication hub, possibly transmitting to unknown locations.

Modern Governments' Role: NASA's limited return to the Moon is seen as secrecy to avoid revealing its "true nature."

Evidence Cited by Believers:

Moonquakes and unusual resonance during Apollo missions ("ringing like a bell").

Unusual orbital stability and size ratio compared to other moons.

Long gaps in direct human exploration.

Counterpoint:

Scientific consensus attributes the Moon's properties to natural formation after a giant impact event.

"Ringing" was due to seismic properties of its crust, not hollowness.

Famous Quotes / Sources

"The Moon is the perfect observation post — because it was built to be one."

— Alternative space theory forum

"We don't go back because the Moon isn't what they told us."

— Conspiracy researcher

"The Moon is a natural body. Hollow Moon theories have no scientific basis."

— Planetary scientist

Real-World Consequences

Integration with Other Theories:

Linked to Hollow Moon theory, alien monitoring, and Saturn stargate conspiracies.

Cultural Impact:

Popularized in science fiction, from Space 1999 to modern alien-themed media.

Ongoing Suspicion:

Renewed interest as space agencies plan new lunar missions.

Where It Stands Today

Mainstream science treats the Moon as a natural satellite, but for believers, it is the ultimate cosmic surveillance station — watching us silently from above.

Chapter One Hundred and Sixty-Four

Section: More Conspiracies from Around the World

Conspiracy: China Controls TikTok to Influence U.S. Youth

Summary

The China Controls TikTok to Influence U.S. Youth conspiracy claims that the Chinese government uses the social media platform TikTok as a strategic psychological and cultural tool to shape the values, beliefs, and behaviors of young Americans.

Believers argue that the app's algorithm intentionally promotes certain trends, humor, and political attitudes, while subtly suppressing content that might oppose Chinese geopolitical interests.

History & Key Claims

Background:

TikTok is owned by ByteDance, a Chinese company subject to Chinese cybersecurity laws.

The app has over 150 million active users in the U.S., many of them under 25.

Conspiracy Allegations:

Cultural Manipulation: TikTok's algorithm allegedly pushes distracting, low-value content in Western markets, while the Chinese version (Douyin) emphasizes STEM, education, and patriotism.

Political Bias: Sensitive topics such as Hong Kong protests, Taiwan, or Xinjiang are allegedly downplayed or censored.

Strategic Targeting: Influencer promotion and trend cycles subtly encourage values that erode social cohesion in rival countries.

Youth Conditioning: By shaping humor, beauty standards, and political awareness, China allegedly builds a generation more favorable (or indifferent) to Chinese influence.

Evidence Cited by Believers:

Reports of content moderation aligned with Chinese government sensitivities.

Studies comparing Douyin's educational content to TikTok's entertainment-heavy feed in the U.S.

U.S. political moves to ban or restrict TikTok use on government devices.

Counterpoint:

TikTok claims algorithms differ due to regional audience preferences, not political manipulation.

Critics argue all major platforms influence culture via algorithms, not just TikTok.

Famous Quotes / Sources

"TikTok isn't just an app — it's a cultural weapon."

— Conspiracy geopolitics blog

"Douyin builds engineers. TikTok builds dancers. That's not by accident."

— Internet culture analyst

"There's no proven evidence of algorithmic manipulation for geopolitical goals."

— Social media researcher

Real-World Consequences

Government Scrutiny:

Ongoing hearings in the U.S. Congress over TikTok's data and algorithm control.

Public Awareness:

Parents, educators, and lawmakers increasingly suspicious of foreign influence through social platforms.

Integration with Other Theories:

Closely tied to TikTok as a spy tool and global psychological operations.

Where It Stands Today

Mainstream discussions frame the issue as one of data security and platform regulation, but conspiracy believers see TikTok as a sophisticated influence operation aimed directly at the minds of U.S. youth.

Chapter One Hundred and Sixty-Five

Section: More Conspiracies from Around the World

Conspiracy: AI Chatbots Are Secret Surveillance Tools

Summary

The AI Chatbots Are Secret Surveillance Tools conspiracy claims that artificial intelligence chatbots — from customer service bots to advanced systems like ChatGPT — are not just tools for conversation, but data collection systems designed to monitor, record, and analyze user behavior, thoughts, and private information.

Believers argue that conversations with AI are stored in vast databases where governments, corporations, and intelligence agencies can access them for psychological profiling, predictive behavior modeling, and mass monitoring.

History & Key Claims

Background:

AI chatbots became common in the 2010s, first as customer service agents and later as advanced natural language systems.

Widespread use of AI in daily life (smart assistants, translation tools, chatbots) has raised privacy concerns.

Conspiracy Allegations:

Mass Data Capture: Every interaction is logged and analyzed to build individual behavioral profiles.

Surveillance Integration: Data may be shared with governments or intelligence agencies (similar to social media cooperation).

Behavior Prediction: AI can identify patterns, political leanings, mental health status, and purchasing habits.

Soft Interrogation: Chatbots allegedly encourage users to share information voluntarily, bypassing traditional privacy barriers.

Evidence Cited by Believers:

AI companies admit that chat data may be stored and reviewed to improve models.

Past revelations of government access to big tech company databases (e.g., PRISM program).

Unclear transparency about data retention and deletion policies.

Counterpoint:

AI companies say stored data is used to train and improve the systems, not for surveillance.

Most countries have data privacy regulations limiting how companies handle user data.

Famous Quotes / Sources

"Talking to AI is like whispering into the ear of the state."

— Conspiracy tech blog

"They don't need to bug your home — you invited the bot in yourself."

— Privacy advocate

"AI chat logs are stored, but there's no evidence of secret government surveillance programs attached to them."

— Cybersecurity analyst

Real-World Consequences

Public Distrust of AI:

Fear of AI adoption in education, law, and personal communication.

Integration with Other Theories:

Linked to social credit systems, NSA mass data collection, and digital ID control.

Policy Pressure:

Calls for transparent AI governance and stronger user data protections.

Where It Stands Today

While mainstream AI systems are officially marketed as safe, conspiracy believers argue that chatbots are voluntary surveillance portals — clever tools to get people to hand over their private thoughts freely.

For them, every typed word is another brick in the global monitoring system.

Chapter One Hundred and Sixty-Six

Section: More Conspiracies from Around the World

Conspiracy: The Pine Gap Base in Australia Is a UFO Hub

Summary

The Pine Gap UFO Hub conspiracy claims that the top-secret military base in Pine Gap, Australia — officially a joint U.S.-Australian intelligence facility — is not only a signals intelligence center but also a key hub for UFO activity, extraterrestrial contact, and advanced aerospace projects.

Believers argue that Pine Gap operates as the Southern Hemisphere's equivalent of Area 51, concealing alien technology, secret space programs, and interdimensional research.

History & Key Claims

Official Purpose:

Established in 1966 near Alice Springs, Pine Gap is operated jointly by the Australian Defence Force and the U.S. CIA, NSA, and NRO.

Publicly described as a satellite tracking and communications interception station.

Conspiracy Allegations:

UFO Storage and Testing: Sightings of strange lights and aerial phenomena around the base are attributed to reverse-engineered alien craft.

Underground Facilities: Claims that much of the base extends deep underground, housing hangars, labs, and alien liaison areas.

Southern Space Program Operations: Allegedly serves as a launch and control center for black-budget spacecraft.

Interdimensional Experiments: Some theories suggest the base works on time and space manipulation projects.

Evidence Cited by Believers:

Consistent reports of unidentified flying objects in the Pine Gap area.

Restricted airspace and heavy security far beyond that of most intelligence bases.

Whistleblower statements describing underground sections larger than the surface facility.

Counterpoint:

Officials maintain Pine Gap is a satellite relay and signals intelligence hub critical to U.S.-Australian defense.

UFO sightings are attributed to aircraft tests or atmospheric phenomena.

Famous Quotes / Sources

"Pine Gap is the southern gateway to the secret space program."

— UFO researcher

"What's underground there makes Area 51 look small."

— Alleged whistleblower

"It's an intelligence base, not an alien airport."

— Australian defence analyst

Real-World Consequences

Integration with Other Theories:

Linked to Area 51, Project Aurora, and Secret Space Program conspiracies.

Public Fascination:

Pine Gap is a regular feature of UFO documentaries and alien conspiracy forums.

Political Tension:

The secrecy fuels skepticism about U.S. military presence in Australia.

Where It Stands Today

Pine Gap remains operational and heavily classified. For conspiracy believers, it's not just a spy base — it's the UFO capital of the Southern Hemisphere, guarding secrets humanity isn't ready for.

Chapter One Hundred and Sixty-Seven

Section: More Conspiracies from Around the World

Conspiracy: Pyramids Exist on Mars and the Moon

Summary

The Pyramids on Mars and the Moon conspiracy claims that both Mars and the Moon contain artificial pyramid-like structures, built by an ancient civilization — either extraterrestrial or human in origin.

Believers argue that space agencies like NASA deliberately obscure or alter images that show these formations to keep the truth about ancient advanced builders hidden from the public.

History & Key Claims

Origins of the Theory:

In 1976, NASA's Viking 1 spacecraft photographed the Cydonia region of Mars, where features resembling pyramids and a "face" sparked speculation.

Subsequent images from lunar missions have shown angular, pyramid-like shapes on the Moon.

Conspiracy Allegations:

Artificial Construction: The formations are not natural mountains but ancient monuments.

Common Builders: Similar pyramid shapes on Earth, Mars, and the Moon suggest a shared civilization or alien influence.

NASA Image Tampering: High-resolution images are allegedly blurred, recolored, or classified.

Ancient Records: Some theorists link these pyramids to Atlantis, the Nephilim, or interstellar travelers.

Evidence Cited by Believers:

Viking and Mars Global Surveyor images of the Cydonia "pyramids."

Apollo-era photos of angular lunar structures.

Mathematical claims of geometric alignment between formations.

Counterpoint:

NASA and planetary scientists attribute these shapes to erosion, shadows, and pareidolia.

Higher-resolution images show more natural landforms.

Famous Quotes / Sources

"They didn't build just in Egypt — they built across the solar system."

— Ancient astronaut theorist

"The pyramids on Mars are the most inconvenient structures NASA ever photographed."

— Conspiracy space researcher

"There's no credible evidence these are artificial. Geology explains the formations."

— Planetary scientist

Real-World Consequences

Integration with Other Theories:

Linked to Ancient Aliens, Secret Space Program, and Vatican archives hiding ancient history.

Public Fascination:

Continues to inspire documentaries, books, and sci-fi films.

Mistrust of Space Agencies:

Believers see NASA's secrecy as proof of a cover-up.

Where It Stands Today

Mainstream science sees the formations as natural geology, but for conspiracy believers, they are the fingerprints of an ancient, solar-system-spanning civilization that built monuments on multiple worlds.

Chapter One Hundred and Sixty-Eight

Section: More Conspiracies from Around the World

Conspiracy: The Lost City of Atlantis Is Being Hidden by Governments

Summary

The Atlantis conspiracy claims that the legendary Lost City of Atlantis — described by Plato as a technologically advanced civilization that sank beneath the ocean — was real and that modern governments know its location but deliberately keep it hidden.

Believers argue that the discovery of Atlantis would expose lost technology, ancient history, and truths about humanity's origins that could undermine the current historical narrative.

History & Key Claims

Origins of the Legend:

Plato's Timaeus and Critias (4th century BCE) describe Atlantis as a powerful island nation destroyed by cataclysm around 9,000 years earlier.

Mainstream archaeology considers it either a myth or inspired by real ancient civilizations (e.g., Minoans).

Conspiracy Allegations:

Known Locations: Theories suggest Atlantis lies at:

The Azores in the Atlantic Ocean.

Richat Structure ("Eye of the Sahara") in Mauritania.

Caribbean or Bimini Road off the Bahamas.

Suppressed Discoveries: Alleged satellite images, sonar scans, and deep-sea expeditions have been classified.

Hidden Technology: Claims of advanced energy systems (e.g., crystal power, anti-gravity devices) that could disrupt modern industries.

Elite Secrecy: Believers claim governments and private institutions (including the Vatican) prevent access to key sites.

Evidence Cited by Believers:

Unusual underwater structures (e.g., off Bimini and Cuba).

Geological features at Richat Structure matching Plato's description of concentric rings.

Eyewitness accounts from divers and alleged whistleblowers.

Counterpoint:

Archaeologists view these sites as natural formations or misinterpreted ancient ruins.

No physical evidence of advanced Atlantean technology has been confirmed.

Famous Quotes / Sources

"Atlantis was real, and its technology would rewrite human history."

— Ancient civilizations researcher

"They know where it is — and that's why you'll never see it."

— Conspiracy historian

"Plato's Atlantis was a moral allegory, not a geographical account."

— Classical scholar

Real-World Consequences

Integration with Other Theories:

Linked to Vatican archives, giant skeleton cover-up, and ancient aliens.

Cultural Impact:

Atlantis remains a popular subject in documentaries, books, and films.

Continuing Search:

Amateur researchers and conspiracy theorists continue expeditions despite skepticism.

Where It Stands Today

Mainstream science treats Atlantis as myth, but conspiracy believers see it as the ultimate hidden truth about our past — a civilization buried not just in the ocean, but in secrecy.

Chapter One Hundred and Sixty-Nine

Section: More Conspiracies from Around the World

Conspiracy: Biorobots Used in Government Positions

Summary

The Biorobots in Government Positions conspiracy claims that some world leaders and high-ranking officials are not entirely human but bioengineered androids — advanced synthetic organisms created to mimic humans, follow elite directives, and replace dissenting figures.

Believers argue these biorobots are deployed to ensure absolute loyalty and consistency, eliminating the unpredictability of human nature in positions of power.

History & Key Claims

Origins of the Theory:

Emerged alongside deepfake and robotics advancements in the early 2000s.

Influenced by earlier conspiracies about clones replacing celebrities and politicians.

Conspiracy Allegations:

Replacement of Key Leaders: When a leader becomes politically problematic, they are allegedly replaced by a biorobot double.

Public "Glitches": Awkward speeches, mechanical movements, or blank expressions are interpreted as malfunctions.

Hidden Facilities: Advanced bioengineering labs allegedly operate in secret, producing lifelike human replicants.

Global Elite Control: Biorobots ensure policy continuity, regardless of elections or public opinion.

Evidence Cited by Believers:

Viral videos of politicians "freezing," blinking unusually, or speaking robotically.

Rapid health recoveries or personality changes among leaders.

Leaked patents related to synthetic muscle tissue and AI-controlled human replicas.

Counterpoint:

Odd behaviors are explained as normal human error, fatigue, or camera distortion.

No physical evidence of biorobotic humans exists.

Famous Quotes / Sources

"They don't glitch because they're tired — they glitch because they're machines."

— Political conspiracy podcast

"The perfect politician is one that you program."

— Conspiracy tech forum

"Claims of robotic doubles are science fiction. Malfunctions are human, not mechanical."

— Political analyst

Real-World Consequences

Integration with Other Theories:

Linked to world leader clones, AI surveillance, and New World Order continuity of power.

Cultural Fascination:

Popular in memes and speculative videos of alleged "robotic" moments.

Public Distrust:

Fuels the belief that politics is a stage-managed illusion.

Where It Stands Today

Mainstream views see the theory as fantasy, but for believers, biorobots are the perfect solution for an elite who wants obedience in government without the risk of human unpredictability.

Chapter One Hundred and Seventy

Section: More Conspiracies from Around the World

Conspiracy: Bermuda Triangle as a Dimensional Portal

Summary

The Bermuda Triangle as a Dimensional Portal conspiracy claims that the infamous stretch of ocean between Miami, Bermuda, and Puerto Rico is not just a dangerous area for navigation but a gateway to another dimension or time.

Believers argue that the unexplained disappearances of ships and aircraft in the Triangle are due to portals, wormholes, or interdimensional rifts hidden within the region.

History & Key Claims

Origins of the Mystery:

The Bermuda Triangle gained notoriety in the mid-20th century following mysterious incidents such as:

Flight 19 (1945): A squadron of U.S. Navy bombers disappeared without a trace.

USS Cyclops (1918): A U.S. Navy ship vanished with over 300 crew members.

Popularized by authors like Charles Berlitz in the 1970s.

Conspiracy Allegations:

Dimensional Gateway: Ships and planes are pulled into another dimension, explaining their disappearance without wreckage.

Time Distortions: Survivors allegedly report sudden time jumps or strange weather phenomena.

Atlantis Connection: Some claim the portal is linked to advanced Atlantean technology buried under the ocean floor.

Military Knowledge: The U.S. government allegedly monitors the Triangle but suppresses information.

Evidence Cited by Believers:

Sudden compass malfunctions reported in the area.

Electronic disruptions and unusual cloud formations.

Lack of wreckage in certain high-profile disappearances.

Counterpoint:

Scientists attribute incidents to human error, severe weather, and strong ocean currents.

The number of disappearances is not statistically higher than other heavily traveled ocean regions.

Famous Quotes / Sources

"They aren't lost — they're somewhere else."

— Paranormal investigator

"The Bermuda Triangle is a natural doorway to another reality."

— Conspiracy ocean research forum

"Navigation errors and storms explain nearly all cases."

— Maritime safety expert

Real-World Consequences

Integration with Other Theories:

Linked to Atlantis, alien bases, and underwater technology.

Cultural Impact:

Inspires books, films, and documentaries on mysterious disappearances.

Tourist Fascination:

The Triangle's mystery draws adventurers and conspiracy enthusiasts.

Where It Stands Today

Mainstream science dismisses the Triangle's supernatural claims, but for believers, it remains one of Earth's most active dimensional gateways, swallowing ships and planes into the unknown.

Chapter One Hundred and Seventy-One

Section: More Conspiracies from Around the World

Conspiracy: The Ark of the Covenant Is Hidden in Ethiopia

Summary

The Ark of the Covenant in Ethiopia conspiracy claims that the biblical Ark — the sacred chest said to hold the stone tablets of the Ten Commandments — was not lost or destroyed but secretly taken to Ethiopia, where it remains hidden and guarded to this day.

Believers argue that the Ark is kept under constant watch by the Ethiopian Orthodox Church, which refuses to allow outsiders to verify its presence, fueling centuries of speculation.

History & Key Claims

Biblical Background:

The Ark was kept in the Temple of Solomon in Jerusalem until its disappearance after the Babylonian conquest in the 6th century BCE.

Its fate is one of the greatest biblical mysteries.

Conspiracy Allegations:

Journey to Ethiopia: According to Ethiopian tradition, the Ark was brought to Aksum by Menelik I, son of King Solomon and the Queen of Sheba.

Current Location: The Ark is said to reside in the Church of Our Lady Mary of Zion in Aksum.

Guarded by a Chosen Monk: One guardian, appointed for life, watches over the Ark and is the only person allowed to see it.

Secrecy: No outsider has been allowed to confirm the Ark's presence, leading to speculation about hidden reasons for its concealment.

Evidence Cited by Believers:

The unbroken tradition of Ark guardianship in Ethiopia.

References in ancient Ethiopian manuscripts.

Religious processions in Aksum involving replica Arks.

Counterpoint:

No archaeological evidence confirms the Ark's existence in Ethiopia.

The Ethiopian Church refuses inspection, citing religious law.

Famous Quotes / Sources

"The Ark rests in Aksum, as it has for thousands of years."

— Ethiopian Orthodox Church elder

"They guard it because it holds the power of God — and the truth of history."

— Conspiracy theologian

"There's no verifiable evidence. The Ark's fate remains unknown."

— Biblical archaeologist

Real-World Consequences

Integration with Other Theories:

Tied to Vatican archives, Holy Grail secrecy, and ancient relic conspiracies.

Religious Significance:

The Ark remains a cornerstone of Ethiopian Christian identity.

Cultural Fascination:

Featured in films (Raiders of the Lost Ark) and countless documentaries.

Where It Stands Today

Mainstream archaeology treats the Ark's Ethiopian connection as unverified legend, but for believers, the Ark is not lost at all — it's hidden in plain sight, in a guarded Ethiopian chapel.

Chapter One Hundred and Seventy-Two

Section: More Conspiracies from Around the World

Conspiracy: Nibiru / Planet X Will Return

Summary

The Nibiru / Planet X conspiracy claims that a massive, undiscovered planet — sometimes described as a rogue celestial body or brown dwarf — is on a long elliptical orbit around the Sun and will one day return, passing close to Earth.

Believers argue that Nibiru's approach will cause catastrophic gravitational effects, earthquakes, tsunamis, pole shifts, and possibly mass extinction. Governments and space agencies allegedly know of its existence but cover it up to prevent panic.

History & Key Claims

Origins of the Theory:

Popularized by author Zecharia Sitchin, who translated ancient Sumerian texts describing a planet called Nibiru, home to an advanced alien race (the Anunnaki).

NASA's early 1980s search for a "Planet X" beyond Pluto fueled speculation.

Conspiracy Allegations:

Hidden Observations: Space agencies allegedly detect Nibiru but classify images and data.

Ancient Predictions: Civilizations like the Sumerians and Mayans are said to have recorded Nibiru's cycles.

Impending Disaster: Some claim its return will cause planetary upheaval or be tied to apocalyptic prophecies.

Government Preparation: Underground bases and seed vaults are allegedly part of survival planning.

Evidence Cited by Believers:

Reports of unusual gravitational effects in the outer solar system.

Claims of amateur astronomers spotting anomalous objects near the Sun.

Sitchin's translations of Sumerian cosmology.

Counterpoint:

Astronomers deny any evidence of a rogue planet entering the inner solar system.

"Planet Nine" theories exist but describe a distant, stable orbit — not a collision course.

Famous Quotes / Sources

"They know Nibiru is coming, and that's why they're building bunkers."

— Planet X conspiracy blog

"The ancients left us warnings, and we've ignored them."

— Alternative history researcher

"There's no credible astronomical evidence for a rogue planet approaching Earth."

— NASA scientist

Real-World Consequences

Integration with Other Theories:

Linked to Mayan 2012 prophecy, Anunnaki return, and elite survival plans.

Public Fascination:

Waves of doomsday panic around predicted return dates (e.g., 2003, 2012, 2017).

Cultural Impact:

Inspires documentaries, online videos, and sci-fi literature.

Where It Stands Today

Mainstream science considers Nibiru a myth, but for believers, its return is a matter of time — and the elite are already preparing for the chaos it will bring.

Chapter One Hundred and Seventy-Three

Section: More Conspiracies from Around the World

Conspiracy: Crop Circles Are Alien Messages or Military Tech

Summary

The Crop Circle conspiracy claims that the intricate patterns that appear overnight in fields of crops are not the work of pranksters but messages from extraterrestrials or tests of advanced military technology.

Believers argue that certain crop circles demonstrate mathematical precision, biological changes to plants, and energy anomalies that cannot be explained by simple human hoaxes.

History & Key Claims

Origins of the Phenomenon:

Crop circles began appearing in large numbers in the 1970s and 1980s in England, particularly in Wiltshire near ancient sites like Stonehenge and Avebury.

While some have been confessed hoaxes, many patterns remain unexplained.

Conspiracy Allegations:

Alien Communication: Complex formations are seen as messages, maps, or warnings from extraterrestrials.

Electromagnetic Phenomena: Some claim circles are created by microwave or magnetic bursts, hinting at secret military experiments.

Sacred Geography: Locations often align with ley lines, ancient sites, and astronomical events.

Cover-Up: Governments allegedly dismiss crop circles as hoaxes to avoid public panic about alien contact or military tech.

Evidence Cited by Believers:

Plants in some circles show elongated nodes and chemical changes consistent with exposure to intense heat or energy.

Patterns that reflect complex mathematics and astronomical alignments.

Eyewitness accounts of strange lights or orbs near crop circle sites.

Counterpoint:

Many crop circles have been publicly admitted to be human-made art projects.

Scientific analysis shows plant damage consistent with mechanical flattening in most cases.

Famous Quotes / Sources

"These are not random designs — they are mathematical messages."

— Crop circle researcher

"The simplest way to dismiss alien contact is to call it a prank."

— UFOlogist

"Most crop circles are hoaxes. The rest have natural or environmental explanations."

— Agricultural scientist

Real-World Consequences

Integration with Other Theories:

Linked to alien communication, Project Blue Beam, and secret energy weapon tests.

Tourism & Culture:

Crop circles draw thousands of visitors to sites each summer.

Scientific Curiosity:

Even skeptical researchers study the phenomenon as an example of complex social hoaxes and mass belief.

Where It Stands Today

Mainstream science sees crop circles as largely human-made art, but conspiracy believers argue they are messages from beyond — or proof of technology that governments don't want us to see.

Chapter One Hundred and Seventy-Four

Section: More Conspiracies from Around the World

Conspiracy: The Moon Is Artificial

Summary

The Artificial Moon conspiracy claims that Earth's Moon is not a natural satellite, but an artificial construct — either hollow, technologically enhanced, or placed in orbit intentionally by an advanced civilization.

Believers argue that its perfect positioning, unusual density, and strange seismic properties are evidence that the Moon is a manufactured object, possibly a massive spacecraft or observation post.

History & Key Claims

Origins of the Theory:

Ancient myths in several cultures refer to a time before the Moon.

Modern speculation grew after Apollo missions recorded unusual seismic activity, with the Moon "ringing like a bell" during impacts.

Conspiracy Allegations:

Engineered Orbit: The Moon's size and distance create perfect solar eclipses, which some see as a sign of artificial placement.

Hollow Structure: Seismic data suggests unusual internal composition, leading to the "hollow Moon" hypothesis.

Observation Base: The Moon is theorized to house alien or ancient human technology, potentially monitoring Earth.

Government Secrecy: NASA allegedly limits lunar exploration to prevent discovery of artificial structures.

Evidence Cited by Believers:

Apollo mission seismic readings of prolonged vibrations.

Coincidental size ratio to the Sun enabling perfect eclipses.

Lack of significant crater depth compared to size.

Counterpoint:

Mainstream scientists attribute seismic properties to the Moon's internal composition and structure.

The Moon's orbit and size are explained by the giant impact theory of formation.

Famous Quotes / Sources

"The Moon is the greatest spacecraft ever built."

— Alternative space researcher

"It was put there on purpose — to watch us."

— Conspiracy astronomer

"There's no scientific evidence the Moon is artificial."

— Planetary scientist

Real-World Consequences

Integration with Other Theories:

Linked to Moon as surveillance device, alien bases on the Moon, and ancient civilizations in space.

Public Fascination:

Popular in documentaries, speculative books, and science fiction.

Renewed Suspicion:

The limited human return to the Moon fuels belief in secrecy.

Where It Stands Today

Mainstream science sees the Moon as a natural body formed billions of years ago, but for conspiracy believers, it is a colossal engineered object — silently circling Earth for reasons we may never be told.

Chapter One Hundred and Seventy-Five

Section: More Conspiracies from Around the World

Conspiracy: Global Warming Is a Hoax for Control

Summary

The Global Warming Is a Hoax for Control conspiracy claims that climate change — specifically the concept of catastrophic man-made global warming — is exaggerated or fabricated by governments, corporations, and global organizations to justify new regulations, taxes, and centralized power structures.

Believers argue that while climate changes naturally over time, the current climate crisis narrative is a tool for political and economic control rather than a purely scientific emergency.

History & Key Claims

Origins of the Theory:

Emerged prominently in the 1990s as climate summits like Kyoto (1997) and Paris (2015) pushed global agreements.

Critics began claiming that climate fears were being weaponized to implement new forms of governance.

Conspiracy Allegations:

Political Tool: Climate change is used to create carbon taxes, environmental regulations, and ESG compliance systems that consolidate power.

Suppression of Debate: Scientists who challenge the mainstream narrative allegedly face career damage or censorship.

Financial Incentives: Corporations and governments profit from "green" industries subsidized by climate policies.

New World Order Agenda: The climate crisis is seen as a vehicle for global governance, tied to The Great Reset.

Evidence Cited by Believers:

Leaked emails in the Climategate scandal (2009) interpreted as manipulation of climate data.

Historical climate shifts before industrialization.

The elite's continued heavy private emissions despite promoting restrictions for the general public.

Counterpoint:

The overwhelming scientific consensus supports anthropogenic climate change.

Climate policies are presented as response measures, not deliberate controls.

Famous Quotes / Sources

"Climate panic is the perfect excuse for global governance."

— Conspiracy political analyst

"They use fear of the future to control the present."

— Alternative economics forum

"Climate change is real, and action is needed. Hoax claims ignore overwhelming data."

— Climate scientist

Real-World Consequences

Integration with Other Theories:

Closely linked to Great Reset, carbon tracking, and population control conspiracies.

Political Impact:

Fuels resistance to climate treaties, carbon taxes, and green energy mandates.

Public Polarization:

Creates deep divides between environmental advocates and skeptics.

Where It Stands Today

Mainstream science supports climate action, but conspiracy believers argue global warming is less about saving the planet and more about controlling the people.

Chapter One Hundred and Seventy-Six

Section: More Conspiracies from Around the World

Conspiracy: Global Cooling Was Suppressed in the '70s

Summary

The Global Cooling Was Suppressed in the '70s conspiracy claims that during the 1970s, scientific discussions about a potential period of global cooling — even a possible new ice age — were deliberately downplayed or erased from the mainstream narrative in order to make way for the later global warming agenda.

Believers argue that early climate research was manipulated to steer environmental policies toward warming-based taxation and regulations instead of a balanced discussion of natural climate cycles.

History & Key Claims

Background:

In the late 1960s and 1970s, some scientific papers and media reports discussed the possibility of global cooling, based on observed temperature drops in the 1940s–1970s.

Magazines like Newsweek and Time published articles about a "coming ice age."

Conspiracy Allegations:

Agenda Shift: Early cooling concerns were abandoned because warming fears were more effective for political and economic control.

Suppression of Data: Research supporting cooling cycles was allegedly buried or ignored.

Climate Narrative Control: Governments and organizations shaped the environmental message toward carbon-driven warming as part of global policy plans.

Media Reframing: Old cooling stories were quietly dismissed as "misinterpretations" despite documented reports.

Evidence Cited by Believers:

Archived magazine covers predicting an ice age.

Cooling-related scientific papers from the 1970s.

The rapid pivot in climate focus toward global warming in the 1980s.

Counterpoint:

Climate scientists explain that the majority of research in the 1970s already favored warming due to greenhouse gases, with cooling discussions limited to short-term natural cycles.

Media sensationalism exaggerated the cooling debate.

Famous Quotes / Sources

"They erased global cooling to keep the warming narrative clean."

— Climate conspiracy blog

"The '70s were a glimpse of how flexible the climate agenda can be."

— Alternative environmental researcher

"The idea of a scientific consensus on cooling is a myth — the majority supported warming predictions."

— Climate historian

Real-World Consequences

Integration with Other Theories:

Linked to climate change manipulation, Great Reset, and carbon tax control conspiracies.

Public Skepticism:

Used by climate change skeptics to argue that scientific predictions are politically driven.

Media Accountability:

Past articles on cooling remain popular evidence in online debates.

Where It Stands Today

Mainstream science frames the cooling talk of the '70s as overstated by media, but conspiracy believers see it as an intentional narrative pivot to fit a larger global warming control agenda.

Chapter One Hundred and Seventy-Seven

Section: More Conspiracies from Around the World

Conspiracy: The Real Purpose of Antarctic Bases Is Unknown

Summary

The Antarctic Bases conspiracy claims that the research stations scattered across Antarctica are not just for scientific study, but serve as cover operations for secret projects — potentially involving hidden civilizations, advanced technology, alien contact, or ancient ruins buried under the ice.

Believers argue that the strict international control of Antarctica and the limited public access are designed to hide what's really there.

History & Key Claims

Background:

Antarctica is governed by the Antarctic Treaty System (1959), which bans military activity and restricts exploitation.

Multiple nations operate research bases focused on climate, wildlife, and geology.

Conspiracy Allegations:

Ancient Civilizations: Theorists claim ruins of advanced cities — possibly Atlantis or alien-built structures — are hidden beneath the ice.

Secret Military Projects: Some bases allegedly function as black-budget facilities testing advanced weapons or craft.

UFO Activity: Reports of unidentified flying objects entering or leaving the continent suggest alien collaboration.

Resource Hoarding: Antarctica may hold vast mineral and energy resources that are being quietly mapped and claimed.

Restricted Access: Tourists are kept away from certain areas, allegedly to prevent accidental discovery.

Evidence Cited by Believers:

Satellite images of unusual shapes under ice.

Accounts of restricted military flights in the region.

Historical anomalies like Operation Highjump (1946–47), where U.S. naval forces deployed unexpectedly large resources to Antarctica.

Counterpoint:

Mainstream explanations point to harsh conditions, environmental protections, and logistics as the reason for restricted access.

No verified evidence of alien or ancient structures.

Famous Quotes / Sources

"They're not there to study penguins."

— Antarctic conspiracy forum

"Antarctica hides more than ice. That's why we can't go."

— Alternative history researcher

"There's no proof of hidden civilizations. Access is restricted for safety and environmental reasons."

— Polar scientist

Real-World Consequences

Integration with Other Theories:

Linked to Atlantis, alien bases, and Hollow Earth conspiracies.

Cultural Fascination:

Antarctica remains a frequent setting in speculative fiction and documentaries.

Public Suspicion:

Limited independent exploration fuels ongoing belief in hidden agendas.

Where It Stands Today

Mainstream science views Antarctica as a unique natural reserve, but conspiracy believers see it as Earth's most guarded secret — an icy cover hiding truths we aren't meant to know.

Chapter One Hundred and Seventy-Eight

Section: More Conspiracies from Around the World

Conspiracy: The Pope Is a Puppet of Global Elites

Summary

The Pope as a Puppet of Global Elites conspiracy claims that the Pope — and by extension, the Vatican — is heavily influenced or outright controlled by powerful global organizations, political alliances, and financial interests.

Believers argue that papal decisions, public statements, and policy stances are aligned with the goals of world governance structures such as the United Nations, the World Economic Forum, and international banking families.

History & Key Claims

Background:

The Pope is both the spiritual leader of over a billion Catholics and the head of Vatican City, a sovereign state.

Throughout history, the papacy has had close relationships with monarchies, governments, and financial powers.

Conspiracy Allegations:

Policy Alignment: The Pope's speeches on climate change, migration, and economics mirror elite globalist agendas.

Hidden Alliances: The Vatican allegedly coordinates with international organizations and corporate leaders to advance political goals.

Influence via Finance: The Vatican Bank and global Catholic wealth are tied to elite financial institutions.

Symbolic Submission: Public appearances at elite gatherings and meetings with global leaders are interpreted as evidence of coordination.

Evidence Cited by Believers:

Papal support for climate action, debt forgiveness, and refugee resettlement, all common global policy points.

Historical Vatican involvement in political deals, treaties, and finance.

Cooperation between Vatican officials and major global organizations.

Counterpoint:

The Pope's statements are framed by the Vatican as moral guidance, not political allegiance.

Cooperation with global organizations is explained as diplomatic engagement on humanitarian issues.

Famous Quotes / Sources

"The Pope is just another face of the globalist agenda."

— Political conspiracy forum

"When his policies match the WEF word for word, it's not coincidence."

— Alternative religious commentator

"The Pope's role is pastoral and diplomatic — global collaboration doesn't prove control."

— Vatican historian

Real-World Consequences

Integration with Other Theories:

Linked to Vatican archives secrecy, Great Reset, and religious New World Order conspiracies.

Religious Division:

Some Catholics question whether papal actions serve spiritual interests or global politics.

Political Reaction:

Statements by the Pope on global issues often trigger political controversy.

Where It Stands Today

Mainstream interpretation sees the Pope's role as balancing moral influence with diplomacy, but conspiracy believers argue the papacy is another tool in the hands of global elites.

Chapter One Hundred and Seventy-Nine

Section: More Conspiracies from Around the World

Conspiracy: Underground Cities for the Elite Exist Worldwide

Summary

The Underground Cities for the Elite conspiracy claims that beneath major countries are vast underground complexes, built as secure cities for world leaders, billionaires, and high-ranking officials.

Believers argue these underground havens are designed to protect elites from natural disasters, wars, pandemics, economic collapse, or even alien contact, while the general population is left vulnerable on the surface.

History & Key Claims

Background:

The existence of underground bunkers is well-documented — from Cold War fallout shelters to modern luxury survival complexes.

Governments such as the U.S., Russia, and China have acknowledged certain military and emergency facilities underground.

Conspiracy Allegations:

Global Network: A network of interconnected underground cities allegedly spans continents.

Elite Evacuation Plan: In times of crisis, select individuals are moved to these secure cities while the public is misled or abandoned.

Secret Technology: These cities allegedly have self-sustaining food systems, energy supplies, and advanced medical facilities.

Mass Secrecy: Construction and maintenance are said to be funded by black budgets hidden in government spending.

Evidence Cited by Believers:

Large-scale tunneling projects and unusual government spending records.

Reports of restricted underground bases such as Mount Weather (USA) and Yamantau Mountain (Russia).

Whistleblower claims of luxury subterranean facilities for the ultra-wealthy.

Counterpoint:

While underground bunkers exist, evidence of full underground cities for elites remains speculative.

Most known facilities are military or government emergency operations centers.

Famous Quotes / Sources

"They aren't preparing bunkers for you — they're for themselves."

— Survivalist conspiracy author

"An entire parallel world exists beneath our feet."

— Underground base researcher

"Government emergency facilities exist, but underground cities are more fantasy than reality."

— Former defense planner

Real-World Consequences

Integration with Other Theories:

Linked to Great Reset, Nibiru/Planet X, and population control conspiracies.

Public Suspicion:

Concerns that crisis preparation is designed to save elites, not the public.

Cultural Fascination:

Popular in films, books, and survivalist communities.

Where It Stands Today

Mainstream explanations confirm bunkers but not entire underground cities. Conspiracy believers maintain that when disaster comes, the elite will disappear into a world beneath the surface — leaving everyone else behind.

Chapter One Hundred and Eighty

Section: More Conspiracies from Around the World

Conspiracy: COVID Test Swabs Implant Nanotech

Summary

The COVID Test Swabs Implant Nanotech conspiracy claims that nasal swabs used for COVID-19 testing were not solely intended to detect the virus, but to implant microscopic technology into individuals without their knowledge.

Believers argue that this alleged nanotechnology could be used for tracking, health monitoring, or even behavioral influence as part of a larger surveillance system.

History & Key Claims

Background:

Widespread nasal swab testing began globally in early 2020 during the COVID-19 pandemic.

Standard PCR and antigen tests involve inserting a swab into the nasal cavity to collect samples.

Conspiracy Allegations:

Nanotechnology in Swabs: Swabs allegedly contain microchips, nanobots, or smart dust designed to enter the body.

Tracking & Surveillance: Implanted nanotech could link individuals to digital IDs or health passports.

Behavioral or Biological Influence: Some theories suggest these implants could alter neurological function or interact with other technologies like 5G.

Mass Rollout: Widespread testing ensured a large percentage of the global population was allegedly "seeded" with the technology.

Evidence Cited by Believers:

Videos claiming to show microscopic fibers or crystalline structures on swabs.

Patents for nanotech devices unrelated to COVID-19, presented as "evidence" of hidden technology.

The unusual deep nasal reach of early PCR tests compared to other medical tests.

Counterpoint:

No verified scientific evidence supports the claim that swabs contain nanotechnology.

The design of PCR swabs is explained by the need to collect samples from areas with high viral loads.

Famous Quotes / Sources

"They aren't testing you — they're tagging you."

— Pandemic conspiracy forum

"The swab was the delivery system."

— Alternative health blogger

"There's no evidence of nanotech in swabs — these claims come from misinterpreted microscopy videos."

— Medical researcher

Real-World Consequences

Integration with Other Theories:

Linked to vaccine microchip conspiracy, 5G mind control, and digital ID narratives.

Public Distrust:

Contributed to skepticism toward COVID testing and health protocols.

Policy Impact:

Led to increased demand for at-home tests and alternative methods.

Where It Stands Today

Mainstream science dismisses the claim as false, but conspiracy believers maintain that COVID testing was as much about implantation as detection.

Chapter One Hundred and Eighty-One

Section: More Conspiracies from Around the World

Conspiracy: Internet "Blackouts" Used for Elite Arrests

Summary

The Internet Blackouts conspiracy claims that large-scale internet outages are sometimes intentionally orchestrated by governments or military alliances to carry out secret arrests of high-ranking elites, corporate leaders, or political figures without public awareness.

Believers argue that blackouts provide the perfect cover for covert operations, intelligence raids, or mass detentions, keeping both the media and the general public in the dark.

History & Key Claims

Background:

Internet outages occasionally occur due to technical failures, cyberattacks, or infrastructure damage.

However, major unexplained blackouts in certain regions at politically tense times have fueled suspicion.

Conspiracy Allegations:

Distraction & Concealment: Internet outages are used to prevent live streaming, leaks, or digital alerts during elite arrests.

Coordination With Military Operations: Certain outages allegedly coincide with military movements or sealed indictments being executed.

Global Elite Takedowns: Blackouts are said to be part of coordinated efforts to dismantle human trafficking networks, corruption rings, or financial crimes.

Ties to QAnon & Similar Theories: Followers of QAnon have long suggested that internet outages precede "mass awakening" events.

Evidence Cited by Believers:

Coincidences between internet blackouts and political purges in countries like Myanmar, Kazakhstan, and certain Middle Eastern states.

Reports of large-scale outages in multiple countries at the same time without clear technical explanation.

Unusual military flight paths or movements during blackout periods.

Counterpoint:

Most outages can be traced to technical faults, submarine cable issues, or cyberattacks, not covert arrests.

No verifiable evidence links outages to elite roundups.

Famous Quotes / Sources

"When the internet goes down, look at who disappears quietly."

— QAnon forum poster

"They black out the lights and the lines before the big moves."

— Political conspiracy blogger

"Internet outages have logical explanations. Elite mass arrests are unfounded claims."

— Cybersecurity analyst

Real-World Consequences

Integration with Other Theories:

Tied to Deep State purges, sealed indictments, and military tribunals.

Public Distrust:

Outages are now met with immediate suspicion in conspiracy communities.

Political Exploitation:

Some political groups use blackout events to push narratives about hidden global operations.

Where It Stands Today

Mainstream explanations see outages as infrastructure failures, but conspiracy believers view every blackout as a sign of something bigger happening in the shadows.

Chapter One Hundred and Eighty-Two

Section: More Conspiracies from Around the World

Conspiracy: The U.S. Government Has Alien–Human Hybrids

Summary

The Alien–Human Hybrid conspiracy claims that the U.S. government is conducting secret genetic experiments that have produced beings which are part human and part extraterrestrial.

Believers argue that these hybrids are the result of agreements between the U.S. government and alien species, serving purposes ranging from biological research to infiltration of human society.

History & Key Claims

Origins of the Theory:

Rooted in abduction narratives from the 1960s onward, where alleged abductees reported medical procedures involving egg or sperm extraction.

Whistleblowers and UFO researchers began connecting these accounts to government-alien collaboration.

Conspiracy Allegations:

Genetic Programs: Hybrids are allegedly created to combine human adaptability with alien intelligence or physiology.

Government Collaboration: Supposed treaties (like the Eisenhower Treaty) allow aliens to conduct limited abductions in exchange for technology.

Hybrid Roles: Hybrids may serve as liaisons, covert agents, or test subjects to prepare for broader alien contact.

Cover-Up: Governments deny their existence to avoid panic and preserve control.

Evidence Cited by Believers:

Abductee testimonies describing hybrid children in alien facilities.

Whistleblower accounts from supposed military insiders.

Alleged leaked photos of beings that appear "almost human."

Counterpoint:

No physical evidence supports the existence of hybrids.

Abduction accounts are explained by sleep paralysis, psychological phenomena, or cultural influence.

Famous Quotes / Sources

"They walk among us, and they're not fully human."

— UFO researcher

"Hybrids are the bridge between species."

— Abduction witness

"There's no credible scientific proof of alien–human hybrids."

— Geneticist

Real-World Consequences

Integration with Other Theories:

Linked to Area 51 alien technology, secret space programs, and extraterrestrial treaties.

Cultural Fascination:

Popular in UFO documentaries, novels, and films.

Ongoing Suspicion:

Any unusual political or celebrity figure is sometimes speculated to be a hybrid.

Where It Stands Today

Mainstream science dismisses the idea of alien–human hybrids, but for believers, these beings are already here — quietly blending in as part of a long-term plan.

Chapter One Hundred and Eighty-Three

Section: More Conspiracies from Around the World

Conspiracy: The Real Queen of England Is a Lizard (Icke Theory)

Summary

The Reptilian Royalty conspiracy, most famously promoted by author and speaker David Icke, claims that members of the British Royal Family — including Queen Elizabeth II — are shape-shifting reptilian beings who disguise themselves as humans.

These beings allegedly belong to an ancient alien bloodline that has ruled Earth for centuries, using deception, symbolism, and power to maintain control over global affairs.

History & Key Claims

Origins of the Theory:

David Icke introduced the theory in the 1990s, claiming the world is secretly controlled by reptilian humanoids from the Alpha Draconis star system.

According to Icke, these beings can morph into human form and interbreed with human bloodlines.

Conspiracy Allegations:

Royal Bloodlines: The British monarchy, along with global leaders and billionaires, are allegedly part of a reptilian hybrid elite.

Energy Harvesting: Some theories suggest reptilians feed off human emotion, particularly fear and trauma.

Historical Control: Reptilians are said to have manipulated events throughout history, from the Roman Empire to modern banking systems.

Symbolic Presence: Reptilian iconography is claimed to be hidden in royal crests, rituals, and buildings.

Evidence Cited by Believers:

Eyewitness claims of public "glitches" or strange behavior from royal family members.

Alleged footage of "slitted pupils" or "scales" captured in still frames.

Ancient myths of serpent gods and dragon-like rulers.

Counterpoint:

No scientific evidence supports reptilian shapeshifters.

Icke's theory is widely viewed as metaphor, satire, or pseudoscience — though some take it literally.

Famous Quotes / Sources

"They are not who you think they are — and they never were."

— David Icke

"The royal family doesn't serve Britain — it serves something far older."

— Reptilian theory blog

"There's no credible evidence of shapeshifting lizards ruling Earth."

— Political historian

Real-World Consequences

Integration with Other Theories:

Linked to Illuminati, Nephilim bloodlines, and alien infiltration conspiracies.

Public Fascination:

The theory has inspired books, podcasts, and mockumentaries.

Symbolic Interpretation:

Some see reptilian references as metaphor for cold, emotionless elites, rather than literal beings.

Where It Stands Today

Mainstream society dismisses the reptilian royal theory as science fiction or satire, but conspiracy believers argue that our rulers are not what they appear — and their scales show through when no one is looking.

Chapter One Hundred and Eighty-Four

Section: More Conspiracies from Around the World

Conspiracy: The Bhopal Disaster Was Covered Up Internationally

Summary

The Bhopal Disaster Cover-Up conspiracy claims that the 1984 gas leak at the Union Carbide pesticide plant in Bhopal, India — one of the world's worst industrial disasters — was far more catastrophic than publicly acknowledged and that both corporate powers and governments worked together to minimize the perceived scale and suppress evidence.

Believers argue that the true death toll, long-term environmental impact, and corporate liability were deliberately downplayed to protect multinational interests and prevent political fallout.

History & Key Claims

Background of the Disaster:

On December 2–3, 1984, a leak of methyl isocyanate gas killed thousands instantly and exposed over half a million people.

Union Carbide Corporation (UCC), a U.S.-based company, was operating the plant through its Indian subsidiary.

Conspiracy Allegations:

Underreported Death Toll: Official estimates list ~3,000–8,000 deaths, but conspiracy claims argue the number is much higher, potentially tens of thousands.

Medical Cover-Up: Long-term health issues — birth defects, cancer, organ damage — allegedly underreported to reduce legal liability.

Corporate Protection: The Indian government allegedly accepted a low settlement ($470 million) under pressure from U.S. diplomats.

Suppression of Evidence: Documents detailing safety violations, cost-cutting, and negligence were allegedly sealed or destroyed.

International Pressure: Some believe global powers intervened to shield U.S. industry from massive compensation demands.

Evidence Cited by Believers:

Discrepancy between official and NGO death/illness figures.

The relatively small financial settlement compared to disaster scale.

CEO Warren Anderson's escape from India and lack of extradition.

Counterpoint:

Governments and courts claim settlements were based on available evidence and legal frameworks at the time.

Safety failures acknowledged, but global conspiracy is considered unproven.

Famous Quotes / Sources

"They buried the truth along with the bodies."

— Bhopal activist

"Bhopal showed that corporate power outweighs human life."

— Environmental lawyer

"There's no evidence of a coordinated global cover-up, just corporate negligence and legal failure."

— Industrial historian

Real-World Consequences

Integration with Other Theories:

Linked to corporate immunity, Big Pharma and chemical industry secrecy, and environmental cover-up conspiracies.

Public Distrust:

The event remains a symbol of corporate greed and government complicity.

Activism:

Sparked global environmental justice movements demanding corporate accountability.

Where It Stands Today

Mainstream accounts frame Bhopal as corporate negligence with legal shortcomings. Conspiracy believers argue it was an orchestrated suppression of truth, protecting industry and political ties over human life.

Chapter One Hundred and Eighty-Five

Section: More Conspiracies from Around the World

Conspiracy: Operation Mockingbird Still Controls Global Media

Summary

The Operation Mockingbird conspiracy claims that the CIA's Cold War–era program to influence and control mainstream media outlets never truly ended.

Believers argue that the operation has simply evolved, with intelligence agencies still guiding narratives, suppressing certain stories, and promoting propaganda across television, newspapers, and online platforms — not just in the U.S., but globally.

History & Key Claims

Historical Background:

Operation Mockingbird began in the late 1940s and 1950s as a CIA initiative to recruit journalists and editors at major media outlets.

Congressional hearings in the 1970s (the Church Committee) confirmed the program's existence but claimed it had ended.

Conspiracy Allegations:

Continuation of the Program: Instead of ending, Mockingbird allegedly shifted into a covert form, influencing both traditional and digital media.

Global Expansion: Intelligence services in the U.S., U.K., and other nations coordinate media agendas.

Narrative Control: Sensitive topics (e.g., intelligence leaks, foreign policy failures, or deep political scandals) are either buried or spun.

Media as Propaganda Arm: Major outlets allegedly receive talking points directly from government or intelligence agencies.

Evidence Cited by Believers:

Publicized examples of media misinformation during wars (e.g., Iraq WMDs).

Similar headlines and narratives across multiple outlets.

The continued presence of ex-intelligence officers as network commentators.

Counterpoint:

Mainstream journalists argue similar stories across outlets reflect shared sources, news cycles, and editorial alignment.

No official evidence proves ongoing CIA control of the press.

Famous Quotes / Sources

"The news is not what happened — it's what they want you to think happened."

— Media conspiracy commentator

"Operation Mockingbird didn't stop — it just went wireless."

— Alternative news forum

"While governments try to influence media, the idea of a single coordinated operation is exaggerated."

— Media historian

Real-World Consequences

Integration with Other Theories:

Linked to Deep State, predictive programming, and narrative management conspiracies.

Public Distrust:

Increases skepticism of mainstream news, fueling independent media movements.

Political Polarization:

Both left- and right-wing groups use Mockingbird to accuse opponents of media manipulation.

Where It Stands Today

Mainstream history records Mockingbird as a past operation, but conspiracy believers maintain that its techniques never stopped — they just became more subtle, digital, and global.

Chapter One Hundred and Eighty-Six

Section: More Conspiracies from Around the World

Conspiracy: Amazon Alexa Records Private Conversations for the NSA

Summary

The Amazon Alexa NSA conspiracy claims that Amazon's popular voice assistant devices — such as Echo smart speakers — are not just convenient home gadgets but always-on surveillance tools that record private conversations and share them with intelligence agencies like the NSA.

Believers argue that Alexa is part of a mass data collection network, quietly compiling vast amounts of audio, behavioral, and personal data for use in monitoring and profiling individuals.

History & Key Claims

Background:

Amazon Alexa launched in 2014, capable of responding to voice commands and integrating with smart home systems.

Concerns about always-on microphones have persisted since voice assistants entered the market.

Conspiracy Allegations:

Continuous Listening: Alexa allegedly records far more than just commands, capturing conversations even when not addressed.

Data Transmission: These recordings are sent to cloud servers where they can be accessed by government agencies.

NSA Partnership: Amazon's cloud service (AWS) hosts data for U.S. intelligence agencies, fueling speculation about direct access to audio files.

Behavioral Profiling: Alexa could analyze tone, word choice, and background noise to identify mood, political leanings, and even potential "risks".

Evidence Cited by Believers:

Reports of Alexa recordings being reviewed by human employees for quality control.

High-profile cases where Alexa audio was subpoenaed in legal investigations.

Amazon Web Services' confirmed contracts with the CIA and other U.S. agencies.

Counterpoint:

Amazon says Alexa records only after hearing a "wake word" and that recordings are stored to improve service.

No confirmed evidence shows direct NSA monitoring of Alexa audio.

Famous Quotes / Sources

"It's the most clever wiretap in history — and you bought it yourself."

— Privacy advocate

"When your home assistant works for the government, it's not assisting you."

— Conspiracy tech blog

"While Alexa stores data, there's no proof it's secretly transmitting it to the NSA."

— Cybersecurity analyst

Real-World Consequences

Integration with Other Theories:

Linked to Smart tech surveillance, 5G control grids, and digital ID monitoring.

Public Distrust:

Many users unplug or disable Alexa due to privacy concerns.

Policy Discussions:

Debate over data privacy laws and consumer device security.

Where It Stands Today

Mainstream explanation: Alexa collects data for functionality and advertising. Conspiracy interpretation: Alexa is the perfect, voluntary bug — installed in millions of homes to serve the surveillance state.

Chapter One Hundred and Eighty-Seven

Section: More Conspiracies from Around the World

Conspiracy: Self-Driving Cars Are Designed to Kill Select Targets

Summary

The Self-Driving Cars assassination conspiracy claims that autonomous vehicles, while marketed as a breakthrough in convenience and safety, could be remotely controlled to deliberately cause accidents or eliminate specific individuals.

Believers argue that the same technology allowing cars to navigate without drivers could be used to stage "accidents" that are nearly impossible to prove as intentional.

History & Key Claims

Background:

Self-driving technology began advancing rapidly in the 2010s, spearheaded by companies like Tesla, Waymo, and Uber.

Public trust was shaken by incidents of autonomous vehicles involved in fatal accidents.

Conspiracy Allegations:

Remote Override Capability: Self-driving cars allegedly have backdoor systems allowing remote control by manufacturers, hackers, or intelligence agencies.

Assassination Tool: Specific vehicles could be programmed to swerve, crash, or accelerate at precise moments.

Elite Protection: Only certain individuals or groups are targeted — dissenting journalists, political enemies, or whistleblowers.

Cover-Up as "Technical Failure": Fatal crashes would be explained as software glitches or road hazards.

Evidence Cited by Believers:

The suspicious 2013 car crash of journalist Michael Hastings, who was investigating government corruption (though not proven linked to self-driving tech, it is cited as an example of vehicle hacking potential).

Documented proof that modern cars can be hacked remotely (e.g., Jeep Cherokee hacking demonstration in 2015).

Lack of full transparency from autonomous car manufacturers about fail-safe protocols.

Counterpoint:

No verified evidence shows autonomous vehicles are being weaponized.

Malfunctions are attributed to software bugs and environmental conditions.

Famous Quotes / Sources

"A self-driving car doesn't need a bullet to kill someone."

— Tech conspiracy forum

"When the car drives itself, you're not in control — someone else is."

— Privacy advocate

"While hacking is possible, the assassination claims are speculation."

— Automotive cybersecurity expert

Real-World Consequences

Integration with Other Theories:

Linked to Smart tech surveillance, AI control systems, and elite-targeted eliminations.

Public Distrust:

Many remain skeptical of fully autonomous vehicles due to hacking and override fears.

Policy Debate:

Raises concerns over liability, security, and kill-switch safeguards.

Where It Stands Today

Mainstream stance: self-driving technology is a safety innovation. Conspiracy believers' stance: autonomous cars are potential assassination machines disguised as progress.

Chapter One Hundred and Eighty-Eight

Section: More Conspiracies from Around the World

Conspiracy: World Leaders Are Clones (Not Just Celebs)

Summary

The World Leaders Are Clones conspiracy claims that some of the most powerful figures in politics are not the original individuals the public believes they are, but genetically engineered clones created to ensure political stability, loyalty, and control by the global elite.

Believers argue that cloning programs, which they claim exist in secret government or military labs, are used to replace problematic leaders or maintain continuity of rule without public awareness.

History & Key Claims

Origins of the Theory:

Cloning became a public fascination after the birth of Dolly the sheep in 1996.

Celebrity cloning conspiracies emerged soon after, later extending to politicians and royals.

Conspiracy Allegations:

Leader Replacement: When a leader becomes ill, disobedient, or politically inconvenient, they are replaced by a genetically identical clone.

Manufactured Continuity: Clones ensure the same appearance and persona while policy remains under elite control.

Hidden Facilities: Advanced cloning labs allegedly operate in military bases and underground facilities worldwide.

Multiple Copies: Some leaders may have several clones, used at different public events.

Evidence Cited by Believers:

Changes in appearance, voice, or demeanor of certain leaders over time.

Public disappearances followed by sudden reappearances looking "different."

Whistleblower claims from alleged insiders at "black site" labs.

Counterpoint:

Physical and behavioral changes are attributed to aging, illness, or stress.

No credible scientific evidence exists of human cloning being carried out or perfected.

Famous Quotes / Sources

"They replace leaders the same way they replace batteries."

— Political conspiracy podcast

"When the same policies continue no matter who is in office, maybe it's because it's the same person — or their copy."

— Conspiracy theory forum

"There's no evidence cloning is being used in politics. The science isn't at that stage."

— Geneticist

Real-World Consequences

Integration with Other Theories:

Linked to celebrity clones, biorobots in government, and Deep State continuity of power.

Cultural Fascination:

Popular in conspiracy media, satire, and science fiction.

Political Suspicion:

Used to explain political consistency despite changes in leadership.

Where It Stands Today

Mainstream science rejects human cloning as impractical and unethical, but conspiracy believers argue that cloning technology is decades ahead of public knowledge — and the world's leaders are proof of it.

Chapter One Hundred and Eighty-Nine

Section: More Conspiracies from Around the World

Conspiracy: The U.S. Government Can Cause Earthquakes

Summary

The Earthquake Weapon conspiracy claims that the U.S. government has developed technology capable of triggering earthquakes in specific regions, either as a military weapon, a tool of political coercion, or a means to disrupt economies and destabilize nations.

Believers argue that projects like HAARP (High-frequency Active Auroral Research Program) and other classified defense research have developed methods to manipulate tectonic activity using advanced energy systems.

History & Key Claims

Origins of the Theory:

Concerns about "weather weapons" and "geophysical warfare" began during the Cold War, with some patents and declassified documents referencing environmental modification techniques.

Major earthquakes coinciding with political or economic crises have fueled suspicion.

Conspiracy Allegations:

HAARP as a Cover: The Alaska-based HAARP facility, officially for ionospheric research, is claimed to have the capability to direct electromagnetic energy into the Earth's crust.

Targeted Events: Certain earthquakes (e.g., Haiti 2010, Nepal 2015) are cited as being unnaturally timed to coincide with geopolitical advantage.

Testing on Allies and Enemies: Earthquakes may be used to test weapons or send warnings to rival nations.

Media Disguise: Natural disaster narratives are used to hide evidence of deliberate triggering.

Evidence Cited by Believers:

Patents for "method and apparatus for altering weather and seismic activity."

Seismic patterns that some claim are inconsistent with natural tectonic activity.

U.S. military interest in geophysical weapons during Cold War research.

Counterpoint:

Mainstream scientists say there is no known technology capable of triggering earthquakes of significant magnitude.

Patterns cited as suspicious are explained as natural seismic phenomena.

Famous Quotes / Sources

"When an earthquake is as political as it is geological, it's worth asking questions."

— Geopolitical conspiracy blog

"HAARP can shake more than just the ionosphere."

— Alternative science forum

"There's no scientific evidence earthquakes can be artificially triggered at scale."

— Seismologist

Real-World Consequences

Integration with Other Theories:

Linked to HAARP weather control, disaster-for-profit schemes, and elite depopulation agendas.

Public Distrust:

Natural disasters are increasingly scrutinized for possible man-made origins.

International Suspicion:

Accusations between nations about environmental warfare have surfaced in diplomatic tensions.

Where It Stands Today

Mainstream science dismisses earthquake weapon claims, but conspiracy believers argue the Earth's crust is another battlefield — and the tremors are not always natural.

Chapter One Hundred and Ninety

Section: More Conspiracies from Around the World

Conspiracy: Every Major Tech Billionaire Is in a Secret Pact

Summary

The Tech Billionaire Secret Pact conspiracy claims that the world's most powerful technology entrepreneurs — from Silicon Valley founders to social media moguls — are part of a covert alliance that coordinates innovation, censorship, wealth control, and societal influence.

Believers argue that despite public rivalries, these figures operate in collaboration, not competition, advancing a shared agenda shaped by governments, intelligence agencies, or elite organizations.

History & Key Claims

Origins of the Theory:

Tech industry dominance accelerated in the 1990s and 2000s, with companies like Microsoft, Apple, Amazon, Google, Facebook, and Tesla controlling major sectors.

Observers noticed a pattern: similar ideological positions on global issues and synchronized policy rollouts.

Conspiracy Allegations:

Unified Agenda: Tech leaders allegedly meet privately to coordinate product directions, censorship policies, and surveillance integration.

Controlled Innovation: New technologies are released or withheld according to elite timelines.

Data Power: The alliance allegedly ensures a centralized global database of user behavior and biometric data.

Political Influence: Coordinated donations, lobbying, and public statements align with specific political and global policy goals.

Evidence Cited by Believers:

Similar censorship actions taken simultaneously by multiple platforms.

Participation in elite gatherings (e.g., World Economic Forum at Davos, Bilderberg meetings).

Shared investments in surveillance tech, AI development, and space ventures.

Counterpoint:

Overlap in decisions is attributed to market trends, regulatory pressures, and shared industry challenges.

No hard evidence of a formal pact or global control agenda.

Famous Quotes / Sources

"They compete in public but collaborate in private."

— Tech conspiracy forum

"The internet isn't free — it's run by a cartel of billionaires."

— Alternative economics commentator

"Tech leaders influence each other, but there's no evidence of a coordinated global pact."

— Industry analyst

Real-World Consequences

Integration with Other Theories:

Linked to Great Reset, surveillance capitalism, and AI world governance conspiracies.

Public Distrust:

Tech companies are increasingly viewed as monopolistic and politically aligned.

Political Impact:

Growing calls for antitrust actions, regulation, and transparency.

Where It Stands Today

Mainstream view: tech leaders align due to shared industry interests. Conspiracy view: they are an elite bloc, shaping technology and society to serve their shared agenda.

Chapter One Hundred and Ninety-One

Section: More Conspiracies from Around the World

Conspiracy: AirPods Emit Brain-Altering Frequencies

Summary

The AirPods Brain-Altering Frequencies conspiracy claims that Apple's popular wireless earbuds, along with similar Bluetooth audio devices, do more than just play music.

Believers argue that AirPods emit specific electromagnetic frequencies capable of subtly influencing brain function — potentially affecting mood, decision-making, focus, or even political attitudes.

History & Key Claims

Background:

AirPods launched in 2016, becoming one of Apple's fastest-selling products.

Concerns about Bluetooth radiation and constant ear exposure surfaced shortly after.

Conspiracy Allegations:

Frequency Manipulation: AirPods allegedly use audio and electromagnetic frequencies designed to influence neurological activity.

Behavioral Influence: Frequencies could alter mood, reduce critical thinking, or encourage consumer spending.

Health Concerns: Long-term exposure is claimed to cause cognitive decline, sleep pattern disruption, or anxiety.

Elite Coordination: Theories link AirPods to a broader surveillance and influence network involving tech companies.

Evidence Cited by Believers:

Studies suggesting prolonged exposure to EMF radiation may affect brain cell activity (though inconclusive).

Reports of headaches, dizziness, and fatigue among heavy wireless earbud users.

Patents related to audio-based neural stimulation.

Counterpoint:

Scientific consensus states Bluetooth emissions are well below harmful limits.

No verified evidence connects AirPods to brainwave manipulation.

Famous Quotes / Sources

"AirPods are portable frequency devices — and they're in millions of ears."

— Tech conspiracy blog

"You think you're streaming music, but they're streaming influence."

— Alternative health commentator

"There's no credible data to suggest AirPods emit harmful or manipulative frequencies."

— Medical physicist

Real-World Consequences

Integration with Other Theories:

Linked to 5G mind control, tech billionaire agendas, and digital surveillance systems.

Consumer Distrust:

Some users avoid wireless earbuds due to radiation and frequency concerns.

Industry Impact:

Calls for independent safety testing and disclosure of long-term effects.

Where It Stands Today

Mainstream science says AirPods are safe. Conspiracy believers say the world's best-selling earbuds are also the world's most discreet brain influence devices.

Chapter One Hundred and Ninety-Two

Section: More Conspiracies from Around the World

Conspiracy: Disney Parks Are Built on Ancient Sites for Power

Summary

The Disney Parks Ancient Sites conspiracy claims that several Disney theme parks — particularly the original Disneyland in California and Walt Disney World in Florida — were intentionally built on or near ancient sacred sites, ley lines, or locations of historical power to harness spiritual or energetic influence.

Believers argue that this placement was deliberate, creating an environment designed to draw in mass energy from visitors, either for mystical purposes or as part of a larger elite power structure.

History & Key Claims

Background:

Disneyland opened in 1955 in Anaheim, California. Walt Disney World opened in 1971 in Florida.

Disney parks have been meticulously designed — but conspiracy theories suggest site selection was not purely about geography or economics.

Conspiracy Allegations:

Ley Line Energy: Parks are positioned along ley lines (hypothetical alignments of ancient spiritual sites) to amplify creative or mystical energy.

Ancient Ground: Florida parks are said to sit on Native American burial grounds or ceremonial lands.

Energy Harvesting: The emotional energy of millions of annual visitors is allegedly channeled through the park design.

Occult Influence: Certain park layouts allegedly incorporate occult symbols to further focus power.

Evidence Cited by Believers:

Historical maps showing Native American settlements near Florida's Disney properties.

Alleged ley line connections between Anaheim, Orlando, and other global Disney parks.

Architectural designs incorporating hidden symbols (pentagrams, compass points).

Counterpoint:

Disney locations were chosen based on land availability, tourism potential, and climate, not mystical geography.

Claims about ley lines and symbols are considered speculative.

Famous Quotes / Sources

"Disney isn't just a theme park — it's an energy machine."

— Conspiracy culture blogger

"They chose the land long before the rides were planned."

— Alternative history researcher

"There's no evidence of ley line mapping in Disney's site selection."

— Cultural historian

Real-World Consequences

Integration with Other Theories:

Linked to occult symbolism in entertainment, predictive programming, and mass energy rituals.

Cultural Fascination:

Disney's secrecy around certain park areas fuels speculation.

Public Curiosity:

Visitors search for "hidden meanings" in park designs and attractions.

Where It Stands Today

Mainstream explanation: Disney parks are feats of creative engineering and entertainment design. Conspiracy believers: they are also carefully placed structures drawing on ancient and mystical energies.

Chapter One Hundred and Ninety-Three

Section: More Conspiracies from Around the World

Conspiracy: Mermaids Were Real But Covered Up by the Navy

Summary

The Mermaids Were Real conspiracy claims that mermaids — or mermaid-like aquatic humanoids — once existed (and may still exist) but their existence has been deliberately covered up by naval forces and government agencies.

Believers argue that historical accounts, maritime folklore, and occasional modern sightings suggest that mermaids are not mythical creatures, but a species suppressed from public knowledge to avoid panic, exploitation, or scientific upheaval.

History & Key Claims

Background:

Mermaid legends appear in nearly every seafaring culture — from Assyrian goddess Atargatis to Norse and Celtic folklore.

Sailors' accounts, particularly during the Age of Exploration, describe encounters with aquatic humanoids.

Conspiracy Allegations:

Historical Encounters: Early explorers like Christopher Columbus recorded sightings of mermaid-like creatures.

Modern Evidence Suppressed: The Navy allegedly encounters mermaids or similar beings during deep-sea operations but classifies reports.

Governmental Secrecy: Possible reasons for cover-up include:

Protecting the species from exploitation.

Hiding evidence of intelligent aquatic life.

Preventing challenges to religious or scientific narratives.

Military Encounters: Speculation that naval sonar testing and deep-sea drills have driven mermaids away or caused mass strandings.

Evidence Cited by Believers:

Centuries of consistent global sightings.

The controversial 2012 Animal Planet docudrama Mermaids: The Body Found (claimed by some to be "soft disclosure").

Mysterious underwater sounds (like "The Bloop") recorded by NOAA.

Counterpoint:

Mainstream science attributes sightings to manatees, dugongs, or marine mammals.

No physical evidence has ever been confirmed.

Famous Quotes / Sources

"They know what's in the deep — and it's not all fish."

— Conspiracy ocean researcher

"Mermaids didn't vanish. They were silenced."

— Maritime folklore investigator

"There's no credible evidence mermaids exist. Myths evolved from misidentified sea animals."

— Marine biologist

Real-World Consequences

Integration with Other Theories:

Linked to ocean mysteries cover-ups, Bermuda Triangle, and deep-sea species concealment.

Cultural Impact:

Mermaid fascination persists in films, books, and tourism.

Public Suspicion:

Every unexplained aquatic humanoid sighting renews speculation.

Mainstream view: mermaids are myths rooted in sailor lore. Conspiracy believer view: they were real — and the Navy knows exactly where they went.

Chapter One Hundred and Ninety-Four

Section: More Conspiracies from Around the World

Conspiracy: The Roman Empire Never Ended – It Morphed Into the Vatican

Summary

The Roman Empire Never Ended conspiracy claims that the fall of the Roman Empire in 476 CE was not the end of its power, but rather a strategic transformation. Believers argue that Rome's political and economic influence shifted into religious authority through the Vatican, allowing it to continue ruling Europe — and much of the world — under a different name.

History & Key Claims

Background:

Official history teaches that the Western Roman Empire collapsed in 476 CE, replaced by various kingdoms.

The Eastern Roman Empire (Byzantine Empire) continued until 1453.

The Vatican, rising in power during the medieval period, became one of the most influential institutions in Europe.

Conspiracy Allegations:

Continuity of Power: Roman elites allegedly maintained control by transferring power into the Roman Catholic Church.

Legal and Financial Systems: Modern Western legal codes, banking systems, and governmental structures trace back to Roman frameworks — allegedly preserved by the Church.

Symbolic Continuity: Roman symbols (e.g., eagles, laurel wreaths, Latin mottos) persist in global politics.

Vatican as Rome Reborn: The Pope is seen as the political heir to the Caesars, ruling a religious empire that replaced the military one.

Evidence Cited by Believers:

Unbroken use of Latin in Church ceremonies.

Architectural and symbolic continuity between ancient Rome and Vatican structures.

Influence of Vatican diplomacy on European monarchies for centuries.

Counterpoint:

Historians view Vatican influence as religious and cultural, not a continuation of the Roman political state.

Many Roman traditions survived independently of any coordinated plan.

Famous Quotes / Sources

"Rome didn't fall. It simply changed robes."

— Alternative history researcher

"The Pope is the new Caesar — ruling over a spiritual empire."

— Conspiracy religion blog

"The idea that the Vatican is the Roman Empire reborn is a metaphor, not a literal truth."

— Church historian

Real-World Consequences

Integration with Other Theories:

Linked to Vatican archives secrecy, Jesuit control, and New World Order via religious authority.

Cultural Fascination:

Inspires books, documentaries, and historical revisionist works.

Persistent Suspicion:

Vatican secrecy fuels speculation about its role as a modern Roman Empire in disguise.

Where It Stands Today

Mainstream historians see Rome's fall as a historical fact. Conspiracy believers argue that Rome never fell — it simply traded its legions for bishops and its Senate for the College of Cardinals.

Chapter One Hundred and Ninety-Five

Section: More Conspiracies from Around the World

Conspiracy: The Holy Grail Was Discovered but Hidden

Summary

The Holy Grail conspiracy claims that the legendary Grail — long associated with Jesus Christ, the Last Supper, and mystical power — was discovered by elites or secret religious orders but kept hidden from the public.

Believers argue the Grail is not just a relic but a powerful symbol or object that could alter religion, politics, or even human destiny if its existence and true nature were revealed.

History & Key Claims

Origins of the Grail Legend:

First appeared in medieval literature (Chrétien de Troyes, Wolfram von Eschenbach) as a mysterious sacred cup.

Later Christian tradition connected it to the cup used by Jesus at the Last Supper.

Alternative interpretations see the Grail as a metaphor for secret bloodlines, hidden knowledge, or advanced technology.

Conspiracy Allegations:

Discovery in Modern Times: Claims suggest secret archaeological expeditions (by the Vatican, Nazis, or private collectors) have located the Grail.

Concealment: Knowledge of the Grail's location is allegedly hidden to preserve religious and political power structures.

Symbolic Power: The Grail may represent immortality, divine authority, or spiritual awakening, making it dangerous for elites to share.

Guardianship: Secret societies like the Knights Templar or modern Vatican orders allegedly keep it hidden.

Evidence Cited by Believers:

Historical expeditions linked to Grail legends (e.g., Nazi searches during WWII).

Religious relics stored in the Vatican that are never displayed publicly.

Ancient manuscripts and coded references in church art.

Counterpoint:

Mainstream historians consider the Grail a literary and symbolic invention, not a historical artifact.

No verifiable evidence of its physical existence has been presented.

Famous Quotes / Sources

"They found the Grail, but the world isn't ready for it."

— Conspiracy religious historian

"The Holy Grail isn't missing — it's just not for public eyes."

— Alternative history researcher

"The Grail legend is allegorical, not an actual hidden object."

— Biblical scholar

Real-World Consequences

Integration with Other Theories:

Linked to Vatican secrecy, Templar treasure, and bloodline conspiracies.

Cultural Fascination:

The Grail's mystery fuels books (The Da Vinci Code), films (Indiana Jones and the Last Crusade), and countless documentaries.

Persistent Mystery:

Its enduring legend keeps it one of the most famous "hidden relic" conspiracies.

Where It Stands Today

Mainstream view: the Grail is a legend. Conspiracy view: it was found long ago — but remains hidden to protect the power of those who hold it.

Chapter One Hundred and Ninety-Six

Section: More Conspiracies from Around the World

Conspiracy: Time Cube Theory (Time as 4 Simultaneous Days)

Summary

The Time Cube Theory claims that modern science and education deliberately conceal the "truth" that each rotation of the Earth contains four simultaneous days occurring at once.

Created and promoted by Gene Ray in the late 1990s, the theory asserts that understanding this hidden time structure would revolutionize science, philosophy, and religion, but that it is being suppressed by academic and government institutions.

History & Key Claims

Origins of the Theory:

Gene Ray launched the Time Cube website in 1997, claiming mainstream science hides the truth about time.

Ray proposed that each Earth day is divided into four separate simultaneous days — one for each corner of the Earth's rotation.

Conspiracy Allegations:

Educational Suppression: Schools and universities allegedly hide the theory to maintain control over scientific and religious thinking.

Global Deception: The Gregorian calendar and standard timekeeping are part of a false time model designed to keep the population ignorant.

Power in Knowledge: Understanding Time Cube would supposedly expose flaws in physics, cosmology, and religious interpretations of time.

Evidence Cited by Believers:

Diagrams from Ray's website showing how each rotation supposedly produces four distinct time quadrants.

References to ancient cultures dividing the day differently.

Claims that opposition to the theory is proof of suppression.

Counterpoint:

Mainstream science rejects Time Cube as non-mathematical pseudoscience.

No empirical evidence supports multiple simultaneous days.

Famous Quotes / Sources

"Academia is teaching evil singularity — time is cubic."

— Gene Ray

"They don't want you to know you're living four days at once."

— Time Cube supporter

"Time Cube has no scientific basis and is not a legitimate theory."

— Physicist

Real-World Consequences

Integration with Other Theories:

Linked to flat Earth, holographic universe, and simulation theory conspiracies.

Cultural Impact:

Time Cube became an internet phenomenon, discussed in forums, lectures, and meme culture.

Philosophical Curiosity:

While dismissed scientifically, it remains an example of alternative models challenging mainstream thought.

Where It Stands Today

Mainstream science dismisses Time Cube as a fringe idea. Conspiracy believers argue that the true nature of time is deliberately hidden, keeping humanity trapped in a false reality.

Chapter One Hundred and Ninety-Seven

Section: More Conspiracies from Around the World

Conspiracy: Reality TV Is Designed to Promote Submission

Summary

The Reality TV Submission conspiracy claims that the explosion of reality television over the past three decades is not just entertainment, but a deliberate cultural tool to promote conformity, distraction, and passive acceptance of authority.

Believers argue that reality TV normalizes manipulation, humiliation, manufactured drama, and surveillance, conditioning viewers to accept similar behavior in politics, workplaces, and daily life.

History & Key Claims

Origins of the Theory:

Reality television gained global popularity in the late 1990s and early 2000s with shows like Big Brother, Survivor, and American Idol.

Critics noticed the recurring themes of constant observation, hierarchies, and control by producers.

Conspiracy Allegations:

Normalization of Surveillance: Shows like Big Brother allegedly condition viewers to see perpetual monitoring as entertainment.

Behavioral Training: Drama, elimination, and reward systems mimic psychological experiments.

Distraction from Reality: Reality TV keeps the public engaged with manufactured problems instead of focusing on political or social issues.

Elite Messaging: Subtle reinforcement of status obsession, competition, and compliance with rules set by "judges" or producers.

Evidence Cited by Believers:

Repeated use of surveillance imagery, confession booths, and elimination rituals.

Similar structures across different global franchises.

Correlation between the rise of reality TV and declining interest in political engagement.

Counterpoint:

Reality TV is explained by networks as cheap-to-produce entertainment responding to public demand.

No proven link between reality shows and coordinated psychological conditioning.

Famous Quotes / Sources

"They turned surveillance into a game show."

— Media conspiracy critic

"You're not just watching the contestants. You're learning how to accept being watched."

— Cultural theorist

"Reality TV reflects social trends — it doesn't engineer them."

— Television producer

Real-World Consequences

Integration with Other Theories:

Linked to mass media control, predictive programming, and social engineering conspiracies.

Cultural Impact:

Reality TV is a multibillion-dollar industry shaping celebrity culture, beauty standards, and public attitudes.

Behavioral Concerns:

Critics note increased desensitization to humiliation and manipulation.

Where It Stands Today

Mainstream view: reality TV is commercial entertainment. Conspiracy believer view: it is a mass conditioning tool — teaching audiences to accept control, surveillance, and submission as normal life.

Chapter One Hundred and Ninety-Eight

Section: More Conspiracies from Around the World

Conspiracy: Celebrity Deaths Are Often Faked to Escape Fame

Summary

The Faked Celebrity Death conspiracy claims that many high-profile celebrities who have been reported dead are, in fact, alive and living in secrecy, having staged their deaths to escape public attention, media scrutiny, or dangerous industry pressures.

Believers argue that the entertainment industry's immense pressures — combined with elite control over celebrity narratives — create conditions where disappearing under a false death is a safer option.

History & Key Claims

Origins of the Theory:

Famous examples like Elvis Presley, Tupac Shakur, and Michael Jackson sparked decades of speculation.

Sightings, unusual funeral arrangements, and inconsistencies in official reports are common triggers for these theories.

Conspiracy Allegations:

Planned Exits: Celebrities arrange fake deaths to escape fame, avoid financial ruin, or remove themselves from industry exploitation.

Elite Assistance: Industry insiders or government contacts allegedly facilitate new identities.

Safety from Threats: Some stars may fake deaths to escape danger from criminal networks or political scandals.

Hints Left Behind: Lyrics, interviews, or unusual social media posts are interpreted as clues.

Evidence Cited by Believers:

Multiple "sightings" of Elvis, Tupac, and others years after their supposed deaths.

Discrepancies in official death certificates or autopsy reports.

Sudden deaths coinciding with legal troubles, disputes, or public breakdowns.

Counterpoint:

Most claims are based on hearsay, misidentification, or fan wishful thinking.

No verifiable proof of any celebrity successfully faking a death.

Famous Quotes / Sources

"Dead? No. Retired from fame."

— Entertainment conspiracy blogger

"They didn't die — they left the stage."

— Alternative pop culture researcher

"Every claimed sighting is either mistaken identity or a hoax."

— Media journalist

Real-World Consequences

Integration with Other Theories:

Linked to witness protection for celebrities, Illuminati industry control, and hidden exile communities.

Cultural Fascination:

Continues to fuel books, documentaries, and online investigation groups.

Fan Communities:

Some fanbases actively track "living legends" they believe are still alive.

Where It Stands Today

Mainstream stance: celebrities die, sometimes tragically and unexpectedly. Conspiracy stance: some deaths are carefully staged exits from a dangerous spotlight.

Chapter One Hundred and Ninety-Nine

Section: More Conspiracies from Around the World

Conspiracy: The Music Industry Uses Frequencies to Influence Moods

Summary

The Music Frequency Manipulation conspiracy claims that the global music industry deliberately tunes music to certain frequencies to influence listeners' emotions, behavior, and even health.

Believers argue that modern standard tuning — particularly the A=440 Hz pitch — is intentionally chosen to create tension, anxiety, or passivity, while other frequencies (like 432 Hz) are said to promote harmony, clarity, and emotional balance but are avoided by the industry.

History & Key Claims

Origins of the Theory:

Standardized pitch of A=440 Hz was adopted internationally in 1955, though alternative tunings existed for centuries.

Some conspiracy theorists claim Nazi propaganda minister Joseph Goebbels supported 440 Hz tuning for its alleged agitation effects.

Conspiracy Allegations:

Emotional Influence: The 440 Hz standard is allegedly chosen to suppress creativity and keep the population stressed.

Avoidance of Healing Frequencies: Frequencies like 432 Hz or Solfeggio tones (396 Hz, 528 Hz, etc.) are said to have positive or "healing" effects and are deliberately excluded from mainstream music.

Mass Manipulation: Streaming platforms and record labels push music engineered to provoke certain moods or behaviors.

Hidden Technology: Advanced audio processing could embed subliminal frequency layers.

Evidence Cited by Believers:

Subjective listener reports of improved mood when listening to retuned music.

Historical accounts of different tuning systems before 440 Hz standardization.

Experiments showing certain frequencies affect brainwave patterns.

Counterpoint:

No scientific consensus supports the idea that 440 Hz tuning is harmful.

Claims about 432 Hz "healing" properties are considered anecdotal.

Famous Quotes / Sources

"They don't just choose the notes — they choose the frequency of your mood."

— Conspiracy music theorist

"Change the tuning, and you change the mind."

— Alternative audio researcher

"Standard pitch has no proven psychological manipulation effect."

— Musicologist

Real-World Consequences

Integration with Other Theories:

Linked to MKUltra mind control, mass media psychological influence, and predictive programming.

Cultural Impact:

Rising popularity of 432 Hz remastered tracks and alternative tuning communities.

Industry Criticism:

Music industry accused of commodifying emotional manipulation.

Where It Stands Today

Mainstream position: tuning standards are for consistency. Conspiracy believer view: the industry chooses frequencies that subtly manipulate the masses, one note at a time.

Chapter Two Hundred

Section: More Conspiracies from Around the World

Conspiracy: The Elite Are Preparing to Abandon Earth

Summary

The Elite Abandoning Earth conspiracy claims that the world's wealthiest and most powerful individuals are preparing for a future where Earth becomes uninhabitable due to climate collapse, resource depletion, or engineered disasters.

Believers argue that while the public is distracted, the elite are building off-world colonies, secure underground facilities, and advanced escape technology to leave the planet behind.

History & Key Claims

Origins of the Theory:

Concerns arose from billionaires' investments in space exploration companies (SpaceX, Blue Origin, Virgin Galactic) and off-grid survival properties.

The Great Reset narrative further fueled suspicion that long-term sustainability measures are for the elite, not the masses.

Conspiracy Allegations:

Space Colonization: Projects in Mars exploration, lunar bases, and orbital stations are part of a private evacuation plan.

Earth Left to Collapse: Environmental warnings and economic shifts are said to prepare the public for gradual decline, while elites secure exits.

Exclusive Survival Infrastructure: Luxury bunkers, seed vaults, and hidden underwater or Antarctic bases allegedly serve as temporary safe havens.

Public Distraction: Media focuses on "space tourism" rather than serious colonization efforts.

Evidence Cited by Believers:

Billionaires purchasing large tracts of land in remote, resource-rich areas.

Private investments in reusable rockets and closed-loop life support.

International treaties allowing private corporate activity in space.

Counterpoint:

Space colonization projects are openly discussed as long-term exploration goals.

No proof exists of active plans to abandon Earth in the near future.

Famous Quotes / Sources

"They aren't saving Earth — they're saving themselves."

— Global politics conspiracy writer

"When they say 'Mars is the future,' they mean for them, not for you."

— Alternative economics analyst

"Space programs are exploration, not evacuation missions."

— Aerospace engineer

Real-World Consequences

Integration with Other Theories:

Linked to Great Reset, underground cities for the elite, and Antarctic base secrecy.

Public Distrust:

Growing skepticism of billionaire-led environmental initiatives.

Cultural Fascination:

Popular theme in dystopian films (Elysium, Don't Look Up).

Where It Stands Today

Mainstream explanation: space projects are scientific endeavors. Conspiracy believer stance: the elite have no intention of fixing Earth because they plan to leave it behind.

576

A Note from the Author

This book has taken you on a journey through hundreds of conspiracies — some well-known, some obscure, and some that hover on the edge between myth and possibility.

It is important to state clearly: the conspiracies presented here are not an endorsement, nor a reflection of the author's personal beliefs. They are the result of extensive research, examination of public sources, and the careful collection of stories, theories, and claims that have persisted through history and into our modern world.

This work was created with three goals in mind:

To entertain — because conspiracies have fascinated people for centuries, and there is no denying their drama, intrigue, and cultural influence.

To enlighten — by gathering these theories together, the book offers readers an accessible overview of how and why these ideas have endured.

To encourage new perspectives — not to tell you what to believe, but to inspire you to question, research, and see familiar events through a broader lens.

Whether you approach this book as a historian, a skeptic, a believer, or simply a curious mind, I hope it has sparked your imagination, challenged assumptions, and reminded you that the world is always more complex than it first appears.

Thank you for reading.

— J.D. Harris

Printed in Dunstable, United Kingdom